D1234670

This study explores the Stuart history play, a genre often viewed as an inferior or degenerate version of the exemplary Elizabethan dramatic form. Writing in the shadow of Marlowe and Shakespeare, Stuart playwrights have traditionally been evaluated through the aesthetic assumptions and political concerns of the sixteenth century. Ivo Kamps's study traces the development of Jacobean drama in the radically changed literary and political environment of the seventeenth century. He shows how historiographical developments in this period materially affected the structure of the history play. As audiences became increasingly skeptical of the comparatively simple teleological narratives of the Tudor era, a demand for new ways of staging history emerged. Kamps demonstrates how Stuart drama capitalized on this new awareness of historical narrative to undermine inherited forms of literary and political authority. *Historiography and ideology in Stuart drama* is the first sustained attempt to account for a neglected genre, and a sophisticated reading of the relationship between literature, history, and political power.

HISTORIOGRAPHY AND IDEOLOGY IN STUART DRAMA

HISTORIOGRAPHY AND IDEOLOGY IN STUART DRAMA

IVO KAMPS
University of Mississippi

Published by the Press Syndicate of the University of Cambridge
The Pitt Building, Trumpington Street, Cambridge CB2 1RP
40 West 20th Street, New York, NY 10011–4211, USA
10 Stamford Road, Oakleigh, Melbourne 3166, Australia

First published 1996

Printed in Great Britain at the University Press, Cambridge

A catalog record for this book is available from the British Library

Library of Congress cataloging in publication data

Kamps, Ivo.
Historiography and ideology in Stuart drama / Ivo Kamps.
p. cm.
Includes bibliographical references and index.
ISBN 0 521 56155 8
1. English drama – 17th century – History and criticism.
2. Literature and history – Great Britain – History – 17th century.
3. Politics and literature – Great Britain – History – 17th century.
4. Historiography – Great Britain – History – 17th century.
5. Historical drama, English – History and criticism. 6. Political plays, English – History and criticism. 7. Great Britain – Politics and government – 1603–1714. 8. Great Britain – Historiography.
I. Title.
PR678.H5K36 1996
822′.309358–dc20 96-14728 CIP

ISBN 0 521 56155 8 hardback

SE

For Deborah

They flutter behind you your possible pasts. Roger Waters, *The Final Cut*

Good my lord, will you see the players well bestow'd? Do you hear, let them be well us'd, for they are the abstract and brief chronicles of the time. After your death you were better have a bad epitaph than their ill report while you live. Shakespeare, *Hamlet*

Contents

Preface

This book is not the first to study the connection between history-writing and the renaissance history play. Not surprisingly, I am therefore indebted to those who surveyed the field before. Three claims in particular that emerge from earlier studies help to frame the present inquiry. First, members of all social classes in the Elizabethan and Stuart epochs turned to history to locate and legitimate personal and family identities that had become unsettled in a climate of unprecedented social and economic mobility and religious and political turmoil. But at the same time that people turned to history for much needed stability and continuity, it became increasingly clear that "Historiographic writing no longer had a direct, unequivocal relation with historical truth. Alternative accounts of historical events and opposed interpretations of their causes and significance now threatened each other's credibility."[1] These two opposing tendencies which are admirably elaborated upon by Phyllis Rackin in *Stages of History*, and which seek for certainty where there is much ambiguity, are exploited magnificently and provocatively by a small number of Stuart playwrights. The third contextual marker of this study – the one that firmly links historiography to the drama – derives from Irving Ribner who, taking his cue from Lily B. Campbell's *Shakespeare's Histories: Mirrors of Elizabethan Policy*, characterized the history play as a type of drama that based itself on one or more of the English chronicles and sought to achieve the *authentic purposes of renaissance historiography*.[2] The crux of Ribner and Campbell's claim is that the drama appropriated not only the substance of history-writing but also its methods and aims – an act of appropriation that, this study seeks to demonstrate, helps to explain the generic shift from the Elizabethan to the Stuart history plays.

Taken together, these three factors drew the historical drama and historiography very closely together, and set the drama in competition with the narratives. In Ben Jonson's *The Devil is an Ass*, Meercraft says to Fitzdottrel: "By my faith, you are cunning in the chronicles, sir," to which Fitzdottrel replies, "No, I confess I have it from the play-books, / And think they are more authentic." No matter how witty and provocative

Fitzdottrel's remark is, the point of this book is not to argue that one genre is more historical than the other, but rather that the close proximity in which the two genres found themselves in the renaissance theater resulted in a dramatic formulation of an acute skepticism about the reliability of historical discourse in general. The status of historical discourse in the theater is the subject of this book.

This book began as a dissertation at Princeton University, under the direction of Lawrence Danson and Victoria Kahn. A dissertation fellowship from the Mrs. Giles Whiting Foundation allowed for its completion in 1990. The idea to write about renaissance conceptions of history and the drama first occurred to me in one of the last seminars Alvin Kernan taught at Princeton. Along the way many friends and colleagues have been kind enough to discuss with me or read various incarnations of my argument. I would like to thank Sharon Achinstein, Hunter Cadzow, Chris Fitter, Ellen Gardiner, Richard Kroll, Robert Mack, Sheila Newbury, Karen Raber, and Jyotsna Singh. I am deeply indebted to Michael Sprinker, who has, over the years, supported my work in every conceivable way, and who took the time to read the manuscript in its entirety, and parts of it twice. At the University of Mississippi, I learned much from the group of students that participated in the Studies in English Drama seminar. For a whole semester I got to try my arguments about Stuart drama on a "captive" audience. Summer grants from the Graduate School and Department of English helped me to bring the book to a conclusion.

At the Folger Shakespeare Library, I benefited greatly from Linda Levy Peck's seventeenth-century history seminar. I am grateful for the Folger's support of my participation in the seminar and my research with a grant-in-aid.

At Cambridge University Press, Ray Ryan was surpassingly helpful and diplomatic in negotiating this study into print. David Sanders has my gratitude for being a very careful yet flexible copy-editor.

My father, Carel F. Kamps, Jr., provided the illustration of a gang of conspiratorial-looking Dutch politicians for the dust jacket. Given avid genealogical interests that usually led him to hard-to-decipher records in Dutch libraries, church registers, and town halls, I suspect he quite enjoyed hunting for pictures.

My greatest debt is to Deborah, to whom this books is dedicated, not least because the good ideas in it are hers. She is both its co-author and most astute critic.

Parts of chapter 4 appeared as "Possible Pasts: Historiography and Legitimation in *Henry VIII*" in *College English* 58 (1996), pp. 56–79, and are here reprinted with permission of the editor of the journal.

Introduction

Admit me chorus to this history. Shakespeare, *Henry V*

I

It is time to fill a void in renaissance drama studies by reconsidering the Stuart historical drama in the context of recent research on the history of renaissance historiography. To be sure, over the last few decades several critics have scrutinized the renaissance history play in conjunction with renaissance historiography, but only Irving Ribner's now inevitably dated investigation extends beyond the works of Shakespeare *and* into the Stuart period.[1] Many critics have slandered the Stuart historical drama by insisting on its inferior status compared to Elizabethan history plays. But such defamations are based less on a thorough appreciation of the Stuart history play on its own terms and in its historical context, than on the unfounded assumption that historical drama ought to be heroical, nationalistic, and more or less ideologically coherent – that it ought to be Elizabethan in character. With the accession of James I, a new set of political ideologies fused with typically Elizabethan modes of representation (including the drama) to foster a decidedly different cultural and literary landscape in England. In appearance and rhetoric, King James presented himself as more autocratic, more convinced of his absolutist powers, than Elizabeth ever had. To sanction this image of himself, James frequently turned to historical modes of argumentation. In part as a response to these changes, the Stuart playwrights begin to rethink and redefine the role of the monarch in their history plays. This process of redefinition, we shall see, is aided greatly by their understanding of renaissance innovations in historiographical theory and discourse. My chief aim will be to unfold the intricate negotiations between the genres of historiography and historical drama in the early years of the seventeenth century, and to relate those negotiations, whenever possible, to the representation of monarchs (or rulers) in the plays. And I will have achieved my goal if this inquiry were to lead to a new appreciation of the Stuart historical drama's conceptual, historiographical, and aesthetic strengths.

The basic argument of this book is that the *forms* of historiography developed in the sixteenth century become part of the *content* of pre-Civil War Stuart historical drama. The playwrights do not embrace these forms uncritically; indeed, they often set these forms against each other for the purpose of causing calculated disruptions in the wildly popular and socially conventional plots common to sixteenth-century historical narratives and dramas, and, in the process, help to make visible the ideological operations which produce these plots. To be sure, a handful of Elizabethan history plays, Shakespeare's *Henry V* in particular, reveal similarly disruptive moments in historiographical discourse, but on the whole their broad actions and sweeping gestures foreground unity and cultural orthodoxy, as depicted through a coherent literary representation of the figure of the monarch, and a utilization of providence.[2] The opposite is true for the early Stuart historical drama, which dramatizes precisely the inadequacy of orthodox socio-historical and providential patterns imposed routinely by the shaping powers of Tudor culture on history's rag-and-bone shop.

This study explores points of friction between the playwrights who write history plays and a state that seeks to control historical discourse. The relationship between the state and the theater, however, is not a binary one. The state did not actually *write* the histories (although it did commission some of them and submitted virtually all of them to censorship) to which the playwrights took exception. The renaissance state's most effective mode of control over historiographical discourse was often less direct, less focused, and less concrete, and had to do more with a shaping of life in general than with any particular aspect of it. Through its religious policies, system of law, social customs, and educational system, the state tried to create obedient subjects that would be accepting of a society with enormous economic and social inequities. That the state was very successful in making its subjects embrace the social hierarchy as an image of God's plan and natural law is evident from the fact that ordinary men and women – educators, artists, poets, dramatists, members of the clergy, lawyers, clerics, historians, and artisans – none of whom benefited from the system the way their social superiors did, actively participated in the perpetuation (or reproduction) of that system (which included, of course, literary production). Whether their stake in the system was sufficient to justify their participation is a different matter, but it is certain that without their participation the Elizabethan–Jacobean state could not have lasted as long as it did.

But even if the state's means of exerting control (law, church, patronage, royal iconography, etc.) generally produced compliant subjects, we also know that in a hierarchical system no amount of social engineering can render absolutely invisible or completely rationalize gross disparities between its subjects. The reason is that although a social system produces subjects of various classes that share a common interest in the reproduction of that system, no two subjects will have all interests in common. This inevitably causes friction, which can be expressed across a wide spectrum of possibilities (depending, in part, on how deeply the state's principles of obedience have been internalized), ranging from silent discontent or personal depression to innocuous social satire to armed rebellion and revolution. Because it understood that its more "benevolent" modes of subject production were not perfect, the state called into being very specific institutions – the censor, for instance, to deal with unruly playwrights and historians – to curb the concrete transgressions of its subjects. We must keep in mind, however, that, despite this outrageously lopsided division of power, the forces that drove the social reproductive process were disseminated throughout the culture, and were not located solely in the hands of the elite.

The bulk of this study's argument flows from a reading of a small number of Stuart history plays in their historical context. By historical context I certainly mean here the political, religious, legal, and cultural milieu of the moment, but especially the pivotal developments that occurred in the field of *historiography* just prior to and concurrent with the period during which the plays were written. The reason for making historiography a centerpiece of this study of the drama is that the playwrights recognized the inherent ideological dimension of history-writing, a recognition which they exploited to marvelous effect in their stage plays. Although most categorical distinctions between the Tudor and Stuart periods ultimately demand qualification, we can be certain that Stuart dramatists conceived of the monarch and his relationship to history in a manner conspicuously different from their Tudor predecessors. In the Stuart drama the monarch is viewed less and less as the primary (earthly) mover of history, and becomes instead a figure who is himself subject to historical necessity.

Following the widely accepted "great men" theory of history, most sixteenth-century playwrights and historians portrayed the monarch as the master and the maker of history. Narrative historians organized their matter according to the reigns of monarchs, allowing the political lives and deeds of the rulers to give shape, order, and meaning to events. Given a universally held belief in the absolute power of divine providence, no one could reasonably deem the monarch all-powerful in all matters, but the ruler's obvious sway over most earthly matters is reflected in Tudor historiography's blatant preoccupation with the actions and motives of "great men," or, on rare occasions, of great women. This preoccupation with "mostly kings, generals, statesmen . . . [and] princes of the church"[3] betrays a certain Tudor perception of the dynamics of history and the basis of power. Power is thought to be held by "princes," and history is the consequence of their wielding it: history is literally "made" by princes (Ferguson, *Clio Unbound*

4); indeed, in a sense, princes *are* the stuff of history, or history itself. On occasion this rather extreme yet commonplace fixation on "great men" takes on an unfeeling, almost callous quality, as when Shakespeare's Henry V names for posterity the English fallen at Agincourt: "Edward the Duke of York, the Earl of Suffolk, / Sir Richard Kettle, Davy Gam, esquire; / *None else of name*."[4] We are not merely talking of Bardolph and Nym here, but of ordinary soldiers (like Court and Bates and Williams) who could have lost their lives in their king's service. Their names matter not. But even men of name may be quickly forgotten, for it is King Henry, or *England* – as some of the speech prefixes in the First Folio identify him – whose fate is synonymous with England's historical fate. When the Chorus, who embraces the role of the historian (see Prologue 32), in the epilogue tells of Henry's death it is clear that the *king* achieved "the world's best garden" (Epilogue 7), and that his premature death changed the course of history and made "England bleed" (12). "Historians in the sixteenth century," David Scott Kastan points out, "were willing to isolate the victorious acts of Henry V from the temporal context in which they occur. From such a vantage point, they saw only the peerless warrior-king, and it is their uncritically heroic conception of Henry that informs the voice of the Chorus."[5]

Needless to say, this "great men" theory of history, which we encounter in Edward Hall, Raphael Holinshed, George Puttenham, and, in less developed form, in Polydore Vergil, was hardly adequate to describe the complex relationship of actual monarchs to power and history. In the early Jacobean period, Sir Walter Ralegh's "immensely popular" *History of the World* stands as a spirited corrective to any idea of princely control over the forces of history (Woolf, "Erudition" 54). However, far from deconstructing or disseminating the power of princes into impersonal historical forces, Ralegh unswervingly emphasizes the "storme-like, suddaine, and violent" powers of inscrutable divine providence and its agent fortune which obliterate the efforts and achievements of even the world's greatest princes (53). Yet despite Ralegh's fervor his views do not constitute a conceptual breakthrough in historical thought. Rather, the difference between Ralegh's and his Tudor predecessors' representation of the prince in history is one of accent: the former fatalistically valorizes providence as an incalculable force which wrecks monarchical accomplishments, whereas the latter more optimistically holds out for greater historical stability and at least a temporary triumph of the prince over history. The key terms in the debate – providence, prince, and history – remain constant.

Perhaps it is incongruous that the *dramatists* found both historiographical models wanting; it is downright ironic that they were the ones whose texts reveal a conceptual breakthrough in historical thinking. The late-Elizabethan Shakespeare and the early Stuart dramatists, I will show, astutely abandon a view of the prince as the repository of power and maker of history in favor of a prince who is an opportunistic manipulator not merely of historical events themselves (many of which turn out to be largely beyond his control) but also, crucially, of their *representation*.

The difference here is not simply one of degree. The point is easily illustrated by again turning briefly to Shakespeare's Henry V. In *King Henry IV, Part 1*, Hal soliloquizes his intent to "redeem time." Such a redemption – if we take the term literally, and I think that Hal wants us to – would require a Christ-like intervention in the course of history. It turns out, however, that all Hal is capable of is fighting wars and praying to God: "O not to-day, [to] think upon the fault / My father made in compassing the crown" (*Henry V* 4.1.299–300). If any time is to be redeemed, if any sins are to be forgiven, God must be the redeemer and the forgiver, not Henry. And, as Henry privately admits, not even his "contrite tears" and liberal charity payments can exact God's redemption ("all that I can do is nothing worth" [309]), because his "penitence comes after all" (310). But despite some highly unflattering self-pity, Henry V is able to shed successfully whatever idealistic historical pretensions he may have embraced as young Prince Hal. In their stead Henry, the son of the usurper, comes to understand that "authority goes to that contender who can seize hold of the *symbols* and *signs* legitimating authority."[6] One of those signs is, of course, historical representation, especially here the attempt to impose on the chaos of civil strife (which characterized the reigns of Richard II and Henry IV) Edward Hall's "*restorative*" conception of history:[7] "O God, thy arm was here; / And not to us, but to thy arm alone, / Ascribe we all!" (*Henry V* 4.8.108–10). The king's professed piety writes him into history, into providence, as God's agent, as the *embodiment* of history, as the *de facto* (but really the *ex post facto*) redeemer of "*England*." Of course, as we shall see in chapter 4, Shakespeare's play as a whole precisely challenges Henry's (and the Chorus's) efforts to use historical representation to transform the "fantasy of . . . ideological [and historical] unity in the sole figure of the monarch."[8] My central point here is that we see Shakespeare represent the king as one acutely concerned with the power of historical representation, not with history itself.

In order to trace this conceptual shift embodied in the renaissance drama, I have limited myself to a relatively small number of plays. From the period between 1519 and 1642 there are some seventy extant plays that have some claim to belonging to the history play genre (Ribner, *English History Play* 319–27). But I have confined my investigation to Stuart history plays and left undiscussed the plethora of acclaimed Elizabethan history plays, which have received, and continue to receive, ample attention, while the Stuart dramas are generally slighted or disparaged. This study closely examines only four Stuart history plays, even though there are at least twenty-four extant history plays written and published between 1603 and 1642 (Ribner, *English History Play* 325–7). Obviously, I do not offer my study as a survey of the field. I have narrowed my inquiry by selecting those plays which treat of the English monarchy directly. The reason for this is plain. If the Elizabethan history play exalted the "great men" view of history, and if the Stuart playwrights come to challenge that mode of representation, then it should be particularly useful to scrutinize the representation of monarchs in the Stuart historical drama. Strictly speaking, *The Tragedy of Sir John Van Olden Barnavelt* may appear to be an exception to this rule (for it does not introduce a monarch), but I will argue that the political and religious ties between England and the Dutch Republic (where the play is set) are so close that the play can be read in terms of James I's foreign and domestic policies, and thus has direct bearing on the monarchy. Also, I have opted to write only about those dramas that deal with "recent" history (as opposed to ancient or legendary history or romance history) of the English monarchy because they exude a more perspicacious and genealogically more urgent connection to the reigning Stuart dynasty than do the plays about ancient English history. The practical consequence of this connection is a more acute ability of these plays to intervene (subversively or otherwise) in contemporary political thought and practice. With the exception of John Bale's *King Johan* and Shakespeare's *Henry V* (both of which are treated as test cases of my basic premises about the negotiations between drama and historiography), none of the plays harkens back further than Henry Richmond's victory over Richard III in 1485. Therefore, each play examined here has keen bearing on the Tudor and Stuart dynasties. I have therefore opted for the following plays: Thomas Heywood's *If You Know Not Me You Know No Bodie* (part 1), Shakespeare and Fletcher's *Henry VIII*, Philip Massinger and John Fletcher's *The Tragedy of Sir John Van Olden Barnavelt*, and John Ford's *Chronicle History of Perkin Warbeck.*

II

Although this study is primarily historical in character, it also engages the vexed theoretical problem of literature's relationship to history. Therefore a word or two should be said about the theoretical underpinnings sustaining my enterprise. As I began to suggest at the outset, my study attempts to show that the Stuart history play differs significantly from its Elizabethan predecessor because it appropriates not only the substance or content of sixteenth- and early-seventeenth-century historiography but also its various conceptual and methodological innovations. Hence, my study is about the relationship between form and content, and I proceed on the assumption that literary form and content stand in a fundamentally dialectical relationship to one another. Form, in the words of Terry Eagleton, is a product of content, "but reacts back upon it in a double edged relationship."[9] What is more, "Forms are historically determined by the kind of 'content' they have to embody; they are changed, transformed, broken down, and revolutionized as that content itself changes" (Eagleton, *Marxism* 22).

We can set aside here the difficult problem of introducing a hierarchy within the dialectic (problematic because form and content are never encountered independently of one other), and instead focus on the dialectic itself. The form–content dialectic is so important to the present study because it offers an antidote to the still common tendency among literary critics to assume too readily that when playwrights, novelists, and poets incorporate materials from other sources, they transform those materials into something essentially literary, effacing their formal characteristics in the process. Many critics would admit that materials taken from, say, myths, folktales, historical narratives, or romances retain some of their original qualities; but such qualities are always down-played, and in those instances where they are too visible in the literary work they are invariably judged detrimental to the literary work, and discussed in terms of a conflict between genres or the author's failure to master his or her sources. Nothing could be more damaging to a consideration of the history play, a genre that, as I will show, self-consciously appropriates formal features from historiography. Several Stuart historical dramas simulate historiographical practices and offer them up for the audience's inspection. To erase or minimize those simulations by describing them as primarily "literary" is to miss the point of some of these plays completely.

The straightforward form–content dialectic is useful in helping us see what is at stake in the Stuart history play, but to comprehend fully what dramatists like Shakespeare, Fletcher, Massinger, Heywood, and Ford are up to, we need to make a further distinction within the dialectic. Before "content" borrowed from a historical narrative enters a history play, it already possesses a dual "form." First, it is part of a narrative structure – say, John Foxe's Protestant interpretation of English history – and its form and meaning are inevitably shaped by that narrative. The gruesome deaths by Marian fire of Protestants Latimer, Cranmer, and Ridley are necessarily acts of heroism and martyrdom, not, as they might be in some other narrative, acts of sheer stupidity. We are dealing with a historical account here, but we can call its form "literary" because its narrative is an expression of a specific ideological interpretation of history. However, before the "content" entered into Foxe's narrative, it already possessed a "form" – a pre-literary "form." It is less the product of a calculated effort by a single author, or small group, trying to impose a pattern on life than it is produced "under pressure of an inner need, of a collective psychological demand which, like everything else . . . has its social roots."[10] What this means is that the "raw" materials (words, jokes, folk stories, history, romance plots) out of which historical and, by extension, literary texts are fashioned do not exist in a vacuum; they are "the very components of our concrete social life itself" and possess what Fredric Jameson calls an "inner logic" – the "inner logic of content" (Jameson, *Marxism and Form* 402, 401–3).[11] Inner logic is not to be understood as a fixed essence, but rather as one of content's elastic features whose particular manifestation depends on the ideological milieu within which it occurs. Or, to put it differently, "content" becomes available to a writer (or anyone else) only when ideology endows it with a form or pattern that makes it recognizable. As Hayden White has aptly observed, the contents of "verbal fictions," be they literary or historical, "are as much *invented* as *found*."[12] The historical "facts" or "contents" of literary works are already culturally produced, that is, prior to their incorporation in the literary text.

Significant for this investigation of the drama is that there often existed a tension between content's inner logic and the literary form into which it was cast by historians. From the perspective of someone like Foxe it was crucial (as we will see below) that readers believed that inner logic and Protestant historiographical form were absolutely identical. Foxe's need to stress the equation stemmed of course directly from the existence of alternate readings that propounded different inner logics and different narratives, suggesting that histories are indeed invented, not found. The Stuart dramatists seize on these tensions and foreground them in their plays, pointing out discrepancies between historiographical practices and various "components of . . . concrete social life itself."

For the dramatists, the process of textual production, then, "is the process whereby ideology produces the forms which produce it, thus determining in general both the instruments and devices which work it, and the nature of the work-process itself" (Eagleton, *Criticism* 84). And it is this understanding of the literary work as "an ideological production to the second power" which grants it its peculiar status with regard to ideology. "For in producing ideological representations, the text reveals in peculiarly intense, compacted and coherent form the categories from which those representations are produced" (Eagleton, *Criticism* 85). Reading a literary text, therefore, is not an ordinary encounter with ideology (even though the text *is* an ideological product); the text draws attention to its own artificial and constructed nature (or to the fact that "naturalness is the effect of a particular production") and thus counteracts ideology's basic drive to conceal the productive modes that "'naturalize' ideological categories, dissolving them into the spontaneity of the 'lived.'" The Stuart historical dramas considered here capitalize on this fact by enacting the ideological work – here, specifically, the work of historical representation – required to produce a king.

Eagleton rightly points out that this "double-production" of ideology may, in fact, "cancel itself out" and "invert itself back into an analogue of knowledge." Such "knowledge," to be sure, is still ideological in character (it does not transcend the context which produces it), but it *can* make visible, to the attentive reader, precisely those operations which ideology conceals. It can help shift ideological horizons. Such revelations are of concern to the student of past cultures, and they are extremely significant at a given historical moment insofar as they can constitute a rational basis for an oppositional stance to a cultural hegemony. Whether or not such opposition is actually subversive or whether it is eventually smothered in the all-encompassing embrace of power (as some new historicists would have it) of course depends on larger and entirely extra-literary conditions of political struggle. No type of "knowledge" is inherently subversive.[13]

The *potential* for seditious historiographical activity, however, was greatly enhanced by innovations in English approaches to the past. Beginning in the early decades of the sixteenth century, under the pressures of internal ideological shifts and continental influences, English historiography metamorphosed from a chiefly unified medieval practice into a methodologically eclectic endeavor: different historians came to embrace different philosophies of history and different historiographical practices. Obviously, the actual events of English history had not changed but the Reformation especially brought about changes in the "inner logic" of the content of history. These changes in turn transformed the literary form(s) of the historical narratives and promoted borrowings from continental historiographical practices. Somewhat surprisingly, this methodologically mixed bag, which produced variant and often contradictory historical accounts, did not initially create the epistemological ambiguity one might look for. On the contrary, it was not until the playwrights seized on historiography's eclecticism by borrowing its *forms* for the stage that historiographical instability was foregrounded to the (playhouse) public at large and linked to contemporary political discourses. In order to explore these matters, however, the history play had to abandon the typical Elizabethan historical narrative with its fondness for strict hierarchies and divine overplots. One way to expose the mechanics of history-writing was to disrupt or displace the ways in which the Tudor conception of history concealed its own production. This was possible not merely because the playwrights carefully studied the historians, but because the "inner logic" of the content of Elizabethan history changed in a Jacobean world with new ideological trends, including ostensibly greater religious tolerance, a policy of peace vis-à-vis Spain, and an intensification of the rhetorics of divine right theory and royal absolutism. By appropriating the content and the form of the narrative histories and incorporating *both* of them into the content of the drama, the playwrights alter the *form* of the history play in two crucial ways: they transform the Elizabethan ideological model (and the literary form which flows from it), and they change the *genre* of the history play.

These changes also spelled the demise of the history play, but not, as has been argued, because of an aesthetic decline; on the contrary, the history play wrote itself out of existence by probing into the nature of historical presentation, which did not go over well with an audience which had grown accustomed to heroic plots that by and large affirmed Tudor orthodoxy. The dramatists, it seems, were responding to a set of cultural and ideological developments (a foreign monarch on the English throne, peace with Spain, and so forth), while the audience was locked into a nostalgic longing for the days of the Virgin Queen during which all could unite with her against a common foe. In other words, the playwrights on the whole reflected the cultural disjointedness of the new Jacobean nation, whereas the public, in the theater at least, apparently harkened back to former times. The growing appetite for the romance plays of Shakespeare, Fletcher, and others may be, as critics have suggested, a reflection of this.

III

Part of what made history plays effective as inquiries into the very process of historical representation is a continuity that existed in the renaissance between the fields of "literature" and "history." The sharp distinction we commonly draw between history and literature (or poetry) is essentially a modern invention. The renaissance did not always insist on this discrimination, or even care to make it. At any time during the renaissance, "history," the *OED* tells us, could mean "A relation of incidents (in early use, either true or imaginary; later only those professedly true). . ." Early usage continued into the early seventeenth century. Measured against a modern yardstick, renaissance usage seems primitive because it falls far short of a conception of history as ostensibly fact-based. It would be grossly misleading, however, to assume that renaissance men and women were troubled per se by the "story" component of history. On the contrary, there are numerous renaissance instances where history and poetry intersect quite naturally. *Hamlet* serves as an excellent example. The Prince Hamlet hails a troupe of traveling players to Elsinore with the recommendation that they be "well us'd for they are the abstract and brief chronicles of the time"

(2.2.525–6).[14] That is, the players are not treated as performers of fictions but as guardians of one's historical reputation. As such they are to be held in high regard, and it is implied that there is a reciprocal relation between how they are treated and how they will depict you in their "brief chronicles." The claim made for the players, and by extension for the playwrights who write the scripts, indeed, for the theater as a whole, is quite extraordinary. It portrays the theater as a history-producing institution, and also foregrounds its power to shape that record as it sees fit. Given this study's concern with the historical representation of kings as well as their ability to control their representation, it is all the more fitting that Hamlet uses his skill as a dramatist (he writes "a speech of some dozen or sixteen lines" [*Hamlet* 2.2.541]) to place before an Elsinore audience his "history" of Claudius's involvement in old Hamlet's death. It is important to emphasize, however, that by folding historiographical practice within theatrical practice, Hamlet also implies a dissimilarity between literature and historiography. Yet this difference is only raised to be razed; it is highlighted only to convey the theater's ability to perform the historian's office. An examination of renaissance attitudes regarding historiographical practices makes it quite clear that thinkers, poets, readers, and playwrights were quite content with, or even indifferent about, a need for stable and unclouded distinctions between the poetic and the historical.

To be sure, there were authors such as Philip Sidney, Jacques Amyot, Thomas Heywood, George Puttenham, William Camden, John Selden, Polydore Vergil, and Jean Bodin, who, with varying degrees of rigor, investigated the theoretical underpinnings of historiographical, poetic, and dramatic practices, but it cannot be said that their labors produced any meaningful consensus or even a systematic survey of the broad spectrum of historiographical practice. In part this was so because during the fifteenth and early sixteenth century history did not yet exist as a distinct and coherent discipline. People certainly had a sense of historical writing as something that had to be "true" but the same was held to be a requirement for poetry, and no one seemed to feel the need to theorize historical practice or even to define its object, "truth," with much precision. If Sidney argued in the 1580s that historians were bound to stick to the particular truth of things (whereas poets were concerned with general truths), there were many notable historians who thought it their duty to sacrifice accuracy of detail in the service of greater philosophical truths.[15] Well into the early seventeenth century, Ralegh could write in his *The History of the World* that "it was well-noted by that worthy Gentleman Sir *Philip Sidney*, that Historians do borrow of Poets, not only much of their ornament, but somewhat of their substance."[16]

Still, Phyllis Rackin and others have rightly suggested that in the course of the sixteenth century, "the traditional union of poetry and history was breaking up" (Rackin, *Stages of History* 22). And by the early decades of the seventeenth century, we can see in the writings of Francis Bacon and antiquarians like William Camden that historiography is making a concerted effort to set itself apart from literature by fashioning itself as a recognizably modern proto-science. We can discern the seeds of modern historiography in the early seventeenth century, but we have to emphasize that they were just that: seeds. These developments did not take hold in the universities, let alone in the public mind. The aims and methods of literature and historiography remained intertwined for much of the renaissance. It was not until the eighteenth century that history and the philosophy of history came to be viewed as respectable, well-defined disciplines distinct in aim, content, and method, from poetry.

In light of these renaissance attitudes about history, it is perhaps paradoxical that cultural materialist and new historicist critics of renaissance literature have had to do so much in recent years to break down traditional barriers between literary texts and historical contexts. Abandoning older conceptions of history as a "background" to literature or of literature as "transcending" the historical conditions that produced it, most historicist critics today argue for a cultural equality and a reciprocal dynamic between the literary text and its socio-historical context. And, what is more, they focus on the complex interplay or "exchanges" between literature and its cultural-historical milieu, often as it is inscribed in texts traditionally held to be extra literary. Yet, while a bounty of exciting historically-based criticism has been produced over the last decade or so, it is also true that the precise nature of literature's relationship to history still presents literary scholarship with a seemingly irresolvable epistemological puzzle. If anything, the richness of recent historical interpretations has shown that literature is apparently so overdetermined by a dense tangle of cultural/historical forces that there may never be a generic interpretative model sophisticated enough to account for all the forces active in the creation and reception of literary texts. In a sense, therefore, historicist critical practice still is, and perhaps always will be, ahead of a (complete and consistent) theory of historicism.

Exchanges between drama and historiography constitute fairly stable points of intersection linking the broader fields of literature and history. It is here that what Eagleton terms "an ideological production to the second power" occurs. I ask in my examination of these plays how *they* conceive of and dramatize their relationship to history.[17] My efforts, therefore, are limited to a special instance of the history–literature question, an instance, the self-conscious character of which locates it in a space *interior* to the broader literature–history question. It is here that the early Stuart historical dramatists manifest a keen interest in the process of historical redefinition. One central conclusion that emerges from this study is that the dramatists often show themselves to be better expositors of history than the historians; they show themselves to possess a clearer understanding of historiography's literary origins and its limitations as a knowledge-producing practice.

If the intersections between the drama and historiography provide a stable site for investigation, I suggest that their analysis contributes to our understanding of contemporary debates over literature's connection to history. Walter Cohen has observed that the new historicism has no "organizing principle" determining relationships between the literary texts and its contexts.[18] Cohen's point is perhaps arguable if applied indiscriminately, but he is right to suggest that numerous new historical studies proceed on the unwarranted assumption "that any one aspect of society is related to any other."[19] One dubious consequence of this, Cohen contends, is an "arbitrary connectedness" which typifies the coupling of literary text and historical context, making them too readily available for a poetics of culture designed to tease out the seemingly interminable links between history and text.[20] This almost-anything-goes type of criticism is of course very seductive for anyone who wants to "do" practical criticism, for it allows for an endless number of *new* connections. Yet, while "arbitrary connectedness" makes for an extremely enabling interpretative model, the resulting interpretations are not always satisfactory – as a scornful Frank Kermode recently remarked apropos the work of one new historicist, "It is easy enough to say something new if you don't care whether it makes any sense."[21]

If the new historicism is guilty of too much hermeneutic freedom, the "old" historicism has been disparaged in recent decades for being far too rigid in its conception of the literary text in culture. The older historicism tends to conceive of history as an essentially static and homogeneous background to literature that nonetheless delineates the range of meanings that can be expressed in works of literature at any given time. As E. W. M. Tillyard (by now infamously) asserted, "Shakespeare used the thought-idiom of his age. The only way he could have avoided that idiom . . . was by not thinking at all."[22] Lifted from its context, this declaration can be construed as extremely progressive, almost Althusserian in its understanding of the deterministic relationship between subject and ideology. In Tillyard's understanding, however, there is only one truly historical language: that of his own rigidly hierarchical Elizabethan World Picture.[23] If we take Tillyard as representative of the "old" historicism, we can say that orthodoxy is its alpha and omega. The present study does not intend to solve the perceived weaknesses in the new or the old historicisms; such solutions would require a completely different kind of investigation. But I do try to demonstrate that the new historicist hermeneutic model need not confine itself to allegorical or anecdotal historicism, nor does it need to rest on an arbitrary connection between culture and the drama. I attempt to strike a more pleasing balance between the synchronic impulse of new historicism and the more traditional emphasis on history's diachronic axis, the axis of historical change (Cohen, "Criticism" 33). In the self-conscious exchanges between drama, history, and historiography, I hope to have located a material connectedness between literature and history that is far from arbitrary. The playwrights appropriate for the stage both substance and method of providentialist, humanist, and antiquarian approaches to history. The first two generally display a strong diachronic tendency, whereas the third is principally synchronic in nature. Moreover, many of these dramatic appropriations serve not only to revise officially condoned and (predominantly diachronic) versions of English history, but also to intervene (primarily synchronically) in contemporary political and religious issues. What these points of intersection represent to me, therefore, are the playwrights' attempts to link their plays to contemporary history by linking them with more distant history and historiographical practices.

The work of theorist Hayden White is important here because it addresses and critiques some common misconceptions about the nature of historical narratives, misconceptions based on a certain reading of Aristotle's *Poetics*. For Aristotle the cardinal difference between drama (or poetry) and history is that the latter is constituted by the contingent, by the "actual" events as they happened, whereas a drama arranges "such things as might or could happen in accordance with probability or necessity."[24] The dramatist organizes incidents into a plot, which must be "whole and complete" (*Poetics* 16). Aristotle also declares that in the dramatist's selection and arrangement of the incidents, "What is impossible but can be believed should be preferred to what is possible but unconvincing" (53). From these admittedly brief remarks, one can conclude that a drama must have a credible syntax which links incidents teleologically, whereas history does not. The historian ought to record not only what is possible and explicable but also those things that appear impossible, inexplicable, and unbelievable. It follows that the totality (or a casually selected set) of historical incidents does not necessarily appear to us either "whole and complete," or as probable or necessary.

Over the years, most Western thinkers, including many renaissance writers, have indeed viewed it as axiomatic that the best histories offer the reader nothing but the "truths" as they happened, unadorned by art or fancy. It is also assumed to be self-evident by almost all renaissance historians that the shape of proper historical narratives – their pattern, or progress, or direction, or system of causation – is contained *in* the historical events themselves. This shape is not considered to be the product of the historian's imagination or ideological pressures; the shape is there, *in* the historical data themselves. The historian is considered, therefore, to be different from the playwright, whose imagination *imposes* a shape or plot on events.[25] On this score, the operations that lead to the production of a history or a drama, it seems fair to conclude, differ fundamentally. Such a conclusion, however, is no longer compelling today, nor was it compelling for the Stuart dramatists.

In recent years, a number of theoreticians, Hayden White among them, have called into question any putatively stable distinction between the domains of the literary and the historiographical. In *Tropics of Discourse*, White contends that "history as a discipline is in bad shape today because it has lost sight of its origins in the literary imagination" (99). When considered as "verbal artifacts," modern historical narratives, despite their aims and claims to be scientific and objective, share some very fundamental features with literary texts. Historical narratives, for instance, are emplotted in essentially the same manner as novels or plays. That is, the historian does not find his narrative *in* the historical "facts"; rather, he imposes a plot on the facts that will make the past accessible to the present. "The historical narrative thus mediates between the events reported in it on the one side and pregeneric plot structures conventionally used in our culture [and, of course, renaissance culture] to endow unfamiliar events and situations with meanings, on the other" (*Tropics of Discourse* 88). Secondly, historiography, lacking the kind of "formal terminological system for describing its objects" that physics and chemistry have, relies on rhetorical or figurative language to construct its narratives in much the same way literature does (94–5). The languages of both historiography and literature, therefore, "presuppose figurative characterizations of the events they purport to represent and explain" (94). In this manner, "historians *constitute* their subjects as possible objects of narrative presentation by the very language they use to describe them" (95). White speculates that historians are convinced that they have "found" the form of their narratives in "the events themselves" because of "a certain lack of linguistic self-consciousness which obscures the extent to which descriptions of events *already* constitute interpretations of their nature." Both of these phenomena – the encoding of events for the purpose of making them culturally meaningful and the purportedly "objective" description of "the events themselves" – we will see, are explored by Shakespeare and the Stuart playwrights.

It will come as no surprise that Hayden White's efforts to draw historiography closer to its "literary origins" were, at least at first, met with considerable skepticism in historians' circles.[26] White reduces their supposedly scientific and objective modes of inquiry to a fundamentally literary enterprise, a study of rhetorical tropes. But when we consider White's arguments in the context of renaissance ideas about history already discussed, they instantly become less controversial. This is not to suggest that all renaissance historians thought about historiography in White's supremely self-conscious and incredulous manner – how could they if historiography had not yet become fully separated from literature and rhetoric? But neither does it mean that renaissance historians were simply naive or confused when they labeled something as a history when *we* would recognize it as a fiction; what it does suggest is that they saw a much closer affinity between literary and historical sensibilities than we do today. This appreciation prodded the late-Elizabethan Shakespeare and the early Stuart dramatists to a keener comprehension of issues of historical representation in ways resembling White's. We can perhaps in part attribute this "negotiation" between the dramatists and the histories to what D. R. Woolf calls "a countervailing tendency in the renaissance mind which allowed it to apply insights borrowed from one sphere of knowledge to problems presented by another" (*Idea of History* 24). Obviously, in this case, the dramatists' borrowing is not a neutral act, but rather one that sharpens and develops the historians' insights in ways that ultimately challenge both historiographical theory and practice.

IV

Hayden White's characterization of historiography as shaped by the culture's "myth, fable, and folklore, scientific knowledge, religion, and literary art" supports a view of history-writing as a fundamentally ideological practice. As we asserted earlier, the very *forms* history-writing takes – for instance a romantic form as differentiated from a tragic form – are determined ideologically. As Barthes, cited by White, notes: "we can see, simply from looking at its structure, and *without* having to invoke the substance of its content, historical discourse is in its essence a form of ideological elaboration. . ."[27]

Ideology should be understood here in its primary types: rationalist and cognitive, the former easily defined "as conscious, well-articulated systems of belief." Cognitive ideology is more complexly defined as something "unconscious" that, in the words of Terry Eagleton, "constitutes the subject's lived, apparently spontaneous relations to a power-structure and comes to provide the invisible color of daily life itself."[28] Although Eagleton bases his definition of ideology on Althusser's famous construal of ideology as the "'Representation' of the imaginary relationship of individuals to their real conditions of existence" (Althusser, "Ideology" 162), he refrains,

I think rightly, from placing too much emphasis on the word "imaginary." Whereas Althusser insists that ideology constitutes "an illusion" which only makes "allusion to reality," Eagleton points out that "False consciousness may mean not that a body of ideas is actually untrue, but that these ideas are functional for the maintenance of an oppressive power, and that those who hold them are ignorant of this" (Eagleton, *Ideology* 24–5). Both Eagleton and Althusser seem in agreement that the study of ideology in literary texts does not lead to knowledge of "the real," but the former places greater value on our understanding of any truth ideology may contain about subjects' relationship to "the real." It is never easy to separate these two types of ideology in literature; they always exist together. However, it seems generally proper to locate cognitive ideology in what Jameson named the "inner logic" of content, in the "pressure of an inner need, of a collective psychological demand which, like everything else . . . has its *social* roots," whereas ideology in its rationalist manifestations can usually be equated with a text's overt theme or subject matter. Significantly, both types produce the work's literary form, and are in the process revealed as doing so. "History" or the "real" does play a crucial role here, but it is disfigured in this process. "History . . . certainly 'enters' the text, not least the 'historical' text; but it enters it precisely *as ideology*, as a presence determined and distorted by its measurable absences" (Eagleton, *Criticism* 72). As will be made clear in the chapters that follow, early Stuart history plays (or any other literary texts for that matter) quite literally do not have the "real" for their object; borrowing from the prose histories, they construct themselves out of representations or significations of the "real." These significations themselves of course do not per se have any firmer grip on the historical real; what is true for the historical drama is true for the historical narrative. Somewhat perversely, then, Eagleton concludes, "Within the text itself . . . ideology becomes a dominant structure, determining the character and disposition of certain 'pseudo-real' constituents. This inversion, as it were, of the real historical process, whereby in the text itself ideology seems to determine the historical real rather than *vice versa*, is itself naturally determined in the last instance by history itself. History, one might say, is the *ultimate* signifier of literature, as it is the ultimate signified."

Written histories cannot be reduced to a culture's dominant ideology even though they are invariably ideological in the rationalist sense, especially when the historian composes a history for a particular monarch or political or religious movement.[29] Polydore Vergil's *Anglica Historia*, commissioned by Henry VII in part to construct a historical basis legitimizing his claim to the English crown, is a case in point.[30] In composing his history, Polydore knew he needed some link, "some connective, superarching theme" to bridge the reigns of the kings of England.

A fairly obvious Lancastrian bias had the advantage of producing dramatic situations which could be exploited – and of course one who favored Henry VII and his son had at least to be anti-Yorkist. But this left the awkward problem of what to say about Richard II. If he were to be considered a good king, then Henry IV had perforce to be a usurper. Even if he were a bad king, still Henry had revolted against him, and no Tudor – least of all the first two – wanted revolution justified. In the end, Polydore blamed the Wars of the Roses on Richard's lack of a male heir, which missed the point entirely – probably deliberately.[31]

Other excellent instances of rationalistic ideological histories are John Foxe's *Actes and Monuments* (first printed in English in 1563), a religiously motivated history that emplots history as an ongoing struggle between good (Protestantism) and evil (Catholicism), and Edward Hall's *The Union of the Two Noble and Illustre Famelies of Lancastre & Yorke* (1548), a history that celebrates the Lancaster – York union and which comes out strongly in support of the Tudor government. Such instances of ideological historiography can be identified not merely by those who have the benefit of historical and cultural distance but also by renaissance readers themselves, especially when the history's ideological thrust has become a source of controversy in the culture. William Tyndale's *Obedience of a Christian Man* (1528), which served as a source for John Bale's history play *King Johan*, illustrates the point well. Writing in opposition to the papists, Tyndale observes:

Reade the cronycles of Engla*n*de (out of which yet they [i.e. the papists] have put a greate part of their wekedisse) and thou shalt fynde them all wayes both tebellious [sic] & disobediente to the kynges & also churlysh & vntha*n*kfull / so that whe*n* all ye realme gave the kynge some what to maynttene hym in his ryghte / they wolde not geve a myte. Co*n*sidre the story of kynge Iohn / where I doute not but they have put the best and fayrest for the*m* / selves and the worst of ki*n*ge Iohn / For I suppose they make the cronycles them selves.[32]

Tyndale's point is straightforward: papists write history in ways that serve their religious and political agenda. And they do so intentionally and cynically. That is, their motives do not even follow from sincere (though erroneous) religious conviction. "Compare the doinges there [in the chronicles] of holy church (as they ever call it)," Tyndale continues, "vnto the lernynge of Christe and of his Apostles . . . Se*n*t not the Pope also vnto the kynge of France remission of his synnes to goo and co*n*quere kynge Ihons realme. So now remission of synnes cometh not by fayth in the testame*n*te y^t^ God hath made in Christes bloude: but by fyghtinge & murtheringe for the popes pleasure" (Adams, "Introduction" 25–6).

The writings of the sincere or honest historian are of course no less ideological. The history of popular martyrologist John Foxe is an excellent case in point. The language of his *Actes and Monuments* assures the reader that the historian believes in the objective truth of his account. The purpose of *Actes and Monuments*, the author tells us, echoing Tyndale, is the edification of those who are ignorant of the history of "the true descent of the church," and those who rely for their knowledge of history on "the multitude of chronicles and story-writers . . . of whom the most part have been either monks or clients to the See of Rome."[33] Foxe's history promises to lay before the reader the evidence of horrible actions committed by the papists leading to "heaps of slain bodies, of so many men and women, both old, young, children, infants, new born, married, unmarried, wives, widows, maids, blind men, lame men, whole men . . . whole households and whole kindreds together . . . whose wounds, yet bleeding before the face of God, cry vengeance!" (509). These heaps of slain bodies are the very "acts and facts" that result from the papists' "errors and superstitious vanities" (509, 512). Foxe's mission is to dispel the "partial dealing and corrupt handling of [other] histories," for without *his* history "man's life is *blind*. . ." (520; italics added). An imperious thinker, Foxe has no difficulty appreciating how someone else may come to internalize a false rationalist ideology and transform into it a cognitive ideology. What is more, Foxe is not merely trying to get his readers to decide between different ways of understanding the world; he is no pluralist. He insists that history demonstrates that there is only *one* way to view the world. Not to view the world his way is to have no view at all; you may as well be blind. Foxe is incapable of envisioning that anyone who has the facts (as presented by Foxe) before him, can possibly come to a different conclusion. The "facts" or "contents" of history are so compelling to Foxe because, in the wake of religious-ideological shifts in English culture, their inner logic has followed ideological suit. This is part of what Althusser means when he defines ideology as the "lived" relationship to the real. It is "lived" because Foxe cannot extricate himself from it (become a "different" individual) for even a single moment in order genuinely to consider an alternative. It is, in Althusser's scenario, always the other who is ideological ("Ideology" 175).

The central point that needs to be made here is that historical narratives or dramas are always ideological in the Althusserian sense. And, what is more, as my earlier citation of Hayden White suggests, a certain set of cultural values is always implied in the very way in which historians (or dramatists) constitute their subject matter (including the "facts" themselves), and in the way they transform their subject matter into a chronologically and causally ordered narrative.[34] Finally, it is therefore important to recognize that a historical narrative or drama does not necessarily express – or appear to express in the reader's mind – cultural or political values which the author embraces or of which he is even conscious. "While it is possible,"

White contends, "to produce a kind of knowledge that is not explicitly linked to any specific social program, all knowledge produced in the human and social sciences lends itself to use by a given ideology better than it does to others" (*The Content of the Form* 81). A written history will always reveal at least certain ideological proclivities, no matter what the author's intent. As such, a historical text is always predisposed to ideological appropriation and is therefore always available to anyone who decides to use it for purposes the author may (or may not) abhor. The practical consequence of this for our study of the drama is that even as the princes in the plays – or, for that matter, James I through his Master of the Revels – sought to control representations of the past, those representations were also beyond the crown's control and therefore fodder for sedition.

In sum, then, written histories are always ideological in the Althusserian sense of the term, despite the fact that the historian may not be consciously peddling a particular political or religious point of view. In fact, since Althusser defines ideology as the spontaneous "lived" relationship to the real conditions of existence, historians are not in a position to recognize all ideological dimensions of their narrative, even though that narrative is the verbal expression of their relationship to the world. The same holds true in literature. Shakespeare's *Richard II* is a case in point, not only because it demonstrates the playwright's Althusserian perceptiveness vis-à-vis ideology, but also because it marks an early moment in the shift *away* from the "great men" theory's understanding of the monarch's relationship to history. Challenged by the Bolingbroke rebellion, Richard labors throughout the play to understand and give expression to his true relationship to his subjects, his world, and his God. But he cannot. It appears that he has lived the "divine right of kings" spontaneously or "innocently." It has never occurred to him that the concept of rule by divine right which he cherishes so much is, in fact, a textbook example of an ideology that oppresses the masses and rationalizes and sanctions as natural a world of grave social inequalities. He fails to see that the success of divine right ideology *depends* not only on his subjects' acceptance of the ideology but also on the monarch's knowledge that divine right theory *is* an ideology. Shakespeare never grants Richard the kind of insight imparted to Lear when, out on the storm-swept heath, the old king senses that *he* could have "show[n] the heavens more just" if only he had taken better care of his suffering subjects (*King Lear* 3.4.36). Richard cannot conceive of a universe in which the monarch's actions determine the subjects' perception of the heavens. It simply never dawns on him that divine right is a theory fabricated and propagated by human beings. It is an ideology he was born into, and which he has come to accept as an accurate image of his (and everyone else's) relationship to reality. When he finally realizes that "grim Necessity" (*Richard*

II 5.1.21) can and will take the crown from God's anointed – and that venom-sucking spiders, heavy-gaited toads, and lurking adders will not rise in his defense (3.2.14,15, 20) – he trades in his heretofore untroubled and absolute metaphysical world view for a nightmarish vision of the world as an existential abyss in which King Richard "straight [is] nothing" (5.5.38). Absolute order or absolute nothingness – those seem to be Richard's only choices.

It is critical here to recognize that Shakespeare's portrayal of Richard II indicates that the playwright understood both the rationalist and the cognitive view of ideology.[35] Indeed, in order to present a Richard II who could not grasp the cognitive view, Shakespeare must have recognized it himself. What we gain therefore from our use of Althusser's conception of ideology is a *place* from which we can bring a character, a play, or a narrative history into focus. The whole of *Richard II*, for example, reveals that Shakespeare understood the operations, the possibilities *and* the limitations of ideology quite well. The play demonstrates how a ruler who himself believes in the fictions that rationalize the power structure will fail miserably; that is, presumably, had Richard *managed* a representation of himself as divine right ruler rather than "lived" it, he would have proved a more reliable king in the eyes of his people and a much tougher adversary for Bolingbroke. But most importantly, for our purposes it shows how literary and historical texts can reveal not just ideology but also the operations by which ideology aims to disguise its own nature.

Shakespeare can offer this kind of perspective on Richard because when he wrote *Richard II* in 1595 England had not yet been touched by the divine right of kings fever James I was to nurture upon ascending to the throne. The theory of divine right was of course known in Tudor times (and was occasionally called on by monarchs to further their authority), but Elizabeth's government is best characterized as a mixed monarchy, where final authority lay with statute law as it was written by monarch *and* parliament. For Shakespeare, therefore, divine right was something of a political relic, something – to use Raymond Williams's word, of a "residual" ideology whose vital currency belonged to a former, and, ironically, to a future epoch.[36] In the course of this study I hope to demonstrate how the history plays discussed here "lift" certain ideological forms from the cognitive to the rationalist (or from the unconscious to the conscious) level – a movement which is aided by the dramatists' keen insights into their culture but also by the historical shifting of cardinal ideological principles from dominant status to residual.

It may ultimately be impossible to determine with certainty *why* Shakespeare and his Stuart colleagues arrived at the kinds of insights vis-à-vis historiography that they did. This study emphasizes the manner in which historiography itself enabled the playwrights, but it is certain that the theater as an institution and the conditions of performance also figure into the equation. First, as Steven Mullaney observes, "public playhouses were born . . . at a time when traditional hierarchies were breaking down,"[37] which allowed them to evolve in unexpected ways. More specifically, the theaters were located in the Liberties, outside of the authority of the city fathers who were, traditionally, vigorously opposed to dramatic performances. The Liberties or suburbs were a culturally liminal area where "the dominant culture [failed] to rearticulate itself in a fashion that would close off gaps and seams opening on the margins of its domain" (Mullaney, *Place of the Stage* 136). These transitory "seams," Mullaney suggests, afforded the theater "a place on the ideological horizon, a marginal and anamorphic perspective on the cultural dynamics of its own time" (136). As a result, Robert Weimann writes, the public theater's geographic location made it "secure enough to defy the authority of the city and, in a cultural sense, broad enough to *complement the representation of the signs of authority with a self-authorization of signs and significations* through which the needs and perspectives of the theater asserted themselves."[38] Historical representation in the drama, to be sure, becomes such a self-authorization of signs and significations. Our earlier example of Hamlet will illustrate the point. Hamlet's ability to write the history of King Claudius's murderous plot parallels and heightens our awareness of Shakespeare's own ability to write the history of kings. This ability, in turn, puts "certain privileged symbols such as representations of monarchy into broad cultural circulation. This stripped those symbols of their sacred aura, making it more possible for spectators to have a critical rather than a merely reverential, attitude toward them."[39]

It should be obvious that the playwrights' interest in historiographical representation would have had little impact on the general public if that public did not have a considerable (though not necessarily critical) knowledge of the writings of English historians. That such popular knowledge of history existed is adequately demonstrated by Louis B. Wright, who argues that while history might at first have been part of any "gentleman's training," it "was soon recommended as a means of inculcating good qualities in the sons of shopkeepers."[40] Hence, if we accept both Woolf's contention that most Tudor historiography preached a fundamentally "conservative ideology" (*Idea of History* xiii) and Wright's claim that these texts were read widely, then we may assume with Robert Weimann that the playwrights' unique social position allowed them to "complement" that ideology with alternative ways of contemplating England's past.

V

So far I have discussed the exchanges linking the drama and historiography (and history). Obviously, the way I conceive of these exchanges is not suggested solely by the plays and historical texts themselves. Hence, it is not amiss to reflect for a moment on the somewhat eclectic theoretical fabric holding this study together. I agree with Raymond Williams that when it comes to marxist meditations on literary form, there is "no abstract theoretical relationship between collective modes and individual projects. The degree of distance between them, within the continuing reality of each mode of consciousness, is historically variable as a function of real social relationships, both general and specific" (*Marxism and Literature* 190). It seems better therefore simply to offer one's readings than to theorize them into some type of harmonious relationship with the dynamic of a broad historical epoch.

Nonetheless, a word should be said about my use of marxist principles and modes of analysis in conjunction with the work of Hayden White, whose work lacks the kind of positivist view of history which is synonymous with marxism. My reasons for this odd pairing are in some measure heuristic. White's unswerving drive toward historiography's literary origins is also a return to a sensibility shared by most renaissance historians. Secondly, marxism, its Althusserian strand in particular, provides the best analytic tools available to date for the scrutinizing of historiography's and literature's ideological dimensions. Nevertheless, despite these heuristic boons, the gap between Marx and White is wide and deep. For Marx, doing history is a science, for White it is an exercise in rhetoric. In Marx's view the historian unveils the iron laws of history, whereas White's historian imposes certain generic (literary) narratives on data in order to make history accessible and meaningful to contemporary readership. For Marx, history is in large measure objective; for White, history never escapes the subjectivity of the historian's culture.

It may be that the tension between marxist positivism and Whitean rhetoric is philosophically irresolvable, insofar as mimetic and post-structuralist conceptions of the world must, in the final analysis, be incongruent. There may, however, be a practical and productive middle ground where a rapprochement between the two positions can be achieved. First, Hayden White's rhetorical understanding of history need not be reduced either to paralyzing subjectivism or to a depressing descent into discourse.[41] White's emphasis on historiography's basically linguistic character does not have to lead us into a post-structuralist abyss where, in Hamlet's words, we have nothing but "words, words, words." In response to Barthes's assertion that "historical discourse is in its essence a form of ideological elaboration" (i.e.

not a representation of the real), White observes that as far as he is concerned this does not "mean the degradation of historiography to the status of ideology or propaganda" (*Tropics of Discourse* 99). His remark, however, appears to be limited to the rationalist view of ideology. This becomes clear when White goes on to suggest that his analysis of history-writing "would serve as a potent antidote to the tendency of historians to become captive of ideological preconceptions which they do not recognize as such but honor as the 'correct' perception of 'the way things *really* are.' By drawing historiography nearer to its origins in literary sensibility, we should be able to identify the ideological, because it is the fictive, element in our own discourse. We are always able to see the fictive element in those historians with whose interpretations of a given set of events we disagree; we seldom perceive that element in our own prose" (99). Although quotation marks render ambiguous references to "objectivity" and the "real," I would argue that White's position is remarkably close to Terry Eagleton's. White clearly believes that one can transcend one's ideology by raising one's self-awareness. And this can mean two things: (1) the historian can increase awareness of his/her rationalist ideologies, and (2) the historian can gain a perspective on his/her cognitive ideologies. The former is often not all that difficult, but the latter does not allow for such simple transcendence because it calls for a transcendence of the *way* we think about the world and the *way* we interact with our environment. Nonetheless, White seems to share the Althusserian view of cognitive ideology when he alludes to the culture's aggregate impact ("myth, fable, and folklore, scientific knowledge, religion, and literary art" – all of which can become integral to consciousness) on the way the historians constitute and comprehend their "facts" and the way they arrange them into sense-making narratives – Althusser might call this the interpellation of the individual as the historian (and narrativist).[42]

In *Criticism and Ideology*, Eagleton adopts a position akin to White's. Eagleton's commitment to language's referentiality is perhaps greater than White's, but he, too, displays a dash of post-structuralism. Though language denotes objects, he writes,

> it does not do so in a simple relationship, as though word and object stood adjacent, as two poles awaiting the electric current of interconnection. A text, naturally, may speak of real history, of Napoleon or Chartism, but even if it maintains empirical historical accuracy this is always a *fictive* treatment – an operation of historical data according to the laws of textual production. . . To say that the 'historical' literary work must operate as fiction is not, of course, to suppress the relevance of the particular history with which it deals, as though this might be *any* history. It is to claim that *this* particular history is being fictionalized – construed in terms of an ideological production of its agents' modes of ideological insertion into it, and so rendered as *ideology to the second power*. (70)

The word "fictive" here carries the same critical sense and interpretative weight as it does for Hayden White. For Eagleton, the analysis of fictionalized history yields "a sort of historical knowledge" of the ideological codes which aid in the production of the fiction (*Criticism and Ideology* 71); while for White the analysis of the fictional element in historiography leads to a "knowledge" of "'the way things really are'" – i.e., of the forms we use to fictionalize our world.

This provisional alliance between White and recent marxist literary criticism should be productive for my inquiry because it stresses the constructed character of historical narratives as well as access to the "knowledge" (codes, ideologies, fictions) of the culture which produced them. This emphasis is ideal for my purposes. Mine is a study of renaissance conceptions of its past, not that past itself. Mine is a study of the ideological and constructed character of those conceptions, and what they tell us about the culture of their origins.

1 Renaissance historiography

I

In *The Idea of History in Early Stuart England*, D. R. Woolf asserts that with the exception of ecclesiastical historiography Tudor and early Stuart historical writing "reflects a conservative ideology of obedience, duty, and deference to social and political hierarchy."[1] Until at least the 1630s, he argues, English historians held "a relatively monochromatic, and almost universally shared, image of the national past." Lest his views are mistaken for Tillyard's, Woolf adds that early Stuart political thinking did permit "a range of opinions on questions such as the relationship of monarch and law, of prince and parliament, and of church and state," but that it did "without ever challenging assumptions about the need for political order, the importance of social hierarchy, and the dangers of rebellion" (xiv). Annabel Patterson's recent book on Holinshed,[2] I think, presents an interesting challenge to Woolf's monochromatic picture of Stuart historiography, but, on the whole, we have to agree with Woolf that although historical writings and historical drama were subjected to government control (and therefore deemed potentially subversive), neither genre is generally known to have incited rebellion or called for radical changes in the monarchy. On the other hand, we should not be lulled into believing that "moderate dissent and subtle shadings in various historians' personal pictures of the past" constitutes anything less than the basis for the "truly dialectical, even confrontational" nature that comes to characterize historiography as we near the English Revolution (Woolf, *Idea of History* 33). That dialectic may not reveal itself fully until the abolishment of censorship in the 1640s, but the seeds for confrontation had long been sown, for what could potentially be more subversive to the stability of the state than "moderate dissent and subtle shadings" on questions of the crown's relationship to the law, parliament, church and the state?

Undoubtedly, on the surface, sixteenth- and early-seventeenth-century historiography presents a broad consensus on issues of obedience and duty, but within that accord we perceive a latent basis for political confrontation. Historians may have cared little to make conspicuous the seeds of their dissent, but these seeds are nonetheless there for anyone who wishes to discern them. The playwrights did just that.

It is a principal impetus of the present study to show that the political consensus Woolf discerns in the narrative histories is already challenged vigorously by historiographical means in the historical dramas of the late Elizabethan and early Stuart periods. A quick illustration will make the point. To underscore his argument about historians' consensual outlook, Woolf observes that "For certain English kings the jury [of historians and their readers] spoke with unanimity. Henry VII was uniformly (and necessarily, under the Tudors) considered a good king, Richard III the archetypal tyrant. Edward I and Henry V were successful, Edward II a failure" (*Idea of History* 31). A brief glance at Shakespeare's portrayal of Henry V, however (I will take up Henry VII in chapter 6), shows Shakespeare challenging the historians' "unanimity" on the success of this king. Woolf calls Henry V a "pious warrior" and quotes Edward Hall to contend that Henry was perceived as "a captaine against whome fortune never frowned nor mischance once spurned" (*Idea of History* 7). In *Henry V*, however, the deep ideological rift between Chorus and many of the king's actions, and the perception of those actions by various characters such as the common soldier Williams, counsels us away from any kind of moral or political consensus regarding Henry's exploits. Shakespeare furthermore identifies the Chorus as a self-professed historian from the outset. "Admit me Chorus to this history" (Prologue 32),[3] the Chorus implores, entreating the audience not only to "Piece out [the theater's] imperfections with your thoughts" (23) but also to enlist its "imaginary forces" on Henry's side in the great patriotic war against France. The fact is that the first thing the audience sees following this ideologically charged invitation are not proud horses and heroically decked-out kings but two conniving churchmen who are instantly implicated in an opportunistic political deal with Henry, in which the king will allow the Church to keep its temporal lands in return for the financing of, and lending its religious authority to, the invasion of France.[4] Clearly, the dialectical clash on politics, which according to Woolf does not occur in historiography until the 1630s, is superbly evident as Shakespeare sets the Chorus' version of history against the dramatic-historical tale that accounts for the rest of the play. Not only is there no historiographical consensus in *Henry V*, the range of opinions expressed ranges well beyond "moderate dissent and subtle shadings . . . of personal pictures of the past" and posits irreconcilable historical views.

My probe into the Stuart historical drama, then, occurs within the context of developing trends in renaissance historiography. I will show how the persistent, yet irregular, development of early modern historiography allows it to emerge as a catalyst furthering the transformation and eventual disappearance of historical drama as England approaches the 1640s. And although there is virtual unanimity among twentieth-century scholars that the history play's demise goes hand in hand with its aesthetic decline,[5] it is my resolve throughout to demonstrate how the development of the historiographical method also had a positive, enriching, and complicating effect on the post-Elizabethan history play – even while making it finally obsolete. Before we can meaningfully explore the ways in which the drama destabilizes historiographical discourse, we first need to turn to history-writing itself.

II

The subject of renaissance historiography has certainly received ample attention from modern historians, yet its centrality to the present study of the drama makes it necessary to review here some of its salient concerns and to give an account of what the terms "history" and "historiography" might have meant to sixteenth- and seventeenth-century readers and writers. My account will not, nor need it, be exhaustive. I will bring to the fore chiefly those aspects of historiography that clearly impacted the drama. Furthermore, since it is less my aim to revise the history of historiography than to locate the historical drama in relation to it, I incur a heavy debt to the work done by modern historians of historiography. [6] My first task will be to identify and briefly characterize the main currents in renaissance historical thought. Next, I will expand upon these characterizations and situate the various historiographical currents diachronically in an attempt to demonstrate their development and interconnection.

One provisional way of coming at the field of renaissance historiographical theory and practice is to carve it into three principal zones: late medievalist (or providentialist), humanist (early and late, Christian and more or less secular), and antiquarian. Medieval historiography was concerned first and foremost with explicating the links between divine providence and human affairs, whereas humanist historiography drew on the texts of classical antiquity for exemplary instances by which to guide moral, literary, and political conduct in the present. Antiquarians, on the other hand, were driven to reconstruct, through study of both textual and physical remains, the past for its own sake (although there were a number of humanist antiquarians, among them John Selden, who viewed the past "with special reference to contemporary legal and political issues" [Ferguson, *Clio Unbound* 58]). Because today providential historiography is often held to be ahistorical and because antiquarian research is frequently likened to an early form of modern historical scholarship, it has been suggested that the trajectory of historiography's progress leads from a primitive focus on God's divine and, in some sense, extra-historical will to an ever-growing scholarly respect (which ostensibly characterizes modern historiography) for the distinguishing qualities (material, psychological, and institutional) of distant civilizations. It must be stressed, however, that such a teleology is at best misleading.

The somewhat bewildering reality of historiography's development does not allow for easy schematization. In actuality, there were often no rigorous theoretical divisions between these approaches (although antiquarians were commonly distinguished from historians insofar as they were not thought of as historians at all, neither by the historians nor by themselves); nor did these approaches follow each other in neat chronological order. In fact, during the period from 1530 to 1640, a single historical text could contain, often without any discernible authorial awareness of methodological contradiction, elements of each of these three main approaches. Hence, the description of renaissance historical practice that follows does more to confound than to authenticate a schematic view. Still, the gradual abandonment (though not the rejection) of providential causes in favor of secondary causes and a philological interest in antiquities does mark a shift in *emphasis* in historical consciousness during the English renaissance (Gransden, *Historical Writing* 426).

For the modern reader it is important to recall that "history" did not become an academic subject in England until the eighteenth century. Its absence from medieval and renaissance curricula is in large measure responsible for its erratic development. Had history become an academic pursuit earlier, scholarly rigor might have regularized it sooner. But, as F. J. Levy points out, "there was no danger that history writing would become an academic subject, since neither its authors nor its readers ever received any formal training in it" (*Tudor Historical Thought* 51). By the early decades of the sixteenth century, there were very few historians in England who grappled with questions of theory and practice, but their number grew gradually throughout the sixteenth century, as the influence of continental theorists of history such as Polydore Vergil, Jean Bodin, Jacques Amyot, Niccoló Machiavelli, Francesco Guicciardini, and others, became more widespread.[7] One undeniable result of these foreign influences was a growing sophistication in the inquiries of individual English historians, but it should be clear that by the early seventeenth century still nothing like a uniform approach either to the nature or to the purpose of history-writing had emerged. In part this was so because, as an academic subject, history had still not risen above its medieval status as an endeavor "subsumed under rhetoric" (9).[8]

By the fifteenth or even the sixteenth century the term "history" had not yet come to refer exclusively to our modern notion of "a record of past events" (13). Even this broad and rudimentary definition is insufficiently supple to contain scholarly and popular understandings of the term as late as the early 1600s.[9] Certainly, many more readers and writers considered history to be "a record of the past" in Francis Bacon's day than in William Caxton's, but it is still relatively easy to find late-sixteenth- and early-seventeenth-century instances (both scholarly and literary) where the term "history" refers simply to "story."[10] As Woolf points out,

> In common parlance, a play could be a history, or a "tragical history," or a "historical comedy," or even, somewhat redundantly, a "chronicle history". . . . Poems were also often considered histories, especially but not exclusively when they versified events generally accepted as having actually occurred. . . . A variety of prose forms was also called history. Besides the obvious candidates. Bacon's *Henry VII* (1622), Camden's *Annales* (1625–27) and the like – narratives of current events, which would now be deemed journalism, were commonly referred to as histories. . . . (*Idea of History* 16)[11]

Moreover, even among those who concurred that history ought to be a "record of past events," there was profound disagreement over what exactly ought to be included in that record and what it ought to be used for.

The advent of humanism in late medieval England complicated matters further.[12] Lacking internal consistency on questions of historiographical method and purpose, humanism not only introduced various new ways of thinking about the past, it also made available to English historians more than one model for writing about it. Historiographical *practice*, however, despite the historians' best intentions, did not always keep up with conceptual innovations. The great chronicles of Hall, Grafton, and Holinshed (which proved so important to the dramatists), for instance, often proclaim prefatorily to embrace rigorous (humanist or even antiquarian) historiographical innovations, but these avowals are scarcely borne out by their old-fashioned and often offhand practices. In their addresses to William Cecil and "the reader" respectively, Grafton and Holinshed are clearly aware of various forms and hierarchies of historical evidence.[13] They distinguish between the claims of preceding historians (Aucthors), reports, eyewitness reports, their learned friends, and their own personal observations and experience. They indicate that these different types of evidence ought to be weighed differently. Holinshed, for example, notes that he has "in things doubtfull rather chosen to shew the diuersitie of [other historians'] writings, than by ouer-ruling them, and vsing a peremtorie censure, to frame them to agree to my liking. . ." (n.p.). Here Holinshed certainly sounds like a cautious modern historian, but his historiographical practice matches the lofty aims of his method only part of the time, which will become clear in chapter 6 when I discuss his treatment of the Warbeck episode. This phenomenon is by no means merely a mark of the "vulgar" compilations of the popularizers of history, for we will notice a similar disparity between theory and practice in Bacon's highly sophisticated and ambitious history of Henry VII (chapter 6).

Historiography's status as a mode of inquiry in renaissance culture is further confounded by the continued cultural currency of older ideas about the past, even when these could have been supplanted by the emergence of newer and more sophisticated conceptions of history. Taken together, this shows that renaissance historiography, unconstrained by singleness of purpose or method (and catering to a seemingly impervious readership), developed eclectically, allowing individual historians to pick and choose from a wide variety of sources to produce versions of England's past commensurate with the political, religious, cultural, and commercial requirements of the day.

But it is not solely a lack of epistemological rigor or consistency that accounts for historiography's uncertain social and scientific status. Indeed, as a social practice historiography's standing was greatly complicated because of its rise as "a matter of public interest, both in the sense that the material of English history was popular material for the emerging national theater, and because (for a set of reasons which included the same popular appeal) the government regarded English historical materials as subject to its own control."[14] The tremendous surge in historical curiosity that produced the great Tudor chronicles and historical dramas (and the simultaneous intensification of government censorship) is not merely a sign of history's growing popularity but also of its escalating social significance in a culture seeking to define itself in terms of its past.[15] The creation of the Tudor dynasty, founded on doubtful historical claims, motivated both government and politically astute subjects to become aware of history as a branch of knowledge that could be manipulated for ideological purposes. Such manipulation was made possible not least by a growing awareness of historiography as a methodologically eclectic and *under*determined practice. This underdetermination opened up a space where discourse was not firmly controlled, and where there was room for conflicting views. Significantly, the underdetermined character of historiographical discourse was not merely a convenient way for the power elite to manipulate bloodlines, family genealogies, claims to properties, inheritances, etc.; for those working in the theater, it also became a site where the otherwise disenfranchised could promote their agendas by retelling and revising the nation's past.

III

Although medieval historical thought is more complex than we are often led to believe, it is not necessary here to offer a comprehensive survey of all its intricacies and nuances in order to convey its profound impact on the historical drama. The prevailing belief among medieval people was that they inhabited a divinely structured universe, that they understood some, but not all, of its details, and that God, in his omnipotence and omniscience, controlled and guided events. The central question to be addressed was how to live a life that would please God and be rewarded with a place in heaven. Convinced that God would not leave humanity wholly to its own devices, medieval Christians believed that "history demonstrated the working's of God's will on earth; as mankind proceeded towards its destiny, the last judgment and eternal life in heaven and hell, God rewarded virtue, punished vice and otherwise showed His omnipotence" (Gransden, *Historical Writing* 454). Of course it was not always possible to demonstrate clear and trustworthy links between earthly events and divine providence, and medieval historians would frequently "adopt a literary structure to reflect the divine scheme" (454–5). Such literary expressions of God's general plan could take various shapes,[16] and although their importance faded considerably in the renaissance, it is clear that like their medieval predecessors, renaissance historians could never completely abandon the thought that providence shapes history.

Taken in their totality, medieval histories span a broad spectrum. They range from non-narrative monastic chronicles detailing daily events of monastic life to ambitious Reformation arguments enumerating the corruptions of Rome and the essential purity of the English Church; from local topographical histories to universal histories; and from moral diatribes against the wickedness of princes to the interpretation of natural events as signs of God's displeasure. But on whatever specifics a given historian might focus, his contribution was always to be understood in light of Christian revelation, which offered, in the words, of Collingwood, "a view of the entire history of the world, from its creation in the past to its end in the future, as seen in the timeless and eternal vision of God."[17]

Notwithstanding the unpredictable nature of life's small details, it was one peculiar consequence of eschatological thought that meaningful historical changes could not occur within God's grand historical scheme. This circumstance left the historian in an unenviable position: his account could never be anything more than "a record of a (more or less restless) anticipation of the detailed disclosure of a pattern of events which God had revealed in outline. Men could pursue what ends they might but they could not alter the framework of their lives. Innovation was the exclusive preserve of God" (Haddock, *Introduction to Historical Thought* 1–2). On this view, history was split into two separate spheres, "one which determines and one which is determined: the abstract law and the mere fact, the universal and the particular" (Collingwood, *The Idea of History* 54). The preclusion of human efficacy on the outcome of God's universal plan could only lead to the embarrassing conclusion that there was precious little of consequence left to do for humankind. As a consequence, medieval historians did not consider it an especially crucial purpose of histories to chronicle the transient stream of human incidents. It also followed that if indeed an individual's earthly sojourn was but momentary and chiefly ought to help him or her achieve a place in heaven, then historiography could have no nobler objective than to aid in this achievement.

Structured hierarchically (as opposed to temporally) and, on the whole, resistant to social mobility and weary of innovation, English medieval society was marked by a deep-seated sense of stasis. One vital consequence of this view was that somehow history had to *repeat* itself. At work here, as Woolf makes clear, are two seemingly contradictory notions of time. "Through Revelation the Judaeo-Christian tradition taught that all events proceeded *sub specie aeternitatis*, in a more-or-less-straight line from Creation to Apocalypse. But classical writers had asserted a different pattern, based on cycles observable in nature" (Woolf, *Idea of History* 5). A highly influential humanist historian, Thomas Blundeville synthesized these two conceptions by arguing that "the Judaeo-Christian view was itself not strictly linear; and the very concept of divine judgment rewarding and punishing individuals, and of the rise and fall of empires and cities, reveals the Christian time scheme as a spiral rather than a straight line" (5).[18] From this it follows reasonably that medieval and some renaissance historians were not particularly bothered by anachronisms, by the blending of fact and fiction, or that they had only a superficial interest in the dynamics of secondary, natural, or human causes. A lackluster concern with secondary causes is quite evident in works as late as George Cavendish's *The Life and Death of Cardinal Wolsey* (1558). Writing the life of his former master, Cavendish shows little interest in the specific and concrete political errors that may have brought the cardinal down. Instead he eagerly reminds the reader of the dangers of the cardinal's hubris, and underscores the *de casibus* shape of history, and the influence of Fortune and of history's primary mover, God. Cavendish observes:

> I have written thus this history at large because it was thought that the Cardinal gave the chief occasion of all this mischief. Ye may perceive what thing so ever a man purposeth, be he prince or prelate, yet notwithstanding God disposeth all things at His will and pleasure. Wherefore it is great folly for any wise man to take any weighty enterprise of himself, trusting alone to his own will, not calling for grace to assist him in all his proceedings. I have known and seen in my days that princes and great men [who] would either assemble at any parliament or in any other great business first would most reverently call to God for His gracious assistance therein; and now I see the contrary. Wherefore me seems that they trust more in their own

wisdoms and imaginations than they do in God's help and disposition. And therefore often they speed thereafter and their matters take such success.[19]

Like the princes and great men of this passage, medieval and early renaissance historians were of course not incapable of understanding "modern" distinctions between primary and secondary causes; but the distinction was ultimately meaningless to them because all secondary causes were finally merely effects of the primary cause, God's providence. For the same reason, the notion of anachronism was also largely insignificant. Because of their conception of history as cyclical, medieval historians "lacked a sense of the past being different in quality from the present. They did not deny that in some ways the past was unlike the present; they knew, for example, that the ancients had not been Christians. But they did not take the difference very seriously" (Burke, *Renaissance Sense* 1).[20] William Caxton and his contemporaries, Joseph Levine notes,

accepted and embroidered an elaborate body of legend, both sacred and secular, and did not seek to differentiate between romance and chronicle or between past and present. The Trojan heroes and Christian saints who helped to populate the first printed books were often entirely imaginary and were almost always portrayed as contemporaries. Caxton understood history primarily as edification, and he did not bother to make distinctions that had no obvious value. (*Humanism and History* 11–12)

Clearly, then, there was no need for a rigorous and systematic analysis of human events in a secular context, and hence there was no good reason for such a model to sprout from the historian's mind. True, medieval histories do occasionally draw on original documents (as opposed to the narratives of other historians) and a few of them even compare various accounts on a single issue (Gransden, *Historical Writing* 461), but they exhibit no uniform rules for the handling of sources and evidence; and they routinely rely on legend, poorly documented chronicles or narratives, as well as on hearsay. Overall, the meaning of "facts" as well as the cause–effect relationships linking them are determined by implicit or explicit religious truth in the final instance. Though quite eager to comment on the "true" meaning of historical events, the attention of the medieval historian was habitually diverted from those events and drawn to the extra-historical divine as the decisive cause of history.

Needless to say, a historical method that attributed final meaning to the mysteries of divine providence was particularly amenable to those pushing a particular ideological agenda. Grand meta-narratives that aim to explain life, we know, often end up rationalizing various social and economic inequalities. This, of course, is especially true for a narrative that promises rewards primarily in the afterlife, because it will implicitly support the social status quo. Nonetheless, until the sixteenth century strong political points of view are rare in English historiography (Gransden, *Historical Writing* 456), and when a political bias is evident, the chronicle is as likely to present a view of history favorable to the central government as against it (456–8). More to the point here, medieval historiography, by virtue of its focus on the progress of transcendent truth and its view of the human condition as essentially unchanging, naturally served the existing socio-political and economic status quo. Even if a historian saw fit to find quarrel with the government, the outlook of providentially informed historical writing, as a whole, was still orthodox. Historians firmly believed in the orderly nature of the universe. No matter how chaotic or disparate events appeared, and no matter how far the historian might stray in his explanations, the "theological framework remained visible" (Levy, *Tudor Historical Thought* 11).[21] This conservativism is especially significant in light of the fact that, generally speaking, historians' accounts of the past were accepted uncritically by other historians as well as by readers (20; also see Gransden 48–9). The most visible medieval legacy in the development of renaissance historical thought, therefore, was the continued acknowledgment of these theological boundaries; it was left to late medieval and renaissance thinkers to start pushing against these boundaries and reduce their prominence in the analysis of the past.

Thomas Blundeville's *The True Order and Methode of Wryting and Reading Hystories* (1574),[22] which D. R. Woolf correctly identifies as the first sustained attempt by an Englishman to explore the theoretical premises underlying historical discourse (*Idea of History* 3), is also the first text earnestly to test historiography's boundaries from within. Strongly influenced by Italian sources that evince an interest in political history, Blundeville's theory combines a novel insistence to identify the "principall [secondary] cause[s]" of events with a thoroughly conventional desire to demonstrate how history is "the providence of god" (*True Order and Method* 165). This dual purpose should have created a tension, but for Blundeville and his contemporaries it did not because they saw no incongruency in historical analysis that explained the complex and concrete causes and unpredictable consequences of political events, and simultaneously staunchly maintained that "[N]othing is done by chance, but all things by his foresight, counsell and divine providence" (165). "As touching the providence of God," Blundeville writes, "we haue to note for what causes and by what meanes hee ouerthroweth one kingdome & setteth vp another. For though things many times doe succeede according to the discourse of mãs reason: yet mans wisdome is oftentymes greatlye deceyued" (165). Blundeville senses no contradiction, perhaps in part because, despite the Italian influences, he is ultimately less concerned with political history than with that strain of continental humanism that gleans moral wisdom from the rising and falling fortunes of princes and states. His aim is not to understand politics in a human context, but to foreground divine approval or disapproval of the behavior of rulers. Even so, Blundeville's application of Italian political thought drew the attention of a number of English historians and they found it increasingly difficult to maintain a credible interpretive balance between secondary and providential explanations. In time, these historians would become absorbed more and more by the import of second causes. Providence, while still invoked with apparent sincerity, would be bracketed from lengthy historical analysis, only to be invoked in *pro forma* fashion in the end.

Providential arguments and explanations are far from anathema to the Stuart historical drama (God's providence is referred to innumerable times), but the drama's interrogation of such arguments and explanations greatly exceeds anything we encounter in Blundeville. In Blundeville and his medieval predecessors we observe a high level of comfort when the consequences of politics, treachery, stratagem, and suffering are ascribed to providence and/or fortune. We sense a certain peace of mind in the assent to a greater, invisible power. The humanist historian Polydore Vergil, for instance, whose *Anglica Historia* stands as an early example of historiographical skepticism and analytical rigor, readily recalls Cadwaller's famous "heavenly" prophecy to bolster the legitimacy of his patron, Henry VII. Polydore observes:

> Thus Henry acquired the kingdom, an event of which foreknowledge had been possible both many centuries earlier and also soon after his birth. For 797 years before, there came one night to Cadwaller, the last king of the Britons (as we have seen in the third book of this history), some sort of an apparition with a heavenly appearance; this foretold how long afterwards it would come to pass that his descendants would recover the land. This prophecy, they say, came true in Henry, who traced his ancestry back to Cadwaller. The same prediction was made to Henry in his childhood by Henry VI (as we have pointed out in the life of Edward).[23]

The "they say" clause distances Polydore slightly from this "heavenly" authorization of Henry's crown, but the very fact that he includes the prophetic-historical passage speaks volumes. Yet when we get to Shakespeare and Fletcher's Jacobean history play, *Henry VIII*, we will see that Archbishop Cranmer's very similar historical prophecy, also spoken at the behest of a king, is subjected to a scrutiny it is unable to withstand. Shakespeare and Fletcher will directly interrogate the kind of "royal" history-writing occasionally exemplified by Polydore.

IV

The transforming influence of humanist thought on English life and letters is multi-faceted but well documented.[24] Historians commonly recognize humanism's rise as the principal force that unbalanced the medieval equilibrium. As soon as it became acceptable practice to combine a classical education with "patriotic and religious motivation" (a practice encouraged by the English Reformation and break with the Church of Rome), "the humanists had once and for all shattered the medieval view that the past was continuous and undifferentiated" (Levine, *Humanism and History* 80). In its broadest sense, humanism has been authoritatively defined as "a cultural and educational program with a special literary preoccupation, a recapitulation of the ancient *studia humanitatis* with its particular cycle of disciplines: grammar, rhetoric, history, poetry, and moral philosophy."[25] Until humanism's rise, the Bible and church authority had been the ultimate source for moral instruction, historical knowledge and precedent, as well as for authoritative examples of many literary genres. The precise reasons why the texts and artifacts of antiquity came to supplement (and, gradually, to replace) the Bible as the primary source to be imitated or emulated are beyond the scope of the present study.[26] Here it suffices to recognize briefly that during the period from the middle of the fourteenth to the early eighteenth century the western world changed decisively and absolutely. Ernst Breisach describes these changes succinctly:

> In the age of discovery the world became global; scholars and philosophers conjured up new visions of nature and the cosmos; the works of classical antiquity were recovered, critically assessed, and adulated to an unprecedented degree; over a thousand years of a united Latin Christendom ended; and the state, emerging as the basic framework for people's lives, provoked discussions of statecraft, collective identity, and laws. (*Historiography* 153)

Perhaps the simplest way of stating the importance of these changes for the development of historiography is that people began to view their own world as substantially *different* from societies of the past. This sense of the past as *other* – of societies with their *own* language, institutions, laws, and customs – combined with the desire to recover valuable aspects of these lost cultures, created a need for new methods of inquiry.

Humanism's sway over historical scholarship was perhaps most visible in a new sort of interest in the texts and, eventually, in the cultures of Roman and Greek antiquity. To be sure, Latin texts in particular had been read and preserved in the medieval monasteries, but their readership had been extremely small because of the limitations in reproduction technology and widespread illiteracy outside the cloister walls. Moreover, as is routinely stated, medieval scholarship had overlaid the texts of antiquity with so "many layers of commentary, allegory and interpretation" that commentary had replaced the text itself as the object of study.[27] In debate, medieval scholars had appealed to the evidence of traditional and accumulated authorities (the Bible, the Church Fathers, Aristotle, the scholastic philosophers), but humanist scholars tried to wipe the textual slate clean so that the original, unadulterated text itself might be studied. Scholars were generally delighted by what they discovered, and there was a growing sense that something authentic, unique, and of considerable value was contained in the remains of past civilizations.

Humanist thought was relatively unconcerned with the abstract shape of providence on an immediate level of analysis, and instead promoted a powerful interest in the specifics of antiquity and its surviving texts, even though, paradoxically, it displayed initially no desire actually to recuperate lost Greek and Roman civilizations in any kind of systematic manner. Instead, the writings of Livy, Sallust, Caesar, Cicero, and others, were treated as source-books for the teaching of grammar and rhetoric. From these texts, it was suggested, "'the boys shall gather the flowers . . .,' that is, the phrases of use to a student of rhetoric" (Levy, *Tudor Historical Thought* 46). The absence of a desire to know history for its own sake and the reduction of historical texts to a manual for style are, ironically, not altogether anachronistic. The Romans themselves had conceived of history as obligated to record truth, but their systematic failure to conduct significant research into their own past, combined with the overriding emphasis on history as a means for promoting civic responsibility, patriotism, and public consensus, designated history-writing foremost as a sub-category of rhetoric. "Truth for Cicero and Lucian, the only Roman writers to make more than casual remarks on historiography, was simply needed to give power of persuasion" (Breisach, *Historiography* 76).[28] The relevance and value of any account of the past was measured by its ability to illuminate and guide conduct in the present. As J. G. A. Pocock notes, the desire of many humanists to "return to the ancient world 'as it really was'" placed them "on the threshold of the modern historical consciousness" (*Ancient Constitution* 4). Yet their reason for doing so – to consider antiquity as a storehouse of examples to be imitated, copied or avoided – assumed a profound identification of antiquity with the present, which made it very difficult precisely to discern what made the past *different* from the present; that is, what made it historical in the first place.

A further crucial feature introduced into English historical thought by humanists is thematic and narrative unity. Medieval chronicles had chiefly been annalist and chronological in character.[29] Consequently, a humanist history like Sir Thomas More's of King Richard III offered readers and historians like the popularizer Edward Hall, who copied More in totem, a unity of theme and purpose hitherto unknown in English historiography. Together with the increase in literacy and improvements in methods for textual reproduction, the imposition of a literary structure (Hayden White's pregeneric emplotment) on the data of the chronicles transformed history into a commanding tool for pedagogically motivated humanists and dynasty-conscious monarchs. Taken together these developments in method and purpose made it possible for some histories to be cautious and reluctant interpreters of the past, while others took the shape of stylized, didactic, philosophical or (in the case of More's *Richard III*) psychological treatises embellished with fabricated speeches and informed only periodically by historical anecdote or fact. But no matter how crucial these differences may appear to us, the important point here is that for renaissance readers and writers both kinds of history were just that: history. There was nothing especially wrong in abandoning the truth of specific facts if this was done to illustrate a greater truth.

The coming of the renaissance to England, however, did not instantly alter historiographical thought or practice. Even after the publication of Polydore's *Anglica Historia* and More's *Richard III*, the two quintessential humanist histories to be written in England, little changed in the overall historiographical picture. For sure, Polydore's and More's histories were ransacked by succeeding authors, but neither the former's historiographical method nor the latter's literary form were imitated (Gransden, *Historical Writing* 469). The changes in historiographical practice were to be incremental, responding only slowly to innovations of continental humanists as well as to the gradual changes in newly emerging social and political conditions of the post-Wars-of-the-Roses England. We are often told about the smooth, linear development of renaissance historiography, but the record shows differently.

Nor should we accept the commonplace about the renaissance that equates the rise of humanism with the steady secularization of English society. For one thing, through the influence of Erasmus of Rotterdam and John Colet of London, Christian humanism made significant inroads into English historical scholarship. Based on the postulate that humanist methodology could be applied to the ancient texts of Christianity, Christian humanism offered Colet a way to avoid the danger of paganization seemingly inherent in classical humanism while at the same time circumventing the "aridity of scholasticism" which relied almost exclusively on logic and disputation (Levy, *Tudor Historical Thought* 41). Colet, for example, approached the New Testament in a manner quite different from his contemporaries. Employing the principles of humanist philology, he studied the text itself, not the commentaries, and tried to interpret its meaning and intent in the original historical context (42, 41).

Nonetheless, the commonplace regarding humanism's secularizing powers is of course not altogether without merit. We should not overstate or leave undefined, however, what is meant by the "secular" here.

Irrefutably, the content of humanist histories takes after its medieval ancestors in many respects. This is not the exclusive result of a pillaging of medieval chronicles by renaissance authors. Indeed, "the humanists, like their medieval predecessors, saw history as the manifestation of God's will on earth; the future was predicted by prodigies and portends, and the Wheel of Fortune continued to turn" (Gransden, *Historical Writing* 427). Where they differed most notably from their medieval precursors was in their deeper consideration of natural or secondary causes. Furthermore, if medieval historians considered it their calling to expound God's divine plan and to offer moral examples helpful in an individual's salvation, humanist historians' focus on secondary causes "led to the careful analysis of [human] motives, especially of psychological, but also of political ones" (427). The new focus accommodated an increased emphasis on human explanations without denying supreme divine oversight. Tudor humanists may have been "emotionally committed to the medieval paradigm of social stability and prone to think of reform as a return to an ideal norm, [but] they were prepared to see the history of civilization as the gradual adjustment of man, as a rational creature, to the circumstances of his terrestrial existence" (Ferguson, *Clio Unbound* 357).

Persuaded of the rationality and educability of humanity, humanists considered it history's chief tasks to teach moral behavior and the art of rhetoric. It is, however, the study of politics that defines humanism's interests best. If medieval historians generally equated historical truth with moral utility, the Italian humanist historians who came to influence their English counterparts turned to the past foremost for political lessons. And it is not surprising that the two historical events affecting English sixteenth-century historiography most markedly are the ascendancy of the Tudor monarchs and the break with the Church of Rome (Gransden, *Historical Writing* 469). When Henry Richmond defeated Richard III in 1485 at Bosworth Field and married Elizabeth of York, Edward IV's eldest daughter, he united the houses of York and Lancaster, ended the Wars of the Roses, and founded the Tudor dynasty. In retrospect, the military and political maneuvers that enabled Henry to grab and consolidate power appear shrewd and effective, but at the time his crown hung precariously in the balance. Henry Tudor and his successors lacked an unclouded and undisputed historical claim to the throne, and were in need of any advantage propaganda could offer. Motivated by a mixture of enthusiasm and fear, historians like John Rous, Robert Fabyan, and Bernard André (Henry VII's chaplain and biographer) took it upon themselves to express in historical writing the official Tudor point of view (Gransden, *Historical Writing* 469–70). The impact on historiographical theory and practice was phenomenal.

Although the repressive attitude of the Tudor government had an inhibiting effect on writers of contemporary history, its propaganda to some extent encouraged the study of the more distant past. The fifteenth century was treated as a prelude to the accession of Henry Tudor. Already John Hardyng had written of the doom which enshrouded the Lancastrian kings because of Henry Bolingbroke's illegal seizure of power and the murder of Richard II. Polydore Vergil expanded this theme: he saw God's vengeance manifested in the alternation of an unhappy reign with a more propitious one, and regarded Richard III as the wickedest of kings. This embryonic historiographical structure reached its full development in the chronicle of Edward Hall, completed in about 1532 . . . He did not adopt the typically medieval divisions of the Seven Ages of the World, nor even, like Fabyan, of the Seven Joys of the Virgin Mary, but used secular divisions, namely the seven reigns of the kings of England from Henry IV to Henry VIII . . .

In its emphasis on secular power and its predominantly secular tone, and in its literary thematic unity, Hall's chronicle resembles a renaissance history. (*Historical Writing* 470–71)

Lest we credit Tudor ideology too much for having a progressive effect on history-writing, we should note that it also brazenly promoted medieval romance historiography. There was a general outcry against Polydore Vergil's efforts to debunk Geoffrey of Monmouth's legendary account, linking the English kings to Brutus, son of Aeneas. The distinguished antiquary John Selden was so "moved by patriotism and loyalty to Henry VIII and his dynasty" that he retarded the development of historiographical progress by publishing a vigorous defence of Geoffrey's *British History* against the contentions of Polydore (*Historical Writing* 472).

Niccoló Machiavelli's pragmatic approach to political science presented the English with a less propagandistic but enormously potent strain of humanist thought.[30] Machiavelli turned his attention to antiquity in search of examples that would illustrate or help shape his views on questions of political prudence in the present. This pragmatic approach to politics led Machiavelli away from the religious tenets driving Christian humanism, but his judgment that historical examples can aid in the understanding of present circumstances has a certain structural affinity with the medieval and humanist moralists. Both depend on a fundamentally cyclical view of the past. Lydgate's *Fall of Princes* and its sixteenth-century successor *The Mirror for Magistrates* both used the wheel of fortune as a structuring device for a series of individual lives, which start out with good fortune and end in tragedy. The cyclicism here consists of a fairly unsophisticated grasp of historical process: one's fortunes can change at any moment, often without a clear warning. What is on top one moment will be at the bottom with a single turn of the wheel. And the wheel can be turned at any time; and it *will* be turned. This inevitability imposes a regularity on the cyclicism. Yet its long view of history consists of little more than an endless string of individual rises and falls: the macrocosm is a series of microcosms, culminating in Final Judgment where all fortunes are ultimately decided.

It has been suggested that the wheel-of-fortune motif does not place individuals entirely at the mercy of fickle fortune. "Insofar as they retain responsibility for their actions, they can hedge against it. That, too, is the message of the *Mirror* and, indeed, its more profound conclusion" (Ferguson, *Clio Unbound* 350). The minimal degree of genuine political and historical analysis offered to explain the enigmas of fortune make the *Mirror for Magistrates* more an occasion for anxiety and fearful humility than a manual on how to wrestle human destiny away from the spasms of chance. Now Machiavelli, too, accepted fortune's dominance over human affairs, and he also believed in the cyclical shape of history. But despite the conventionality of these beliefs, Machiavelli made an outstanding contribution to historical and political thought by observing that the cycles of history contain within them very clear patterns of development, and claimed that an understanding of those patterns can fortify princes to some extent against the whims of fortune. In his *Discourses on the First Decade of Titus Livius*, for instance, Machiavelli describes the birth of monarchy, then traces its decline into tyranny, followed by rebellion and the establishment of aristocratic government, which then in turn declines into an oligarchic tyranny, when the children, "not knowing the variations of fortune, never having experienced evil," succeeded their fathers. [31] Rejecting the tyranny of the few, Machiavelli argues, the people establish a popular form of government – democracy. Licentiousness soon follows, however, when, "after the death of the generation that established it," the state rapidly lapsed into abuses of liberty:

> there was no fear either of private or public men, so that since each one lived as he pleased, every day a thousand wrongs were done. Hence, forced by necessity, or according to the suggestion of some good man, or to escape such abuses, they returned once more to princedom; and from that, step by step, things went on again toward abuse of freedom, in the ways and for the reasons given. (*Discourses* 198)

Recognizing the pattern could help the prince in preventing conditions that would drive the cycle. Now since England had been a monarchy of some sort since time immemorial, it is not surprising that sixteenth-century historians express only the most cursory interest in alternative forms of government. The case of the English dramatists, however, is quite different. On them Machiavelli's ideas exerted a tremendous influence by kindling their interest in non-monarchical forms of state, in the conditions determining changes in the government of the state, in political causality, in the question of hereditary sovereignty, and in the importance for princes to have first-hand experience and a precise knowledge of history.

Shakespeare's fascination with alternative modes of government is evident in plays like *Coriolanus* and *Julius Caesar* that depict clashes between the patrician Caius Marcius and plebeians, and between idealistic republicans and the powermonger Caesar. These dramatic meditations on the proper distribution of power between government leaders and citizenry were of course not without contemporary resonance in absolutist England, where increasingly antagonistic debates between parliament and crown over right of impositions, imprisonment, individual liberties, and other constitutional matters eventually led to a radical change in government structure. Even a play like *King Lear*, which begins *and* ends with monarchy, draws a highly perceptive and unsettling picture of momentous developments within monarchy: we move from the feudal state of Lear, which functions on the basis of Lear's brand of honesty, loyalty, duty, honor, and reciprocity, to the England of Edgar, who rules, much like Machiavelli's prince, by guile, disguise, and manipulation, and who embraces the dangers of military involvement only when doing so becomes unavoidable. The same argument can be made for *Macbeth*. Other plays such as Ben Jonson's *Cataline* and *Sejanus* and Shakespeare's *Henry V* and the *Henry VI* plays can be added to the list, but of the plays discussed in this study, Massinger and Fletcher's *Tragedy of Sir John Van Olden Barnavelt* is probably the most Machiavelli-inspired drama of the period in its treatment of the Dutch republic's perceived metamorphosis into a monarchy.

Machiavelli also taught English historians and playwrights an important lesson about the political use-value and epistemological status of religion in society. He pointed out that Christian morality can often be incompatible with "actions dictated by the rules of politics."[32] As Felix Gilbert observes, Machiavelli's "central point was that man must choose: he could live aside from the stream of politics and follow the dictates of Christian morality; but if man entered upon the *vita activa* of politics, he must act according to its laws" (*Machiavelli and Guicciardini* 197). Victoria Kahn makes the point even more sharply when she argues that in *The Prince* "prudence has become . . . a technical skill divorced from ethical considerations" (*Rhetoric, Prudence, and Skepticism* 186). Gilbert, however, rightly observes that Machiavelli never promotes amoral behavior for its own sake (*Machiavelli and Guicciardini* 196).

Machiavelli's understanding of religion as ideology in the world of politics made available a point of view that is lacking in writers like Tyndale, Foxe, and Bale. Foxe's *Actes and Monuments*, for instance, critiques Roman Catholicism by pointing out that its unprecedented and therefore unwarranted innovations create a historical context that transforms established and time-honored Christian practices into heresies. Foxe clearly sees that some institutions possess the power to rewrite or recreate historical contexts in a way that radically changes the meaning of religious doctrine. Foxe, however, is unable to recognize that the same logic applies to the tenets of his own religion, which of course also produces historical contexts that aggressively transform other Christian practices into heresies. Foxe's application of principles of historical relativism to the Church of Rome is based not on a faith in the validity of his method but on the religious conviction that Rome has corrupted the Church. He discerns hidden behind perverted Rome the true Church to be recovered, and supplants one metaphysics with another. Machiavelli, on the other hand, does not of course reject one type of Christianity in favor of another. He recognizes Christianity as one group of belief systems among many, each of which has its usefulness in the maintenance of the state; yet none can be granted a transcendental status on epistemological (though perhaps on purely pragmatic) grounds.

Machiavelli's grasp of the separation of political utility or prudence from Christian morality can hardly be exemplified more graphically than it is in the Duke of Gloucester's use of religious symbolism and rhetoric in Shakespeare's *Richard III*. Thwarted by a recalcitrant crowd of "tongueless blocks," ambitious Gloucester and Buckingham secretly decide to clear the way to the crown by presenting Richard as the paragon of Christian piety. Extreme devotion to God, they feel, is the only thing that will convince Lord Mayor and citizens of London that Richard is suitable to be monarch. Buckingham advises Richard to "stand between two churchmen . . . / For on that ground I'll make a holy descant. . ." (*Richard III* 3.7.47–9). After repeated entreaties from co-conspirator Catesby, Richard indeed shows himself "*aloft*," flanked by two bishops, "prayer book in his hand," and explains his reluctance by his "earnest service of my God," which "Deferr'd the visitation of my friends" (3.7.98, 106–7). The people, which were not persuaded by Richard's earlier attempts to paint King Edward's son as illegitimate, are swayed by the charade and give their "amen" to "King Richard, England's worthy king!" (3.7.241, 240).

Shakespeare's decision to allow Richard successfully to deploy religious spectacle and sentiment in this way is all the more pointed because it is absent from his source. Thomas More asserts skeptically that the "stage play" contrived by Richard and the Duke of Buckingham failed to fool the crowd gathered outside Baynard's Castle.[33] The reason the people went along with it, More contends, is that they were afraid what might happen to them if they were to interfere in the proceedings. More's suggestive analogy implies utter contempt for Richard: "in a stage play all the people know right well that he that playeth the sowdaine [sultan] is percase a sowter [shoemaker]. Yet one should can do little good to show out of season what acquaintance he hath with him and call him by his own name while he standeth in his majesty, one of his tormentors [torturers] might hap to break his head, and worthy, for marring the play" (83). More and Shakespeare are equally contemptuous of Richard and skeptical of his ambitions, but the analysis of the role of religion belongs to Shakespeare alone. In Shakespeare religion becomes a tool with *use* value (and no inherent value) in a political contest. In this study, Massinger and Fletcher will offer a Jacobean variation of this Machiavellian theme in their remarkably sympathetic stage portrayal of the Dutch Arminian Johan Van Oldenbarnevelt and his princely Calvinist counterpart, Maurice, both of whom are among Machiavelli's brightest students when it comes to using religious doctrine as a political tool. *The Tragedy of Sir John Van Olden Barnavelt* is something of a civics lesson in the political utility of religion.

It has been argued convincingly that Machiavelli's historicism does not so much urge his readers to imitate one historical example and shun another as it seeks to engage and sharpen the reader's "activity of judgment" so that he could deal more effectively with the never-ending contingencies of human affairs (Kahn, *Rhetoric, Prudence, and Skepticism* 186). But despite his sophistication and skepticism, Machiavelli's view of history as cyclical and of human nature as essentially stable (another feature that he shared with Christian humanists) invited cogent criticism of his innovative countryman Francesco Guicciardini, who argued that examples were inextricably linked to their unique historical context and could not be treated as if they were transhistorically applicable.[34] Guicciardini maintains that it is a terrible mistake to

> cite on all occasions the example of the Romans! To do as the Romans did, we would need to have a city circumstanced like theirs and govern likewise. To attempt it with means so inferior as ours is to require of the ass the fleetness of the horse . . . It is most misleading to judge by examples; for unless these be in all respects parallel, they are of no force, the least diversity in the circumstances giving rise to the widest divergence in the conclusions. To discern these minute differences requires a just and clear eye.[35]

A century later, Francis Bacon found himself struggling with the same problem. Although, as Dean points out, Bacon was unable to move beyond the idea of modeling "one's conduct on historical examples,"[36] he was aware that examples taken out of context and granted too much prominence can adversely affect the merit of an argument. As a remedy, he suggested that "examples alleged for the discourse's sake [should be] cited succinctly and without particularity, and carry a servile aspect toward the discourse which they are brought in to make good."[37] Bacon, therefore, while agreeing with Machiavelli on the instructional value of the example, insisted (at least in his theoretical writings) with Guicciardini's adamancy about the integrity of the historical example. In chapter 3 we will see Thomas Heywood dramatize Guicciardini's insight and underscore the importance of historical context for political meaning.

V

Antiquarians were humanists insofar as they too were occupied with the recuperation of the texts and artifacts of classical antiquity. Their pursuit of the past, however, was more scholarly inclined.[38] The impetus for antiquarian research was born of the rediscovery of antiquity, and stimulated by a belief that an "exact memory" of the objects of antiquity could be restored (Levine, J., *Humanism and History* 73, 77). "The efforts to restore the classical authors was advancing on all fronts [and] as these texts were read and imitated, the problems of their exact meaning and interpretation became more pressing, and renaissance philology was born" (76). Lorenzo Valla's exposure of the "Donation of Constantine" as a fraud on philological grounds is probably the best-known renaissance instance of the use of linguistic analysis to date a text. Relying on his knowledge of the history of the language, Valla established that the idiom and vocabulary of the document did not fit the linguistic characteristics of the early fourth century.[39] Moreover, to aid in the illumination of the literature of the ancients and the rise of the arts in classical antiquity in general, Italian humanists like Poggio Bracciolini and Flavio Biondo undertook the systematic description and "cross-examining" of "old remains" like monuments, coins, and road maps in connection with the written sources (76–77). For the most part, however, antiquarians, despite their occupation with matters of textuality, viewed their labors neither as part of a rhetorical tradition nor as a source for moral or political *exempla*. Foremost they were concerned with the *actual* objects (monuments, road maps, inscriptions, coins, etc.) and documents of the past, and not for any ulterior pedagogical or didactic purpose. They wished to study these artifacts primarily for their own sake and for what the objects could tell the investigator about the character of peoples and societies of another time. And while the humanist narrative historians ordinarily organized their information in a diachronic or "chronological order," renaissance antiquarians wrote, as noted by Arnaldo Momigliano, in a synchronic or "systematic order."[40] This is so because the objectives of narrative historians and antiquarians are different. Narrative historians typically "produce those facts which serve to illustrate or explain a certain situation; antiquarians collect all the items that are connected with a certain subject, whether they help to solve a problem or not" (Momigliano, "Rhetoric of History" 3).[41]

In the course of the sixteenth century, this practice, which led to a variety of innovations, was introduced to English historical studies by John

Leland, William Camden, John Selden, and others. Leland especially understood early on "that the many new devices of Italian humanism could be employed not only to resuscitate classical antiquity but to recover the whole of the British past" (Levine, J., *Humanism and History* 82). Following the same principle in his *Britannia* (1586), William Camden constructed a topographical history of Roman Britain, emphasizing Britain's roots in Roman civilization rather than its legendary connection to Troy. And antiquarians Selden and Sir Henry Spelman showed themselves able and willing "to distinguish things human from things Divine" and thus created a practice sophisticated enough to be called "social history" (Ferguson, *Clio Unbound* 117).[42] Looking back on these achievements, many today are tempted to herald antiquarian respect for the artifacts of history, its restraint in interpreting them, and its suspension of providential or other narrative frames, as the coming of modern historiography. This is no doubt correct, but, ironically, the antiquarian scholar was not viewed as a historical visionary in his own day, and his work was rarely even considered to deserve the name of "history" at all.

In the context of the English renaissance, it would be patently false to view the development of historiography as a linear progression from medieval providentialism to humanist antiquarian scholarship. Its actual development is much too erratic. Nor would it be judicious to follow the lead of J. G. A. Pocock and valorize the scholarly side of historiography (that is, antiquarianism and legal studies) at the expense of the narrative histories. Pocock chastises those who have studied the history of historiography "as if it could be identified with the history of those literary works which bear the title of histories" (*Ancient Constitution and Feudal Law* 7). From a modern vantage point Pocock is certainly correct. The practices of antiquarians can tell us much about the origins of modern practices. It is also indisputable that many narrative histories of the renaissance are driven (consciously or unconsciously) by political and religious agendas, and are shaped by literary and rhetorical considerations that would embarrass a modern historian in search of factual accuracy and objectivity. But here it is of overriding concern that renaissance men and women, historians and readers alike, thought of narrative histories *as* histories. To cast them aside in favor of what *we* would consider to be bona fide histories is to be ahistorical.

In fact, as Pocock and other modern historians have noted, renaissance humanists in particular nurtured a clear prejudice *against* antiquarians, whose enterprise was described as that of "imperfect historians who helped to salvage relics of the past too fragmentary to be the subject of proper history" (Momigliano, "Rhetoric of History" 7). Most renaissance thinkers did not consider antiquarian research "really history at all" (Ferguson,

Clio Unbound 5).[43] In Philip Sidney's *Apology for Poetry*, skepticism about the historian's pursuit of "mouse-eaten records" is joined by a sarcastic assessment of the stereotypical antiquarian as one who is "better acquainted with a thousand years ago than with the present age."[44] And Bacon writes that antiquarians are "entitled however to the less authority, because in things which few people concern themselves about, the few have it their way." "History that did not teach was utterly inconceivable, and if any changes occurred during the course of the sixteenth century, these had to do not with whether history should teach but with what it taught" (Levy, *Tudor Historical Thought* 7). Views such as these assured that until the late seventeenth century, narrative and antiquarian methods were only sporadically combined.[45] Hence, while it may be profitable for a modern historian in search of the origins of scholarly history-writing to scrutinize the works of antiquarians and legal scholars, it would be misleading to magnify their sway over a renaissance sensibility of the past; it would be to streamline retrospectively the truly erratic and varied history of historical scholarship and present it as a teleological march toward a modern historiography. The truth of the matter is that the overwhelming majority of the reading public took the term "history" – when it referred to a written account of the past – to designate literary history. Even so, antiquarians did become increasingly active in the period, and they were of course not altogether without influence. It is wise, therefore, to adopt a balanced view of the situation. It is fine, on the one hand, to assume that the English humanists, "in their reverence for antiquity, continued to write their ordinary history in direct imitation of the classics as a branch of rhetoric, often heedless of the new methodology of the antiquarians and unwilling or unable to incorporate their results" (Levine, J., *Humanism and History* 13), as long as we do keep in mind that antiquarians and legal scholars like William Camden, John Selden and Sir Edward Coke produced and published innovative work, and that their ideas and methods were already anticipated in Polydore's *Anglica Historia* (which employed innovative scholarly practices to refute Geoffrey of Monmouth's myth of Britain's Trojan origins), and were partially and haphazardly incorporated by historians like Holinshed, Grafton, Hall, and George Buc – even though these practices were not fully appreciated or systematically embraced by narrative historians until after the Restoration of the monarchy.

At the very best what we can say is that "beginning in the early seventeenth century, history as a literary form on the one hand, and that type of philological or antiquarian knowledge which can be broadly fit under the rubric of 'erudition' on the other, grew more familiar with each other, both in practice and in theory" (Woolf, *Idea of History* xii). This familiarity, however, is difficult to define, and its importance unmeasurable. The coexistence of the various historiographical theories and practices is a better index of what historiography was to become than what "it" was.

The opening sentences of John Stow's second edition of *The Survey of London* (1603) can here serve as a final and typical and illustrative instance of historiography's strange, if not perplexing, status:

> As the Roman writers, to glorify the city of Rome, derive the original thereof from gods and demi-gods, by the Trojan progeny, so Geoffrey of Monmouth, the Welsh historian, deduceth the foundation of this famous city of London, for the greater glory thereof, and emulation of Rome, from the very same original. For he reporteth that Brute, lineally descended from the demi-god Aeneas, the son of Venus, daughter of Jupiter, about the year of the world 2855, and 1108 before the nativity of Christ, built this city near unto the river now called Thames, and named it Troynovant, or Trenovant. But herein, as Livy, the most famous historiographer of the Romans, writeth, antiquity is pardonable, and hath an especial privilege, by interlacing divine matters with human, to make the first foundation of cities more honourable, more sacred, and, as it were, of greater majesty.[46]

But in his dedication to Robert Lee, Lord Mayor of London, Stow contends that "the discovery of London" is his aim, and that "what London hath been of ancient time men may see here. . . ." Stow here speaks the language of the antiquarian endeavoring to construct an exact memory of London's past through the study of geography, etymology of place names, and physical remains. Yet, paradoxically, he also defends Geoffrey's right to trace London's origins back to the demi-god Aeneas, even while implicitly conceding that Geoffrey's account is less a history than a labor to make London "more honourable, more sacred, and, as it were, of greater majesty." Such mixing of myth with history is admissible, Stow argues in good humanist fashion, because similar conflations were created by Roman historians; that is, Geoffrey has a classical precedent (even though he was of course no humanist). Stow apparently does not think it prudent to address Polydore Vergil's almost seventy-year-old debunking of the myth of Trojan origins. Thus, while claiming to offer a schematic and fact-based history containing "The original, antiquity, increase, modern estate, and description" of London, Stow's preface, in fact, easily combines fervid chauvinism with a fondness for the medieval national myths of origins, justified by an invocation of Roman precedent. In the process, he ignores Polydore's "advancement" of historical knowledge. Renaissance historiography was, as this 1603 example indicates, a thoroughly eclectic practice, a discourse unconcerned to embrace what we (and a number of renaissance thinkers) would consider grave contradictions in theory and method.

It should be pointed out that critics and historians have at times painted a much tidier picture of historiography's identity in the English renaissance. Phyllis Rackin, for instance, writes that

> at the beginning of the sixteenth century, English writers made no clear distinction between poetry and history, either of which could be in prose or verse, both of which freely mingled fact and legend, event and interpretation, and endowed characters from the past with customs and manners of the present. By the seventeenth century, all this had changed: history had become an autonomous discipline with its own purposes and methods, clearly distinct from myth and literature, and accountable to different formal requirements and different truth criteria. (*Stages of History* 19)

Rackin's description of the sixteenth century is on target. It is also accurate to say that in the seventeenth century historiographers' statements of *principle* began to include the articles mentioned by Rackin (and that historiography became thought of by Bacon and others as a knowledge-seeking science), but it is impossible to find a single historian who faithfully applies these principles in his narrative – and this includes Bacon in his celebrated history of King Henry VII, which draws at different points on humanist, antiquarian, and, on rare occasions, providential methods. The point to be stressed here, before we embark on a discussion of the Stuart drama, is that the concurrent availability of various historiographical practices offered the playwrights a unique opportunity to exploit the epistemological, historical, and political ambiguity latent in such methodological variety.

2 Historiography and Tudor historical drama: the example of Bale's *King Johan*

Just as we have to resist the temptation to construe renaissance historiography in an orderly model of linear development, so we must withstand the urge to build a model of smooth and progressive development for the historical drama. But if we look for general tendencies rather than historical absolutes, we can assert that, under the influence of a growing sophistication in historical thought in general, the historical drama of the Stuart period exhibits a more complex historical consciousness than did its Elizabethan predecessor. As D. R. Woolf observes, "Over the first four decades of the seventeenth century, as more histories came to be written, and as the newer antiquarian scholarship began gradually to influence the writing of narratives, the interpretative corridor began to expand: cracks even appeared in the walls."[1] It should not be inferred, however, that the Tudor playwrights were simple-minded providentialists and the Stuart playwrights perspicacious antiquarians. In the narrative histories, the methodological innovations for the recovery of the past awkwardly share textual space with more traditional and ostensibly less rigorous approaches to history. The same holds true for Stuart historical drama. All the plays dealt with in this investigation accommodate features of medieval and early humanist historiography, even while disclosing simultaneously an early modern and deepening skepticism about the immediate import of divine providence, the stability of historical knowledge, and the objective truth or monolithic nature of historical accounts. The vital point of distinction here is that while the narrative histories usually do not seem particularly bothered by the coexistence of these contradictory approaches to the past,[2] the Stuart drama self-consciously exploits them in order to intervene in the construction of the English past.

Both Tudor and Stuart historical dramas reveal a close affinity between historical and dramatic writing, but the Tudor drama is noticeably less radical and less innovative in its *conception* of history and historiography than its Stuart counterpart. The drama in both periods considers itself a vehicle for historical discourse; the concrete difference lies in the distinct understandings of the nature of that discourse. The form of many of the

Tudor plays, for instance, reveals a certain sameness of historical consciousness that we no longer encounter in works like Shakespeare and Fletcher's *Henry VIII* and Ford's *Perkin Warbeck*. As Alvin B. Kernan puts it,

> History was discovered by Tudor historians to have the sameness of ritual: a weak or saintly king makes political mistakes and is overthrown by rebellious and arrogant subjects; the kingdom becomes a wasteland and society a chaos in which every man's hand is set against his fellow; after a period of great suffering, reaction against the forces of evil occurs, and a strong and good king restores order. The pattern – so similar to the Eden pattern of disobedience, fall and redemption – governed not only the writing of chronicle history but became through repetition a ritual pattern in the numerous history plays extending from the earlier *Gurbodoc* and *Cambyses* through such works as *The Life and Death of Jack Straw* (c. 1588) . . . and Shakespeare's earliest plays, the three parts of *Henry VI* (c. 1588–92).[3]

This Tudor understanding of history (variously labeled as providentialist, medieval, the Tudor myth, and the Elizabethan world picture) certainly did not instantly fade from the ideological horizon of English consciousness after the death of Queen Elizabeth. We find it expressed, for instance, in *Macbeth* and in *King Lear*, although less to affirm the pattern's validity than to underscore its failure to delineate historical reality accurately.[4] Indeed, what changes in the course of the English Renaissance is the *conception* (really conception*s*) of history (and historiography). It is absolutely crucial to recognize that during the Tudor and the Stuart eras the playwrights do not so much change their understanding of the relationship between drama and history, as acquire a new understanding of history (and, of course, history-writing) and *therefore* reach a new understanding of historical drama's form and possibilities. The relationship between historical drama and history remains one of sameness. As Kernan makes clear, the pattern observed in history (and historiography)[5] is also expressed by the history play; in the post-Elizabethan period the failure of that pattern and the instability and inscrutability of history (which in itself constitutes a conceptualization of history) manifest themselves in the historical drama. Quite early in the Tudor period, writers discovered that it was a virtue of the medieval morality play that it "could be used to fulfill what the Renaissance considered primary historical functions" (Ribner, *English History Play* 41). For some authors, to write historical drama *is* to write (or to rewrite) history. This is as true for the Tudor polemicist-playwright-antiquarian John Bale in 1538 as it is for popular dramatist John Ford in 1634.[6] Bale's play about King John's troubles with Pope Innocent III is no less sophisticated or complex in its treatment of the drama–historiography relationship than Ford's daring refutation of the officially condoned narrative accounts of the notorious Warbeck affair (discussed in chapter 6).

Since John Bale's *King Johan* is an early Tudor text, it does not really belong with the plays that constitute the body of evidence here. Yet, for a number of reasons it makes good historical sense to inspect this exceptional work before marching down the Stuart path. First, Bale's drama is the first in the English language to appropriate historical discourses for the stage. As such it is an archetypal text in the context of my argument, and the foundation and source for many of the attributes we find in later history plays. Secondly, *King Johan* powerfully illustrates the marxist dictum (central to my study) that literary form and content stand in dialectical relationship to each other; the drama's *literary* form changes under the ideological pressure of its socio-historical content and *historiographical* form. Thirdly, *King Johan*'s complex treatment of the literature–history nexus clearly cautions us against constructing a history of the genre based on a teleological version of the genre's ever growing sophistication. Later treatments of the literature–history nexus by Shakespeare, Fletcher, Massinger, Heywood, and Ford may be more elaborate and far-reaching, but Bale's is easily as innovative and sophisticated.

Written at a time when separate categories for literature and history were only just materializing, Bale's *King Johan* (c. 1538)[7] seizes on this difference precisely to highlight and to put to political–religious use the underlying affinities between the categories. Bale did not proceed in the manner of, say, Geoffrey of Monmouth, in whose *History of the Kings of Britain* history and fiction are so thoroughly fused that readers, unless they possessed independent knowledge (which was extremely unlikely), had no means of telling myth, legend, and pure fabrication, from the work's historical component.[8] Instead of immediately shrouding the historical and the fictional in an uncritical veil of sameness, *King Johan* turns its back on the fanciful historicism of Geoffrey and makes its audience *aware* of itself as a morality-play–history hybrid by showing where literature and history intersect. Thus Bale anticipates many of the later historical dramas which capitalize on the genre's difference from and tantalizing link to history.

In my introduction, I touch on Hayden White's noteworthy efforts to bring to our attention historiography's origins in literary sensibility. Bale's whole treatment of the historical impasse and subsequent clash between King John and Pope Innocent III over the question of papal versus royal authority depends on an assumed *difference* between drama and historiography, but only to undo that difference and show a fundamental sameness of dramatic and historical writing. What Bale realized, Irving Ribner points out, is that "the morality play contained elements admirably suited to the dramatic presentation of history in such a way that the didactic ends of Tudor historiography might be served" (*English History Play* 40). One of *King Johan*'s most remarkable features is that "All of the morality vices whom John opposes represent actual historical figures, and during the course of action they take the names of those figures" (37). The transformation of allegorical figures into historical ones is slow and deliberate. As David Bevington observes, except for a brief mention of John's name in the opening scene, there are no historical references to the thirteenth century "for nearly one quarter of the play's considerable length. . . . An essentially nameless king faces the recurrent backsliding of his people, nobility, and clergy." "The historical personages of Stephen Langton, Pope Innocent III, Pandulphus [a cardinal], and Simon of Swinsett are reserved for much later."[9] *King Johan* shows us the slow and extraordinary birth of historiography in literature.[10] The drama's internal metamorphosis is effected by a twofold maneuver: on the dramatic-generic level it translates allegory into history (one genre into another genre), and on the historiographical (and pedagogical) level it abandons a medieval morality-based exemplarity in favor of a humanist predilection for a historical-political exemplarity.

The birth of historiography in drama is an immediate result of Bale's and the Tudor state's ideological needs and the historical and literary climate in which those needs are to be satisfied. First, the advent of the Reformation had introduced an embryonic yet unwelcome sense of "democracy" in the Tudor state. Protestant doctrine maintained that the Bible (now no longer the Vulgate Latin edition but available in English translation) explicated itself to *all* readers. Although this dogma aided the English crown in its efforts to undermine Rome's interpretative monopoly, it also weakened the crown's position vis-à-vis its subjects because it decentralized interpretative authority in general. The Protestant reformer Thomas Cranmer understood the problem and wrote *The Book of Homilies* (1547) to curb the worshippers' interpretative freedom.[11] Designed as a "guide to Christian living" – as an authorized means of interpretative restraint – *The Homilies*, John King asserts, was one of the most powerful channels of government control (124, 132). Cranmer justified his act of intervention by arguing that while most parts of the Bible are "easy and plain for the understandyng," there are also "'obscure mysteries' [that] can only be understood by the learned" (King, *English Reformation Literature* 132).

The question of the Reformation's success and English religious autonomy was far from settled. "In December of 1538 [at the time the play was first performed, if not actually written], the long-suspended bull excommunicating Henry was at last published, and throughout the autumn the government had frantically prepared for Catholic invasion and supporting insurrection of Catholic nobles at home" (Kastan, "'Holy Wurdes'" 270). As an emergent ideology, Reformation truth first needed to acquire a reasonably privileged status in English culture independent of the play. Bale and other Reformation historians believed this could best be achieved through a mooring of their views in history. Antonia Gransden and Levy go so far as to suggest that Bale undertook the study of medieval historiography *chiefly* to ferret out information that could support the pro-monarchy, anti-papist views of the Henrician apologists (Gransden, *Historical Writing* 473; Levy, *Tudor Historical Thought* 97).

Unquestionably, the Reformation could have seriously jeopardized the continuity of English religious history. Despite its wealth of institutions and dogmas, the Church of England could easily "have found itself rootless, unable to derive either strength or prestige from the past" (Gransden, *Historical Writing* 472). To assail this dangerous condition, pro-Reformation historians tried to demonstrate on the basis of historical precedent that "the Catholic church in medieval times was corrupt, and . . . that the reformers of the sixteenth century had precursors in the earlier period" (472). Henry VIII, for instance, commissioned antiquarian John Leland to search the libraries of monasteries and universities for "ancient writers." In a report to the king outlining his progress and future plans, Leland indicates he planned to preserve "evidences of the medieval past, to ensure that 'the holy Scripture of God might both be sincerely taught and learned, all manner of superstition and craftily coloured doctrine of a rout of the Roman bishops totally expelled out of this your most catholic realm.' And he claimed to have discovered 'full many things . . . concerning the usurped authority of the Bishop of Rome and his complices, to the manifest and violent derogation of kingly dignity'" (473). In the effort to preserve the monastic library collections, Bale was Leland's partner, and their collaboration led to the publication of two comprehensive bibliographical works listing all writings by British authors.[12] Dramatic art, Cranmer and Bale realized, could also be used as propaganda and perform a control function similar to that of the *Homilies*. Bale's *King Johan* has to be understood in this context.[13] The play was first performed at Thomas Cranmer's residence, and was, as David Scott Kastan observes, if not devised "explicitly in response to [Richard] Morinson's call for new entertainments to be written to promote the Reformation . . . clearly conceived in a similar spirit."[14]

Before issues of theological doctrine, the fundamental Reformation tenets of the Tudor government stressed loyalty to the English crown and independence of Rome. That Bale shared these concerns is beyond doubt. In *The Image of both Churches*,[15] written during his exile after the death of his protector Thomas Cromwell, Bale declares that the shape of history is determined by the battle between the "true" church which "had maintained faith and worship based upon the gospels ever since the apostolic age, and the 'false' church, which . . . was subverted by the Antichrist in 607 when Pope Boniface III obtained recognition from Emperor Phocas as head of the church of Rome."[16] To argue the purity of the English Church, Bale draws on legendary historical accounts that speak of a "secret disciple of Christ, whose arrival predated the mission from Rome of St. Augustine of Canterbury" (Happé and King, "Introduction" 15). In *The Vocacyon of Johan Bale to the Bishoprick of Osserie in Ireland*, Bale concludes:

> Untruly therfore are we reported of the Italyane writers / and of the subtylle devysers of sanctes legendes / that we shulde have our first faythe from Rome / and our christen doctryne / from their unchristen byshoppes. *From the schole of Christe hymselfe / have we receyved the documentes of our fayth.* From Jerusalem / & not from Rome / whome both Peter & also Christe hath called Babylon / for that she so aptely therunto agreeth in ministryng confusion to the world.[17]

Both these texts reveal that Bale readily turned to historical forms of argumentation to promote English autonomy. Since *King Johan* was to serve the same ideological aims as *The Image of both Churches* and *The Vocacyon* we should not be surprised there to encounter the same trope of history. *King Johan* places its materials in a historical frame that is apocalyptic in structure and that depicts history in terms of a "perennial opposition between the forces of Christ and Antichrist as expounded mystically in the Apocalypse."[18]

Now in general the English moralities make "significant use of one or more traditional allegories or extended metaphors which exist *independently* of the play itself" (Adams, "Introduction" 58; emphasis added). Because such tropes habitually apply equally to all human beings and because they contain universal *truth*, they are excellent structural and didactic devices. A common trope in medieval literature is that of the journey, which structures the plot of *Everyman* and speaks to all. After centuries of coherent Catholicism in England such tropes were plentiful and shared by virtually all believers. From a pedagogical vantage point such independent metaphors and allegories can serve the playwright (and the status quo) well because they help organize the materials of history or everyday life into a frame whose truth is *a priori* and indubitable. The apocalyptic trope that structures *King Johan* is of course extremely familiar to sixteenth-century men and women (regardless of their position on Protestant reform), but the purpose to which that trope is put by Bale and his fellow reformers is absolutely antithetical to the institution of the (Catholic) Church that possessed the sole privilege to determine its meaning for centuries. In other words, if the trope is to convey Bale's Reformation meaning to its audience, then that audience must be prevented from backsliding to the traditional truths that are evoked by the various "allegories or extended metaphors" that occur in morality plays but that mean and exist "*independently*" of those plays. Indeed, the determination of the trope's meaning must take place within the literary text itself because outside Bale's play centuries of Catholic authority and intimately familiar dogma stand ready to pounce on and overwhelm the ambivalent Christian. The need to reinterpret the meaning of the allegory or trope presents Bale with both the need and the opportunity to transform the shape of the morality play. Bale responds to this need by introducing "history," significantly, not by imitating Geoffrey's legendary history of England, nor by anticipating the "historicall fiction" offered by Edmund Spenser roughly fifty years later,[19] but by achieving a type of *internal* historicity that will, instead of allowing the reader to speculate about the implications of the allegory or have it comprehended in a Catholic context, shut down any allegorical ambiguity with the historical concrete.

As Bale's abstractions gradually take on historical flesh, Sedition is metamorphosed into a monk (and future Archbishop of Canterbury) by the name of Stephen Langton; Private Wealth is transmuted into Cardinal Pandulphus; and Usurped Power assumes the attire, paraphernalia and identity of Pope Innocent III (s.d. l. 983). Allegory becomes history before the audience; the universal is converted into the historical particular. And this drive away from the universal and the abstract toward the historical particular for the purpose of the reader's (or spectator's) edification constitutes a shift away from a medieval typological historiography and a step (as far as the drama is concerned) into the future toward a historiography rooted in the humanist postulate of exemplarity (even though one could easily assume that it is Bale's purpose to indoctrinate his audience to the point that Protestantism achieves the type of independent truth status that would allow it once again to determine the meaning of a morality play *a priori*).

A biting piece of propaganda, the play's central ambition is difficult to miss: its politics are largely pro-Tudor and its religious stance is assiduously pro-Reformation (see Bevington, *Tudor Drama* 98–105). "Bale holds up King John as a model for Henry [VIII] – and later for Elizabeth [I] – to emulate; they too must resist the power of Rome and assert the independence of England" (Ribner, *English History Play* 40). Indeed, as Andrew Hadfield observes, "Bale has conflated the whole of national history into the idealised self of the monarch and the implication is that just as the devil's history can be written as a series of lives of the popes or English votaries, so can God's history be written as a series of lives of Protestant saints and good rulers."[20] When we look at the choric "interpretour's" closing speech at the end of Act 1, its technique and substance appear conventional enough in that it is cyclical, typological, and animated by divine providence much like other morality dramas.

> Thys noble kynge Iohan, as a faythfull Moyses,
> Withstode proude Pharao for hys poore Israel,
> Myndynge to brynge it out of the lande of Darknesse.

But the Egyptyanes ded agaynst hym so rebell
That hys poore people ded styll in the desart dwell,
Tyll that duke Iosue, whych was our late kynge Henrye,
Clerely brought vs in to the lande of mylke and honye.

As a stronge Dauid at the voyce of verytie,
Great Goyle, the pope, strake downe with hys slynge,
Restorynge agayne to a Christen lybertie
Hys lande and people, lyke a most vyctoryouse kynge,
To hir first bewtye intendynge the churche to brynge,
From ceremonyes dead to the lyuynge wurde of [th]e lorde.[21]

The "intepretour's" speech is thoroughly conventional in its deliberate elision of most of the specifics contained in the book of Exodus passage on which it draws (Ex. 7.8–12). There is no mention of rods being turned into serpents, plagues of frogs and locusts, thunder and hail, or the deaths of all first-borns; nor is the Pharaoh's motivation examined; only "Darkness" is mentioned but in such a way that, like the "desert," it becomes an all-purpose metaphor. Bale's reason for effacing the historical specificity is to posit an (a)historical analogy: King Johan (Moses) may be able to deliver England from the Pope's (the Pharaoh's) tyrannical control, but it is left to Henry VIII (Joshua) to bring the people through a period of trial and confusion (the Reformation process) into the promised land (the one true Church). Thus the preordained journey of the Israelites from bondage to deliverance becomes a blueprint for English religious and political history, and English monarchs become doubles of their biblical antecedents. But how can Bale be sure that this is the interpretation that audiences will assign to the analogy? The "interpretour's" speech is commonplace and compelling enough in its illumination of the apocalyptic struggle between the forces of good and evil, but how should audiences arrive at the specific reading that the Pharaoh is the Pope who keeps the English in religious bondage?

Apparently Bale is not confident that audiences will spontaneously arrive at his peculiar reading of church history. To drive his reading home, Bale, just prior to the "interpretour's" speech, initiates the play's transformation from morality to history, most shockingly through the transmutation of Usurped Power into the Pope and the appearance of Stephen Langton. Before the "interpretour" articulates the religious and political state of affairs in John's (and Henry's and Elizabeth's) England and forecasts the events of the second Act, we are told that the Pope shall compel King Johan to surrender his crown (1017–18) and that "The popys powr shall be abowe [th]e powrs all" (1019). Still not certain that the audience will grasp the agenda, the "interpretour," immediately after the Pope leaves the stage, proceeds to tell us that John was appointed by God to govern "thys same noble regyon" and to "see mayntayned the true faythe and relygyon" (1089–90). To eliminate any lingering doubt about the vital connection between John and Henry, the "interpretour" then reminds us that John will be excommunicated for his noble efforts to "prouyde *reformacyon* / In the Church" of the realm (1094–5; emphasis added).

In the absence of a widely disseminated and culturally entrenched Protestant reading of history, Bale must interpret his morality drama within the confines of the play itself; he must reinterpret apocalyptic history by anchoring it in specific historical moments that are narrated in the text. Morality Vices must be identified by their historical names. Only then can Bale hope to accomplish his aim, which is to have his audience question "their conditioned responses to the external signs of religious truth in an age when competing institutions were laying exclusive claim to it" (White, P., *Theatre and Reformation* 35). Only then will the balance of truth begin to be tipped in favor of the Bale–Tudor agenda.

This formal shift in the morality genre, driven by religious politics, is accomplished in part by a subtle shift from Christian typological historiography to a humanistic concern with secular exemplarity. Humanism, especially in its earliest forms, utilized historical texts primarily as an inexhaustible source of examples on which to base conduct in the present. The emphasis here was almost always on civil conduct, and, in the case of William Baldwin's *Mirror for Magistrates* and Machiavelli's *The Prince*, aimed predominately at the education of rulers. *King Johan*'s typological presentation of John as type of Henry VIII (who appears as Imperial Majesty to restore order at the play's close) can be understood in terms of humanistic exemplarity insofar as for pedagogical purposes it constitutes an analogy between two distinctly political historical moments by underscoring their basic similarity (and thus implying a cyclical view of history). A crucial difference between the Christian typology and humanist exemplarity is that the former points toward divine truth while the latter preaches civic truth; the former always moralizes events, greatly emphasizing the sway of Fortune and providence sway over human affairs; the latter draws on a wide range of historical texts, including non-Christian ones, and emphasizes the importance of grappling with secondary causes; the former relies on prefiguration, the latter primarily on coincidental similarity. But this is of course no surprise for, as Barry Adams asserts, while the structure of *King Johan* may owe "much to a theory of history which is fundamentally religious, Bale's ultimate concern is not so much religious as political. Both plot and theme center on Pope Innocent's appointment of Stephen Langton as Archbishop in opposition to John's wishes" (Adams, "Introduction" 64). Doctrinal changes introduced by the Reformation are barely touched on in the play.

More significant than any of this is that the play appeals more to the audience's nationalistic sense of outrage over foreign intervention into English affairs than to its desire for religious purity. England is besieged from abroad by wicked forces that have managed to corrupt and lead into rebellion vital elements at home. It is this civil rebellion that causes most of the problems in *King Johan*. Speaking to the repentant Nobility, Civil Order, and Clergy at the end of the play, Imperial Majesty emphatically asserts that religious purity can only be achieved after clarity in political hierarchy and authority are established.

> The adminystracyon of a princes gouernance
> Is the gifte of God and hys hygh ordynaunce,
> Whome with all your power yow thre ought to support
> In the lawes of God, to all hys peoples comfort.
> First yow, the clergye, in preachynge Gods worde;
> Than yow Nobilyte, defendynge with the sworde;
> Yow, Cyuyle order, in executynge iustyce.
> Thus I trust we shall seclude all maner of vyce,
> And after we haue establyshed our kyngedome
> In peace of the lorde and in hys godly fredome,
> We wyll confirme it with wholesom lawes and decrees,
> To the full suppressynge of Antichristes vanytees. (2634–45)

As these lines underscore, the questions of religion and social stability can of course not be separated, but the kind of prominence afforded to the prince who governs with God's ordinance, and who needs the support of the nobility, civil order, and the clergy – all working together toward a single goal – anticipates Canterbury's beehive metaphor of national unity in Shakespeare's *Henry V*.

At the same time that Bale looks with a humanist eye on the past, he also reveals his historiographical rootedness in the medieval tradition. When, for instance, Nobility acknowledges that God punishes seditiousness, he cites Brutus, Cataline, and Cassius (along with Absalom) as examples (2605–6). Taking a swipe at humanism, Baldwin in *The Mirror* claims that he "nede not go eyther to the Romans or Grekes" to prove that "the goodnes or badnes of any realme lyeth in the goodnes or badnes of the rulers."[22] English history offers enough instances to make the point. But despite intimations of humanist exemplarity, Nobility's use of classical examples to illustrate God's justice is much more reminiscent of the "mixed" world of Geoffrey of Monmouth's historiography than it is of, say, the great humanist historian Thomas More.

Bale's blend of historiography, however, is less a result of the dramatist's flashes of progressive insight followed by historiographical backsliding than an indicator of his ability to match historical method with political need. The character Verity's highly self-conscious presentation of history illustrates my point. Toward the end of *King Johan*, Verity offers a striking instance of Bale's mixing of medievalism and humanism, of morality and history:

> I assure ye, fryndes, lete men wryte what they wyll,
> Kynge Iohan was a man both valeaunt and godlye.
> What though Polydorus [Vergil] reporteth hym very yll
> At the suggestyons of the malicyouse clergye?
> Thynke yow a Romane with the Romanes can not lye?
> (2193–7)

Verity then proceeds to list a number of medieval and early renaissance historians – "Sigebertus, Vincentius and also Nauclerus; / Giraldus and Mathu Parys with hys noble vertues take – / Yea, Paulus Phrigo, Iohan Maior and Hector Boethius" – all of whom are said to support Verity's estimation of John (2200–6). An examination of these writers, however, demonstrates that the claim is "at best highly misleading" (Adams, "Introduction" 27).[23] In fact, scholars have been unable to locate a single medieval history defending either John's cause or his character (Adams, "Introduction" 30). The practice of critically comparing diverse historical sources for the purpose of producing an accurate account of past events belongs primarily to humanist and antiquarian practices. Bale's Verity implicitly *claims* to follow this same practice with the aim of discrediting humanist historian Polydore Vergil, who had reported King John "very yll / At the suggestyons of the malicyouse clergye." It appears that Bale takes on Polydore on the latter's own terms, for it was, we recall, this Italian humanist who had made a genuine scholarly effort to demystify Geoffrey's history of England's Trojan origins by comparing various contradictory accounts on the matter (Levy, *Tudor Historical Thought* 58–9). Verity claims that Polydore is unreliable because he has been refuted by many other historians. Yet while Bale appeals to a humanist practice of critically comparing sources, he, in fact, also proceeds the way a medieval author would, trying to settle a dispute by calling on the spectator's reverence for authority, without offering a critical account of method or credibility. As noted by Thomas Greene, "The author (*auctor*, *actor*, *autor*) . . . was a writer whose work had commanded respect for so many centuries as to have become an authority (*autorita*), to be read as an *authentic* source of knowledge."[24] It appears, then, that Bale the antiquarian and dramatist puts enough stock in humanist historiographical practice (or at least he believes that his audience does) to pretend that he is using it against the humanist Polydore. Indeed, he uses its cachet to claim precisely the opposite of what would be the likely outcome of a genuine humanist–antiquarian investigation. Yet in essence his method is subordinated entirely to his political and, secondarily, but simultaneously, to his inseparable religious agenda. Both humanist and medieval historians treated history "as a repository for moral *exempla*," but they did so with different attitudes.[25] As we saw in the previous chapter, humanists became gradually less concerned with moral exemplarity than with examples that could shed light on matters of political conduct, and their medieval preoccupation with salvation was eventually displaced by an interest in man as a political creature (Gransden, *Historical Writing* 428). Hence Bale's decision to use King John, a figure from extra-biblical history, as exemplar to instruct Henry VIII and Elizabeth I on how to handle Rome and papal authority is at once medieval and humanist in nature, because it combines political advice on issues inexorably bound to religious questions. The Reformation did *change* the abstract and independent truths hitherto conveyed through the morality play tradition.

Could Bale's new Protestant truth be the "tenor" of a traditional "vehicle" like the morality play that predated the Reformation? Perhaps Bale could have turned to a more complex allegorical form (as did Spenser) or he might have followed the example of Geoffrey and presented a suitable fiction as history, but neither of these would have been effective under the circumstances.[26] The different historical circumstances of each author help to explain their different literary choices. Geoffrey's efforts to link the English kings to Aeneas were motivated foremost by patriotism, a quality shared by most readers of his Latin text. His history was received by a receptive culture of rulers and aristocrats pleased to be told of their proud heritage. Moreover, until Polydore took him on, very few readers of Geoffrey's history were knowledgeable enough to challenge its conclusions. The cultural climate and level of popular historical knowledge made possible the kind of history Geoffrey wrote. Similarly, when Spenser publishes the first three books of the *Faerie Queene* in 1590, religious stability has returned (the Reformation has taken hold), and a formal distance between England and Rome has become the norm. The Reformation vision of apocalyptic history has gained great currency in English culture, and Spenser can assume that certain allegories will once again almost automatically point the reader toward a truth that exists in English culture independently of the epic itself.

Bale's historical circumstances, however, were very different and called for an adaptation of the morality play genre. Together with like-minded reformers, he had to undo centuries of Catholic indoctrination that had led people to believe that certain metaphors and allegories derive directly from God, through Scripture and as interpreted by the Church. The morality genre relied for its success on this widespread belief. For Bale to propagate his new-found Reformation truth successfully, he had to swerve from the morality form and legitimate the new truth by linking it to a new interpretation of specific moments in human history. Bale's drama therefore is an instance of literary-historical innovation (though it fights against *Romish* innovation). But even more striking is Bale's obvious awareness of the negotiations between literature and history. Indeed, as a literary artifact, Bale's history–morality play is an excellent illustration of what Hayden White has in mind when he argues for the recognition of historiography's literary sensibility. White, we will recall, contends that histories derive their structure from the various types of emplotment available in the historian's own culture. Moreover, White holds that those plot structures prefigure what will become the very building blocks – the "fact" or "events" – used to fill out the narrative. Similarly, Bale's politico-religious itinerary not only shapes his overarching narrative, it also refigures the shape of a specific generic feature (a building block) of the morality play genre: its concept of *character*. In the morality drama, characters are personifications or allegorical figures that not only conceptually predate the specific dramas in which they occur but that are also timeless within a Christian scheme of things. As Baldwin observed in *The Mirror*, one does not need to search into far recesses of history to dig up examples of good and bad rulers; virtue is virtue and evil is evil, always and everywhere. In Bale's play, however, the status of character becomes almost analogous to that of the "independent" plot or allegory that shapes the structure and meaning of the individual morality play. Morality characters, too, appear to have an existence independent of historical particulars (as long as a certain Christian ideology continues to hold sway over the culture). When monarch and government change course and begin to exert their political will to make adjustments in the dominant ideology (for instance, people's understanding of church history) it becomes necessary for a dramatist, antiquarian, and resolute propagandist like Bale to revise and historicize not only the master narrative but also the concept of character itself. Indeed, the historicization of character follows directly, if not inevitably, from the need to reinterpret historically the master narrative. Derived from God, the allegory, which under a pre-Reformation version of Christianity was revered timeless, now feels the pressures of political and historical change and descends into history. (The historicization of character is, in reality, of course a *re*historicization because no matter how abstract and ahistorical personifications may appear, they are clearly concretizations of values that are rooted in historically contingent ideologies.)

The reason that the morality play is so easily transformed into an embryonic history play flows from the basic *structural* kinship between medieval and humanist historiography. Members of both schools of thought were happy to regard history as a treasure chest of moral examples. Hence, the medieval apocalyptic history evident in *King Johan* strongly suggests a direct analogy between King John and Henry VIII; that is, the transference of a biblical typological trope to a "secular," political context. But it also offers Henry VIII, in familiar humanist context, a historical example (regardless of religious doctrine) for the purpose of guiding him in a fundamentally political struggle with Rome.

This mixing of religious concerns and political questions occurs in several historical and non-historical dramas throughout the Elizabethan period. When, in the waning days of Elizabeth's reign, Thomas Dekker et al. present their historical drama *Sir Thomas Wyatt* (first performed in the autumn of 1602), its subject matter accents a distress similar to Bale's over the threat of England's subjugation to foreign religious authority, and underscores its continuing link to a core anxiety in Tudor culture.[27] With the impending death of Elizabeth and no successor named, the threat of Catholic Spain (which has replaced that of Rome) once again loomed large. In *Wyatt*, Dekker et al. reach back to the reign of Mary to affirm a clear hierarchy between religious authority and political independence. Wyatt in the play defends Mary's right to rule England as, despite her Catholicism, she is the *legitimate* monarch (designated so in her father's will). Yet when Mary intends to marry Philip of Spain, Wyatt raises a rebellion. Upon his capture, his last words on his way to the scaffold are:

> Then here's the end of *Wyats* rising up,
> I to keepe Spaniards from the Land was sworne,
> Right willingly I yeelde my selfe to death,
> But sorry such, should haue my place of birth.
> Had *London* kept his word, *Wyat* had stood,
> But now King *Phillip* enters through my blood. (5.2.32–7)

Because Mary is a woman, Wyatt fears that "the throne of England might pass to a foreign king" (Bevington, *Tudor Drama* 293). The play's insistence on English autonomy from Catholic control links it, across five or so decades, to *King Johan*. In the next chapter we will see that the first Jacobean history play, Thomas Heywood's *If You Know Not Me You Know No Bodie* (Part I),[28] turns on the same troubling issues.

There is no good reason to view Bale's *King Johan* as a rejection of literary form (the morality genre) in favor of "history." We have to remember that the manipulation of historiographical practices takes place *within* the boundaries of a text that remains recognizably literary. For Bale as well as his Stuart successors, the literature–history problematic is less an either–or issue than it is a question of a growing understanding of the conceptual and imaginative affinity between the two genres. This affinity clearly follows the ideological shifts taking place in the culture and has its impact on the literary form of the drama. At first, as the content of history, with its own internal Reformation logic, becomes inscribed into the drama, the resemblance between the two modes of expression is certainly not meant to diminish the authority of either: for Bale, both proclaim the same profound truth. Yet when we enter the post-Elizabethan era, the playwrights become increasingly skeptical in their exploitation of the literature–history nexus. The hybrid offered by Bale the polemicist imitates the Protestants' historical search for indisputable precedents, and hence strives to conceal the ideological strategies which affect to present the reader with "history" itself. The Jacobean playwrights, on the other hand, become increasingly determined to lay bare those strategies by publicly exploring their literary and ideological coordinates.

A significant by-product of *King Johan*'s excursion into historical understanding (one that appears to adumbrate a more full-fledged Jacobean skepticism) is the potential corrosion of the authority of the monarch as the renowned "great man" of so many Tudor histories. Taking note of Bale's efforts to promote the Tudor agenda, we would expect him not to stray far from the "great men" model. King John of course is overcome by concrete powerful historical forces, but even the much more powerful Henry likewise is indirectly portrayed as *subject* to political (as opposed to divine) history. When Henry (in the guise of Imperial Majesty) enters the play near its conclusion to restore a sense of order, we must recognize that Bale presents us a vision of a possible *future*. The play intimates – and history bears this out – that at the moment of the play's performance, Henry and Britain are under pressures they may not be able to withstand; *Tudor* history hangs in the balance, and an adverse outcome is not unthinkable, as the spine-tingling account of John and twelfth-century England's defeat surely means to imply. Though *King Johan* surely looks to Henry as a "great man" in the Tudor historiographical tradition, we cannot overlook the play's obvious insinuation (contained in its advice to Henry) that he is a great man, a maker of history, thus far only *in potentia*.[29] But even this intimation is somewhat qualified by Bale's advice to the king on how to gain the upper hand on history by embracing and proselytizing the radical, apocalyptic historical narrative recommended by Bale the historian-playwright himself. He urges the king to do as he does: to wrest the issues from the opposition by seizing control of historical and, what amounts in political terms to the same thing, of religious representation. The delicious irony in all this, as Hadfield shrewdly observes, is that although Bale conspicuously distorts his own sources he attributes the reason for John's poor reputation to the distortions perpetrated by "clerical chroniclers subservient to the papacy" (*Literature* 78). Witness Nobility's words to Clergy:

> He that dothe hate me [th]e worse wyll tell my tale
> Yt is yowr fassyon soche kynges to dyscommend
> As yowr abuses reforme or reprehend.

> Yow pristes are [th]e cawse [th]at Chronycles doth defame
> So many prynces and men of notable name,
> For yow take vpon yow to wryght them euermore;
> And therfor kyng Iohn ys lyke to rewe yt sore
> Whan ye wryte his tyme, for vexcyng of [th]e clargy. (582–9)

The passage clearly anticipates Verity's later speech (2193–7; already quoted) and echoes a sentiment expressed by Foxe in *Actes and Monuments* (discussed in my introduction). The question of whether Bale is an early English Machiavel hinges crucially on his ultimate conviction about the relationship between religion and politics; which takes precedence? If religious fervor carries Bale's agenda there is less room for manipulation; if his counsel is chiefly political (as many critics believe) then the religious dimension of the Reformation may be little more than a tool for "state-building" (Kastan, "'Holy Wurdes'" 269). But we cannot look into Bale's heart, and even if we could, we may not find an answer to our question since for most, issues of politics were inseparable from those of religion, a condition which appears endemic for much of English renaissance culture because state-building and the establishment of the Reformation Church were in many ways inextricably linked in mid-sixteenth-century England, one thought impossible without the other.

3 Thomas Heywood and the Princess Elizabeth: disrupting diachronic history

I

Written on the brink of the Stuart era, Thomas Heywood's very popular *If You Know Not Me, You Know No Bodie; or, The Troubles of Queene Elizabeth* (1603–4),[1] which apparently was performed for "overflow houses,"[2] offers a tenuous break with the Elizabethan past by engaging both diachronic and synchronic representations of the past. The play still draws on the hallmark traits of the Elizabethan history play by telling a nostalgic, diachronic tale of an English princess in distress, but it also offers an unmistakable sample of the type of synchronic approach which is to blossom in the course of the seventeenth century, and which squarely undercuts the diachronic story. Based on the play's content it is unlikely that Heywood is trying to be particularly radical. Nevertheless, the presence of these two historiographies, each driven by its own ideological agenda, invests the drama with both incongruence and tension. Therefore, the play offers a fairly cautious and conservative political message (perhaps to the newly crowned King James) and simultaneously exposes the ideological dimensions of historiographical propaganda under the Elizabethan and Jacobean regimes. Structurally as well as politically, one could call *If You Know Not Me* a confused play, but whatever confusion there is it is certainly not of the aesthetic variety. Rather, it reveals a change in the "inner logic" of the genre – a subtle mutation which still gives the audience the powerful diachronic and cathartic narrative described by Alvin Kernan (see chapter 2), but which also draws the attention away from the play's and culture's heroine, Elizabeth.

It is hardly surprising to find Heywood's historical play *If You Know Not Me* wrought with an acute awareness of historiography; the author's remarkable oeuvre contains several others texts that deal directly with history-writing. Among those texts, and directly relevant to *If You Know Not Me*, are his *Englands Elizabeth: Her Life and Troubles, During her Minoritie, from the Cradle to the Crowne*[3] (a prose history that includes accounts of most of the events rendered in the play), the well-known *An*

Apology for Actors (1612), and a translation of the fourth chapter of Jean Bodin's *Easy Method for the Comprehension of History*, which was published in 1608 as a "Preface to the reader" prefixed to his translation of Sallust. As a group these texts constitute a unique corpus among renaissance writers. Heywood is probably the only author of his time to have written on the subject of history in so many genres: dramatic history, prose history, and the theory of historical writing itself.

If You Know Not Me offered its London audience a representation of the ordeals of Elizabeth during Queen Mary's reign. It commences with the Bishop of Winchester implicating Elizabeth in the (Sir Thomas) Wyatt insurrection (staged in support of a Protestant government to be headed by Elizabeth and Edward Courtenay),[4] and concludes (following an account of her several close brushes with death) with her ascension to the English throne after Mary's death in 1558. Heywood greatly emphasizes the powers and benefits of Elizabeth's Protestant faith, which aid her as she is rudely dragged from her sickbed in Ashridge and made to endure not only imprisonment (including a stint at the Tower) but interrogations and uncharitable treatment at the hands of her Catholic persecutors, Queen Mary, Winchester, the Constable of the Tower, and Sir Henry Bedingfield. The importance of her Protestant faith is underscored in the play's closing scene, in which she kisses an English translation of the Bible – an abomination in Catholic eyes – that is presented to her by the Mayor of London. This histrionic gesture can be understood as a metonymic response to John Bale's urging (in *King Johan*) Henry VIII to defy Rome and vigorously to embrace Protestant reform and to seize upon the diachronic system of historical representation that is part and parcel of it. *If You Know Not Me* thus makes for a comfortable ideological tale for a patriotic, Protestant London theater-goer. Peter Lake rightly argues that English religious sovereignty was challenged by Catholic threats for much of Elizabeth's reign. And although James made peace with Spain, this hardly meant the end of the story, because, as Tom Cogswell observes, when the general consternation over "the Spanish match is added to the traditional list which stretches from the Armada, through the gunpowder plot, the various invasion scares of the 1620s and the Irish revolt, then every generation of English people between the 1580s and the 1640s had personal experience of a popish assault on English independence."[5]

If You Know Not Me certainly presents Elizabeth's steadfast religious choices and her triumph over adversity as exemplary. In this respect, Heywood's representation of the princess (despite her gender) fits fairly in the Tudor historiographical mode of "great men" who through perseverance bend historical circumstances to their will. Peter Burke rightly claims that in the renaissance popular heroines "were admired not so much for what they did as for what they suffered" (Leggatt, *Jacobean Public Theatre* 213n. 6) – and suffer she does – but this tells only part of the story for Elizabeth certainly was not, nor was ever presented as, a typical Elizabethan female. The iconography sustaining her public images as well as her self-representation aimed at a much more active and masculine posture – something which is born out in exemplary fashion by her legendary public appearance, "*compleatly armed*" and possessed of "a masculine spirit" at Tilbury, which Heywood dramatizes in detail in the Armada scenes of *If You Know Not Me*, Part Two (337).

Yet the play has political and religious ambitions beyond simply singing Elizabeth's praises and celebrating her triumph. Despite indulging the familiar Tudor narrative, the play's opening lines do not allow the spectators to settle in too comfortably. They carefully elicit and manipulate audience anxiety by propelling onlookers into a curious and mixed experience of past and present political and religious turmoil. "Touching the Queene, my lord," Lord Shandoyse asks Lord Tame, "What thinks the realm of *Philip*, th' Emperours sonne, / A marriage by the Councell treated of?" (*If You Know Not Me*, Part One, 193–4). The question is a highly volatile one because it compresses an awareness of several pivotal moments in the reigns of Mary, Elizabeth, and James I. What *does* the realm – i.e., the theater audience – think of a marriage between their Queen and the future King of Spain? Indeed, what Queen are the Lords of Tame and Shandoyse talking about? Mary or Elizabeth? Can anyone tell? The presence of the Lords of Howard and Sussex (only identified by family name and earldom respectively) and a nameless Lord Chamberlain fails to provide the necessary historical clues. The Lord Chamberlain's reference to "the Cardinal of *Winchester*" conjures up a Catholic context, but the man in question, Stephen Gardiner (as he is later identified), was the *Bishop* of Winchester, and never a cardinal. Even the naming of the relatively unknown Sir Henry Beningfield does little to clarify the situation. In the tomes of Foxe and Holinshed, Beningfield, a minor member of the Privy Council, is identified as "Bedingfield" and "Benefield," making it quite difficult (if not impossible) for even those members of the audience well versed in recent history to determine the exact context of the conversation.[6] So how did an audience understand these opening lines in 1604 or 1605? And what did the audience believe it was witnessing on the stage?

Almost certainly, the assembly that paid their money that day expected to be entertained by a play about Elizabeth I. In a prologue to *If You Know Not Me*, Heywood refers to it as "the Play of Queene Elizabeth," leading Madeleine Doran to suggest that possibly "more authority attaches to the sub-title" than to the main title.[7] Although the prologue did not appear until 1637 – and then not even as an addition to the play – each printed edition, beginning with the first in 1605, had "The Troubles of Queene Elizabeth" as its subtitle.[8] If Heywood wished to refer to Elizabeth as "Queene" out of common courtesy, he could have identified her fittingly as "Princess," a term which could mean either queen or princess at the turn of the century,[9] and so honor the monarch as well as maintain descriptive accuracy. Of course, we do not know by what title the performances were advertised, but it seems reasonable to believe that spectators were drawn to the theater by the promise of a drama about their recently deceased monarch. All this is important, but also rather peculiar, because the play deals with Elizabeth's days as *princess*, not with her reign as queen.

It becomes clear that the ambiguity is probably intentional when we consider that the title of Heywood's prose history, which is concerned with many of the same events in the life of Elizabeth, is notably more accurate: *Englands Elizabeth: Her Life and Troubles, During her Minoritie, from the Cradle to the Crowne*, leaving no doubt as to what part of her life the history deals with. The "error" in the play's subtitle did not result from an oversight since Heywood, as already noted, refers to it as "the Play of Queene Elizabeth" as late as 1637 – after the publication of *Englands Elizabeth* (1631) – which strongly suggests he did not want to remove the ambiguity.

The play's title, then, makes it feasible that for a brief, uncomfortable moment the crowd believed that Tame and Shandoyse are discussing a marriage between Elizabeth I and Philip II, between the English defender of the Protestant faith and the Catholic aggressor dedicated to its destruction. Everyone knew, of course, that Mary, and not Elizabeth, married Philip. But before realizing that the Queen in question is Mary (as becomes clear only a few lines later in the play), audience anxiety would have been kindled further by recalling the seemingly ever present "threat" of a marital union with the Spanish royal family. In October of 1545, Henry VIII had sought to arrange a marriage between Philip and Elizabeth; and shortly after the death of Mary in 1558, Philip himself proposed to Elizabeth (Ridley, *Elizabeth I* 30–1, 79–80). Even so, the crowd's uneasiness would give way almost instantly to a sense of relief if it were founded solely on a former peril that had been averted. There is every reason to assume, however, that the possibility of a marriage between Elizabeth and Philip had a deeply troubling and powerful resonance for many in the early Jacobean political and religious milieu. The very notion of a far-reaching alliance with the Spanish Catholics was anxiously perceived as an urgent threat to English Protestantism.

In 1604, in an attempt to consolidate further the peace with Spain, James I ventured to negotiate a marriage between Prince Henry, Prince of Wales, and the Infanta Anne, daughter of Philip III. The Spanish were optimistic that they might be able to coax James into allowing Prince Henry to be instructed in Catholic doctrine,[10] and Pope Clement, heartened by the fact that James's wife, Anne, was a Catholic, urged the King to educate Henry in "the old faith" (Lockyer, *The Early Stuarts* 282). Nothing came of the idea because the children were as yet too young, but the thought of a Catholic heir to the English throne was distressing if not simply intolerable to a London theater audience.[11] (As much is made clear in *Sir Thomas Wyatt* [c. 1602], a play in which Heywood had a hand, when the titular hero raises a patriotically inspired rebellion in response to Queen Mary's intention to marry Philip of Spain.)

The historical associations are therefore no less inflammatory when in *If You Know Not Me* Beningfield mentions "*Wiat* and the Kentish rebels" and the "Dukes, / That fought by all meanes to proclaim Queen *Jane*" (194), or when it becomes clear that the unfolding action belongs to the early days of Mary's reign, and that Mary is the mystery Queen in question.[12] In Heywood's England, the memory of Mary was surpassed for public disapproval only by that of Richard III, and the official line on her reign, aptly expressed in Holinshed, was that she "abused" her throne for "the destruction of Christs church and the people."[13] Save for the 40,000 remaining English Catholics (Lockyer, *The Early Stuarts* 281), most people would recall with horror the days of religious persecution and public burnings of Protestant heretics. Spoon-fed an ideology of hereditary monarchy, Elizabethans, including Heywood and Holinshed, never doubted the legitimacy of Mary's rule, yet it was precisely her right to the throne that made her or any other Catholic with the same right so deeply objectionable to English Protestants.[14]

Audience response to the opening scene of *If You Know Not Me* would therefore have been shaped by a feeling of genuine apprehension about James I's perceived tolerance in questions of religion. The new monarch had been raised in the strict Calvinist tradition, but widespread rumors prior to his arrival, as well as some of his first statements and decrees as King of England, had Protestants intensely worried. Before ascending to the throne, he communicated to Henry Howard, the future "Earl of Northampton, and the unofficial spokesman for the English catholics, that he would not 'persecute any that will be quiet and give but an outward obedience to the law.' On the contrary, he would be more than willing 'to advance any of them that will by good service worthily deserve it.'"[15] And to Elizabeth's Secretary of State, Robert Cecil, he wrote: "I will never allow in my conscience that the blood of any man shall be shed for diversity of opinions in religion" (Lockyer, *The Early Stuarts* 281).[16] These correspondences were supposedly secret, but this hardly means that James's views were unknown in England. While still in Scotland James spoke to a Catholic priest by the name of William Watson in such a way that "Watson came away satisfied that James would extend religious toleration to the English Catholics. Back in England Watson championed James so ardently among his co-religionists that his enemies tauntingly referred to James as 'Watson's king.'"[17] What is more, Queen Elizabeth herself was openly suspicious of James's apparent Catholic leanings. In 1586, Elizabeth and James had made a sealed agreement to the effect that the Queen "would do nothing prejudicial to his [James's] claim [to the English throne] unless he provoked her into doing so, but further than this she would not go."[18] For James this hardly meant the "security that in due course he would be bequeathed the crown," and, as Elizabeth was told by her informants, the King "aimed at making foreign monarchs look favorably on his candidacy, [even] when this led him into contact with Catholic powers who were hostile to Elizabeth" (Somerset, *Elizabeth I* 562).

But most unsettling was James's first address to the English Parliament in 1604, in which the new king stated: "I acknowledge the Romane Church to be our Mother Church, although defiled with some infirmities and corruptions." Further report had it that James said he "would be gladly reunited with the Roman church and would take three steps in that direction if only the church would take one."[19] He seemed "resolved to accord toleration to the catholic laity,"[20] and he reduced recusancy fines significantly, despite the fierce opposition of the 1604 Parliament, "which passed an Act calling for the 'due execution of the statutes' . . . against 'any manner of recusants'" (Lockyer, *The Early Stuarts* 283).

In retrospect, there is no reason to believe that James was trying to advance the Catholic cause at the expense of the Church of England.[21] At least one historian maintains James was merely "out to win friends in England" (Akrigg, *Letters* 39). He favored peaceful co-existence between England's main religious currents, but he "would also be lo[a]th that, by too great connivance and oversight unto [the Catholics], they might at last increase . . . as, by continual multiplication, they might at last become masters" (Lockyer, *The Early Stuarts* 282). He confirmed that he believed the Pope to be the Antichrist, and he banished seminary priests and the Jesuits. He also reinstated recusancy fines, failed to grant toleration to the Catholic laity, and dashed Catholic hopes at the Hampton Court conference.

What mattered to Protestants at the time, however, "was not so much the facts of the case as the general impression" of a king whose behavior they judged to be overly permissive. One subject wrote that "it is hardly credible in what jollity they [the Catholics] now live. They make no question to obtain at least toleration if not alteration of religion; in hope whereof many who before did dutifully frequent the [parish] church are of late become recusants" (*The Early Stuarts* 283). The miscarriage of the Gunpowder Plot in November 1605 brought an abrupt end to all this Catholic "jollity."

If You Know Not Me traffics in anxiety about a perceived growth in Catholic power, but it also does much to ameliorate that anxiety by presenting Philip in a remarkably positive light. Not only is the marriage between Queen Mary and the man who was to send his Armada against the English people described as "treated first in heaven," but he is also shown to be instrumental in saving Elizabeth from a plot against her life and in bringing about her eventual reunion with the Queen. The play's apparent rapprochement with Philip runs contrary to its anti-Catholic impulse, and can perhaps be explained in the context of the economic hardships caused by the prolonged struggle with Spain.[22] The last decade in particular of the war with Spain demanded financial sacrifices from all levels of society, while "the standard of living of working men and women in town and country reached its lowest level in the whole of recorded English history" (Smith A., *Emergence of a Nation State* 235). We need only contrast this state of affairs with "the trade boom which followed the ending of the Spanish War in 1604 and lasted until 1614" (252) to understand just how important peace was for a London theater audience.

Nevertheless, however crucial peace had become to economic survival, it did not require a *marriage* for "*Spain* and *England*, two populous kingdomes / That have a long time been opposd / In hostile emulation, be at one" (*If You Know Not Me* 202). For most Englishmen, the desire for peace with Spain was very much circumscribed by equally deep feelings of suspicion toward a nation that had not changed all that much since the time of the Armada, and a marriage was considered a far too invasive and irreversible solution. Besides, the Treaty of London had come about without a wedding. Making peace was one thing, inviting the enemy into the palace quite another. Heywood signifies as much in the scene following the defeat of the Armada, featured in the Second Part of *If You Know Not Me You Know Nobodie* (but which may originally have been a part of the conclusion to Part One [Doran, "Introduction" xii-xviii]), in which Elizabeth announces that "Towards London march wee to a *peaceful* throne: / We wish no warres, yet *we must guard our owne*" (344; italics added).

In Part One of *If You Know Not Me*, Heywood underscores the point by essentially dissolving the Catholic union between Mary and Philip at the very moment that the Catholic queen and her Protestant sister are happily reunited. The playwright, in this respect, goes well beyond the matter provided in his sources. "Whatere you think, arise and kisse our hand," Mary tells an anxious Elizabeth, clearly allaying lingering fears about her sister's allegedly treasonous or Protestant thoughts. Philip steps from behind the arras to "applaud this unity," and to hear Mary say to her sister, "To-morrow for the country; you are free" (236).

Philip's next words mark both his exit from the play and his departure from English soil. It is as if saving Elizabeth was his sole purpose for being at the court. In parting, he says to his wife:

> My soul is ioyfull that this peace is made;
> A peace that pleaseth heauen and earth and all,
> Redeeming captiue thoughts from captiue thrall.
> Faire Queene, the serious business of my father
> Is now at hand to be accomplished.

Mary responds prophetically, "My soul diuines we neuer more shall meet" (237). The two hundred or so lines following Philip's departure recount the sudden deaths of the Bishop of Winchester, Cardinal Poole, and, finally, of Queen Mary herself. Thus Heywood marks the end of their marital union, and the beginning of a new era which, according to Winchester, shall see "true religion . . . decay" in favor of "heresy" (237).

Heywood's primary sources, Foxe and Holinshed show considerably more restraint than the playwright in reporting the supposed conciliatory meeting between queen and princess. Holinshed and Foxe do not combine several and separate events into a single cataclysmic moment that dramatically shifts the historical tide: "And so [the princess and the queen] departed [*separated*], with very few comfortable words of the Queen in English. But what she said in Spanish, GOD knoweth! It is thought that King Philip was there, behind a cloth [*tapestry*], and not shewn; and that he shewed himself a very friend in that matter."[23] In *Englands Elizabeth*, Heywood reports that Elizabeth did not even know how to interpret the conference: "not one word of comfort could she imagine to have proceeded from her sister." Heywood also delays the moment of Elizabeth's freedom until some seven days after the meeting, and indicates that she was released "by the intercession of som eminent friends" (100), without suggesting that Philip was among them. In addition, he attributes a motive to Philip for aiding Elizabeth that is significantly absent from the play. In *Englands Elizabeth*, the King "is worried about his own life. His rationale is that if the English can seek the life of a native who is sister to the Queen, 'they would then make it small scruple of conscience to assault him and his followers, being mere aliens and strangers.'"[24] In the drama, however, Philip is not so disposed and appears to be moved solely by adulation for the woman whom he perceives as a "Mirror of vertue and bright Natures pride! / Pity it had beene such a beauty should haue dide" (236).

Here Heywood has seized upon a few enigmatic lines in his sources and unpacks them in a way that runs contrary to the Elizabethan stereotype of Philip II as the man who, many felt, was primarily responsible for the burning of the martyrs. Heywood's strategy of revising the historically received image of Philip is compatible with his manipulation of the unnamed "Queene" in the opening scene. Both instances playfully destabilize the orderly progression of formalistic Christian and humanist historiography. This is not to say that everything in the play conspires to this purpose; on the contrary, the heroic tale of a queen whose ultimate faith in providence eventually triumphs over the Machiavellian efforts of her Catholic opponents fits squarely in the tradition of Heywood's sources, Holinshed and Foxe. Addressing only this dimension of Heywood's work led Louis B. Wright to construct an image of him as a "popularizer" of historical knowledge and "an apostle of simplicity."[25] It seems quite clear, however, that Heywood's political and religious itinerary also places him at odds with a simple and streamlined presentation of history.

II

In fusing the exemplary tale of the innocent Lady Elizabeth with such problematic ambiguities as the identity of the "Queene" and the sympathetic portrayal of Philip II, Heywood's historical drama delineates two diametrically opposed ways of generating history, and, more specifically, two opposed ways of producing historical sequences. In its formal approach to history (of which the exemplary story of Elizabeth is an instance par excellence), the play arranges its material *diachronically*, but it also employs an alternative, more poetic and *synchronic* approach to history in its representation of the "Queene" and Philip.

A diachronic, formal method of producing history operates on the basis of a predetermined historical code – moral, providential, political – to which it subordinates historical entities. Guided by the principle of equivalences ("similarity and dissimilarity, synonymity and antonymity"), it selects and substitutes different historical entities (events and figures) into the categories of the larger, predetermined code for the purpose of instruction or elucidation. The predominantly diachronic works of Foxe and Holinshed, for example, readily yield lessons about the "miraculous preserving" of the virtuous and righteous Elizabeth under "the mighty protection of our merciful God," and offer "an admonition to all Christian rulers" not to emulate Queen Mary who strove "against the Lord and his proceedings" (Foxe, *Imprisonment* 363; Holinshed, *Chronicles* 140). The "historical entities," Elizabeth and Mary, here function as concrete instances or exemplifications of the formal category "monarch" which helps to constitute the larger, predetermined "code" of the Reformation as envisaged by Protestant providentialist historians. Within this particular paradigm of history, it is theoretically possible to substitute any Protestant ruler for Elizabeth and any Catholic one for Mary, and the essential lesson and meaning of the historical equation (Protestant rulers are with God,

Catholic rulers are against him) remains the same.[26] Heywood's depiction of Princess Elizabeth, of course, corresponds closely to this kind of formalist approach to historical presentation.

A synchronic history, on the other hand, has, as I suggested earlier, greater kinship with the antiquarian impulse. A synchronic history proceeds horizontally and seizes on events and figures that roughly coincide in time. It orders its "historical entities" on the basis of "contiguity," rather than on the basis of their selection or substitution into a predetermined code. The work of Hayden White is of heuristic value here. White's astute analysis[27] of Roman Jakobson's much celebrated essay, "Linguistics and Poetics,"[28] reveals how the tension between different modes of historical representations perceived by Heywood resonates in contemporary debates over historical criticism. White distinguishes between an older, formalist approach to literary history and the recent method advocated by new historicists by characterizing formal historical criticism as a diachronic activity – that is, as a transhistorical activity that occurs on the vertical axis – and new historicism as a synchronic enterprise occurring on the horizontal axis and centering on events that transpire at roughly the same point in history.

White associates diachronic historiography with Jakobson's idea of the "metalingual" function of language (which belongs to the vertical axis) and synchronic historiography with the "poetic" function thereof (which belongs to the horizontal axis). The "metalingual" is the code of language (the set of rules and conventions that makes language possible) that invokes De Saussure's conception of *langue*. Jakobson contrasts the "metalingual" with "object language," that is, the concrete, ordinary, and everyday expression of the "metalingual," and argues that while the "poetic" function of language does manifest itself in "object language," it does so in a very particular manner. According to Jakobson, an ordinary linguistic utterance (as opposed to a poetic utterance) results from two processes: selection (or substitution) and combination.[29] Selection takes place on the vertical axis for the purpose of selecting, on the basis of similarity and dissimilarity, synonymity and antonymity, the proper words from the available lexicon. These words are then positioned in a sequence based on "contiguity" (word order), which occurs on the horizontal "axis of combination."

In its poetic function, by contrast, language borrows the principle of equivalence (the process of selection and substitution) from the vertical axis and *displaces* it onto the horizontal axis of combination (Jakobson, "Linguistics and Poetics" 95). In White's reading of Jakobson, poetic language results from, and is structured by, a fusion of "equivalence" and "contiguity." Here White returns to literary history to suggest that formal historical criticism relies on a metalingual-like code to perform its operations, whereas new historicism creates its historical sequences by exploring equivalences between seemingly unrelated events (unrelated, that is, according to available codes). Consequently, White argues, the pattern of new historical sequences is "distinctively poetic" in nature, and can be called poetic history.[30] Hence, Greenblatt's bold assertion that "shadow stories" of transvestism in Switzerland "haunt" Shakespeare's *Twelfth Night* is a most vivid instance of poetic historicizing.[31] It is fair to criticize Greenblatt and other new historicists as Dr. Johnson criticized the metaphysical poets, and suggest that they yoke together by violence heterogeneous ideas. It is also fair to point out that no matter how synchronic new historicism tries to be, it often presupposes coherent models of culture and its development. But it is also wise to remember T. S. Eliot's response to Johnson and to suggest that certain minds are capable of "amalgamating" seemingly disparate experiences and shaping them into "new wholes" that allow us to perceive previously invisible connections established by what Greenblatt calls "social energy."[32]

Obviously, diachronic and synchronic descriptions of the past each have their advantages and disadvantages, and each necessarily contains some characteristics of the other. It is, however, not my purpose here to elevate one over the other. In the context of my discussion of Heywood's play, it is the relationship between the two approaches that matters. The chief aim of synchronic history is to represent events and situations that drop out of a diachronic account because they appear unrelated to its central interest or theme. Synchronic history's second aim (and this is especially true for new historicists) is to tell a type of intimate, idiosyncratic story a diachronic master narrative *cannot* tell. New historicism obviously lacks the drive for an exhaustive record of the past we see in antiquarianism, but both approaches produce tensions when set *against* diachronic texts. In *If You Know Not Me* Heywood offers the reader a diachronic and exemplary tale of Elizabeth; but he also demonstrates the shortcomings of the diachronic model and the importance of a synchronic approach. The aim is achieved through the crossing of the diachronic and the synchronic axes, which produces something that may be called "poetic history." Diachronic historiography, we saw, relies on the principle of equivalences to make selections and substitutions for the purpose of maintaining its historical equations. Heywood's initial presentation of the unnamed "Queene" sets in motion a complex process of selection. The diachronic process falters when the audience is unable to pin down conclusively a historical figure who fits into the category "Queene." Audience confusion could lead, as I argued, to the contemplation of several marriages (all of which were at one point historically plausible): Elizabeth I and Philip II, Princess Elizabeth and Philip II, Mary and Philip, and even, by further association, Prince Henry and the

Spanish Infanta, or the religious uncertainty of the union between the Calvinistic James and his staunchly Catholic Queen Anne. Taken together, Heywood's failure to identify the "Queene" and the audience's desire to resolve the riddle frustrate the diachronic process of selection and substitution. The utter lack of historical specificity precisely demonstrates the urgent need for it, and emphasizes that monarchs and their marriages are *not* interchangeable. The Queene's lack of identity *results* from an insufficient historical context, and underscores the importance of a synchronic perspective because it prompts us to view monarchs as products of historical conditions, not moral, providential, or exemplary categories.

Moreover, the very instant the process of diachronic substitution breaks down, the audience (or reader) is faced with a typically poetic situation. The unresolved search for equivalences – the search for similarities and dissimilarities – turns out to be the *only* organizing principle or "pattern" of the search for the correct monarchs (Jakobson, "Linguistics and Poetics" 95; White, H., "New Historicism" 300). And poetic history can thus be envisaged as "a complex interaction between two kinds of syntagmatic processes: one corresponding to the [diachronic] dimension of Jakobson's linguistic model, the other corresponding to the 'poetic' [or synchronic] dimension thereof" (White, H., "New Historicism" 301).

The power of Heywood's poetic history resides, in part, in its subtle difference from the more typical turn-of-the-century models that rely on exemplarity (or diachrony). Except for the historical accounts produced by antiquarians and skeptics, the most popular renaissance histories operate along the diachronic axis for the explicit purpose of substituting persons and events into an overarching code of history in which events supposedly repeated themselves. The pedagogical and ideological strengths of this approach are that the code (which is almost inevitably conducive to the reproduction of the existing socio-political hierarchy because it elides those aspects of history that do not fit) remained fundamentally unaltered by historical and cultural changes. This model, in which the code is not required to change significantly to accommodate historical "anomalies" (rather, historical examples are selected to *fit* the code), posited an unfailing continuity between certain historical occurrences and present political circumstances.

Heywood's *If You Know Not Me* has what could be termed a pedagogical purpose, but it conveys that purpose differently. Degory Wheare, the first man to hold a chair in history at Oxford University, confirmed a popular notion when he pronounced history to be "nothing but moral philosophy, clothed in examples."[33] For Wheare historical particulars are by definition subordinate to general moral categories. Heywood's ambiguous opening scene, however, conflates actual marriages and proposed marriages from the past and present to raise anxiety about England's political and religious future. The reason trepidation is raised in this manner is that these marriages and their consequences for English religious and political life are vastly different. It is their difference that makes the conflation so alarming. Not naming the "Queene" is Heywood's distinctly poetic choice, a choice which is alien to the historian. The latter would identify the "Queene" precisely for the purpose of erecting interpretative boundaries that will prevent the reader from roaming outside of history's codes.

III

The poetic dimension of Heywood's historiography, its apprehension of the past's applicability to the present, becomes even clearer when we consider the remarkable conversation between the three White Coat soldiers assigned to guard the Lady Elizabeth, who surmises that she has reached the low point in her life. Having failed to convince the Queen and the Bishop of Winchester of her loyalty and innocence, she understands her relocation to "that fatall place," the Tower, to be the signal for her certain death. In carefully chosen words and sometimes thinly veiled allegorical terms, the soldiers contemplate Elizabeth's predicament, and unwittingly offer a meditation on the unique character of historical context.

While passing around "a jacke of beere," they wonder what "a man may say, without offence" (*If You Know Not Me* 209). They agree there is no harm in toasting one's friends or in syllogistically suggesting "that the Lady *Elizabeth* is both a lady and *Elizabeth*." They think it may even be acceptable to speak in the subjunctive mood and ask: "if I should say she were a verteous princess, were there any harm in that?" Perhaps there is not. In Marian England it seems possible to get away with a *conditional* statement of praise, but, as the second soldier states, one "must beware of talking of the Princess" because it is not wise to "meddle with the State." It is safer, he suggests, to "meddle with our kindred; there we may be bold." The first soldier retorts with a brief tale: "Well, sirs, I haue two sisters, and the one loues the other, and would not send her to prison for a million. Is there any harm in this? Ile keepe myselfe within compasse, I warrant you; for I do not talke of the Queene; I talk of my sisters"; and he adds, "Why, sir, I hope a man may be bold with his own. I learned that of the Queen" (209–10).

The soldier's tale ostensibly shifts from the political sphere to the domestic sphere by the substitution of his "sisters" for the Queen and the Princess. Albeit indirectly, he is obviously criticizing the actions of his queen, and he is meddling with the state. Yet he seems to believe that his act of substitution alters the context of the situation enough to safeguard him against the wrath of the authorities, while still making it clear that one sister should never imprison another, even if one of them is the queen. But the third soldier clearly does not think the substitution is effective. "That word sister goes hardly down," he says. And, indeed, if a representative of state power were to overhear their words, it is quite conceivable that these soldiers would be punished severely. In other words, we have here two competing conceptions of interaction between historical contexts. The third soldier seems to believe that the substitution of sisters for queen and princess produces an equivalency on the diachronic axis, while the first soldier relies on equivalences that create a pattern of associations belonging to the synchronic axis.

"Is there any harme in all this?" is the scene's recurring question. The answer is "yes" and "no"; it all depends on the historical context into which the scene is inserted. There is obvious harm in all this from Mary's point of view. As everyone knew quite well, Princess Elizabeth enjoyed her greatest popular support among English Protestants, and since she was a designated heir to the crown under Henry VIII's will, she, as a focal point of Protestant resistance, presented a threat not only to Mary but also to foreign Catholics like Charles V and the future Philip II, who took great pains to transform England into a stable Catholic ally. Charles and his ambassador to England, Renard, put great pressure on Mary to eliminate Elizabeth as a political force. They doubted the sincerity of Elizabeth's conversion to Catholicism early in Mary's reign. They sought her life, and when this proved too bold a move for Mary's divided Privy Council, they suggested passing a new Act excluding her from the crown, as well as "marrying her to some [foreign] reliable catholic husband who would keep her in order" (Ridley, *Elizabeth I* 49–52). The Constable of the Tower reminds the audience of this very fact when he asserts:

> rather could I wish
> She were married to some priuate gentleman,
> And with her dower conuaid out of the land,
> Then here to stay, and be a mutiner.
> So may your highnesse state be more secure;
> For whilst she lives, warres and commotions,
> Foul insurrections, will be set abroch.
> I thinke twere not amisse to take her head:
> This land would be in quiet, were she dead.
>
> (*If You Know Not Me* 225–6)

That *If You Know Not Me* was licensed for performance and publication early in the reign of James signals a fundamental shift in the attitude of the state. That "times change" is in and of itself not all that surprising, but Heywood's drawing our attention to the fundamental mutability of historical contexts *is*. Within the immediate dramatic-historical context created by the play, the White Coat soldiers *are* engaging in treasonous speech. They go unpunished because they express their views privately; their meddling with the state goes undetected. Yet their subversive speech is also made extremely public, on the public stage of a different historical time. The result is not merely a superficial realization that "times change," but that a historical occurrence can mean radically different things in different settings; that the response of the state to any given point of view can vary from calling it treasonous to licensing it for public consumption; and that historical representation exists not only on the diachronic axis but also on the synchronic axis, where historical accounts are not exemplary because they represent "discrete" and "unique" moments. The "code" or "fundamental structure" on which formal diachronic historiography relies to produce historical sequences and meaning is shown to be not separate from historical events, but itself transmutable, ever bound up in the (changing) ideological–historical conditions that it seeks to describe.

The scene suggests that although poetic history *does* build "a sequence [out] of discrete moments," it also recognizes that the "pattern" of the sequence is only retroactively discernible, not "prospectively predictable." There may therefore be a "code" or "fundamental structure" (as in the formalist version of literary history) to historical sequences, but, unlike the formalist critic/historian, the poetic historian does neither subordinate "historical entities to that code," nor appeal to the code "to account for the unique features of specific moments in the series that comprises the sequence" (White, H., "New Historicism" 301).

Heywood again foregrounds the contingent character of history when the Earl of Sussex questions the cruel treatment afforded to Elizabeth by the Constable of the Tower. "But if this time should alter," the Earl protests, "marke me well, / Could this be answer'd?" Surely, the question is not intended to invoke merely a medieval conception of fortune, suggesting that individuals rise and fall in unexpected ways as determined by God's providence. What Sussex's question drives at is the fundamental instability of social, political, and ideological structures: the Marian cultural system can be transformed by another. The Constable defends his actions by noting that they are at "the Queene's commands," and, moreover, that "the Queen is young, likely to beare / Of her own body a more royall heir." "She shall," he insists, "be vsed so still (214)." A Jacobean audience need only recall Henry VIII's gruesome marital and divorce schemes to perpetuate his line, and, indeed, Elizabeth I's own marital politics, to realize that royal bodies may fail to produce the desired "royall heir[s]." And as both Mary's reign and the play draw to a close, as Philip II departs for Spain, as Winchester and Cardinal Poole are both dead, and as Mary falls "exceeding sick," Sussex's remarks carry very specific political and religious import when he proclaims that: "The *State* begins to alter" (240; italics added). With the benefit of hindsight, a Jacobean audience can roughly discern the historical pattern that culminated in their contemporary world; but they would also be aware of the Constable's inability to predict the political future, and the Earl's reluctance to bank on the stability and continuance of the present political structure. The audience would have been especially attuned to these matters because they reverberated in contemporary society. With the recent arrival of the new King and the peace treaty with Spain, the English state was altering once again, and many people were uneasy and uncertain about the precise direction and consequences of the changes.

IV

Because Sir Philip Sidney is such an important and eloquent figure in the late sixteenth century, critics have found it tempting to believe the conceptions of history, philosophy and poetry offered in *The Defence of Poesy* to be representative of the English renaissance. Perhaps the temptation looms so large because our modern understanding of these ideas until recently corresponded roughly to Sidney's own. The historian, Sidney tells us, is tied "to the particular truth of things [and] his example draweth no necessary consequence."[34] The philosopher, on the other hand, has no such limitations. He deals in "abstract consideration," in "the general reason of things." "The peerless poet [however] perform[s] both: for whatsoever the philosopher saith should be done, he giveth a perfect picture of it in some one by whom he presupposeth it was done; so as he coupleth the general notion with the particular example" (Sidney, *Sir Philip Sidney* 221). The primary purpose of Sidney's argument is not merely to draw out differences among poetry, history, and philosophy, but also, and more importantly, to demonstrate poetry's superior capacity to educate its readers and to spur them on to noble action.

A glance at other renaissance views on the subject immediately reveals that not everyone shared Sidney's conviction concerning poetry's superior pedagogical character. Thomas North, translator of *Plutarch's Lives of the Noble Grecians and Romans*, dedicated his efforts to Elizabeth I, and begged humbly for her "protection" on the grounds that while "these lives of Plutarke" could not teach the wise Queen anything, they contained numerous historical "examples" capable of teaching her "subjects" "so much honor, love, obedience, reverence, zeal, and devocion to Princes."[35] Jacques Amyot, who translated Plutarch from Greek into French and whose preface to the reader North adds to his edition, further contradicts Sidney by claiming that the examples from history teach "with greater weight and gravitie, than the inventions and devises of the Poets: bicause [history] helpeth not it selfe with any other thing than with the plaine truth, whereas Poetry does commonly enrich things commending them above the starrs and their deserving, bicause the chiefe intent thereof is to delight" (North, *Plutarch's Lives* 11).[36]

Thomas Heywood stands in a peculiar and complex relationship to these positions. If we go by his translation of Bodin's "Of the Choice of History," Heywood seems to agree with Sidney about history's limited scope. "Historie ought to be nothing but a representation of truth, and as it were a Map of mens actions, set forth in the publicke view of all commers to bee examined."[37] Nevertheless, while he agrees with Sidney about history's inability to teach effectively, he positively disagrees with him about the domain to which moral education belongs. "And to their opinions, that suppose the praises of vertue, and the display of vices to be the fruit of History, I answere, that it may more truely and properly bee handled by Philosophers (to whose element it pertaineth) then by Historiographers" (Bodin, "Choice of History" 19).

However, the philosopher's prerogative in Heywood's translation of Bodin (to expound virtue and vice) emphatically becomes the dramatist's license in his *An Apology for Actors*. The staging of "domesticke hystories" can be "so bewitching a thing" that it possesses "power to new mold the harts of the spectators and fashion them to the shape of any noble and notable attempt."[38] Heywood's public theater emerges as a genuine extension of the state apparatus:

> Playes are writ with this ayme, and carryed with this methode to teach the subiects obedience to their King, to shew the people the vntimely ends of such as haue moued tumults, commotions, and insurrections, to present them with the flourishing estate of such as liue in obedience, exhorting them to alleance, dehorting them from all trayterous and fellonious strategems. (sig. F3^{v})

Heywood's conception of the uses of the theater closely resembles those articulated for history in Amyot's preface and North's dedication to Queen Elizabeth, but it is altogether different from Bodin's. Differences become blurred, however, when Heywood's defense of the acting profession appropriates for the stage history's objective as defined in his translation of Bodin. "Playes," he insists, "haue made the ignorant more apprehensiue, taught the vnlearned the *knowledge* [my emphasis] of many famous histories, instructed such as cannot reade in the discouery of all our *English* Chronicles" (sig. F3^{r}). In other words, Heywood's idea of historical drama combines the affective powers Sidney attributes to poetry with those that Amyot and North grant to history, and also appropriates what Bodin conceives of as history's function, "to be nothing but a representation of truth."

This multi-purpose definition of historical drama contains a clear contradiction. How can historical drama provide instruction in truth *and* serve as an instrument of state ideology? The question cannot be resolved on a conceptual plane, and, perhaps, need not be resolved at all because we cannot be positive that the contradiction is of Heywood's own making. First, we do not know enough about Heywood's reasons for translating Bodin. Surely he found much of merit in the *Method*, but it is impulsive to claim that "undoubtedly Bodin summed up Heywood's own conceptions of the historical method" (Wright, *Middle-Class Culture* 290), for the simple reason that Heywood was a professional writer and translator who often wrote for money simply on a publisher's request. Likewise, it's difficult to determine how sincere he is in the *Apology* when he offers the Earl of Worcester, the former patron of Queen Anne's Company, an image of the theater as a willing instrument of state power. As a principle sharer and actor in the company, Heywood had much to gain from secure relations with the authorities in an era that saw both the number and identity of London companies tightly controlled.

But even if the idea of historical drama that emerges from these texts is not necessarily and wholly Heywood's, we still have in *If You Know Not Me* a play that manifestly embodies these contradictory views. The play's grand gesture is clearly diachronic in its approach to history; it offers a traditional, providentialist interpretation of Elizabeth's path to the crown, culminating in the triumph of the true religion. Foxe, Hall, and Holinshed would be proud of such a model. To support further this historical outcome, the play is critical of Mary's treatment of her sister, but careful never to question the legitimacy of her rule. Indeed, to question Mary's right to the crown (a right recorded in the will of Henry VIII) would equally unsettle Elizabeth's right and confound the clarity of the Tudor myth, a myth which still had considerable purchase on Heywood and the English nation at this moment. Thus the play energetically professes political values and ideals that belong to the Elizabethan age. Nevertheless, when viewed in its early Jacobean context, Heywood also injects the story with synchronic impulses that interrupt the continuity of a meta-narrative of history with a more poetic version of history.

One such impulse that meets the diachronic, linear version of history head-on centers on Elizabeth's identity. In *Englands Elizabeth*, the diachronic historian Heywood begins his tale of the princess by insisting that, "The better to illustrate this history, needfull it is that wee speak somthing of the *Mother*, before we proceed to the daughter" (9). He in fact inaugurates the history of Elizabeth with the match "concluded betwixt Prince *Arthur* the eldest Sonne and Heyre apparant to *Henry* the 7th, King of England, and the Infant *Katharine* daughter to the King of *Spaine*." His concern is clearly with genealogy, with a causal sequence that establishes the royal credentials and identity of the princess. It determines how she fits into the larger version of history – the stabilizing version of history designed to unite England (in a very specific manner) following the coronation of Henry VII. But in the play there are several occasions where lineage and ancestry are decidedly ineffectual in establishing Elizabeth's political credibility and innocence. Accused of treason by Winchester and the Constable of the Tower, she exclaims:

> Treason, Lords! If it be treason
> To be the daughter to th'eight *Henry*,
> Sister to *Edward*, and the next of blood
> Vnto my gracious Soueraign, the now Queene,
> I am a traitor . . . (207)

Elizabeth is urgently attempting to draw on the powers and dignity of a former age, but the irony of her predicament is, of course, that her ancestry is as much her enemy as her ally. "Madam," the Constable responds like a true interrogator, "The Queen must heare you sing another song, / Before you part with us." Elizabeth's words may win her a Jacobean audience's sympathy and underscore her credibility in their minds, but they also aptly summarize why she is a legitimate threat to Mary. A further historical association suggests that Elizabeth's appeal to her parentage would ring true to early Jacobeans who, along with their parents and grandparents, had been educated and raised in the Elizabethan system, but that it would also recall that Henry VIII had declared Elizabeth a bastard, taken away her title of Princess, and sought passage of the "Second Succession Act" which "entailed the Crown on the King's yet unborn heirs by his third wife, Jane Seymour" (Smith, A., *Emergence of a Nation State* 379; also see Ridley, *Elizabeth I* 25–6, 85). In other words, Heywood again demonstrates the inevitable difficulties involved in diachronic substitutions. In ever-changing historical contexts the song does not remain the same; what is true can also be treason.

To what extent is *If You Know Not Me* a subversive text? On the basis of new historicist practice, Hayden White observes that a poetic approach to history serves "as a means of identifying those aspects of historical sequences that conduce to the breaking, revision, or weakening of the dominant codes" (White, H., "New Historicism" 301). The providential plot of Heywood's drama, however, certainly promotes the continuity and stability of the existing socio-political order. And even those aspects of the play that challenge the permanence of that order – not naming the Queen, the conversation between the White Coat soldiers, the sympathetic portrayal of Philip II – also seek to promote rather conservative goals: namely, to preserve the true religion and to oppose what remained of Ralegh's war party in favor of economic prosperity. The play's subversive bent is contained in its synchronic (poetic) treatment (for conservative political ends) of events and relations commonly understood in a diachronic frame. Rather than suggest here that a conservative Heywood (inadvertently?) undermines conservative modes of history-writing and play-writing, I would submit that he presents his audience with two ways of thinking about the past, one traditional and diachronic, the other, conceptually radical and perfectly compatible with the poetic. Although there is no doubt that the fusion of drama and history inevitably results in a type of poetic history that conflicts with the linear, diachronic nature of formalistic history, it seems that Heywood considered them equally useful, which in itself is an anti-authoritarian consideration because it originates outside the halls of power and shows the figure of the monarch to be subjected in a cultural system. In the context of new historicist criticism, the play presents an interesting problem. For some new historicists, the play's subversive impulses – its presentation of moments of synchronic history that run counter to state-sanctioned diachronic history – would have to disclose themselves eventually as instruments of state power. In one sense, of course, they do because they *are* geared towards the preservation of Elizabethan policy. On the other hand, as the Elizabethan state is just beginning to be transformed into the distinct Jacobean state, the play speaks in favor of some of those anticipated transformations (for instance, peace with Spain) but against others (changes in religion). The question is, in 1604 and in a period of acute political changes, what counts as complicity and what as subversion? Jonathan Dollimore has argued that "a writer can be intellectually radical without necessarily being politically so. In the individual writer or text subversive thought and political conservativism may seem to be harmonized in a way which belies the fact that historically the two things relate dialectically: the former relates to the latter in ways which are initially integral to it yet eventually contradict it."[39]

The long-range implications of *If You Know Not Me* treatment of historical discourses are certainly anti-authoritarian, a fact borne out by the plays to be treated in following chapters. Thomas Heywood does not merely enact or produce a play containing diachronic history – an act which reveals the operations by which ideology produces itself – but he further draws the viewer's attention directly to that "double production" and its operations by "crossing" it with a different mode of historical production. The act of "crossing" is of supreme importance here because, as Eagleton points out, a text does not always display "its ideological categories on the surface."[40] If *If You Know Not Me* merely told the heroic story of the princess, the play would resemble Elizabethan historical dramas which "naturalize" their ideological conception of history. But of course it does not and crosses the two historical axes, which can only point to the artificiality of that conception. The foregrounding, via the emerging field of historiography and drama, of the constructed and ideological nature of something that purports to be natural makes available to the public a mode of analysis capable of questioning the authority of official versions of the past, and hence constitutes a potential blow to the state's power to create and control the past and, by extension, the present.

V

Basic distinctions between history and poetry, as understood by a tradition of thinkers extending from Aristotle to Sidney, are called into question by *If You Know Not Me*, because it makes important claims for its own historicity but also ranges well beyond "the particular truth of things" (Sidney, *Sir Philip Sidney* 89). For the most part, literary critics in this century have opted to characterize "history plays" as a special literary genre that draws on histories or chronicles only to transform their subject matter into something distinctly literary which is at best of marginal historical interest. Others, Ribner prominent among them, have maintained that a play is a history play if it "appears to fulfill what we know Elizabethans considered to be the legitimate purposes of history."[41] The crucial difference between these two views is that the first considers a historical drama to be foremost a literary or poetic text, a text that presses certain historical facts and events (as they are preserved in the prose histories) into the service of poetic creation, whereas the second suggests that history plays are shaped by the same principles we observe in the supposedly authentic histories written by Italian and English humanists, as well as by medieval providentialist historians. Thus, in the latter view, a history play is "an adaption of drama to the purposes of history" (Ribner, *English History Play* 29), and not an adaption of history to the purposes of drama. But what are the legitimate purposes of history? That, of course, is the vexing question because, as I tried to demonstrate in chapter 1, there was, especially as the sixteenth century drew to an end, genuine confusion and disagreement about the procedures and proper aims of historical discourse. The main approaches to history – providential, rhetorical, humanist, antiquarian – did not evolve into a single, even a dominant, historical method. Consequently, a play like Heywood's is not a straightforward imitation of history-writing or another history of Elizabeth, but an exploration of the coexistence of multiple historiographical discourses. What is more, as both a dramatist and a writer of prose history, Heywood must have been acutely aware of the fundamental affinities between literature and historiography. The renaissance generally held that there were defining distinctions between literature and historiography, but our examination of programmatic statements by historians indicates that the methodological dividing line between them is a fluid one. Historiography's roots in classical rhetoric align it naturally with literature; its humanistic use of examples link it to moral or political philosophy as well as literature (in the tradition from Horace to Sidney); and its emerging antiquarian concerns draw it closer to science. In the melting pot of the public theater, Heywood's *If You Know Not Me* easily embraces all three. Undermining the diachronic and exemplary tale of Elizabeth and the triumph of the true Church by crossing it with destabilizing synchronic axis, draws our attention to the "literary" shape of much traditional historiography. Indeed, if we again return to Hayden White, we can suggest that a play like *If You Know Not Me* draws "historiography nearer to its origins in literary sensibility."[42] That Heywood considered the boundaries between literature and historiography permeable is underscored strikingly by an unusual material exchange between two texts on Princess Elizabeth. When Heywood came to write *Englands Elizabeth* at least two decades after *If You Know Not Me*, he returned to his own drama and used it as a source next to Holinshed, Foxe, and Faybian. Both the dramatic and the prose accounts are obviously based on either Holinshed or Foxe or both, but a phrase like "he made their pates ring noone" which occurs in *Englands Elizabeth* (80) is found in the play ("make their pates Ring noon" [222–3]) but not in Holinshed, Faybian or Foxe (see Foxe, *Imprisonment* 354, Holinshed, *Chronicles* 129). In other words, the "normal" exchange between historical source and literary text has been reversed.

The end result of Heywood's "mixed" play-text is an exceptional kind of history play, one that does not construct itself in good Aristotelian or Elizabethan fashion and disallows its parts ultimately to produce a single historiographical or dramatic effect. The diachronic tale has to coexist with skeptical voices that deconstruct it – that is, voices that challenge the validity of its very structure or form. One way of explaining this phenomenon is to speculate that because what Jameson calls the "inner logic" of Elizabeth Tudor's story is no longer so absolutely sacred and compelling in the early moments of King James's reign, Heywood can exploit its nostalgic power at the same time that he can manipulate the story to serve a new agenda. We can assume that with the arrival of the new king and peace, the cultural and political landscape changed enough that the materials of the Princess Elizabeth story no longer dictated a single history. This is not to say that while Elizabeth was alive her story was always an uncontested one. When, for instance, John Stubbs in 1579, claiming to be motivated by "the affection of my heart, which must love my country and my Queen,"[43] publicly advised his queen (in writing) not to marry the Catholic Francis, Duke of Alençon (advice which Elizabeth eventually followed), he had his offending right hand lopped off for meddling in affairs of state. Yet when Dekker in *Sir Thomas Wyat* (1602) and Heywood in *If You Know Not Me* (1603) offer a less vitriolic version of the same message there are no such consequences. The once explosive question of Elizabeth's marriage schemes has lost most (but not all) of its volatility, and can now be used in a strategy of theatrical indirection to caution the new monarch about how he will arrange a marriage for Prince Henry.

I should note that in addition to concrete political considerations, the queen's gender is also a contributing factor to the destabilization of the "great men" model of historiography. Although Elizabeth ultimately triumphs over adversity, she is, for the most part, a victim throughout the play. As such, her status reflects the prevailing notion of popular heroines who "were admired not so much for what they did as for what they suffered" (Leggatt, *Jacobean Public Theatre* 213n. 6). Given late-sixteenth-century conceptions of gender, the portrayal of a woman in a historical discourse founded on the "great men" principle automatically undermined that principle because "great women" were by *definition* not the makers but the patient endurers of history. Hence the happy outcome of history in *If You Know Not Me* appears due less to the princess's decisive actions, than to factors beyond her control (the inexplicable support of Philip, the timely death of her childless sister Mary and the sudden death of the fanatical churchmen, Winchester and Poole). But it is also true that Elizabeth undergoes a marvelous transformation upon her coronation. Fear, anxiety, and self-pity give way to kindness, forgiveness of her jailer, Beningfield, and a bold embrace of the English Bible. In fact, I think that unlike Shakespeare's Prince Hal, who tries to convince us (perhaps unsuccessfully) that he will mature into the job, we are to infer that Princess Elizabeth is England's monarch already. Despite the ambiguity of the opening scene, Heywood's Elizabeth is instantly identified as the *Queen Elizabeth* in the play's title, and is never allowed to waiver from what is historically most important to her and England's identity: the Protestant faith and her loyalty to the English nation. The princess may only be the princess, but the queen is already contained in her; history becomes (retroactively) preordained. Thus, even while she is powerless and being dragged around the countryside by her enemies, Heywood grants her the same centrality that a historian might afford a male monarch.

For this reason it is interesting to speculate that Elizabeth's famous Tilbury address, which Heywood dramatizes in the sequel to *If You Know Not Me*, may initially have served as the ending of part one (Doran, "Introduction" xii–xviii). The queen appears before her troops "*compleatly armed*," and her speech directly addresses the question of her gender, and has the effect of masculinizing her.[44] "Know, my subjects," she declares, "Your Queene hath now put on a masculine spirit" (337). But she then complicates her gender position further by comparing herself to the eastern Queen Zenobia who "in the field incounter'd personally, / *Aurelianus Caesar*," and in conclusion expresses the wish that "had God made vs manlike like our mind, / We'd not be here fenc'd in a mure of armes, / But ha' been present at these sea alarmes" (338). If these speeches indeed formed the ending of Heywood's original play, the playwright compressed thirty years of history into a single scene (from coronation to Armada), no doubt to create a dramatic ending that makes us simultaneously see Elizabeth aspiring to a type of masculinity that draws her closer to the "great men" historiographical model, and also calls our attention to the fact that Elizabeth very much remains a woman – and a successful one at that – which calls into question the traditional notion that monarchs must be men who bend history to their will.

4 Shakespeare, Fletcher, and the question of history

> The Kings Players had a new Play called *All is True*, representing some principle pieces of the Reign of Henry 8. which was set forth with many extraordinary circumstances of Pomp and Majesty, even to the matting of the stage; the Knights of the Order, with their Georges and Garter, the Guards with their embroidered Coats, and the like: sufficient in truth within a while to make greatness very familiar, if not ridiculous.
>
> Henry Wotton[1]

I

Shakespeare's *Henry VIII* (1612–13), a play presumably written in collaboration with John Fletcher, has often been chastised for being episodic and lacking a strong hero. In many cases, the basis for this judgment is a comparison of this *Jacobean* text with Shakespeare's supposedly more successful Elizabethan history plays: "the weakness of *Henry VIII* results from its failure to embody an over-all consistent philosophical scheme such as makes cohesive unities out of all of Shakespeare's earlier histories, including *King John*."[2] This type of comparison is ill-conceived because it rests on the unfounded assumption that Shakespeare and Fletcher were trying (or ought to have tried) to compose an Elizabethan history play. It ignores the fact that when a genre alters under the pressures of the changing times, our readings must be attentive to the new historical conditions that went into its making. I will argue therefore that far from giving "us a coherent and meaningful philosophy of history" (Ribner, *English History Play* 191), *Henry VIII* tackles two problems central in the development of Jacobean historiography: it undercuts and revises the Tudor conception of history *as* the history of great men, and it shatters the Tudor propensity for unified (often providential) historiography. It achieves these ends in large part by dramatizing in a single text the contradictory character of various modes of historical representation readily available in the early seventeenth century. In the closing scene of *Henry VIII*, Archbishop Thomas Cranmer puts forth a determined effort to portray Tudor–Stuart history as a providentially guided succession of powerful individuals, but his historical approach stands in such sharp competition with other modes of historiography dramatized in the play;[3] and Cranmer distorts "known" history to such an extent that it is extremely unlikely that Jacobean audiences would have accepted his version without question.

In order to understand the gravity of the new historical awareness embodied in *Henry VIII*, we need to look back at Shakespeare's Elizabethan histories, for it is there that we witness the beginnings of shift in historical thought from its familiar Tudor form to its eventual Jacobean manifestation. This Tudor form, we recall, is aptly articulated in *The Arte of English Poesie* (1589) by George Puttenham, who suggests that it is the task of "historical Poesie" to record the "famous acts of Princes and the vertuous and worthy lives of our forefathers."[4] Arthur B. Ferguson extends this observation to just about all Tudor historiography when he contends that it displays no interest whatsoever in "man's collective interests, his customs, laws, institutions, and beliefs," and instead concerns itself with *res gestae*; that is, the acts and motives of "great men" ("kings, generals, statesmen [and] princes of the church") and little else that reaches "beyond . . . the acts, the ambitions, and the tragic dilemmas of the actors themselves."[5] Alvin Kernan consolidates these kindred views when he describes the typical historical pattern for Tudor historical dramas as follows: "a weak or saintly king makes political mistakes and is overthrown by rebellious and arrogant subjects; the kingdom becomes a wasteland and society a chaos in which every man's hand is set against his fellow; after a period of great suffering, reaction against the forces of evil occurs, and a strong and good king restores order."[6] If we add to the argument that the good or strong king who restores order is invariably guided by God's providence, we have virtually exhausted the list of historical causes – i.e., providence and human agency – that the mainstream Tudor historians thought they needed to incorporate into their accounts.

It can be said that a concern with providence and the actions of great men generally characterizes the historical drama of the Tudor Shakespeare. The first tetralogy offers mostly Machiavellian explanations (i.e., the motives and actions of individuals) for most of the misfortunes that befall the infirm Henry VI, Talbot, Clarence, Hastings, Edward V, Buckingham, and others, and concludes by dramatizing the rise and fall of a single, powerful character who is defeated by the agent of God's providence, Henry Tudor. The harsh world of *Realpolitik* depicted in *King John* (c. 1594–5) surely harkens back to the three *Henry VI* plays, although Shakespeare's story of John withholds the providential resolution offered in *Richard III*. It seems that these plays offer two primary visions of history: one in which providence "constructs an unbroken chain of historical causation," and another where "a Machiavellian view [almost always temporarily] interrupts that chain, constructing each age as unique, the product of Fortuna, or accident, and individual will."[7]

Here I would suggest, however, that Shakespeare's last history plays, *Henry V* and especially *Henry VIII*, although still very much concerned with the actions and failures of "great men," *begin* to demonstrate a substantial interest in what Georg Lukács referred to as the "social-historical basis" of human character.[8] Commencing with *Henry V* and burgeoning in *Henry VIII*, Shakespeare (and Fletcher) explore the fundamentally *im*personal forces – "the regulative features of . . . social collisions and contradictions" (Lukács, *Historical Novel* 154) – that determine history and the lives of individuals in ways ultimately beyond the control of even the most powerful princes. Neither play advances a systematic analysis of English renaissance institutions, customs, or laws, but both plays do break away significantly from an exclusive focus on the acts of famous Princes and/or God's providence. In two prior history plays, *1 Henry IV* and *2 Henry IV*, Shakespeare shows us how Prince Hal believes himself able to manipulate events in a manner that will allow him to remain above the historical fray; and in some respects he is successful. But in *Henry V* Shakespeare decides to give us a king who, his ingenious manipulations and rhetorical brilliance to the contrary, is ultimately incapable of transcending history, and all that that entails. On the eve of the Battle of Agincourt, Henry is unequivocally pulled down into history by the soldier Williams, and afterwards the King is unable to conceive of himself either as God's agent (à la Richard II) or as the crafty politician capable of transcending history's material and ideological conditions at will. The difference between Henry V and his predecessors, Richard II and Henry IV, is that the latter two, during their final moments, very much understand their somber fate in the Tillyardean terms of "Providence, fortune, and human character."[9] Henry V, however, although he emerges triumphantly from battle, realizes he is a diminished figure; neither divinity nor human skill allow him to rise above the historical fray. As "subject to the breath of every fool," the King finds himself firmly rooted in the very historical quagmire he has sought to escape. He learns he is a monarch who does not simply rule *over* the historical process; it also rules him. And no matter how many times he proclaims *publicly* that it was God's arm "alone" that carried England to victory (*Henry V* 4.8.108–14),[10] we know from his *private* prayer that Henry does not expect God to be on his side since contrition comes after the crime against God's anointed, Richard II (*Henry V* 4.1.309–11).

As Dollimore and Sinfield observe in their landmark essay on *Henry V*, once we view King Henry as a bearer of ideological and historical *structures*, the question of his personality or integrity becomes less crucial. This is a notable insight for it allows us to follow Shakespeare's deviation from

Tudor historiographical norms, and to abandon conventional criticism's desire to explain the plays exclusively in terms of the actions of great men and the powers of providence.[11] It further enables us to postulate that Shakespeare and some of his contemporaries were quite capable of expressing an *independent* view of English history, a view of history that differs factually, conceptually, and ideologically from versions endorsed by the culture's hegemonic forces.[12] It allows us to see that as the "new historiography, which developed in British intellectual life between 1580 and 1640, moves beyond Ciceronian platitudes," history plays come to embody "their own internal dialectic . . . begin to view history as a process of change, as self-determined, as a struggle between aristocratic houses and the monarchic state, between military and civilian interests, as a conflict regarding matters of succession and inheritance – a view of history, in a word, founded in ideological confrontation."[13]

All of Shakespeare's history plays of course disclose ideological conflict, but the early plays tend to disguise such conflict in terms of oppositions between good and evil men, strong kings and weak kings, providence and fortune, order and rebellion. When we get to *Henry VIII* we see that Shakespeare and Fletcher dramatize a radically different conception of history, a conception in which a complex network of largely inscrutable forces drive historical events. Older notions about "great men" and providence are still evoked but only as two of many ways to represent or reconstruct a fundamentally inaccessible past. To appreciate the magnitude of the shift in historical thinking from Elizabethan Shakespeare to *Henry VIII*, it will be useful to examine the relationship of monarchs to history in the second tetralogy. For in this history cycle we can observe a movement away from the personal to the providential and an increasing concern with ideological conflict in impersonal terms.

II

I want to examine the remarkable predicament King Henry V finds himself in on the eve of Agincourt, because it offers a radical insight into the monarch's relationship to history that can serve as an important reference point against which to measure subsequent developments in *Henry VIII* (and the Stuart historical drama in general). From the encounter with the common soldier Michael Williams, a bitterly disappointed Henry learns that a lowly subject is capable of *subjecting* the King, a subjection made possible by the reciprocal nature of the ideological structures that comprise social relations in the play. The moment in which the King recognizes himself as a subject and product of a historical process (which is neither random, providential, nor wholly subject to the human will) is, as far as I can tell, unique in the Elizabethan drama, and emblematic of an emerging historical consciousness more fully elaborated in the Stuart period. It suggests that even a victorious king like Henry, who is certainly reminiscent of the "great man," can utterly fail in his attempts to control his own perception in history. And here we have to recognize that for Henry control of that perception is virtually the same as controlling history itself.

Prince Hal, for the better part of his career, thinks he can operate outside of history. Or, to put it more precisely, he acts as if he can interact with history without being affected in any significant way by the ideological structures which comprise history at any given moment. Henry's confidence in his ability to write his own history is perhaps best demonstrated in the commissioning of a genealogy which establishes Henry's legal and historical right to annex France. For all practical purposes, Henry writes history to accommodate his personal wishes. He cautions the Archbishop of Canterbury not to "fashion, wrest, or bow [his] reading [of history] with misinterpretation, yet long before we have heard the whole of the archbishop's lengthy speech we recognize the extreme casuistry out of which it is built" (Lindenberger, *Historical Drama* 160).

As Stephen Greenblatt and others have made clear, Hal, from the very start, adopts a privileged position vis-à-vis his environment.[14] His decision to withhold knowledge about his "true" identity and his political aims creates a strategic distance between Henry and every other character in the plays. "How much better than my word I am," he soliloquizes.[15] "I'll so offend, to make offence a skill, / Redeeming time when men think least I will" (Shakespeare, *1 Henry IV* 1.2.211–12). As an audience we are asked to believe that whatever happens or however badly Hal may *appear* to be out of control, there is no need for worry because he will redeem all. Among other things, Hal's claimed ability to redeem time is a historical claim. His choice of Christian language suggests that time has fallen or that history has somehow strayed from its providential path.[16] Hal announces he can redirect the course of history, reaffirm England's teleology. In Christian terms, the redemption of time points toward ultimate salvation; in political terms it denotes greater stability for a nation torn by ceaseless civil strife. The primary function of the Christian language is to reinforce the political goal, no doubt, but Hal's claim nonetheless clearly oversteps the traditional limits placed on a human being's powers over the trajectory of providential history. Prince Hal ties the direction of English history directly to his person, and asks the audience to have faith not in God or country but in *him*. The decision as to when the time-redeeming scheme will come to fruition is not, as Hal makes clear, based on God's signal or public need, but on his understanding of public relations; that is, the moment Hal looks best, when he will "attract more eyes / Than that which has no foil to set it off" (*1 Henry IV*, 1.2.209–10).

Marx's finely balanced pronouncement that "men make their own history, but they make it not as they please; they do not make it under circumstances chosen by themselves, but under circumstances directly encountered, given, and transmitted from the past"[17] can serve here as a warning against Hal's extreme self-confidence. Whether we conceive of history as providence or a materialist dialectic, Hal's assumption that he can manipulate or transcend history as if he were not in the least constrained by actual and ideological circumstances invites us to view his character as god-like and, at least to some extent, supra-historical. And when Hal does throw off his loose behavior, many of his actions (defeating Hotspur and the rebellious forces, convincing his father of his worthiness, and invading France with an army that shows some semblance of national unity) can indeed be construed as a cunning design to bring about the redemption of time. Yet there are also moments in Hal's journey from the tavern to Agincourt that directly or indirectly challenge his self-assigned position of privilege, and which threaten to disclose this transcendent king's roots in ideology and history.

It is one of ideology's characteristics to "interpellate individuals as subjects." In essence, this means that there are no radically free, economically, ideologically, and socially unconstrained individuals. It is a matter of choice whether we think of this as an instance of oppression, but to the extent that all individuals are inevitably part of a society with its own economic, political, and ideological organization, all individuals are "subjects" of that system. A subject's awareness of his or her interpellation can sometimes be as simple as "the most commonplace everyday policeman (or other) hailing: 'Hey, you there!'"[18] Notwithstanding this apparent simplicity, it is crucial to recognize that interpellation is not an intermittent empirical phenomenon carried out primarily by individuals. As Michael Sprinker explains, "The discourses in which subjects 'recognize' themselves operate on the individual prior to birth," and although the discourses may change in time, the process itself never ceases. "It is possible," therefore for Althusser, "to conceive of the human individual not as a unitary terminal of an 'imaginary' subject, but as the support of the decentered complex of practices and statuses which have distinct conditions of existence."[19] Nonetheless, as Althusser's example of "the everyday policeman (or other)" makes quite clear, it is possible for one subject to serve as a social or ideological agent and interpellate another person. Falstaff and Williams, we will see in a moment, are such agents.

Now Hal, to be sure, does not conceive of himself as a subject in the Althusserian sense. The society of the plays certainly exerts its pressures on the prince, but there is no evidence (until after the encounter with Williams at night) that he considers himself subjected by anything. In part, this may be so because Hal has adopted a theatrical mode in which he is not himself. As long as he upholds "the unyok'd humour of . . . idleness" (*1 Henry IV*, 1.2.191), his "true self" is hidden and unavailable to be hailed by anything or anyone. There is indeed an eerie sense in which there may not be a "core" to Hal's personality at all; it may be that the very concept of a "true self" is nothing more than a clever aspect of his gift for "theatrical improvisation" (Greenblatt, "Invisible Bullets" 33–4). In the tavern world, Falstaff, who is the spokesman for that world and its values, could address him in a variety of ways because Falstaff, unlike the audience who has been let in on the redemption scheme, does not really *know* to whom he is speaking; the fat knight's words do not *really* address the individual at whom they are directed. This unbridgeable space between Hal and the men he traffics with is made even more inaccessible by the realization of the anticipated military and political successes which reinforce Hal's image as redeemer of all. The final separation from his "former self[s]" occurs when he succeeds his father on the throne, a privileged position which should certainly protect him from anyone hailing him: "Hey, you there!"

And yet this is precisely what Falstaff does at the close of *2 Henry IV* when he calls out: "My king! My Jove! I speak to thee, my heart."[20] The appellation, the familiarity of which, despite the recognition that Hal is now king, belongs clearly to the tavern world, tries to surmount the distance between the old knight and the new king by an appeal to their shared history. However, the king's earlier words, "My Lord Chief Justice, speak to that vain man" (44), clearly disclose not only the rejection of Falstaff but also a refusal to be recognized, historicized, or subjected by his former drinking partner. Henry elects to transcend the present circumstance by denying both the knight *and* himself (although Henry would like to think of it as his "former" self). "I know thee not, old man," he says, and "presume not that I am the thing I was" (47, 56). The self-denial only *appears* to contradict Althusser. Henry *is* an interpellated subject (as he will learn later), he just does not recognize it at present because he believes he has successfully avoided Falstaff's too familiar salutation. The audience may or may not recognize this. It will depend on whether or not *we* are immersed in Henry's time-redeeming scheme. If we are, then Henry remains for us outside of ideology (precisely because we are *in* it); he becomes a god-like entity that creates and manipulates history but is not subject to it. If, on the other hand, we assert that Henry cannot now awake from the *dream* he despises (51) because that dream *is* part of his history and because he has shown himself to be awake to *all* his actions since his first soliloquy in *1 Henry IV*, then we can see that there is no honest distinction between his "former self" (58) and his newly acquired royal self.

I am not suggesting that Henry is just like Falstaff or that they relate to the tavern world in the same manner, only that Henry is bound inextricably to Falstaff, the tavern, and the cultural matrix they stand for (or against). Ever since Hal's grim warning, "I do, I will" (*1 Henry IV*, 4.2.475) Falstaff's expulsion has apparently been unavoidable. However, the very act of banishing Falstaff from the new national "unity" confirms that the King *does* know the "old man," the very judgment discloses his connection with the dejected and befuddled knight. It is therefore a mistake to believe that Hal is just like Falstaff; he is not at all like Falstaff. But it is also a mistake to believe that the King can entirely transcend Falstaff's world. "What really takes place in ideology," Althusser writes, "seems to take place outside it. That is why those who are in ideology believe themselves by definition outside of ideology: one of the effects of ideology is the practical *denegation* of the ideological character of ideology by ideology: ideology never says, 'I am ideological'" ("Ideology" 175). If Henry V believes to have escaped Falstaff's interpellating cry after the coronation, he is less fortunate when one of his soldiers, Michael Williams (echoing Althusser's policeman), calls out to him on the eve of Agincourt: "Who goes there?" (*Henry V* 4.1.90–91). This apparently innocent query inaugurates a debate in which Williams, speaking from his own peculiar subject position in the social hierarchy, becomes the (inadvertent) agent of an ideology that interpellates and defines the King. After identifying himself as "a friend," Henry joins his soldiers in conversation. In the ensuing exchange, the King, *in absentia*, becomes the topic of debate. And it is precisely Henry's "absence" which distinguishes Falstaff's "hailing" of the monarch from Williams's. At the close of *2 Henry IV*, the King had his royal power and ceremonial presence to "transcend" the disagreeable voice; here he has neither.

Incidentally, but appropriately ironic, as Williams's hailing initially places the dark figure under suspicion, so it becomes crystal clear that the soldiers are leery of their king. By hiding his identity, Henry can move freely among the troops, but it also exposes him to the type of inquisition from which his power and elevated office ordinarily protect him. The soldiers wonder if the King's cause is good or bad, and what a king's responsibilities are with regard to the fate of his fighting men. "Every subject's duty is the king's; but every subject's soul is his own," Henry says as part of a lengthy response (*Henry V* 4.1.182–83). Henry's words are self-serving and his logic is shoddy;[21] but they also announce a certain understanding of the distribution of power and responsibility in the social structure. Every subject is the king's subject, *but* no subject can subject the king because the fate of the subject's soul is between the subject and God, and does not involve the king in any way. Somewhat surprisingly, Williams grants Henry's argument, and if the king had been allowed to sneak back to his tent here, it appears he would once again have managed to stay above the historical fray. The crucial exchange, however, recommences:

K. Hen. I myself heard the king say he would not be ransomed.
Will. Ay, he said so, to make us fight cheerfully; but when our throats are cut, he may be ransomed, and we ne'er the wiser.
K. Hen. If I live to see it, I will never trust his word after.
Will. You pay him, then! That's a perilous shot out of an elder-gun, that a poor and a private displeasure can do against a monarch. You may as well go about to turn the sun to ice with fanning in his face with a peacock's feather. You'll never trust his word after! come, 'tis a foolish saying. (4.1.197–208)

Williams, of course, does not realize how his private displeasure has dealt Henry a truly perilous shot. The cloaked king does not have ready another patient "rational" response. Instead, he says: "Your reproof is something too round: I should be angry with you if the time were convenient" (209–10). Clearly, Henry has no argument to transcend or subdue Williams's subversive jab. Of course, Henry could reveal his royal persona at this moment, but pulling rank would hardly win the case on the basis of merit. Having momentarily given up his royal power and privileged spot at the apex of the social hierarchy, Henry finds himself (much like Lear after he divides his kingdom) unable to enforce the ideology of kingship that legitimizes and presents as benevolent the king's rule and the socio-political structure. When words and manipulation fail Henry, he seeks to resolve the situation through violence, or the threat thereof, in the form of a duel. Just as Hotspur, who would not be domesticated by the new post-feudal regime, had to be destroyed in battle, so the upstart Williams may have to be eliminated.

The matter appears to be settled thus, left to the future, but when the soldiers leave their king, a new side of him that we have not seen before emerges. Before the meeting with the soldiers turned argumentative, Henry explained to his men that the King, "ceremonies laid by, in his nakedness he appears but a man" (105–6). The central idea conveyed here is that the trappings and the suits of kingship are mere attributes that can be laid aside so that the essential man may be studied. Such a premise is of course consistent with the image of Henry as a consummate actor, politician, and redeemer: the king whose brilliant adoption of many shapes and postures allows him to be outside of ideology and to know and rule all. Yet following Williams's assault on transcendent kingship, Henry speaks privately in an altogether different vein which reveals that he cannot separate himself from the suits and trappings of his office:

> Upon the king! let us our lives, our souls,
> Our debts, our careful wives,
> Our children, and our sins lay on the king!
> We must bear all. O hard condition!
> *Twin-born* with greatness, subject to the breath
> Of every fool, whose sense no more can feel
> But his own wringing. (236–42; emphasis added)

First there is the self-pity and resentment occasioned by a newly understood connection between the conception of kingship and the king's person. Whereas prior to his encounter with the soldiers the king's person was the sole effective power in the interaction with reality, it has become clear that a crosscurrent has disturbed the smooth flow of power. Williams the subject has, in fact, subjected the King. As a result, Henry reluctantly comprehends that he is himself also a *bearer* (and not just the creator or controller) of the ideological structure named kingship. A king's subject has made Henry "subject to the breath of every fool," and so produced a conception of the king that the King himself cannot transcend. Anticipating an Althusserian understanding of individuals as subjects always-already (even in the womb) in ideology, Henry now sees himself bound up inevitably, "twin-born," with the ideological subject-position defined by his royal office. It is because of the "decentered complex of practices and statuses" (Sprinker, "Politics and Theory" 1004) that "Like his subjects, he is a man under obedience."[22]

In this respect, Henry V is markedly different in kind from Richard II and Henry IV. Whereas Henry V is brought down from his autonomous, supra-ideological, god-like position at the top of a socio-political structure to recognize that he in fact occupies a semi-autonomous position produced by that structure, similar moments of crises in the reigns of Richard and Henry IV merely cause these rulers to abandon one metaphysical world view for another.

Richard is so firmly entrenched in the ideology of divine right (while also being wholly oblivious to its ideological nature) that he unwittingly undermines his own power when he confiscates Gaunt's lands to finance war. Similarly, upon his return from the Irish campaign, he expects nature itself to rise in support of the king and crush the unnatural forces of rebellion raised against him in his absence. When loss of the crown and imprisonment finally force him to comprehend that kingship is neither divinely bound to his person nor sanctioned by nature, his grasp of the situation does not reach beyond the insight that he is an actor who plays "in one person many people" (*Richard II* 5.5.31). He emerges from the ensuing identity crisis by exchanging a divinely ordered universe in which he is God's anointed for one that is chaotic and meaningless and in which he is nothing. Having been "unking'd by Bolingbroke" (37), Richard rejects his metaphysically sanctioned Elizabethan world picture and replaces it with an equally metaphysical nihilism. He finds some peace in this newly acquired belief: "whate'er I be, / Nor I, nor any man but that man is, / With nothing shall be pleas'd, till he be eas'd / With being nothing" (38–41). If a rejection of the essentialist view followed here, Richard could – as did Henry V – recognize himself as a bearer of ideological structures. He does, in fact, acknowledge that outside forces shape his life, but he can only conceive of those forces in abstract, metaphysical terms: "I wasted time, and now does time waste me; / For now hath time made me his numb'ring clock; / My thoughts are minutes, and with sighs they jar / Their watches on unto mine eyes, the outward watch, / Whereto my finger, like a dial's point, / Is pointing still, in cleansing them from tears" (49–54). The complex networks of material and psychological causes responsible for Richard's undoing are here abstracted and made remote in the word "time," which turns Richard into a clock, an impersonal mechanism. The material and psychological facts of the play show, however, that not "time" but Bolingbroke, Northumberland, and King Richard himself took the crown away from Richard. But he never grasps this reality; his staunch belief in divine right of kings, as one historian puts it, renders "history immaterial."[23] He is convinced that history cannot touch him. In this, of course, he resembles the pre-Agincourt Henry V, albeit for quite different reasons. For Henry V everything becomes ideology, whereas for Richard II nothing is ideology: one believes himself to be time's redeemer, the other time's fool.

Even though Henry IV (as a less fortunate prototype of Henry V) is radically different from Richard, their final thoughts share a similar world view. From the moment of his triumphant return from banishment, Bolingbroke is an individual on the move, a man eager to shape his own destiny. In *2 Henry IV*, however, we encounter him as an ailing and tormented monarch who, worn down physically and psychologically by feuds and perpetual rebellions, pictures the universe as a vast and impersonal terrain that changes continuously and aimlessly and mocks the controlling efforts of individuals:

> O God, that one might read the book of fate,
> And see the revolution of the times
> Make mountains level, and the continent,
> Weary of solid firmness, melt itself
> Into the sea, and other times to see
> The beachy girdle of the ocean
> Too wide for Neptune's hips; how chance's mocks
> And changes fill the cup of alteration
> With divers liquors! O, if this were seen,

> The happiest youth, viewing this progress through,
> What perils past, what crosses to ensue,
> Would shut the book and sit him down and die.
>
> (3.1.45–56)

Kernan reads these lines as Henry's rejection of "obedience," "tradition and ritual," and established social hierarchy. The rejection is closely followed by Henry's discovery that "freedom leads, ironically to . . . the tragic necessity of history, which forces you to endure the unsuspected consequences of what you are and what you have done."[24] This is true enough, but it is not at all clear that Henry IV himself comprehends his predicament in these terms. Like Henry V and Richard II, he recognizes that he does not control his own fate, but he emulates only Richard when he *abstracts* the real and material forces of history into the "revolution of the times," hidden in the book of fate. However, this almost existential, impersonal conception of fate which levels mountains and melts continents into the sea is also infused with distinct and concrete echoes of the Tudor myth. Afraid and desperate, Henry recalls Richard's prophecy, "Foretelling this same time's condition" (3.1.78). But instead of discarding the prophecy as the silly superstition of a former time or accepting Warwick's suggestion that Richard's was "a perfect guess" (88), Henry relapses into the traditional and teleological universe of the Tudor myth. He trusts the prophecy uttered by the spokesman for the divine right of kings, and resolves, with "dogged courage" (Kernan, "*The Henriad*" 262), that if the "time's condition[s]" are "necessities . . . / Then let us meet them like necessities" (92–3). In other words, individualism gives way to metaphysical (not historical) determinism; instead of analyzing his position in its immediate context of political and military strife, Henry opts for the larger, more removed explanation: politics and ideology give way to metaphysics and meta-ideology.

Surprisingly, in the final lines of his soliloquy, Henry V himself shows signs that he too might regress into some version of the "naturally" ordered world of the Tudor myth. "Not to-day, O Lord! / O not to-day, think upon the fault / My father made in compassing the crown!" (*Henry V* 4.1.298–300). He proclaims to have Richard's body "interred new," and "to have bestow'd more contrite tears," and to have "built / Two chantries, where the sad and solemn priests / Sing still for Richard's soul" (301, 302, 306–308). The sentiment is of course quite religious, but the soliloquy's closing lines, "Though all that I can do is nothing worth, / Since that my penitence comes after all," should be read as an equivocal rejection of the importance of atonement in the outcome of the military struggle. As Sigurd Burckhardt has noted, "Shakespeare does his dramatic best to keep God out of it until *after*" the battle has been fought.[25] Henry "has to face his trial – ambiguous as for human beings these always are – in full consciousness, and *alone*. He may pray but he is not answered . . ." (Burckhardt, *Shakespearean Meanings* 197; emphasis added). In significant contrast with Richard and Henry IV, the absence of manifest divine support for England's claim does not cause Henry to become defeated in despair. Nor does his subjection by Williams discourage him enough to pack up and go home. The newly gained knowledge of his limitations as king allows him to adjust, and, somewhat ironically, to continue his time-redeeming project. The important difference is that Henry and the audience now know that the project is not equivalent with a process of historical inevitability flawlessly guided by a monarch who acts in history and who is not acted upon by history. The historiographical myth must be, if not rejected, rethought.

Yet it would be wrong to overestimate Henry's knowledge. His insight is not into the dynamics of ideology qua ideology. He could say in Althusserian parlance, "I was in ideology" (the ideology of the transcendent, manipulative, God-king), but he could say so only from within a new ideology (of the king who has become more deeply cognizant of how the dynamics of power affect him from below). What his confrontation with Williams has shown him and us is that the king is as much a part of the historical process and the reciprocal nature of the ideological structures that comprise it as is the common soldier. To subject the ruler in this manner is quite unique in the drama of the Elizabethan period. Ordinarily, the focus is on the monarch's moral nature and his ability to rule, and he is valorized or chastised accordingly. In *Henry V*, however, Shakespeare seems as interested in the king's position in a reciprocal socio-political structure as he is in exploring the character's personal qualities. This tendency to explore issues of power becomes increasingly pronounced in the Jacobean drama, particularly in Shakespeare and Fletcher's *Henry VIII* (a play without a protagonist), written in a period of heightening tensions between monarch and parliament on fundamental issues such as the royal prerogative, personal liberties, and powers of taxation.[26]

This somewhat narrowly conceived reading of Henry V's plight is meant to suggest that already in 1599 Shakespeare is initiating a clear break with the Tudor tradition of history-writing marked by a focus on "the moral nature of man and the Providence of God," and "the acts, the ambitions, and the tragic dilemmas of the actors themselves" (Ferguson, *Clio Unbound* 5). In collaboration with Fletcher, Shakespeare continues his exploration into historiographical modernity in his final historical drama, *Henry VIII* – a play without a clear protagonist or "great man," and without the presence of a stabilizing concept of providence.

III

As I noted earlier, it was until recently a critical commonplace to label *Henry VIII* an aesthetic failure. The grounds for this judgment were the weak performance of the play's titular hero and its episodic structure (which may have suited some earlier renaissance dramatists, but not the mature Shakespeare). The latter failing, it will be recalled, was attributed by Irving Ribner to a lack of any cohesive philosophy of history. The following pages will show that while *Henry VIII* indeed does not promote a single view of history, this is part of its dramatic strength and not of any aesthetic failure.

It must be conceded that unlike his order-restoring appearance as Imperial Majesty in John Bale's *King Johan*, Shakespeare and Fletcher's Henry VIII fails to meet expectations raised by both Tudor historiographical practice and historical drama. The king is neither Puttenham's "great man," nor Kernan's "strong and good king [who] restores order," and Joseph Candido describes him as a "well-intentioned yet strangely inattentive king" who fails "to address himself to the deep religious and political differences that divide his ministers."[27] He is "blithely superficial" in his approach to the "grave and divisive issues of his reign" and too out of touch "to inspire our confidence in quite the same way that Henry V or even Bolingbroke does" (Candido, "Fashioning Henry VIII" 57). The central question here of course is whether Shakespeare and Fletcher are trying to portray the traditional "weak ruler" or are they aiming at something altogether different?

Secondly, is the play's episodic structure due to a lack of "consistent dramatic design" (Ribner, *English History Play* 289–91), or is it the result of a deliberate effort to portray history differently? How we answer these questions hinges greatly on how we view the play's final scene and how we read Archbishop Cranmer's speech at the christening of Princess Elizabeth. Ostensibly at heaven's bidding, the Archbishop of Canterbury foretells the Age of Elizabeth as a golden world. She shall shower on England "a thousand thousand blessings;" "every man shall eat in safety / Under his own vine what he plants, and sing / The merry songs of peace to all his neighbours;" and "God shall be truly known" (5.4.19, 33–5, 36).[28] The nature of this speech is so important because after the turmoil portrayed in the play – the opportunistic removal of the loyal Queen Katherine, the equally expedient execution of the Duke of Buckingham, and the timely fall of the powerful and corrupt Cardinal Wolsey – Cranmer tries to restore social order in the Henrician state by proffering a prophetic history of the next seven or eight decades. He links the Elizabethan past (which flows from the Henrician past) to the Jacobean present: "Nor shall this peace sleep with her" because her successor, James I, shall be "as great in admiration as herself," inherit her "blessedness," and "He shall flourish, / And like a mountain cedar, reach his branches / To all the plains about him: our children's children [i.e., James's generation] / Shall see this and bless heaven" (39, 42, 43, 52–5). In this decidedly teleological oration it is the *promise* of the reigns of Elizabeth I and James I which underwrites the appropriateness of Henry's rule. But what is a promise to Cranmer's audience in 1533 is of course *history* to his audience in 1613. In short, how we respond to the play as a whole depends greatly on how we respond to Cranmer's rendering of Tudor–Stuart history.

Commentators who repudiate claims that the play is an aesthetic failure have indeed turned to this final scene to unify the play's various elements into a meaningful whole. Paul Dean, for instance, contends that while the "falls" of Buckingham, Katherine, and Wolsey and the "rises" of Anne Bullen and Thomas Cranmer are not unrelated, they are best understood "as a translation into dramatic terms of the undulations of the Wheel of Fortune which controls the action."[29] Dean acknowledges and then unifies the play's episodic structure by invoking the medieval *de casibus* tradition, thus explaining a Jacobean history play in terms of an essentially medieval theory of history. Frank V. Cespedes argues "that the structure of *Henry VIII* is designed to force upon its audience an awareness of two things at once: the fortunate march of English history toward the reign of Elizabeth [and James], and the 'sad,' 'woeful' story . . . of individuals during Henry VIII's reign who unwittingly helped to shape, and perished in the unfolding of, this historical process."[30] Thus the play presents the Jacobean viewer with "a conflict between historical ends and means" (415) of an essentially "'good' historical process" (437). Matthew H. Wikander simply notes that the Buckingham, Katherine, Wolsey episodes "befog" the "play's historiography," which really "celebrates the stability and continuity of the monarchy in a manner even more providential than that of the Tudor chronicles."[31] If Cranmer constitutes the standard of historical judgment in the play, then Dean's and Cespedes's readings are compelling; but I think we ought to resist granting the archbishop such special status. Indeed, I want to do what neither the play's detractors nor those who try to save its reputation do, which is consider the possibility that Shakespeare and Fletcher give us not a disunified play about history but a play about disunified history.[32] The latter alternative, rather than harkening back to medieval notions of history, looks to the more "modern" world of Jacobean historiography to illuminate the play. Choosing it allows us to see that despite the christening scene's power and pathos, Cranmer's effort to produce dramatic and historical closure is an ideological move that is undercut by other historical "voices" of the play.

Frances A. Yates has eloquently argued that the play recommends a return to the Foxean way of viewing "Tudor reform of the Church as an imperial reform" (Yates, *Shakespeare's Last Plays* 68, 67–82), but we should not be too quick in conceding that a nostalgia for things Elizabethan necessarily led a Jacobean audience to embrace uncritically the archbishop's narrowly medieval, providential version of history. Since Cranmer is without a doubt the king's mouthpiece (he is instrumental in providing the legal means for the divorce), we do well here to remember Jean Bodin's admonition voiced in the *Method for the Easy Comprehension of History* (translated into English by Thomas Heywood in 1608) against looking for "the truth of history . . . in the Commentaries of Kinges, for they are given to speake largely of their own praises, but to make no use of those Observations which are little or nothing interessed in their praise or disgrace."[33] If this edict applies to Henry, it must also apply to his agent Cranmer.

What is more, the fact that Cranmer is supposedly divinely inspired when he prophesies England's glorious future complicates the historiographical nature of his speech. Around the time Shakespeare and Fletcher wrote *Henry VIII*, Edmund Bolton in "Hypercritica, or a Rule of Judgment for Writing or reading our Histories," explicitly warned against placing too much faith in historians who serve a Christian agenda first. Bolton first criticizes pagan historians for failing to note the presence of divine providence in human history, but he then goes on to say that "Christian authors, while for their ease they shuffled up the reasons of events in briefly referring all causes immediately to the will of God, have generally neglected to inform their readers in the ordinary means of carriage in human affairs."[34]

There is reason to conclude that Cranmer's unifying historiography sounded archaic and unsophisticated not only to more learned Jacobeans but also to those who were raised on the popular histories of Holinshed, Hall, Grafton, and others. From their own reading of the histories, Shakespeare and Fletcher certainly understood that Cranmer's conception of history was dated, and, to make sure the viewer understood the same, they set Cranmer's ideologically driven "good" historical process in competition with other, more recent methods of historical representation. Specifically, I am referring to the episodes detailing the fortunes of Queen Katherine, the Duke of Buckingham, and Cardinal Wolsey. In each of these episodes, Shakespeare and Fletcher draw on distinct and at times theoretically incompatible "schools" of renaissance historical thought. The Buckingham episode confronts questions of eyewitness evidence and hearsay; Katherine's divorce and disgrace center on questions of historical (and legal) precedent versus innovation; while Wolsey's plunge from power in the play is in part facilitated by an antiquarian appeal to evidence that speaks for itself.

One notable effect of dramatizing these historiographies is a highlighting of their acute differences as knowledge-producing practices – differences that produce not historical clarity or certainty but epistemological ambiguity. Such ambiguity was a relatively new phenomenon in the late sixteenth and early seventeenth centuries. As Phyllis Rackin observes, "Historiographic writing no longer had a direct, unequivocal relation with historical truth. Alternative accounts of historical events and opposed interpretations of their causes and significance now threatened each other's credibility, a process intensified by the development of the printing industry and the spread of literacy. . . ."[35] As we witness in *Henry VIII*, such historiographical pluralism is flexible enough to serve the state as it disposes of a duke with pretensions to the throne, a queen who is too old to bear a male heir, and an increasingly powerful and autocratic cardinal. Yet since James I himself increasingly turned to historical argumentation to assert himself unequivocally on such momentous issues as royal prerogative and the crown's relationship to the law of the land,[36] it is easy to see how any epistemological ambiguity stemming from historiographical eclecticism could also destabilize the monarch's authority on such matters. Hence, in *Henry VIII* the Henrician state first exploits historiographical diversity, and then tries to provide historical closure and clarity by trying to erase or, at the very least, suppress the ambiguities sprouting from that diversity. In the scene depicting Elizabeth's christening, Cranmer's providential account of royal genealogy appropriates and reorders the discontinuous elements of Tudor (and Stuart) royal history under the all-embracing rubric of God's plan for England. The problem of course is that the historiographical eclecticism of the play strongly resists such a totalizing move. Taken as a whole, therefore, the play focuses not on the inevitable outcome of a historical process, as Cranmer submits, but on the various historiographical strategies that can be employed to make the outcome *appear* inevitable. *Henry VIII* draws our attention to the operations whereby historiography produces a past, and the ways in which historiography and/or historians mystify those operations by sanctifying them.

When *Henry VIII* is viewed in light of its serious interest in the process of historiographical representation, we can begin to dislodge the play from this "Elizabethan" context in which so many critics have deemed it aesthetically inferior, or to which critics have tried to make it conform. Although, as several critics have observed, Henry VIII does sporadically seem active behind the scenes, he is a far cry from the protagonist of the Elizabethan history play who, in the words of Leonard Tennenhouse, is able to "seize hold of the symbols and signs legitimizing authority and wrest them from his rivals, thus making them serve his own interests."[37] This presentation of the king, however, is quite deliberate. Far from being a successful or failed

Elizabethan heroic play (in which a strong protagonist like Henry V or Henry VII triumphs over historical conflict), Shakespeare and Fletcher's account of the reign of Henry VIII precisely emphasizes the impotence of "powerful" individuals in the face of a network of mostly "invisible" and inscrutable historical forces that besets them from all sides.

In the play's network of forces and discourses, God's providence (the first and final cause of much Tudor historiography) figures as a prominent "escape" for several characters who have difficulty harmonizing their personal fate with common notions of causality and the distribution of social justice. As a ubiquitous force, providence can serve them as the supreme signifier and final determinant in a system where signification seems to have become arbitrary. Yet, while positing God as transcendental signifier situates him as a source of solace, it does not render God knowable or providence visible to the degree that these characters gain any specific knowledge about the deeper reasons for their circumstances. The play discloses a tension between providence's simultaneous status as ultimate signifier and as empty signifier.

As a heuristic device, Foucault's concept of power is helpful here because it reassigns "power" from the conventional categories of "providence" and "human agency" to a much wider cultural field in which power "is exercised from innumerable points, in the interplay of nonegalitarian and mobile relations."[38] An analogy between Foucault's "power" and providence is especially useful in this context because both have purpose and agency but no *known* goal or agent. What is more, since Shakespeare and Fletcher concern themselves with multiple forms of historical representation and the apparent inaccessibility of raw history itself, Jameson's conception of history as "the experience of Necessity" is also pertinent here.[39] It is the experience of Necessity which makes it impossible to reify or thematize history "as the mere object of representation or as one master code among many others" – a fact borne out by Shakespeare and Fletcher's play from which no true or "real" history emerges. As the "inexorable *form* of events," Necessity functions as the "formal effect" of an "absent cause." It is this absent cause which shapes history but which remains invisible. Concretely, "History is what hurts, it is what refuses desire and sets inexorable limits on individual as well as collective praxis, which its 'ruses' turn into grisly and ironic reversals of their overt intention. But this History can be apprehended only through its effects, and never directly as some reified force" (Jameson, *Political Unconscious* 102).

I will argue that the play's political, aesthetic, and generic ambiguities stem directly from the playwrights' refusal to mold their materials into a dramatically and ideologically coherent (Tudor) version of the reign of Henry VIII, a refusal that is fed by a Jacobean cultural milieu becoming less and less receptive of narrowly etiological historiographies (Rackin, *Stages of History* 13).[40] Perhaps more than any other drama of the period, *Henry VIII* focuses on the problems of historiographical production and explores the process whereby interested individuals and institutions transform the contiguous moments of the past into purposive, unified discourses, and how the construction of such discourses relates to self-legitimation. Thus the play draws our attention to the operations whereby ideology produces itself, and how those operations are camouflaged. Moreover, it will become clear that the play's supposedly flawed dramatic form is due less to an aesthetic lapse than to the potency of the "form" already contained within the play's "materials" (their logic prior to incorporation into the play – to use Jameson's concept), a form that resists both the ideology and generic features of the Elizabethan history play.[41]

Although *Henry VIII* does not offer an easily identifiable oppositional voice, it should not be said that it is an apolitical text. Rather, in what resembles a Foucaultian sensibility, Shakespeare and Fletcher avoid casting the play's multiple historiographies in the context of a binary power structure that organizes them in terms of true versus untrue, good versus evil, authoritative versus subversive, or "accepted discourse [versus] excluded discourse." As in Foucault, historiography is a discourse in which "power and knowledge are joined together" (*History of Sexuality* 100), but no particular historiography becomes permanently linked to any particular concentration of power (the king's person, his office, the law, cardinal, archbishop, or the people); nor do Shakespeare and Fletcher forge a necessary union between any particular historiography and a specific ideological agenda. Hence, *Henry VIII*'s use of historiographies serves as an excellent test case for the new historicist creed that "no cultural practice or critical practice is simply a politics in disguise, that such practices are seldom intrinsically either liberatory or oppressive, that they seldom contain their politics as an essence but rather occupy particular historical situations from which they enter into various exchanges, or negotiations, with practices designated 'political.'"[42] As an instance of such a cultural practice, *Henry VIII* is neither a simple expression of dominant Jacobean ideology nor a rebellious voice. Some of the play's deeper complexities surface when we examine what Greenblatt calls the "acquisition through simulation" of several historiographical practices which assist greatly in structuring the play. The acquisition of historiographical methods in *Henry VIII* is largely symbolic because their appropriation occurs through a process of *simulation*, i.e., their appropriation into a different literary genre. Such symbolic acquisition occurs when "a social practice or other mode of social energy is transferred to the stage by means of representation."[43] Greenblatt emphasizes theatrical self-consciousness when defining "acquisition[s] through simulation" as "complex simulations of the histrionic elements in public ceremonials and rituals," but with a helpful minor adjustment this category can also incorporate the simulation of social practices which do not possess an inherent theatrical component, i.e. the simulation of history-writing. In the case of *Henry VIII*, Shakespeare and Fletcher arrange elements of at least four recognizable historiographical methods – providential, antiquarian, early humanist, and humanist – into a textual collage, but they do so in the context of their dramatic medium, the stage. They refrain from offering their play as a substitute for Holinshed or Foxe or Hall or Camden. In its Prologue, *Henry VIII* asks the audience to "*Think* ye see / The very persons of our noble story / As they were living" (25–7; emphasis added). Like the opening Chorus of *Henry V*, the invitation draws the audience into the theatrical illusion, it solicits the audience's *complicity* in the production of historical representation, yet it simultaneously "insist[s] upon the difference between its representation and the 'real' ['history' or accounts of it], only to draw out the analogy or proportion linking them" (Greenblatt, *Shakespearean Negotiations* 10).[44] The result of this simultaneous presentation of multiple historiographies within the conventions and expectations of the theater is that *Henry VIII* is much more effective in scrutinizing the premises of historical discourses and ways in which they are deployed to legitimize political projects than traditional narrative history could ever hope to be; it shows that the materials out of which the playwrights fashion a theatrical representation *already* constitute a (historical) representation – and a constructed one at that.[45]

Although the epistemological ambiguity laid bare in *Henry VIII* does not take the shape of a concrete ideological agenda, its presence does present a challenge to the use of historiography in the royal legitimation process, a use that we can trace back to Polydore Vergil's *Anglica Historia* (1534), a work commissioned by Henry VII for the construction not merely of an official history for England but also of a compelling foundation for the Tudor dynasty.[46] Henry VIII himself was no less aware of history's utility. In his 1533 Act in Restraint of Appeals – a document produced primarily for the very specific purpose of establishing England as an autonomous nation independent from Rome – Henry appeals to the authority of "histories and chronicles" to authenticate the position of the monarch.

> Where, by divers sundry old authentic histories and chronicles, it is manifestly declared and expressed that this realm of England is an empire, and so hath been accepted in the world, governed by one supreme head and king having the dignity and royal estate of the imperial crown of the same, unto whom a body politic . . . be bounden and owe to bear next to God a natural and humble obedience. . .[47]

What is more, bringing the issue into the Jacobean period, evidence abounds to support J. G. A. Pocock's contention that apropos the King's relationship vis-à-vis the law, "historical criticism became one of the sharpest weapons of monarchy" (*Ancient Constitution* 17).[48] As Richard Halpern notes, James had already argued in *The Trew Law of Free Monarchies* that the kings of Scotland preceded "any estates or ranks of men . . . any Parliaments . . . or lawes."[49] The kings and no one else, James maintained, erected states, devised and formed governments, and "were authors and makers of the Lawes" (Halpern, *Poetics* 223). In the *Trew Law* James admits "that in the first beginning of Kings rising among the Gentiles . . . men choosed out one among themselves . . . to maintaine the weakest in their right," virtually conceding that historically speaking the monarch owes his powers to the people. But he then goes on to expound that this scenario hardly applies to Scotland.

For as our Chronicles beare witnesse, this Ile, and especially our part of it, being scantly inhabited, but by very few, and they as barbarous and scant of ciuility, as number, there comes our first King *Fergus*, with a great number with him, out of *Ireland*, which was long inhabited before us, and making himself master of the countrey, by his owne friendship and force, as well of the *Ireland-men* that came with him, as of the countrey-men that willing fell to him, hee made himself King and Lord . . . . Thereafter he and his successors . . . made and established their lawes . . . . So the trewth is directly contrarie in our state to the false affirmation of such seditious writers, as would perswade vs, that the Lawes and state of our countrey were established before admitting of a king. . . .[50]

The English and Scottish situations were of course hardly identical (making for a weak analogy), but when James assumed the English throne he nonetheless inflamed the debate over this thorny constitutional issue. The argument over who preceded whom historically, and who therefore had the right to exercise power over the other, centered on the monarch's position vis-à-vis the ancient constitution and the Norman Conquest. The lawyer Sir Edward Coke insisted that English common law has its roots in an ancient constitution which dated back to time immemorial, long before the institution of monarchy arose. The practical consequences of Coke's influential view were that historically James's royal prerogatives did not originate from the king himself and were therefore circumscribed by the law of the land and parliament. On the other side of the argument, historians like Henry Spelman took a line more favorable to James when he argued that parliament post-dated the Norman Conquest. The chronology here is paramount, for prominent figures like Coke, the Civil lawyers, and Sir John Davies, James's Attorney-General for Ireland, agreed that if a king acquired land through conquest he "acquired power over his vanquished subjects not from their consent but from God alone. . . . As Richard Hooker put it, 'Kings by conquest make their own charter: so that how large their power . . . is, we cannot with any certainty define . . .'" (Sommerville, *Politics and Ideology* 66).[51]

The probable reason why critics of *Henry VIII* have dealt with issues of royal conduct rather than royal legitimacy may be twofold: even when reading Jacobean dramas, critics cannot quite abandon their search for the "great men" of the Elizabethan plays; and, secondly, as the accepted view has it, neither King Henry nor King James suffered significant legal challenges to their right to wear the crown, but were, instead, habitually criticized for being less than perfect, or even nonchalant administrators who left important matters of state to ambitious men such as Thomas Wolsey and the Jamesian favorite, Robert Carr. Indeed, Leonard Tennenhouse – the only critic who does take up the issue of legitimacy – bases his efforts to distinguish between the Elizabethan and Jacobean historical drama on the historical claim that the anxiety over the succession during Elizabeth's reign (which resulted from her refusal to marry or name a successor and which fueled a certain kind of political adventurism among her courtiers)[52] was virtually eliminated by the dynastic stability provided through the accession of James I, a father of two young sons.[53]

Nonetheless, it is my intention here to go against the critical grain because below its pro-Stuart veneer, Shakespeare and Fletcher's play teases out some of the politically significant ambiguities inherent in projects of royal legitimation, and, by inference, in James's claim to England's throne. The disclosure of these ambiguities will become apparent shortly, after an exploration of Cranmer's closing prophecy and the events and attitudes surrounding the reversals of fortune of Buckingham, Katherine, and Wolsey. Moreover it will become manifest not only that Henry contrasts sharply with the Elizabethan "great man" who triumphs over the forces of chaos, but also that his birthright is hardly sufficient to present him as the paragon of dynastic stability and royal legitimacy – as Tennenhouse would have us believe ("Strategies of State" 123). What we will find is that Shakespeare and Fletcher probe so deeply into the murky depth of political force and agency that ambivalence and overdetermination rather than clarity of purpose and individual human will emerge as the shaping forces of historical representation.

IV

The judicial proceedings against Buckingham, Katherine, and Wolsey manifest none of the disinterestedness, uniformity, and stability one might hope to expect in a nation of law. Although conducted – at least in name – on behalf of the state, the three trials reveal a variety of motivations and methods of legal protocol, in particular with regard to the composition and treatment of evidence. The purpose for this variety is to show how radically different legal and historiographical discourses are able to exercise power and claim knowledge (or what passes therefor) all under a single rubric, i.e. justice or truth or law.

Although many of the events that bear on the fates of these three characters do not lie in the distant past, common historiographical principles apply because, as D. R. Woolf observes, the kind of "current events, which would now be deemed journalism, were [then] commonly referred to as histories."[54] In understanding the trials of Buckingham, Katherine, and Wolsey it is therefore significant that renaissance historians were generally dubious about the construction of reliable accounts of current or recent history. Bodin observes: "Sure those that will write of the present, can hardly write truly, but [because] they must touch the credit and reputation of some men" ("Choice of History" 11). Annabel Patterson, among others, has argued credibly that Bodin's point about the power of men of reputation was not lost on Shakespeare and his contemporaries.[55] And Raphael Holinshed himself, a principle source for *Henry VIII*, openly bemoans the historian's inability to be a witness to all that happens himself, and the unfortunate need "to inquire of moderne eie-witnesses for the true setting downe" of what he delivers.[56]

In *Henry VIII*, the case against the Duke of Buckingham is shaped by the historiographical concerns just described. During a pre-trial hearing held at Cardinal Wolsey's instigation, Henry seals the Duke's fate on the basis of a single character's testimony, that of the Duke's former Surveyor. We hear of a formal trial (conducted by the Duke's peers) during which additional witnesses are heard before the Duke is officially sent to the scaffold, but it is the pre-trial hearing before the King that procures the death sentence.[57] The oral testimony of a disgruntled employee is relied on to reconstruct the past speeches and intentions of his former master.

Buckingham is arrested on charges of "high treason" against the King's person (1.1.201) only moments after declaring his aim to inform the King of Wolsey's treasonous political stratagems. But before turning to the scene in which the Duke's Surveyor brings the "evidence," Shakespeare and Fletcher insert another scene – clearly for the purpose of juxtaposition – in which Wolsey himself stands accused of shadowy dealings. And if we compare the case against Buckingham with the initial assault on Wolsey's reputation, we instantly notice alternative ways of handling historical evidence. Early in Act 1, when he is accused of levying unprecedented taxes on the people and thereby causing a popular uprising, the Cardinal bitterly complains that he is "Traduc'd by ignorant tongues, which neither know / My faculties nor person, yet will be / The chronicles of my doing"

(1.2.72–4). Wolsey has good reason not to want anyone to narrate the history of his activities, for he has few reliable allies at the court where there are many interested parties who would not hesitate to bring him down. But with Henry on his side, maybe Wolsey need not worry how his actions are chronicled. Katherine, who appears in the sympathetic role of the people's advocate, and who has little trouble exposing the Cardinal as the driving force behind the exorbitant "commissions, which compels from each / The sixth part of his substance, to be levied / Without delay" (1.2.57–9), is incapable of convincing her husband to acknowledge that Wolsey's act of indiscretion is a sign of his fundamentally corrupt character.[58] The King immediately rescinds the tax measure and in that respect takes the evidence against the Cardinal seriously, but when it comes to the Cardinal himself, the charges against him are, for all practical purposes, treated as if they were, indeed, but slander from the tongues of ignorant accusers. The contradiction is never resolved.

In sharp contrast, Buckingham's pre-trial hearing before the King – the very next event in the same scene – shows us precisely how devastating an effect oral testimony can have on a person's reputation and fate. The Duke stands accused of treason by a single person, his former Surveyor, a man the Duke believes is now on the Cardinal's payroll (1.1.222–3). The Surveyor claims to have heard the Duke "discharge a horrible oath" in which he swore he would assassinate the King "were he [the Duke] evil us'd" (1.2.206, 207). The Surveyor, however, offers no material or corroborating evidence. His only attempt to bolster his credibility is to relate how the Duke was incited to these villainous thoughts by a "vain prophecy" (149), which promised that "the duke / Shall govern England" (170–1). Queen Katherine is obviously disturbed by the developments, and she (echoing Bodin) points out that the Surveyor may well be motivated by a desire for revenge against his former master, who dismissed him from "office / On the complaint o'th'tenants" (172–3). The Queen's observation also recalls the earlier complaint against Wolsey, who, like the Surveyor, was charged with wrongdoings by anguished subjects (56–7). The similarity heightens the contrast between the two "trial" scenes, and the difference between the judges. Under roughly similar circumstances, the Duke dismissed his Surveyor, while the King retains his Cardinal. And to top it off, the King pronounces the Duke a "traitor to th'height" (214) solely on the basis of the testimony of a man of dubious motivation and reputation.

Holinshed was clearly not convinced of Henry's justice in this matter (even though he enumerates *more* "evidence" against the Duke). Recalling one of his own guidelines for history-writing, Holinshed concludes his recapitulation of the indictment against Buckingham with the following remarks: "These were the speciall articles & points comprised in the indictment, and laid to his charge: but how trulie, or in what sort prooued, I haue not further to say, either in accusing or excusing him, other than as I find in [Edward] Hall and Polydor[e Vergil], whose words in effect, I haue thought to impart to the reader, and without anie wresting of the same either to or fro" (Holinshed, *Chronicles* 661). Holinshed does not always show himself such a paragon of historiographical prudence (as I argue in chapter 5), but here his assessment accords with that of modern historians,[59] and Shakespeare and Fletcher follow this chronicler's lead by inserting a scene in which two gentlemen agree that "By all conjectures" (2.1.41) "the cardinal is the end of this" (40), that is, of the Duke's fall. That the King may be implicated in the biased proceedings against Buckingham is suggested by Henry's words to Cranmer in Act 5: "at what ease / Might corrupt minds procure knaves as corrupt / To swear against you? such things have been done" (5.1.131–3).[60]

But there is a further consideration to be reckoned with in assessing the "justice" doled out by the King, one that makes it critically perverse to view this episode as merely a clash between "great men." Buckingham himself offers a complex reading of his fate. When first arrested, he stoically professes that "The net has fall'n upon me; I shall perish / Under device and practice. . . . / It will help me nothing / To plead mine innocence, for that dye is on me / Which makes my whit'st part black. The will of heav'n / Be done in this and all things: I obey" (1.1.203–4, 207–10). There is an intriguing irony at work here. Buckingham is apparently so convinced of the efficiency of Wolsey's plots ("device and practice") against him that he believes it useless to resist (regardless of his actual guilt or innocence). He also implies, however, that if his impending death is indeed a certainty (and *only* if it is a certainty), then it must be God's will that he dies. Consequently, in the Duke's world view, the effectiveness of Wolsey's machination becomes equated directly with providence because only providence can be a certainty.

These views do not change as Buckingham's execution draws near. In the aftermath of the trial he still professes his innocence, but also states that he bears the law (a third facilitator in his downfall) no malice for his death, and that "his vows and prayers / Yet are the king's" (2.1.62, 88–9). The law, he says, "has done upon the premisses but justice" (63), and thereby he appears to validate the process which has brought him down, even though he still implicitly challenges the evidence and says he "could wish more Christians" those who have "sought" the judgment against him (64). This dichotomy continues to haunt his final thoughts. "Heaven has an end in all" (124), he proclaims, but then warns that if you "are liberal of your loves and counsels, / Be sure you be not loose; for those you make friends / And give your hearts to, when they once perceive / The least rub in your fortunes, fall away / Like water from ye" (126–30).

Simultaneously, Buckingham asserts the omnipresence of providence and holds out for the efficacy of an individual's actions. If we posit that the Duke believes his predicament to be shaped by binary powers – divine determinism versus independent human agency – we can only conclude that he has given up on a unified vision of the world in which contradictions are only apparent. This paradoxical view of reality becomes less vexing, however, when we consider Foucault's conception of power as a field of forces without traditional notions of agency, and from which there is no escape: "Where there is power, there is resistance, and yet, or rather consequently, this resistance is never in a position of exteriority to power."[61] The apparent paradox contained in the Duke's views resolves if we do not insist on situating them in the context of a binary clash between freedom and determinism. Although Buckingham clings to the prospect that his fate might be an effective example to others – and even implies that if he had known then what he knows now things might be different – this hardly means that if he had not trusted his Surveyor and if he had not been convicted of treason, providence would have been altered in any way. As far as he or any human being can know, *that* would have been providence in all its inscrutable inevitability. The Duke's dilemma rests in his desire to hold out for some form of human agency while he is unwilling to assert his independence of God's ways. Hence, his vision of resistance in the face of Wolsey's plots resides wholly within an always deferred and unknowable providential scheme.

The case against the Duke, then, is conducted according to established legal principles, some of which overlap with those of humanist historians. Henry's divorce proceedings against Queen Katherine – who "like a jewel has hung twenty years / About his neck, yet never lost her lustre" (2.2.31–2) – are of a distinctly different character. In the Duke's trial, we saw the prosecution try hard to follow entrenched principles – although without great rigor vis-à-vis witnesses and evidence – and the Duke saw fit to sanction the trial in the narrow legal context, as well as in terms of providence. In the legal procedures against Katherine, however, law, church, and history all fail the King, leaving him to his own ingenious devices. Founded generally on the principle of custom and (religious and secular) authority, English society demanded some type of legal precedent in cases of divorce. If the appropriate precedent was not immediately apparent, a historical investigation for one could follow. Historical inquiry of some sort, therefore, was a routine aspect of most legal cases (many humanist scholars fed right into this ancient practice by arguing that the primary function of history was to guide legal, moral, and political conduct in the present). Shakespeare and Fletcher's Henry explicitly confirms this basic principle in his response to the Wolsey-taxation case. When notified of the Cardinal's scheme, the King instantly revokes his secretary's actions and asserts that "Things done without example, in their issue / Are to be fear'd. Have you a *precedent* / Of this commission? I believe, not any. / We must not rend our subjects from our laws / And stick them to our will" (1.2.90–4; italics added). The argument can be expressed simply: nothing can be done without a historical precedent because we, like our subjects, must observe the law.[62] This view, while it gains him admiration from his subjects, does not serve Henry once he has decided to divorce Katherine and marry Anne Bullen. There is no historical precedent upon which the divorce can be granted. Katherine has borne him an heir, and there is no doubt she has been obedient and faithful to him in every conceivable way. Neither Henry's desire for a male heir, nor the burden of a guilty conscience, nor his desire to marry another woman constitute a precedent for divorce in renaissance England. Therefore, what is required, if the divorce is to take place, is an act of innovation. Traditional legal avenues must be abandoned in favor of unknown territories. But such ventures are not without peril. As J. G. A. Pocock notes apropos of Machiavelli's political historiography, "nothing was more difficult than innovation; if ancient customs existed, they were almost impossible to change; if they did not, they were almost impossible to create" (*Ancient Constitution* 285). Faced with Rome's refusal to grant special dispensation for the divorce (which in a way was not surprising, since Rome had granted special permission for the marriage between Henry and his late brother's wife),[63] Henry resorts to the creation of "a precedent of wisdom" (2.2.85) by commissioning written opinions on the matter from the theologians of Oxford, Cambridge, and a host of European universities.

The Queen, on the other hand, has the authority of history and custom on her side. Not only does she make a convincing case for having been the perfect Queen and wife (2.4.11–42), she also unwaveringly invokes the historical events and figures that authorized her marriage to Henry.

> The king your father [Henry VII] was reputed for
> A prince most prudent, of an excellent
> And unmatch'd wit and judgment: Ferdinand
> My father, King of Spain, was reckon'd one
> The wisest prince that there had reign'd by many
> A year before. It is not to be question'd
> That they had gather'd a wise council to them
> Of every realm, that did debate this business,
> Who deem'd our marriage lawful. . . . (2.4.43–51)

To Katherine (or to anyone in concord with Tudor law, culture, and decorum), the case against her can only be profoundly baffling. Henry VII – patriarch and founder of the Tudor dynasty – and the King of Spain were the architects of her marriage, Rome gave it its blessing, and an international council imparted its judicial approval. Therefore, with "history" so overwhelmingly on her side, it is really not surprising that Katherine rejects what is to her the most unseemly of proceedings, and departs from the court prematurely and dramatically (ignoring the King's summons), refusing to submit herself while contending that she has "here / No judge indifferent, nor no more assurance / Of equal friendship and proceeding" (2.4.14–16). Katherine only barely fits the typical renaissance category of the heroine as patient victim; she endures her fate but she also boldly defies her king and judge, stretching the definition of female heroism to the breaking point, and remaining noble and sympathetic throughout.

The King's claim consists of a guilty conscience (resulting from a change of heart about the legitimacy of his marriage), the possibility that the absence of "male issue" is evidence of God's censure of the marriage, and the opinions collected by Thomas Cranmer. In other words, in a clear departure from his ruling in the Wolsey-taxation matter, Henry counters Katherine's perfectly solid, legally sound, and traditional defense with an intangible appeal to conscience, providence, and manufactured "evidence." Appropriately, it is precisely at the moment of legal stalemate that we first learn of Henry's desire for the return of "well-beloved Cranmer." "With thy approach, I know / My comfort comes along," he asserts. "Approach" here means Cranmer's physical return to the court, but it also denotes his new and alternative "approach" to the divorce, the invention of which is often credited to him.

The innovation lies in the King's method, not in the grounds on which he seeks the divorce. At Blackfriars, he implicitly draws on biblical precedent when he attributes the lack of issue in his marriage to God's disapproval of the union. This type of explanation is a direct allusion to the punitive consequences promised to all who violate Leviticus's prohibition against a union between a man and his deceased brother's wife. However, Henry does not cite his source – which is essential if the argument is to have the force of a precedent – nor is he, sensing "the dilatory sloth and tricks of Rome" (235), any longer content to have the matter adjudicated by the Pope. Partially, he therefore does seek the divorce on conventional grounds. Yet his actions take the controversy out of the ecclesiastical courts (where it traditionally belongs, thus circumventing the authority of Rome), and transform the King's great matter into a "direct" appeal – legitimized by commissioned opinions – to God's law.

In this way, it is not established authority or church law or custom but individual will and disputation produced by selected university theologians which constitute the legal basis for the King's decision to press ahead with the divorce. The abandonment of both the humanist predilection for precedent and the Catholic deference to authority (as well as Henry's rejection of Katherine's direct appeal to the Pope for judgment [2.2.117]) in favor of theological wranglings here inevitably results in a rewriting of the past: the marriage that was first deemed politically desirable, legal, and holy turns out to be really politically dangerous, illegal, and incestuous.

If the cases against Buckingham and the Queen are based on tainted testimony and acts of legal and historical innovation, the welcome fall of corrupt Thomas Wolsey requires neither the unscrupulous handling of evidence, nor the creation of it. In fact, the removal of Wolsey calls for only the most minimal participation by king or state authority because the Cardinal himself has committed to paper an incriminating chronicle of his doings: an inventory of his inordinate wealth (which extends beyond "possession of a subject"), and a piece of correspondence in his hand "writ to th'Pope against the king" (3.2.128, 287). These documents come into the King's possession and initiate a process of law against the Cardinal that differs greatly from the proceedings conducted against Buckingham and Katherine. The King's use of these written artifacts invokes an antiquarian approach to the past. Antiquarians typically set themselves the task of describing the physical remains (documents, monuments, coins, and other artifacts) of former times. Unlike renaissance humanist historians, they were unwilling, or at best reluctant, to engage in the writing of narrative history. If it was the humanist's fundamental aim to proclaim history's utility as a pedagogical tool, it was the antiquarian's primary purpose to resuscitate and preserve the past in order to learn about the past itself, not about its relevance to the present. Hence, when an antiquarian like William Camden did try his hand at something that resembles a narrative – "an Historical Account of the First Beginnings of the Reign of Queen Elizabeth"[64] – he provoked Wallace T. MacCaffrey to charge him with exercising too much interpretative restraint. Camden's

> book is conceived as a monument to the achievement of Queen Elizabeth and her government. This purpose he seeks to accomplish not by praising her merits but, more obliquely, more delicately, by laying out the record of her reign. To him that record is self-evident; its very recital will command the admiration of the world and posterity. What Camden did not quite grasp is that the record by itself, unadorned by interpretation or examination, is intellectually unassimilable by his readers. The relentless flow of historical facts informs their minds without illuminating their understanding.[65]

Aside from the value judgment implied in this passage, it is undeniable that Camden's history, and the fruits of antiquarian scholarship in general, were no feast for those who nourished themselves on the more user-friendly narratives of Hall, Grafton, Holinshed, and others. What is of concern here, however, is the interpretative soberness attributed to Camden, a soberness that marks the essential character – at least in theory – of the antiquarian enterprise.

Henry's handling of the Wolsey documents emulates, certainly in its external manifestations, Camden's interpretative forbearance motivated by the desire to let the artifact *speak for itself*. Henry never directly accuses Wolsey of any misdoings. He interrogates him about his loyalty, duty, and holiness, but never asserts his guilt. Instead, when the Cardinal (who does not know his papers have been intercepted) professes his undying loyalty, the King merely hands him the inculpating documents and leaves. In an emotional soliloquy, it is Wolsey *himself* who reads the papers and declares his own guilt and fall from glory. In the context given, the evidence speaks for itself. However, the playwrights undercut the antiquarian approach at the very same time that they allow Henry to employ it triumphantly. Peter Rudnytsky shrewdly observes that even though the matter of the "crossed letters" derives from Holinshed, it pertains there *not* to Wolsey but to Thomas Ruthall, Henry VII's Bishop of Durham (Rudnytsky, "*Henry VIII*" 49). Moreover, the case against Wolsey, which appears just if we limit our consideration to the documents themselves, is equivocal at its very core. The Cardinal's post-dismissal repentance and regeneration have led many commentators to put a positive spin on his fate by viewing his rise and fall in terms of the *de casibus* genre, but if we consider that Henry may well be turning against Wolsey not because of his indiscretions in general – the King was apparently not all that distressed over the taxation measures – but for a particular indiscretion: opposing the divorce – then we have to abandon a morality-play version of history.[66]

In the proceedings against Wolsey, Katherine, and Buckingham, then, we have three different legal or historiographical approaches to the recovery of past events. And while it may be tempting to compare these approaches qualitatively and rank them according to their capacity to produce truth or justice, it is important to note that they all hold equal purchase in the Henrician state. Shakespeare and Fletcher do not seem interested in valorizing any particular approach. Indeed, Shakespeare and Fletcher arrange their materials so that it is impossible to tell if any of these trials is put on to yield truth or justice, or if they serve some ulterior motive(s). Yet judgments are doled out, heads roll, and a queen abdicates.

Despite the antiquarian restraint that marks the Wolsey episode, elusive providence is invoked to explain the inexplicable (as it was in the trials of Buckingham and Katherine). Commenting on the King's discovery of Wolsey's treasonous papers, the Duke of Norfolk asserts that "It's heaven's will; / Some spirit put this paper in the packet / To bless your eye withal" (3.2.128–30). Wolsey first attributes the situation to "negligence," and, subsequently, to a "cross devil." The juxtaposition of heavenly "spirit" with "devil" simply demonstrates two ways in which differently motivated characters can construe an act indifferent, an instance of "negligence."

Throughout the play there are speeches suggesting that God withholds from Henry insight into Wolsey's ways, but the Cardinal's stratagems (i.e., the arrest of Buckingham just as the Duke is about to apprise the King of Wolsey's intrigues [1.1.190–202] and his ability to control Henry with the "witchcraft" of his tongue [3.2.15–19]) can just as easily, and more revealingly, be called on to account for Henry's inaction. Moreover, Henry's first detection of Wolsey's "contrary proceedings" is hardly suggestive of a moment in which God lifts a veil from his eyes. Shakespeare and Fletcher do not give the slightest indication that Henry's new awareness is occasioned by a divine stirring. It simply occurs at the close of the trial of the Queen, when Campeius's refusal to pass sentence after the Queen leaves the court leads Henry's political acumen to conclude that "These cardinals trifle with me" (2.4.234).

In all three legal cases, then, providence is invoked, but its invocation inevitably signals a moment of human powerlessness, an instance in which the players lose control over the circumstances of their situation. Buckingham acknowledges providence because he conceives of his fate as imminent and certain. Neither his innocence (if he is innocent) nor his reason or rhetoric can help him escape Wolsey's net; therefore it *must* be God's will. Likewise the nobles wait patiently for the moment that God lifts the veil from Henry's eyes (2.2.41–3). They see themselves as impotent in the matter. Henry evokes providence to explain why he does not have a male heir, a situation over which he perceives himself powerless as long as he is married to Katherine. At a loss for a substantial case against his wife, he also appropriates providence as a cause why the divorce must become a reality.[67]

In its exploration of various historiographies active in the legitimation process, *Henry VIII* (in the scenes discussed so far) treats providence either as another tool (in Henry's case) in the political process, or as an ultimate but untraceable metaphysical sign to which characters appeal when they are threatened with becoming marginal to or are about to be eliminated from the legitimation process. Buckingham, Katherine, and Wolsey all resist, but their "resistance is never in a position of exteriority in relation to power" (Foucault, *History of Sexuality* 95). For them, providence comes to mean something very similar to Foucault's "power." They acquiesce to the realization that the "multiplicity of force relations immanent in the sphere in which they operate" constitute "their own [inscrutable] organization" (92). They experience these relations as "intentional" but also as "nonsubjective" (94); that is, they do not consider them to be random, but the ultimate inscrutability of God's intention also makes them nonsubjective (in the sense that they do not originate from a knowable subject). Hence, they perceive that "power is [never] exercised without a series of aims and objectives"; yet their surrender to state authority, coupled with a continued dedication to the King, discloses a recognition that the operations of power finally do not result "from the choice or decision of an individual subject" (95), that is, the King's person. Foucault writes that "if it is true that Machiavelli was among the few . . . who conceived the power of the Prince in terms of force relationships, perhaps we need to go one step further, do without the persona of the Prince, and decipher power mechanisms on the basis of a strategy that is immanent in force relationships" (97). Shakespeare and Fletcher, it seems, beat Foucault to it.

V

Since we know that both the theater and the state drew on the practices and methods of historians, it stands to reason that there may be significant points of intersections between *Henry VIII*'s manipulation of history and James I's own efforts in the same arena. Those intersections would have pertained to the question of historiography's relation to questions of royal legitimacy and privilege, for it is in those areas that James was most active. The work of Leonard Tennenhouse is relevant here because it deals explicitly with *Henry VIII* and questions of literary and royal legitimation. Tennenhouse is one of a group of new historicists whose conventional wisdom it is that renaissance theater played a crucial (and inevitable) role in the legitimation of the monarch and the state. However, the historiographical independence and eclecticism I have tried to disclose in *Henry VIII* suggest that this drama may have had less predictable consequences for a Jacobean understanding of the relation between royal legitimation and historical representation.

Although my conclusions about *Henry VIII* differ significantly from Tennenhouse's, I will spend some time reviewing his argument because the remainder of this chapter is dedicated (directly and indirectly) to its modification. Tennenhouse starts from the assumption "that the opposition between literary use of language and a political use of the same linguistic materials is largely a modern invention," and argues that the theater and the state share the same rhetorical strategies in idealizing state authority.

> As political circumstances changed and presented the monarch with new forms of opposition, then the strategies for legitimizing that authority changed. In the Elizabethan history play, art authorizes genealogy. That is, to legitimize blood one must acquire the signs and symbols of authorization, which is to question the iconicity of the king's body and entertain the possibility of its arbitrary relation to laws and ceremonies of State. Shakespeare's only Jacobean history play declares

itself a contradiction in terms by emphatically canceling out this notion of power. Genealogy authorizes art in this play, and the production of art consequently comes under the political imperative to display wealth and title. ("Strategies of State" 125)

In Tennenhouse's argument, the crucial difference between Elizabethan and Jacobean historical drama (and between Elizabethan and Jacobean conditions of political legitimacy) is that the former displays an individual monarch's ability to triumph temporarily over social and political disorder, whereas the character of Henry VIII (starring in a *Jacobean* play), like the historical James I, need not go through a process of self-legitimation.

According to Tennenhouse, Elizabeth, even though she ascends the throne by birthright as well as her father's will, must engage in a relentless process of self-legitimation because of Henry VIII's decision to inaugurate dual principles of succession in his will, which was granted the legal force of a statute by Parliament. The king's will introduced a legal distinction between succession through blood (or primogeniture) and succession by fiat. Allowed to treat the crown as personal property, Henry specified that it should pass from Edward to Mary to Elizabeth, and, if none of them produced offspring, "to his younger sister's children in the Suffolk line and not to his older sister's children in the superior hereditary Stuart line" (113). When Elizabeth became Queen of England in 1558, her "ascendancy could be justified according to her father's will and primogeniture both [and] her very person temporarily reconciled the competing viewpoints formulated during the debates concerning her succession" (113). All the same, Tennenhouse argues that factionalism endured because the two succession principles had created "competing interest groups during the succession debates" (113). Elizabeth hence became a paradoxical figure for although she embodies both succession principles "she could no longer be understood as a mediatory figure between inheriting the crown and inheriting property as it drew authority from blood and bestowed that authority upon the law" (113). Furthermore, the duality of the succession principle created a dangerous ambiguity regarding the future transference of royal power. This, together with Elizabeth's much-discussed refusal, despite the entreaties of Parliament, either to marry and produce an heir or to name a successor, created factionalism, political infighting, and even an occasional coup attempt.

Elizabeth's rule reflected these historical conditions insofar as her marriage politics, her favoritism, and her often unpredictable actions as supreme patron indicate she felt "it better served her interests to maintain a situation which frustrated all competing factions and alienated none of them" (114). The literature of the period enacted and idealized these historical conditions through the portrayal of strong individuals capable of uniting in their person the different, warring factions. As a logical extension of this approach to the idealization of state power, generally only those works of art were promoted which in turn authorized state power. The instances of Richard III's rise to power, his defeat by Henry Tudor, the rise of Bolingbroke at the expense of Richard II, and Henry V's bringing together of several British factions into a semblance of national unity, all serve to illustrate this point: in "each case state authority does not descend directly through blood" (121), and art ends up authorizing genealogy (125).

If, then, the Elizabethan history play contends that "authority goes to that contender who can seize hold of the symbols and signs legitimizing authority and wrest them from his rivals, thus making them serve his own interests" (121), a Jacobean work like *Henry VIII*, according to Tennenhouse, demonstrates the very opposite. At first, however, the genealogical statuses of Elizabeth and James do not appear to be very different: "By naming her successor, the Queen acted in accordance with a view of the crown as an object of property, which was therefore dispensed according to the will of its owner. By naming James rather than an English claimant, however, she also acted according to the law of primogeniture" (114). But, more importantly, when James arrived in London in 1603, he was already in the possession of a male heir, Prince Henry, signaling "a rebirth of the powers of blood" (116). No act of will was required to designate Prince Henry the next ruler of Britain, thus removing uncertainty and anxiety surrounding the next succession. Jacobean Shakespeare therefore turned to the reign of Henry VIII because neither James nor the second Tudor monarch had to legitimize his blood. Like James, Shakespeare and Fletcher's "Henry VIII does not have to overpower those who possess the symbols of authority to make his line legitimate. Quite the contrary: in possessing the blood, his body is in fact a living icon in relation to which all other signs and symbols acquire meaning and value" (123). *Henry VIII* therefore is authorized by genealogy. Unlike the epilogue to *Henry V*, which forecasts war and turmoil, "The blessing of the infant Elizabeth heralds the fulfillment of divine prophecy and guarantees the corporate nature of the Crown in perpetuity. It does not usher in a period of controversy and misrule over which a new contender will triumph. The poetics of Jacobean politics aim at transforming all such change into continuity. The fulfillment of this prophecy is none other than King James, whom Cranmer's speech unites with both Elizabeth and Henry VIII in the corporate identity of the crown" (125).

Tennenhouse's argument is attractive because it brings a fresh approach and a daring answer to an old critical crux, but it is flawed. Its case rest on two important premises. To be able to conclude that genealogy authorizes art, Tennenhouse maintains that James I's claim to the throne was beyond dispute, and assumes that the Henry VIII–Elizabeth–James genealogy presented by Cranmer in *Henry VIII*'s closing scene is the genealogy endorsed by the drama. Both premises are misleading and neither withstands close scrutiny.

It is of course true that James had a son when he came to the English throne, and this provided considerable security, but at the time *Henry VIII* was staged in 1613 Prince Henry had died (1612), and the stable genealogy of which Tennenhouse speaks no longer existed.[68] James had a second son, Charles, but this feeble young man could not live up to the mythical status of the crown prince. It was thought shortly before the time of Henry's death that the end of the world was near, and that the prince was a type of Christ. John Donne addresses this matter directly in his "Elegy upon the untimely death of the incomparable Prince Henry," when he writes: "But this faith [in Henry as a type of Christ] is heresy: we must / Still stay, and vex our great-grandmother, dust."[69] Rudnytsky therefore prudently interprets the closing lines of the Prologue of *Henry VIII* – "And if you can be merry then, I'll say / A man may weep upon his wedding day" – "as an ironic commentary on the play to follow, [which] takes on a tragic aura when it is recalled that [Princess] Elizabeth's marriage [to Frederick of Bohemia] took place in the aftermath of the period of mourning for Prince's Henry's death" ("*Henry VIII*" 56). Furthermore, James did not come to the throne under the same terms as Elizabeth. The Queen, as Tennenhouse notes correctly, came to the crown both by Henry's will and by the principle of primogeniture. James of course belonged to the Tudor line via Henry VII's sister Margaret (who was his great grandmother), but it is strictly a matter of speculation that Elizabeth named him as her successor. Indeed, as Howard Nenner has recently demonstrated, the legal and political issues surrounding the succession were quite murky (*The Right to be King*, 13–25). Robert Cecil and James had already made private arrangements for the transfer of power, and legend has it that "they went through the formality of pretending to consult her on the matter," and that when she was asked on her deathbed "if she wished the King of Scots to succeed her, and she raised her hand and touched her head . . . they chose to interpret [this] as a sign of her assent."[70] When James received word of the Queen's death, he immediately wrote Cecil but did not mention anything about having received Elizabeth's blessing. Instead, he expressed his satisfaction "that the whole state, by the good advice and grave judgment of *those that have voice in council*, had uniformly consented to proclaim us her lawful successor and to be their king, for the which we offer first our most hearty thanks to God."[71] Given the uncertainty and anxiety surrounding the question of the succession, the Queen's dying voice would obviously have strengthened James's claim considerably, and one would suspect he might have mentioned it. Anne Somerset reports that there was "skepticism" about

Elizabeth giving James VI her dying voice; and John Clapham, "who wrote an account of Elizabeth's death shortly after James's accession, commented, 'These reports, whether they were true indeed, or given out of purpose by such as would have them so to be believed, it is hard to say. Sure I am they did no hurt.'"[72]

More importantly, James's rights by blood were legally impotent because Henry VIII's Third Act of Succession (1546) decreed that the crown would be inherited by a member of the Suffolk line, into which Henry's younger sister Mary had married. "The Scottish Stuarts, descendants of his elder sister Margaret, who had married James IV of Scotland, were ignored."[73] Hence, as Alan G. R. Smith notes in a statement that corrects Tennenhouse, "in 1603 hereditary right to the throne triumphed over the provisions of statute law" (380).

Even James's blood right was not beyond dispute. The unfortunate marriage between Arbella Stuart and William Seymour in 1610, two or three years before the performance of *Henry VIII*, serves as a telling instance of James's insecurity. His excessive and defensive manner in dealing with the marriage allowed to surface acute feelings of anxiety about the stability of his royal station. Arbella Stuart, who was, as S. R. Gardiner points out, "also descended from Margaret, the sister of Henry VIII, had a better title, as she had been born in England, whereas James had been born in Scotland. It was a maxim of the English law . . . that no alien could inherit land in England. If, therefore, James was incapable of inheriting an acre of land south of the Tweed, he was still more incapable of inheriting the whole realm."[74] Arbella showed no interest in politics, and, initially, James treated his cousin well, but when it was rumored she was about to marry a foreign potentate, he had her arrested on the fear that "after such a marriage she might be made use of by someone who would in her name lay claim to the crown of England."[75] During the hearing, Arbella apparently assuaged James's fears, and he, in turn, "assured her that he would have no objection to her marriage with any subject of his." The one subject, William Seymour, that Arbella subsequently happened to fall in love with, however, "was perhaps the only man in England to whom James would have objected as a husband for Arabella [*sic*]" (Gardiner, *History of England*, vol. II, 115).[76]

William Seymour was a direct descendant of the Suffolk line to which Henry VIII had bequeathed the crown of England in case his own offspring – Edward, Mary, and Elizabeth – were to die without a successor. Therefore, since none of Henry's children's children survived after 24 March 1603, the union of Arbella and Seymour consolidated a claim of blood and one of law to the throne of England. James forbade the marriage, and when it came out that the young lovers, though apparently without political ambitions, had married anyway, Arbella was taken into custody and Seymour was sent to the Tower (117). The young lovers' story ends tragically when, during an attempted escape to the continent, Seymour reaches Ostend but Arbella is captured and committed to the Tower, where she was to die in 1615.

James's behavior in this matter was well known at the time, and it is therefore not uninteresting to read Shakespeare and Fletcher's handling of the Buckingham matter in light of James's paranoid trepidations. It is not inconceivable that Shakespeare and Fletcher present in the characters of Buckingham and Henry VIII versions of King James in pre- and post-1603 circumstances.

In theory, Buckingham had certainly as good a claim to the throne of England (in the event of Henry VIII's death) as did James VI of Scotland on 24 March 1603. Buckingham was one of the most powerful men in the land, a descendant of Edward III, and his name had been mentioned as a possible successor around the time of Henry VII's death (Ridley, *Henry VIII* 33, 123). James too was a descendant of Edward III with a hereditary right to the crown, and he had been named as Elizabeth's possible successor long before the turn of the century.[77] Yet neither one of them could claim to be either the undisputed or the legal heir to the crown. James had to bide his time as King of Scots, and wait – although not passively – and see how history would unfold itself. Buckingham, Shakespeare and Fletcher stress initially, like James, did not seek the English crown through violent means. The Surveyor's testimony describes the Duke's wait-and-see attitude and recalls him to have said "that if the king / Should without issue die, he'll carry it so / To make the sceptre his" (1.2.133–5).

However, if James could have seen a younger version of himself in the claimant, he, as King of England, would certainly also have empathized with Henry VIII's explicit concern for the legal foundations of Buckingham's claim:[78] "How grounded he his title to the crown / Upon our fail?" There is no suggestion here, as with James in the Arbella Stuart affair, that the "pretenders" are, in fact, threatening to seize control of the crown. Therefore, this kind of comparative interpretation should not be pushed too far for fear of reducing the play to a neatly planned allegory on contemporary events. However, the similarities I have noted do intimate anxieties about threats to the reigning monarch's legitimacy that lurk just below the surface, even if the enemy claimant lacks the actual capability or intention to pursue a "legal" coup d'état.

Moreover, Shakespeare and Fletcher also illustrate the less-than-stable nature of James's claim by setting up the Buckingham pre-trial scene as the inevitable subversion of Archbishop Cranmer's closing speech. The historiographies of the two scenes roughly coincide, but their relation to truth is judged to be opposite, thus creating an epistemological dilemma. In response to Henry's question concerning the legal grounds of Buckingham's claim, the Surveyor comes up with an intriguing answer: "He was brought to this / By a vain prophecy of Nicholas Henton. . ., a Chartreux friar, / His confessor, who fed him every minute / With words of sovereignty" (146–9). The import of such an answer for the trial is twofold: it gives an expedient plausibility to the Surveyor's testimony because it attributes further motivation to Buckingham, and, secondly, it also completely discredits Buckingham's claim because a "vain prophecy" could never constitute a legal ground. Ironically, it is the very same genre of speech – a prophecy – that sanctions James's accession to the crown at the conclusion of *Henry VIII.*[79] How can anyone assess the truth content of either speech? One voice suggests that Henton "might be deceived . . . by th'devil's illusions," but Queen Katherine quickly points out that this voice belongs to a man who used to be "the duke's surveyor," who lost his office "on the complaint o'th' tenants," and who may well be venting his spleen (178, 179, 172–3). Cranmer's prophecy is not labeled "vain," but Shakespeare and Fletcher insure that we do not forget that the zealous Archbishop does Henry's bidding by reminding us that it was he who collected the opinions against the Queen, "which have satisfied the king for his divorce" (3.2.64–5). And while the cold task of persuading the Queen to accept the fait accompli falls to Wolsey and Campeius, it is Cranmer who rises to the Canterbury seat in 1533, just in time to perform, against the will of Rome, the divorce and the marriage that followed hard upon it.

It will not do to argue that we all "know" that Cranmer serves the historically "right" cause, and that Buckingham and Katherine had to "step aside" to let history run its course.[80] It is precisely this type of misplaced confidence in a continuous, teleological reading of history that Shakespeare and Fletcher are vigorously resisting.[81] To accept Cranmer's prophetic version of the past as the one condoned by the play, therefore, is to celebrate an ideologically skewed version which is borne out neither by the events of the play nor by history as it was presented in the contemporary histories and chronicles read by many Jacobeans.

Deliberately, the play provides no sufficient grounds to make a meaningful epistemological distinction between the speeches of Nicholas Henton and Thomas Cranmer. Henry's interpretation of their speeches is purely opportunistic, designed to produce overtly ideological readings that serve the interests of those who have the power, Henry VIII and, by extension, James I. However, despite the obvious differences between Buckingham's case in the early decades of the sixteenth century and James's in the year 1603, the correspondences between the characters as portrayed by Shakespeare and Fletcher highlight how similar histories and circumstances may bring one man death and another a crown. Hence, Shakespeare and Fletcher's dramatic presentation draws attention to the malleable nature of historiography and historical contexts as instruments of royal legitimation.

VI

But James is not the only monarch whose position is called into question in *Henry VIII*. If we turn to the historiographical representation of the figure of Elizabeth, we encounter a similar but perhaps more subtle ambivalence, one caused by a prejudicial anxiety about the gender of monarchs. There is no doubt that Cranmer's final eloquence captures the ideas and images that helped decades earlier to construct the ideology of the cult of Elizabeth. In fact, when we view it as a purely prophetic speech (which, in 1533, the moment of its dramatic-historical utterance, it is supposed to be), we can think of it as an imaginary, archetypal moment out of which was born the cult of the Queen. Nonetheless, when we consider parental expectations prior to Elizabeth's birth history, as well as her reception into the world as it is presented in the play, we learn that this "royal infant" who shall be "A pattern to all princes living with her, / And all that shall succeed" (5.4.17, 22–3) is not without her perceived defects.

The sex life of the male Tudor and Stuart monarchs was certainly not submitted to profound moral scrutiny, but the adulterous conception of Princess Elizabeth takes on a greater significance because in the play Henry deliberately and explicitly conflates his desire to marry the pregnant Anne Bullen with the interest of the state. During the divorce trials at Blackfriars, Henry cites a comment by the French ambassador about the possible illegality of his marriage as the moment that first "shook the bottom of [his] conscience" and made it "a tender place" (2.2.142–3). Historically, this encounter took place in 1527, at least one and perhaps two years after Henry fell in love with Anne Boleyn (Ridley, *Henry VIII* 157–8).[82] Clearly, Henry had been "moved" long before he began to formulate the scenario that would yield him Anne and, perhaps, a male heir for the throne of England. More important than this historical chronology, however, is the play's chronology. Shakespeare and Fletcher position the masque at York Place, during which Henry first becomes enamored of Anne, *before* both Henry's defense of the divorce and the scene in which two gentlemen first introduce "A buzzing of a separation / Between the king and Katherine" (2.1.148–9), thereby implicitly identifying not religious or national considerations but sexual appetite as a main cause for the birth of Elizabeth as a princess and heir to the crown. Hence, the play lends special weight to Suffolk's assessment that it is not the King's "marriage with his brother's wife / [that] Has crept too near his conscience" but that "his conscience / Has crept too near another lady" (2.2.16–18).

Moreover, the somber aura surrounding the character of Elizabeth is not merely limited to the inspection of Henry's murky motives themselves. The causal connection between Henry's decision to discard and humiliate Katherine and Elizabeth's rise to the throne – although these events occur a quarter of a century apart – is always there as a pivotal part of history, and casts a long and palpable shadow over both Anne's coronation and Elizabeth's christening. The more acute genealogical tension, however, lies in Shakespeare and Fletcher's comparison of Katherine and Anne, a comparison which works in two ways. On the one hand, focusing attention on Anne (and not Elizabeth) as Katherine's successor, steers some of the negative connotations of Katherine's removal in the direction of Anne (ostensibly to shield the reputation of Elizabeth). Yet any blackening of Anne's character also produces the opposite effect, namely the discrediting of Gloriana's mother, a process which precisely calls attention to a less-than-perfect genealogy which casts a blemish on the daughter. Pushing the comparison between the two women, Shakespeare and Fletcher unambiguously *follow* the scene of Anne's coronation with the contrasting scene in which Katherine, shortly before her death, is crowned with a garland by heavenly angels. They clearly do not want us to gloss over the fact that England had for a while – although of course not legally – two queens. Katherine's final request is to be interred "although unqueen'd, yet like / A queen, and daughter to a king" (4.2.171–2). Placing these two scenes, which in actuality took place some three years apart, in such close proximity to one another greatly emphasizes their causal connection and underscores Katherine's dignity and royal bearing. Also, we should not underestimate the collective memory of a Jacobean audience which might very well remember that the year of Katherine's historical death (1536) also witnessed, ironically, the execution of the mother of Elizabeth on dubious charges of adultery, further calling into question the justness of Henry's marital maneuvering. Indisputably, Shakespeare and Fletcher's portrayal of Anne Bullen does nothing to enhance the reputation or genealogical credentials of England's great Gloriana.

But the play goes further in diminishing Elizabeth's stature. The old lady who brings Henry the news of Elizabeth's birth teases him by announcing the child is a "lovely boy" (5.1.164). Upon learning the baby's true sex the King does not express himself verbally, but the old lady's outspoken dissatisfaction with the "hundred marks" allotted her by Henry is a strong indicator of the father's disappointment with his child's gender.[83] As historian Jasper Ridley notes, "It was very important for Henry that Anne's child should be a boy. Not only did he need the male heir for whom he had been waiting for so long, but he and his supporters had argued that Catherine's failure to produce a surviving son was proof that God had condemned their marriage" (Ridley, *Elizabeth I* 22). Shakespeare and Fletcher's Henry similarly explains he believes he "stood not in the smile of heaven" because "my lady's womb, / If it conceiv'd a male-child by me, should / Do no more offices of life to't than / The grave does to th' dead: for her male issue / Or died where they were made, or shortly after / This world had air'd them" (2.4.185, 186–91). Moreover, we should not forget that if Katherine had borne Henry a son, Elizabeth would likely never have been born, and, if she had been, in all probability, not as a legitimate member of the Tudor royal family. As Ridley declares, Elizabeth was "probably the most unwelcome royal daughter and most celebrated woman in English history" (*Elizabeth I* 323). And it is precisely this double mood – this deeply anxious wish that she had been a male combined with the utmost respect and admiration for her accomplishments – that shines through in Shakespeare and Fletcher's juxtaposing of Cranmer's discourse and the reasons for and the responses to Elizabeth's birth.

In this context, Cranmer's exaltation of James takes on a special dimension insofar as he becomes the son, the male heir that Henry and England always wanted. As such James is elevated above Elizabeth, and is apparently valued more than Elizabeth, although this should not lead us to conclude that James's popularity rivaled Elizabeth's or that he was esteemed the better ruler. The sentiment should be understood in terms of deeply ingrained cultural attitudes about gender and authority in a patriarchal nation ruled – except during Mary's brief reign – by a prolonged succession of kings.[84] In order to negotiate the prejudices that often needed to be dealt with if she was to enjoy the confidence of her subjects, Elizabeth on occasion had to escape the cultural aura of her own gender and represent herself "as an androgynous martial maiden, like Spenser's Britomart."[85] Hence, in reading misgivings about the gender of Anne's child back into history, Shakespeare and Fletcher voice certain trepidations concerning the gender of the monarch that existed in 1533 as well as in the playwrights' own day. The disclosure of these cultural anxieties about gender raises serious doubts about the authenticity of Henry's invocation of God's judgment on his marriage to Katherine, which, in turn, subverts Cranmer's concept of Tudor history as right and inevitable.

VII

Judith H. Anderson astutely observes that "looking back from Cranmer's vision to the rest of the play, even in the absence of an intentional signal from the playwright[s], we should have difficulty not wondering whether so nice a vision is not merely rhetorical. . . ."[86] At the christening of the infant Elizabeth, Archbishop Cranmer's exalted historical vision of a Golden Age to come is plainly intended to erase the historiographical eclecticism and inscrutability of history itself that the play has given voice to up until that point. As behooves the king's impromptu historian, the divinely inspired Cranmer presumably furnishes special insight into the "deep structures" of history by suggesting that while certain historical moments and figures may fade, essential patterns and attitudes remain.[87] He craftily links James I to Henry VIII and Elizabeth I through the image of the phoenix, declaring that when "The bird of wonder dies, the maiden phoenix, / Her ashes new create another heir / As great in admiration as herself" (5.4.40–2). The image certainly constitutes a potent compliment to James, not in the least because it designates him the heir not merely of the Queen's crown but also of the qualities of "peace, plenty, love, truth, [and] terror" (47) associated with her. That the phoenix image is material to James's genealogical status in the play is undoubted. Elizabeth, Alexander Leggatt asserts, "is connected to the play at the level of action; every important event leads to her birth. [But] James has no such connection, and here the links are established [only] through imagery."[88] And yet, if we listen critically to the churchman we notice that even in the speech that most eloquently invokes a providential view of Tudor–Stuart legitimacy and continuity (5.4.14–55), its controlling metaphor – that of the phoenix – undermines the very genealogy it is meant to reinforce.

The editor of the Arden edition of *Henry VIII* notes that the phoenix is "a common image of the royal succession" (Foakes 175 n. 40–1). And so it is, but it is vital to note that the phoenix's power to identify the identity of any particular monarch is wholly retroactive or historical and not predictive or prophetic. The coronation behind, the image of the bird that rises from its own ashes bolsters the authority of the new ruler as the one who replaces the deceased one in the never-dying office of the monarch. But the image of the phoenix can never identify the new ruler before he or she has ascended to the throne, not even if the person is designated by law and blood to inherit it. The natural body and the corporate body do not merge until *after* the coronation. The phoenix image denotes an abstraction, a quality, "the Dignity" of the monarch qua monarch, and "the singularity of the royal office"; and it is simply not designed to select any particular *individual* to become king or queen.[89] Ernst Kantorowicz, the author of the monumental *The King's Two Bodies*, turns to *Macbeth* – that other Shakespeare play purported to flatter James I – to illustrate his point:

> By maintaining the fictitious oneness of the predecessors with potential successor, all of whom were present and incorporated in the actual incumbent of the Dignity, the jurists constructed a fictitious person, a "corporation by succession" composed

of all those vested successively with that particular Dignity – a fiction which makes us think of the witches in Shakespeare's *Macbeth*, who conjure up that uncanny ghostly procession of Macbeth's predecessor kings whose last one bears the "glass" showing the long file of successors. (*The King's Two Bodies* 387)

Significantly, the royal images Macbeth sees in the mirror held by the eight kings remain as nameless as the "ghostly procession" of the kings themselves. Macbeth indicates that some of the kings in the mirror carry "twofold balls and treble scepters" (*Macbeth* 4.1.121), possibly connoting James's double kingship of England and Scotland and his title as King of Great Britain, Ireland, and France. James, however, is not mentioned by name. And even if, as some critics speculate, at a court performance the "glass" of the eighth king[90] may have reflected the face of James I, we must still conclude that the play's line of royal successors does not extend beyond the mortal monarch alive at the time of its production (in other words, the play in no way designates Prince Henry as James's successor, which certainly would have been a popular thing to do). In *Macbeth*, as in *Henry VIII*, prophecy therefore does not range beyond what is historically "known." Insofar as it refers to the Dignity, the image of the phoenix is capable only of predicting the perpetual continuation of that Dignity, and quite unable to designate specifically any future heirs to the throne or to lend added force or credibility to any individual in possession of the crown. Its use may well flatter the king, but it does not serve as a particularly powerful image of royal *legitimation* in either the prophetic (Henrician) or the historical (Jacobean) context.

Hence Cranmer's speech, which, spoken in 1533 (in historical time), is clearly intended to be prophetic, is severely hampered by the phoenix in its aim to designate a *natural* body as monarch, and therefore impotent when it comes to adding any legitimacy to the individual who will possess the crown in the future (i.e., the Jacobean present) to which Cranmer alludes with such aplomb. Had they wished to do so, Fletcher and Shakespeare could have emphasized James's *blood* connection to Elizabeth Tudor (Henry VII's sister Margaret was James's great grandmother). Although that blood connection was the very reason that Henry's will barred the Stuart line from the throne of England, mentioning it would have given a sense of the rightness and inevitability of James's reign. It certainly would have pleased James, whose claim to the English throne was based solely on primogeniture. As Maurice Lee observes:

The claims of primogeniture were overriding: whatever English common law or Henry VIII's will or the English parliament might say, James, at the moment of Elizabeth's death, would become king of England by hereditary right. Since this right had not been explicitly recognized in England, it was necessary for James to spell it out clearly and publicly for all the world to acknowledge. This was a major (though not the only) reason for writing *The Trew Law* – and for James's insistence, in his exposition of the doctrine of the divine right of kings, that the right attaches to the *person* of the king, not merely to the office.[91]

Although not everyone in England saw it this way, from James's point of view a Cranmer allusion to his hereditary right would have underscored the inevitability of the mortal James on the throne of England.

Shakespeare and Fletcher, however, have Cranmer make a different, highly controversial genealogical move. Rather than acknowledging the potentially troublesome blood tie through Margaret Tudor, Cranmer exploits the phoenix as "the image of asexual procreation"[92] to insinuate a startling mother–son bond between Elizabeth and James. Phoenix lore has it that when the queen dies, the bird of wonder dies, and from *its* ashes – i.e., not from the queen's – another monarch mysteriously emerges to take her place. In this representational scheme, the reproductive function belongs to the phoenix. Cranmer's deployment of the phoenix image abandons the customary figure of metaphor (which allows for a recognition of the body politic and body natural to be recognized as distinct even while they are mysteriously one) for the figure of simile. The effect of this rhetorical move is subtle but significant. Cranmer says: "Nor shall this peace sleep with her [Elizabeth]; but, *as* when / The bird of wonder dies, the maiden phoenix, / Her ashes new create another heir / As great in admiration as herself" (5.4.39–42; emphasis added). The choice of simile over metaphor changes the relation between the body natural and the body politic from *identification* to one of *likeness*. In the case of metaphor, two entities temporarily coexist in unity, but in the similetic instance certain traits from one entity (the phoenix) are transferred to the other entity (the queen). In this particular example, then, Cranmer transfers the reproductive function of the phoenix to the body natural of the queen. It is not the phoenix that creates itself anew, but the queen who *like* the phoenix from "Her ashes new create another heir." Cranmer's linguistic sleight of hand implies that Elizabeth will give birth to James, which is of course quite ironic since Elizabeth chose to remain single and childless, but also strangely appropriate because so many of her subjects longed for her to marry and produce an heir and stabilize the succession. Cranmer's provocative move may appeal to an audience's wishful memories and lingering regrets over Elizabeth's denial of their wish.

Perhaps a Jacobean audience did not grasp the intricacies of Cranmer's maneuver, but its general sense – the intimate association between Elizabeth and James – must have been obvious to them. And some members of the audience may well have been swayed by the speech, but anyone not caught up in the moment could instantly recognize how Cranmer grossly distorts even the most basic understanding of English royal genealogy. What is more, as Roy Strong observes, "James I and his Queen, Anne of Denmark, had deliberately rejected the mythology of Elizabeth [of which phoenix lore was an integral part], erecting in its stead one which was harder, more assertive, and totally unambiguous in its claims."[93] He abandoned the Elizabethan cult of romance, mysticism, and chivalry in favor of a more legalistic and historical approach that relied heavily on stories from the Old Testament and medieval conceptions of divine right monarchy, which shifted the focus of questions of legitimacy away from ancestral genealogy and located them in the unique and private (and hence equally equivocal) bond between king and God.[94] For those acquainted with this shift in royal self-presentation, Cranmer's manipulation of Elizabethan ideas and images almost certainly had a nostalgic effect, but it would not have lent a powerful voice to Jamesian legitimacy in 1613.[95]

More blatantly damning to Cranmer's efforts before a Jacobean audience to blend Tudor ideology and providence into a unified and compelling whole may be the *type* or *genre* of his historiographical speech. Given that *Henry VIII* draws heavily on historical sources, sometimes simply versifying Holinshed, it may be somewhat alarming to realize that Cranmer's all-important prophecy does not have a historical source. The speech is made up entirely. There are of course many instances in the play where Shakespeare and Fletcher introduce materials for which we have no source, but Cranmer's speech deserves special attention in this respect because the speech, by offering its Jacobean audience a summary representation of the previous eighty years, draws attention to itself *as* a historiographical representation. To present a fictional speech as history is not necessarily to overstep the legitimate bounds of renaissance historical representation, but this particular manifestation, we will see, turns out to be suspect.

Driven by a desire to educate their readers, early humanist and medieval historiographers studiously imitated the propensity of ancient historians to invent speeches where they felt this was appropriate. Relying on classical precedent, they believed that

> The instructional value of history should be increased not only by the exposition of motives but also by the rhetorical manipulation of material in order to emphasize those elements which have the greatest moral or political significance. The most important rhetorical device is the set speech, which gives intensity to the narrative, and so produces a greater effect upon the reader. Long and important speeches should be constructed according to the rules of ancient oratory. Whenever possible, they should be based on factual evidence, but it is permissible to invent them so long as they are probable, are appropriate to the situation and to the character of the speaker, or reproduce the supposed essence of actual speeches. They should normally be introduced only into crucial situations and attributed only to eminent personages. They may serve as dramatic vehicles for the historian's exposition of his character's motives, or, indirectly, for his judgment and opinions.[96]

Without a doubt, Cranmer's prophecy is such a set speech. In its prophetic mode, his oration hits stock Tudor and Stuart themes – political and religious – and draws freely on traditional pastoral imagery, biblical allusions, and the religious imagery associated with the cult of Elizabeth.[97] Cranmer's brand of history therefore, although it strictly speaking belonged to an earlier period, would be recognized *as* historical by a Jacobean audience. And if Shakespeare and Fletcher had opted to shape their play about the reign of Henry VIII wholly in accordance with these early humanist historiographical principles, there would be cause to join with those critics who exalt Cranmer as Shakespeare and Fletcher's official historian.

To embrace any one historiography as true, however, would require us to ignore the competition for privileged historical representation the play dramatizes. Moreover, adopting Cranmer's vision of history means empowering a version of the past that is too simple and omits too much. The Archbishop's Tudor–Stuart genealogy fails to stand up under even the most basic scrutiny. His history pictures an uninterrupted connection between Henry, Elizabeth, and James, tacitly posits Henry's actions leading to the birth of Elizabeth as the original impulse of the Reformation, and links them gracefully to the Jacobean Church of England. His seamless genealogy is silent about both the reigns of Catholic Mary (1553–8) and Edward VI (1547–53), nor does it mention that the historical counterpart of Shakespeare and Fletcher's Henry (who declares his daughter's birthday a "Holy-day" [5.4.76]) was to execute the mother and declare Elizabeth a bastard, legally barring her from the succession – all in pursuit of the elusive male heir. The latter events do not take place within the historical parameters of the play, but Shakespeare and Fletcher do allow Katherine a poignant deathbed petition to Henry on behalf of their daughter Mary. She commends, she says, to "his [Henry's] goodness / The model of our chaste loves, his young daughter / (The dews of heaven fall thick in blessings on her)" (4.2.131–3). The mere acknowledgment of Mary's existence challenges the ideological and genealogical continuity of Cranmer's pro-James historiography. But the ultimate irony is of course that Cranmer himself, as everybody knew from Foxe's fantastically popular *Actes and Monuments*, was burned at the stake by Bloody Mary for his heretical Protestant beliefs. The Archbishop's history of England therefore erases his own tragic death; it tries to silence the queen who was to silence him.

Another reason exhorting against valorizing Cranmer's providential model of history is that, although early humanist historiography still enjoyed some credibility, a number of its essential characteristics had fallen largely in disrepute in the playwrights' day. Despite historiography's erratic development, historians like Francis Bacon, John Selden, William Camden and others became increasingly sophisticated in their methods precisely by bracketing questions of divine truth from historical inquiry, not because they did not value them but because they considered them neither appropriate nor especially helpful to the fields of civil and political history. The liberal usage of invented speeches had come under constant attack from all but the most old-fashioned historians. In Heywood's translation of the *Method*, Jean Bodin finds fault with "many Historiographers, who in the midst of their discourses, fall off from their entended Narrations, to play Orators or Rhetoritians, so deluding the expectations, and confounding the memories of their readers" (16). Even earlier, in 1574, Thomas Blundeville had published his translation of the Italian treatise on history by Francisco Patrocio and Accontio Tridentio. It is the historiographer's office, Blundeville translates, "to tell things as they were done without either augmenting or diminishing them, or swaruing one iote from the truth. Whereby it appeareth that the hystoriographers ought not to fayne anye Orations nor any other thing, but truely to reporte euery such speach, and deede, euen as it was spoken or done."[98] Similar quotations can be drawn from antiquarians like Camden or even from popular historians like Holinshed and Grafton.

VIII

Notwithstanding these various challenges to Cranmer's brand of historiography, *Henry VIII* never rejects the possible existence or power of providence. Nor, however, does it illustrate or exalt that power, or even show a definite instance of its involvement in human history. In a perverse way, providence – the ultimate truth of Christian history – becomes as abstract and remote a concept as Foucault's idea of power, which, detached from its effects, is so inscrutable that it has to be defined only in terms of its effects or in terms of what it is not. What Shakespeare and Fletcher are interested in are not the origins of power or the meaning of God's providence. Their conception of history is not one that calls for a justification of God's ways to humankind. On the contrary, in *Henry VIII* when a character turns to providence it is always to escape a particular conception of history that seems suddenly to have been rendered futile and powerless or simply inconvenient in the context of God's unknowable plan. Nonetheless, Shakespeare and Fletcher do not appear to promote a nihilistic view of life; the play never indicates that there is no "actual" history that exists behind or beyond linguistic representation – just that that history is not accessible. In *Henry VIII*, they explore how the *manipulations* of historical discourses and the inscrutable complex of motives that drives those manipulations can bring characters to just such a moment in which they feel only the unknown can account for (though not explain) particular historical circumstances. And since providential history by definition extends to the end of human history, it is significant that it manifests no prophetic power in *Henry VIII*. Cranmer divines the future but, even aside from his historical errors, he is in fact rewriting history for a Jacobean context. Providence becomes history – ideological history – after the fact, and subsequently takes on a life of its own.

This does not make *Henry VIII* a subversive text in the ordinary sense. The play is not overtly embroiled in specific political controversies of its day, but this hardly makes it an apolitical text.[99] It eschews micropolitics for a more profound and far-reaching consideration of the relationship between political authority and historiography. Yet it is not especially fanciful to suggest that the play's politics of historiography have considerable resonance in the context of the crucial seventeenth-century legal struggle between king and parliament over the nature of English law and the monarch's prerogatives. In a passage about King Fergus from *The Trew Law of Free Monarchies* already quoted, James revealed his understanding of his relationship to the law of the land. As Sommerville notes, "historically, said James, kings had come to power by a variety of means, including election and conquest. But he thought that however monarchs had at first acquired their crowns, their authority was derived from God alone."[100] As God's "lieutenant" on earth, the king was "therefore countable to that great God" alone (James I, *Trew Law* 55). James did not abandon these views once he became King of England. He stood by the idea that kings were the makers of laws (and could therefore break them anytime they felt compelled to do so), and that whatever political privileges subjects enjoyed were necessarily derived from the monarch (Sommerville, "James I" 63). Moreover, to "prove" his "whiggish" case, "The king used history selectively, and to support conclusions which he had reached by other means" (63). Richard Halpern maintains that James went so far as to assert that Parliament had no authority of him because "kings ruled and even *owned* Britain before there were parliaments" (*Poetics* 228). As far as James was concerned, "the crown [and indeed the entire kingdom] was a piece of inherited property" (221).

The common law lawyers who strongly opposed their king on this matter argued that "both monarch and subject draw their power from an ancient constitution" (Sommerville, "James I" 63). Whether one surmises, as Pocock does, that this was "the nearly universal belief of Englishmen," or agrees with Sommerville that common-law ideology was just one of "*several* ideologies . . . current in early Stuart England,"[101] it is easy to see how much this position differed from the king's, and how, like the king's, it relied on historical argumentation, especially since "Englishmen believed that they could discover the ancient constitution which alone defined the right of the king and the liberties of the subjects" (Sommerville, "James I" 56).

Henry VIII does not appear to take sides in this or any other debate, except insofar as it has a sobering or debunking effect on anyone contemplating these historiographical searches for political truths. The theatrical acquisition of historiographical practices through their simulation on stage constituted an available, if not actual, threat to any party or individual intent on accruing power on the basis of historical argumentation. In my discussion of *Henry V*, I cited Arthur B. Ferguson to suggest that Tudor historians cared little about social customs, institutions, and beliefs, and perhaps even less about secondary and largely informal causes, or anything else that reached "well beyond the history of states as told in terms of the acts, the ambitions, and the tragic dilemmas of the actors themselves" (*Clio Unbound* 5). In many respects, Shakespeare and Fletcher are Tudor historians, but *Henry VIII* also continues the all-important break, initiated in *Henry V*, with this tradition by looking for ways to detach the course of history from both providence and the enigmatic desires of individuals. Repeatedly, *Henry VIII* highlights the (ineffectual) role of human agency most strongly at precisely the moments when (inscrutable) providence is called forth. Shakespeare and Fletcher eliminate neither providence nor individual motivation from the play, all the while creating enough of a space between these "agencies" and the play's total action to cast serious doubts on the utility of the kind of historical explanation Ferguson considers to be the Tudor norm. The literary result of Shakespeare and Fletcher's foray into historical thought, we have to keep in mind, is not a flawed imitation of an Elizabethan history play, but a uniquely Jacobean response to and enactment of the complex historiographical discourses of the moment of its creation.

5 “No meete matters to be wrytten or treated vpon”: *The Tragedy of Sir John Van Olden Barnavelt*

. . . when ere your politick *Prince* putts
his hooke into my nose, / here must he
put his Sword too. –*Barnavelt*[1]

I

“Monday, 13th May, 1619. Today was executed with the sword here in The Hague, on a scaffold thereto erected in the Binnenhof before the steps of the great hall, Mr. John of Barneveldt, in his life Knight, Lord of Berkel, Rodenrys, etc., advocate of Holland and West Friesland, for reasons expressed in the sentence and otherwise, with confiscation of his property, after he had served the state thirty-three years two months and five days since 8th May, 1586; a man of great activity, business, memory, and wisdom – yes, extraordinary in every respect. He that stands let him see that he does not fall, and may God be merciful to his soul. Amen.”[2] So reads a formal entry in the register of the states of Holland, marking the public execution of perhaps the most accomplished statesman in the history of the Dutch Republic. The single most important charge against the seventy-one-year-old Advocate referred to in the register – high treason – did, however, not appear in the sentence. The authorities maintained that “he had been looking toward the enemy” (Spain), but that, in light of his decades of service to the nation, they had “spared him the rack” – or, as they put it, a “sharper investigation” (Motley, *Life and Death*, vol. XIV, 228). In essence, Oldenbarnevelt was executed on a charge which neither had been proven nor to which he had confessed.[3] Indeed, the condemned man’s last words on the scaffold were spoken in “a loud, firm voice to the people: ‘Men do not believe that I am a traitor to the country. I have ever acted uprightly and loyally as a good patriot, and as such I shall die’” (226–7).[4]

This nasty affair did not go unnoticed in England. Maurits, the Calvinist Prince of Orange (and friend of the late Henry, Prince of Wales) who had been Oldenbarnevelt’s chief adversary and the prime engineer of his fall, was something of a popular hero in England. For the public, Maurits was cast in the mold of the soldier-courtier – a throwback to the days of Sir Philip Sidney – who enjoyed the endorsement of James I. Still there was also a much broader interest in Dutch affairs in early-seventeenth-century England. Although England was at peace with Spain, the English had been at war long enough with the Catholic kingdom to retain a strong residue of hatred for that nation. Hence many English could easily muster sympathy for the Dutch, who had been in a bitter off and on military conflict with Spain since 1566.[5] English soldiers had even fought on the side of the Dutch, either under English command or as mercenaries in Dutch regiments. When justifying her financial and military support to the Dutch in their struggle against Phillip of Spain, Elizabeth I had publicly spoken of "mutuall Bondes" between England and the Republic (based on "sundrie autentique Treaties and Transactions for mutuall commerce, entercourse and straight amitie of ancient times") and of the "natural unions" of their peoples.[6] The English also had a good deal in common with the Dutch on questions of religion; both nations were fundamentally Protestant. But perhaps most important were the strong commercial ties and rivalry that had developed between the nations during Elizabeth I's reign. As a result, the English had an important stake in the economic, political, and religious fate of the Dutch Republic and had even developed some grudging admiration for this nascent underdog nation desperately seeking to survive the persistent assaults of the Goliath Spain. One outcome of this interest was a flourishing news exchange between England and the Dutch Republic;[7] the sensational story of the execution reached London almost overnight. On 17 May, only four days after the beheading, a pamphlet entitled *The Picture of Barneveltes Execucon* was entered in the Stationers' Register. The overall printed record suggests that Oldenbarnevelt's untimely death was not received with particular sadness. The popular (though not universally held) English view of the Oldenbarnevelt affair was expressed crudely in a contemporary ballad entitled "Murther Unmasked." Exploiting a common Jacobean analogy between Arminianism (a sect of which Oldenbarnevelt was said to have been a member) and popery, the balladeer portrayed Oldenbarnevelt as a man who had "of grace . . . no touch" and who "did consult with Hell / impiously" to murder not only "men, wives, and children" but also the noble Prince Maurits himself.[8] The moral of the ballad is all too clear, as the balladeer not only lambastes the Dutch politician but also seizes the opportunity to urge all Englishmen to embrace the one true faith:

> You Politians all,
> carefully, carefully,
> Be warn'd by *Barnviles* fall
> midst his fowle actions . . .

And let each English heart
speedily, speedily,
From Poperie depart
as from fell poyson.

Unquestionably, the balladist exploited a perceived analogy between Oldenbarnevelt and Catholic sympathizers in England. This common sentiment was, perhaps somewhat surprisingly, shared by important members of James's government. Jan den Tex points out that "In England, where Oldenbarnevelt's support of the heretic Arminians could only be explained in terms of a secret allegiance to Spain, especially [the English Ambassador to the Dutch Republic Sir Dudley] Carleton judged [Oldenbarnevelt's death] to be the triumph of a good cause. In London, the Advocate was portrayed as a statesman who was blinded by false pride, burdened by guilt, and who had dug his own grave."[9] Moreover, Oldenbarnevelt was quickly cast as the Machiavellian stereotype, as the insidious man of intrigue and policy; Prince Maurits, on the other hand, was portrayed as apolitical and frank, a military hero of noble descent without secrets.

It is therefore quite startling that not long after the publication of *The Picture of Barneveltes Execucon* – no more than 104 days, to be exact[10] – audiences at the Globe theater were presented with a play that dramatized the tangled events leading to Oldenbarnevelt's death, but which presented them from a markedly different, potentially explosive point of view. The play in question, Philip Massinger and John Fletcher's *The Tragedy of Sir John Van Olden Barnavelt*, is an ideologically charged work with distinct republican and anti-authoritarian connotations. What is more, the play conveys these meanings, in part, by playfully engaging with the contemporary debate on historiography. The play pits a version of providentialist historiography against a Machiavellian (humanist) historiography, and uses models of humanist exemplarity to help the viewer understand the play's political stance.

II

It must have been quite difficult for playwrights and historians in the first two decades of James's reign to predict with any kind of precision what the government's response to their historical writings was going to be. As the reign of Queen Elizabeth drew to a close, increased state control over the theater and history-writing accompanied a steady decrease in the number of historical dramas in the repertoire of the public playhouses. A Bishops' Order of 1599 reaffirmed earlier prohibitions when it declared that "noe English historyes be printed" unless special permission to do so was first obtained from the Privy Council. In 1614 James I shut down the

Elizabethan Society of Antiquaries, a group of scholars whose broad research entailed a foray into, among other disputatious topics, the origins of the royal prerogative. No doubt, "the political situation of the realm was reaching a point where a search into the origins of various institutions had political overtones regardless of the motives of the searchers."[11] A long-time favorite of Elizabeth I, Sir Walter Ralegh suffered (to his apparent surprise) the monarch's indignation when King James judged his *History of the World* (1617) "too saucy in censuring princes." And Ben Jonson's infamous historical play, *Sejanus* (1603), earned its author an appearance before the Privy Council for treason. It was suggested that Sejanus referred to Essex and that the brutal Tiberius therefore stood for Elizabeth. Although Jonson apparently found a way to get from under the charge, it is clear that those practicing historiography of any sort were closely monitored by state authorities. When Jonson published the play in 1605 he was sure to add the following disclaimer, which, incidentally but probably not accidentally, perfectly echoes King James's own attack on resistance theory as declared in his *Trew Law of Free Monarchies*:[12] "This [the fall of Sejanus] do we advance as a mark of terror to all traitors, and treasons; to show how just the heavens are in pouring and thundering down a weighty vengeance on their unnatural intents, even to the worst princes: much more to those, for guard of whose piety and virtue, the angels are in continual watch, and God miraculously working."[13]

Yet even if writing history had become a politically dicey, if not dangerous, endeavor, there was also a sense in which "history" was a semi-respectable shield behind which an author could hide to protect himself from government charges. The famous case of Sir John Hayward's history of *Henry IV*, which incurred the Queen's severe displeasure, is a case in point. When Hayward (a member of the Essex circle) found himself accused by the lawyer Sir Edward Coke of inserting invented materials "in order to make his narrative point more directly at contemporary intrigue," the historian defended himself by claiming that "he was following accepted practice when he shaped his narrative and interlaced it with political generalizations translated from [the Roman historian] Tacitus."[14] Apparently, Hayward's defense helped him little because, as Annabel Patterson reports, he was sent to jail for his offense. But this does not mean that his defense was, in fact, unreasonable for the time. Patterson quotes from William Camden's response to the affair, who writes that Hayward was treated "as if [the history] had beene written as an example and incitement to the deposing of the Queene," suggesting that Elizabeth objected to Hayward's politics, not to his historical method. The event demonstrates the Queen's power to ignore scholarly conventions, not necessarily a disrespect for historiography as such. Had Elizabeth nonetheless had a deeper familiarity with the works of Tacitus, she might have been more outraged; and perhaps rightly so for Tacitus, whose writings gained prominence in the early Jacobean decades, became the center of a "'Tacitist' literature (which included historiography) with satirical and occasionally republican overtones."[15] Still, the fact that Hayward cited a historian's writings as a precedent for his own is of course quite significant in assessing the credibility of the figure of the historian. Not only does it posit a historian as a credible authority, it also validates the search for precedent itself, a search which constitutes the very essence of the humanist historiographical enterprise. Hence it is not all that surprising that, as Patterson points out, playwrights often used "historical or other uninvented texts" precisely to limit "authorial responsibility for the text."[16]

In writing the *Barnavelt* tragedy, Massinger and Fletcher are clearly trying to maneuver within this complex and sometimes unpredictable labyrinth of dramatic and historiographical censorship. Avoiding a direct treatment of English history almost completely, the playwrights select a contemporary but foreign controversy between two leading Dutch officials, Johan Van Oldenbarnevelt and Prince Maurits. The reasons for their choice – other than that the fall and death of Oldenbarnevelt made for pretty good commercial drama – must therefore have been, in part, strategic. By circumventing English history or classical history altogether, the drama might not be thought to comment on present English circumstances. Contemporary events in a foreign country, it seemed, would fall outside the existing (humanist) historiographical mold, even though "the news-books which reported events on the continent" were sometimes also referred to as "histories."[17] Secondly, the play's foreign setting allows the playwrights to take seriously Jean Bodin's warning to historians insofar as none of the living characters portrayed in the drama holds any direct power over them.[18] Moreover, to report in a play events that had actually taken place did allow Massinger and Fletcher to limit their "authorial responsibility" somewhat.

This is not to suggest that Massinger and Fletcher's particular choice of a plot portraying recent foreign events was without risk. On the contrary, the English-language news pamphlets and the popular ballad which openly linked the Oldenbarnevelt account to English religious (and therefore also political) affairs *afforded* the story contemporary relevance and therefore aroused special interest from the censor. Moreover, a 1559 ordinance issued by Elizabeth I did not merely prohibit the theatrical staging of intentionally rebellious attitudes and events; it also declared matters of church and state to be off limits, no matter what the intent of the author or the performers. The ordinance expressly forbade the staging of a drama "wherein either matters of religion or of the gouernaunce of the estate of the common weale shalbe handled or treated, beying no meete matters to be wrytten or treated vpon."[19] The substance of this Elizabethan ordinance was still very much in effect in James I's England, and speaks with an uncanny directness to the content of *Barnavelt* which deals in matters of state and religion, and which, as we shall see, has strong bearing on the English "common weale." What is more, the fact that only a handful of renaissance plays based their plots on contemporary events may be explained by the staging of Chapman's *Byron* (1602), a play that alluded controversially to "the domestic arrangements of the French king," and which presumably caused the banning of "plays whose subjects were taken from contemporary history" (Chambers, vol. I, 327). In any event, this murky context can be cleared up somewhat as follows. If, like Massinger and Fletcher, you were a dramatist with a political agenda (or were perceived to have one by the authorities), it was safer to base your play on an "uninvented text" or "true" set of events than it was to be the creative originator of your story. It was also safer to write about foreign events than it was to write about English events, despite the fact that certain prohibitions did exist against the former. And, finally, there was, as the cases of Jonson's *Sejanus* and Middleton's *A Game at Chess* ought to illustrate, a measure of safety in trying to avoid the appearance (regardless of intent) of writing a historical allegory. The perceived intent of historical allegory of course coincided with the humanist historiographer's dictum that historians ought to read the past in order to comment on and elucidate the present. Therefore it was in some sense probably wiser to write about the present directly (provided this was not the English present) than to write about the past – English or classical.

This said, Massinger and Fletcher clearly realized that the Oldenbarnevelt saga, despite its recent occurrence, *was* a historical saga; potentially it was the archetypal Tudor historiographical narrative of two great men (one good, one evil) and their actions, with order, Calvinism, and monarchy ultimately triumphing over treason, popery, and republicanism. Massinger and Fletcher clearly saw this potential and were attracted to it, if only to subvert it. What may have drawn them further to the story was its foreign setting which provided an English audience with a certain geographical distance and its attendant sense of "otherness" which fulfills a function very similar to that of chronological distance insofar as it creates a safety buffer between the playwrights and their product. A final attraction for Massinger and Fletcher must have been the fact that the English government had taken a political position on the Oldenbarnevelt affair, thereby opening the door for any historian-playwright to offer a counter-interpretation. In short, for the activist dramatists a history play about Oldenbarnevelt had most of the advantages and relatively few of the risks associated with a more conventional history play. In deciding how to handle the situation, the crucial questions for Massinger and Fletcher must have been: how much of a stake does the crown have in the Oldenbarnevelt affair, and how radical can our version be before we draw the ire of monarch and censor?

There is little doubt that Massinger and Fletcher pushed right to, and sometimes clearly past, the limits allowed by the censor. Set for its first performance at the Globe, *Barnavelt* was initially kept off the stage by the Bishop of London who deemed its content unsuitable.[20] After a series of revisions were made by the Master of the Revels, Sir George Buc,[21] performance was allowed to go on; but seventy-one markings on the *Barnavelt* manuscript display the close scrutiny to which the censor subjected it. As T. H. Howard-Hill observes, "No other play of the period . . . bears so many explicit traces of the censorship to which plays were subjected before performance."[22] Nonetheless, as we shall see, Buc's intercession clearly failed to excise the full political sting from the play. London publishers were still wary of *Barnavelt* (Bentley, *Profession* 258), and it was neither printed in quarto, nor included in the 1647 Beaumont and Fletcher folio, even though it enjoyed considerable success on the Globe stage (Bentley, *Jacobean* III, 416).[23] Everything indicates that the play was perceived as controversial and perhaps as dangerous in its time.

In my discussion of the play I want to do two things: to analyze the presentation of the play's two main adversaries, Prince Maurice and Barnavelt; and to explore the playwrights' use of historiography in a play dealing primarily with recent events. The two issues are closely related since Massinger and Fletcher confer upon the two characters competing historiographies, giving the self-serving Prince of Orange to expound a providentialist historiography and allowing the ambitious Barnavelt to embrace, with a definite measure of skepticism, a humanist approach to the past. This done, I will consider the play and its subversive implications in their historical context, and show how King James's religious policies are inscribed in the play-text and how his conception of kingship is stringently challenged.

III

In censoring *Barnavelt*, Howard-Hill points out, Buc was "bound by official attitudes: the noble Prince had preserved the infant republic from the machinations of the heretical Machiavel. The Prince of Orange was to be magnified, Oldenbarnevelt vilified, and his death justified by his faults" (Howard-Hill, "Buc" 56). Beginning, however, with the play's very first speeches, Massinger and Fletcher begin to dissolve the seemingly rigorous distinctions between the heroic Prince and the despicable Advocate:

between the consummate politician and the noble Soldier-Prince. Initially, we do not trust Barnavelt's cutting critique of the Prince since he is supposed to be the Machiavellian antagonist; yet as the events unfold, it becomes apparent that the Advocate's pride, emotion, and ambition have not unduly distorted his negative assessment of the Prince. We realize that we have been witnessing a play with not one but two Machiavels. At the outset, most of the other characters present the Prince as magnanimous, larger than life. His military exploits have made him a living legend among his troops. In "the peoples Language," he is described as the "Arme, & Sword, [to which] the *Prouinces* owe / their flourishing peace. . . [And] that hee's the Armyes soule / by which it moves to victorie."[24] His followers assert that without the Prince, "dispaire, and ruyn / had ceaizd on all, and buried quick our safeties" (12–13). Indeed, "had not [the Prince] in Act, betterd or Counsailes / and in the execution set them of, / all we designd had ben but as a tale / forgot as soon as told" (14–17). Conversely, Barnavelt, the principal author of those councils, receives no such grandiose language. It is suggested that the politician is nothing without his superior, the man of action, the soldier who betters the politician's "tale" and turns it into reality. It is precisely this conception of the relationship between the Prince and the Advocate that the latter objects to vehemently: he maintains that the Prince's "stile of Excellencie" was the "guift" granted to him by the politician. "Money, the strength and fortune in the war, / the help of England, and the aide of France" (37–9) were the fruits of the Advocate's political labors and not solely or even primarily of the Prince's military doings. Hitherto the Prince and the politician had worked in relative unison for the Republic, but now the Prince is pronounced "the Father of his Cuntrie" (5), leaving his former partner "scarce holding / the second place" (29–30). Barnavelt will not endure this loss of honor (should I "with a boorish patience suffer / the Harvest I labord for, to be / anothers spoile?"), and he resolves to build his own army (of *waardgelders*[25]) and to resist Maurice's military might. For this and several related charges, he is arrested, tried, and executed. Appearances conspire to shape a simple moral tale: the deceptive politician with Arminian loyalties is brought to justice by the noble Prince.

In the final act, however, while Barnavelt has truly remained forthright and steadfast about his motives, the Prince is revealed as a figure deeply engaged in various stratagems in order to disguise his true political will and identity. As Frijlinck notes, the dramatists depart from historical fact when they portray Barnavelt as "a friend of the people," whose house the burghers decorate with flowers on Mayday (Frijlinck, "Introduction" cxxxii, [4.4]). It may have been the playwrights' dislike for absolutism, William Appleton suggests, that helps to explain why Maurice, who appears "wise, sympathetic, tolerant and just" in the first four acts of the play is overshadowed in the final act by Barnavelt, who, though portrayed as a "proud malcontent" in acts one through four, is rendered significantly "more appealing" in the play's conclusion.[26] All the Prince's plans have come to fruition: Barnavelt has been captured, sentenced, and is about to lose his head. Upon learning that "th'Executioners, like hungry vulturs / haue smelld out their imployment," the Prince of Orange speaks: "let them haue it: / and all that plot against the generall good / learne from this mans example, great in age, / greater in wealth, and in authoritie, / but matchles in his worldly pollicie, / that there is one aboue, that do's deride / the wisest counsailes, that are misaplide" (5.1.2704–12). This epitaph explicitly ties the earthly estate to a divine order. Not Prince Maurice but "one aboue" has supposedly overcome this proud man who misapplied his "wordly pollicie" against the "generall good." We may view the Prince as humble and his speech as a pious invocation of a late-medieval and early renaissance historiography which chooses ultimately to explain earthly causality in terms of God's providence. Such piety, however, rings hollow to many in 1618, especially when uttered in an acutely political context. But perhaps more importantly, *nothing* in Massinger and Fletcher's play suggests that "one aboue" had anything to do with the denouement; it does, however, demonstrate that the Prince vigorously pursued the Advocate's demise. Manifestly, the Prince's providential view of history is at odds with his actual practice, which is virtually indistinguishable from Barnavelt's practice. Ironically, the religious differences between the Calvinist Prince and Arminian politician, which at first appear to underscore the difference between the two characters, become relatively meaningless in this historiographical context. As Nicholas Tyacke submits, "for many people in the early seventeenth century the basic issue as between Protestantism and Catholicism [or Arminianism] was that of divine determinism versus human free will."[27] Maurice's increasingly insincere invocation of a providential determinism, however, emphasizes both his reliance on free will and his concealed affinity with Barnavelt's position.

Imprisoned by Maurice and having confessed his part in the "treason" against the Prince, Barnavelt's accomplice, Leidenberch, expresses a sentiment that shares the Prince's token providentialism: "the heavie hand of heaven, is now vpon vs, / and we exposd, like bruizd, and totterd vessels / to merciles, and cruell Seas, to sinck vs" (3.4.1453–5). But Barnavelt immediately expresses an alternative point of view: "our Indiscreations, are our evill fortunes, / and nothing sincks vs, but want of providence" (1456–7). The Advocate's words can be taken either as a denial of the existence of providence or as an equation between providence and the good fortune of Barnavelt's cause. Both meanings of course reject the traditional meaning and controlling influence of providential history. In its immediate context, Barnavelt's declaration is part of a calculated argument to make Leidenberch commit suicide and prevent him from testifying against Barnavelt. All the same, Leidenberch accepts the Advocate's philosophy of free will before he commits suicide.

Even when his own end is near, the Advocate persists in his view that one's fate in life is a result of one's actions. Like Maurice, the Lord of State who accompanies the Advocate to the scaffold invokes a divine order when he chides the prisoner for not confessing his faults. "*Play* not with heaven" (italics added), he cautions, but Barnavelt retorts: "my Game's as sure as yors is: / and wth more care, and inocence, I play it: / take of my doblet: and I prethee, fellow / strike without fear" (5.3.2957–61). To play the game innocently means to play the game without mystification of its rules. This Barnavelt has done from the very start. Wrongly portrayed as a man who conceals his pride or is blinded by it (Appleton, *Beaumont and Fletcher* 89), he willingly admits: "I will preserve / each glory I haue got, with as much care / as I acheivd it; read but ore the Stories / of men most fam'd for courage, or for counsaile, / and you shall find that the desire of glory / was the last frailety wisemen ere putt of: / be they my presidents" (1.1.126–32). The early humanist historian, we recall, invariably cites examples from the past in order to encourage proper conduct in the present. Here, Barnavelt follows this method, but in a marvelously perverse manner. He announces that he will intentionally follow "negative" precedents. The Advocate's distinctive move can be read in two ways: he is trying to reclaim the power to write his own history, a power that he feels is rapidly slipping away from him; but he is also asserting that even the wise men who are our historical precedents have their weaknesses. The second meaning, no doubt, is both an affirmation of his own humanity and a jab at Orange who is deemed infallible by his political supporters. The Advocate goes on to speak of his movements in the "labourinthes of pollicie," and asserts that the Prince's military victories would not have been possible without the statesman's political efforts.[28] Furthermore, as a self-professed republican, he is especially worried about the effects of Maurice's military successes on the political organization of the country. Before his arrest he argues passionately against accommodating the Prince's recent aspirations with a crown. Nonetheless, faced with the reality of the Prince's superior military forces, Barnavelt can only urge the Lords of State to resist the Prince passively and in doing so persuade him that he is perhaps not yet all-powerful. In an emphatic plea, the Advocate tries to remind the Lords of State that *they* are the root of the Prince's power, and that the Prince ought not to be converted into an icon, an absolute ruler who embodies and mystifies state-power in his person. He urges: "this Prince of *Orange* / is but as *Barnauelt*, a Servant to / yor Lordships, and the State: like me maintained: / the pomp he keepes, at yor charge: will you then / wayt his prowd pleasure, and in that confes / by daring to doe nothing, that he knowes not / you haue no absolute powre?" (1.2.304–10).

While Barnavelt and the Lords of State are devising policies to "sinck" (1.2.331) Maurice, the Prince, made to wait outside the council chamber, is already displaying signs of a mounting friction between his newly acquired "Greatnes" and his role as humble servant to the state. "What I haue don, I look not back, to magnifie," (1.3.349) he modestly responds when praised lavishly by his followers. Yet the Prince's humility means very little because it is preceded by his strategic invocation of the memory of Prince William of Orange-Nassau, the aristocratic founder of the Dutch Republic. At this moment in the proceedings, when the Prince's relationship to the state is about to be newly defined, for the Prince to foreground his "happynes / [at] . . . being sproong from such a noble Father" (1.3.335–6), can only insinuate that the son ought rightly to follow in the father's footsteps. It is the articulation of a genealogy of power and blood for the purpose of exercising political power. Eventually, the Netherlands were to become a constitutional monarchy ruled by the House of Orange, but Prince Maurits did not have a birthright in law to the stadholdership of Holland and Zeeland, or any other offices his father formerly held. Yet shortly after Maurits was born a promise was made by the States to the father that his son would eventually inherit the governorship (Rowen, *Princes of Orange* 32). Hence, the play enacts Maurits's gradual and extra-legal but inevitable rise to power.[29]

On the surface, the "humble" Prince appears to resist such labels as the "arme oth' war," the "Soldiers sperit" and the "dooer" (1.3.358, 371–3), and when his followers persist he should no longer accept a subservient role in the state because he is "master of more mindes, that love, & honor" (1.3.379) him, the Prince implores: "I pray ye, no more; as you love me, no more / stupid I neuer Was, nor so secure yet / to lend my patience to mine owne betraying: – *Guard at dore.* / I shall find time and riper cause (1.3.382–5). Despite the Prince's assumed modesty, these words are an unmistakable first sign that he considers himself to be more than just the tool and servant of his country. They show that he possesses private political ambitions that anticipate a proper time and riper cause to manifest themselves.

To attain and then solidify the political zenith in the Republic, the Prince must, however, proceed with caution. Before openly taking control over the downfall of the Advocate, he essentially adopts a cunningly deceptive passive role, hoping to create the impression that the actions that further his cause are urged on and brought about by others. The council scene in which Barnavelt's fate is sealed is a good example of this.

When the council meets – this time with the Prince in charge of the proceedings and without Barnavelt in attendance – Maurice's forces have taken Utrecht, captured Barnavelt's co-conspirator Leidenberch (who has at this point revealed part of the secret plot), and a second co-conspirator, Modesbargen, has fled for Germany. Benevolently, Maurice offers to forgive Barnavelt: "For as *Barnauelt* is / a member of this body politique, / I honor him . . . / and, though my Enemie, while he continues / a frend to his owne fame, and loyall to / the *State*, I love him" (3.2.1191–6). The Prince's rhetoric makes him appear moderate and merciful: by his own definition Barnavelt is no longer loyal to the Republic. He has already accused the Advocate of intentionally causing religious controversy, of raising illegal armies, and of promoting a campaign of confusion in the towns and garrisons to shake the union of the Republic (1.3.519–29). He also has Leidenberch's confession, and even though the Secretary of Utrecht has apparently not yet named Barnavelt as one of the conspirators, there is every indication in the conversations between the Prince and his followers that they "know" the Advocate's part. For these reasons the viewpoints of two of Maurice's devotees, Vandort and Bredero, appear contrived mostly because they are intended to lessen the Prince's share in the persecution of his former partner and as yet to preserve his image of benevolence. The two noblemen urge the Prince to keep one (i.e., Barnavelt) that is "suspected" and "vnfit" from their councils. And Maurice of course submits, saying that he wants to please those who have looked out for his safety (3.2.1199–1216).

The Prince next suggests that for the sake of peace and quiet in the nation the rebels should be left "to the scourge of their owne consciences" (1249) and not brought to trial. But the Lords again resist, claiming that "such mild proceedings in a Goverment / new settled" are "vnsafe and scandalous" and would to ourselves be "tirranie" (1254–5, 1258, 1266). Not surprisingly, the Prince relents with the simple words: "I obey you" (1279). Yet, after agreeing that Modesbargen, Grotius, and Leidenberch should be tried, he still claims he wants to stop there "and leave out Barnauelt" (1289). Again Bredero counters that "yf he be guiltie / he's to be nam'd and punishd with the rest" (1290–1). The Prince's cousin, *Graaf* (Count) William, suggests that they bring Modesbargen back from Germany because "out of him, the truth of all, / may be wroong out" (1297–8). "Since you approve it," the Prince responds, "leave that to me" (1306–7). These words *appear* to signal a slight but concrete change in the Prince's attitude. Only moments earlier he professed to be against prosecuting the Advocate, yet now he has become actively involved in bringing about his rival's downfall by seeking to arrest someone whom he believes can testify against Barnavelt. I use the word *appear* advisedly here because we know from the

Prince's earlier call for a "sodaine, and strong prevention" (545) that action against the Advocate has long been foremost on his mind.

The scene in which Maurice learns of the suicide of his prisoner, Leidenberch, is an example of a Machiavellian political sensibility increasingly noticeable in the Prince's activities. Fully conscious of the extensive popular support Barnavelt and his faction enjoy, the Prince shrewdly coaches Vandort, Bredero, and other Lords of State on how to minimize the political fall-out that may result if the people hold the new government responsible for the prisoner's death. Ironically, it is Barnavelt, not the Prince, who is responsible for the suicide. Yet this irony only implicates the Prince even more deeply as a political strategist who exercises his free will; instead of relying on the truth and the "divine determinism" that produced it, or on justice, or on the special honor of the Soldier-Prince, he opts for a manipulative approach to the situation:

> I moued your lordships
> to a mild, and sweet proceeding in this business
> that nothing might be construde in't malitious,
> and make the world beleeue or owne ends wrought it,
> now it concernes ye to put on more strictnes
> and with seveerer eyes to looke into it,
> you robb yorselves of yor owne rightes els, Iustice
> and loose those pious names, yor Cuntries safeties:
> and sodainely this must be don, and constantly
> the powre ye hold els, wilbe scornd, & laughd at
> and theis vnchristian stroakes, be laid to yor charge.
> (4.2.1824–34)

In this analysis worthy of Machiavelli's best students, the Prince demonstrates that he has no illusions about the true basis of political power. Justice, rights, pious names, power, and the safety of the country are all considered to be directly dependent upon a carefully contemplated and managed political course of action. The reference to "these vnchristian stroakes" marks a simple but powerful contrast between Maurice's public persona and his behind-the-scenes actions because it emphasizes precisely how *un*-Christian his strategies and procedures are. Lest we are not persuaded by these instances, Massinger and Fletcher offer a brief yet potent clue during a debate between Barnavelt's executioners. The executioner from Utrecht proudly proclaims to possess "the Sword that cutt Pompeis head" (2738), which shall shortly "moaw the head of Monsieur *Barnauelt*" (2742). The Utrechter indeed wins the job in a game of dice; but Pompey, it will be remembered, was not tried, sentenced, and executed by any court of law. Fleeing from Julius Caesar and seeking asylum in the court of Ptolemy, he was betrayed and *assassinated* brutally in full view of his wife.

The detail can hardly be accidental, and places the assassin's sword – not the sword of justice – in the hands of the Prince of Orange.

I am of course not suggesting that private action and providentialism are mutually exclusive. What I am suggesting is that the Prince himself expounds an *extreme* providential view, a view that excludes personal action. Indeed, Maurice's divine explanations are even less palatable than those of that other well-known invoker of God's "arm," Henry V. Unlike Henry's invocations, which are really not designed to conceal Henry's own hand in the military victory (they are intended to obscure the illegitimacy of his crown), Maurice's jarring invocations are meant to camouflage his political chicanery. Or, perhaps more appropriate given the references to Pompey, we should consider an analogy between Shakespeare's Julius Caesar and the Prince of Orange. Eager to portray himself as the reluctant ruler, Maurice resembles Shakespeare's Caesar who repeatedly refuses the crown that he longs for with all his heart, and which he eventually intends to accept.

In the course of the drama, then, Fletcher and Massinger dissolve the image of the heroic Captain-General who only wishes to serve his country, and they substitute for it a picture of a highly skilled political manipulator who gradually seizes complete control over the Republic, and who comes to be addressed as "yor Highnes" (5.1.2633). However, as I have attempted to demonstrate, we get glimpses of the seeds of the Prince's political ambitions already in the early parts of the tragedy. Hence the playwrights are perfectly consistent with *their* version of the Prince's character when they freely deviate from history and explicitly identify Prince Maurice – rather than the tribunal of twenty-four judges – as the source of Barnavelt's death sentence.[30] Indeed, Massinger and Fletcher's silence about the judicial panel is clearly strategic. Historically, the panel was obviously intended to deflect the responsibility for Oldenbarnevelt's death away from Maurits. As scholars have determined, however, the panel itself was unconstitutional. "Never before . . . had anyone been arrested in any province by the States General without the prior approval of the States of that province, and the resolution itself [to arrest Oldenbarnevelt] was formally invalid, lacking as it did the vote of Holland. For all Maurice's concern to keep legality on his side, the arrest was an act of revolution" (Rowen, *Princes of Orange* 50). Maurits's was an act of legal innovation, and therefore it makes good sense for Massinger and Fletcher to eliminate the tribunal from the historical scenario and stress to the audience who the actual driving force behind the proceedings is.

Accordingly, Massinger and Fletcher do not present the Advocate's punishment as an act of divine or even social justice; rather they offer it as an act necessary for the maintenance of political power. "To affright the rest," the Prince asserts, "I hold it fitt, that *Barnauelt*, one that has / most frends, and meanes to hurt, and will fall therefore / with greater terror, should receive his Sentence, / then dye as he deserves" (5.1.2564–8). Maurice clearly intends to utilize the public execution of the Advocate as a theatrical event the "terror" of which will "affright" his political opponents at this volatile historical moment. The dramatists add emphasis to this point by yet another deviation from the historical proceedings. A historical court of justice convincted Leidenberch (then already seven months dead) of a capital offense, and sentenced him (that is, his "unburied corpse, reduced to the condition of a mummy"[31]) to be hanged, but in the play it is Maurice himself who comes up with the grisly idea. So that "the world shall know, that what's iust we dare do," the Prince declares, Leidenberch's coffin shall be "hangd vp on the publique Gallowes" (5.1.2700, 2703) next to Barnavelt. Maurice then goes on to assert that hanging Leidenberch's coffin will have maximum impact on the people. His words are simple: hang the coffin so that all may learn that there is "one aboue" who punishes evil. The acknowledged causality of course gives the Prince away. God's judgment follows the horrific human spectacle, and not the other way around. God's judgment is visible only after human spectacle; and what we see here is the depreciation of providential historiography.

These gruesome details aside, it is important to note here that in exposing a profoundly manipulative dimension in the Prince's character, Massinger and Fletcher are not denouncing political behavior per se. Rather, they seem intent on exposing those who efface the political process which sustains their power. And what better place to conduct this exposition than the theater, the place that "stages" the mechanics of power naturally by virtue of its own conventions. "I shall not play my last Act worst," (5.1.2694) says Barnavelt when he receives his death sentence. He knows and acknowledges the nature of his role. Those "that are [Barnavelt's] Iudges now, like Clyents / haue wayted on him, the whole Court attending / when he was pleasd to speake, and with such murmors / as glad Spectators in the Theater / grace their best Actors with" (5.1.2474–8). The relationship between the Advocate and his spectators is well defined. He performs, as does an actor, and the audience applauds. In the case of Prince Maurice and his audiences, the relationship is more ambiguous and more complex because he mystifies the basis of his power and legitimacy by locating it in a realm that is extra-social and ultimately controlled by "one aboue." Barnavelt fears that he may be losing his audience, and hence lose his ability to write his own history, but he is still quite capable of debunking the Prince's providentialist rhetoric.

The play certainly has no sympathy for the Advocate's motives of anger and frustrated pride, but it does offer unqualified praise of his lifelong political accomplishments (4.5.2179–80, 2312–17, 2247–9). The elder statesman himself announces repeatedly that the Republic will be lost without him. In one of those instances in which the haughty are right, he says to Maurice: "And here I prophecie, I that haue lyvd / and dye a free man, shall, when I am ashes / be sensible of yor groanes, and wishes for me; / and when too late you see this Goverment / changd [to a Monarchie][32] to another forme, you'll howle in vaine / and wish you had a *Barnauelt* againe" (4.5.2441–6). Although the Dutch Republic did not officially become a monarchy under the rule of Maurits, Barnavelt's political prophecy is born out since by 1625, the year of Maurits's death, the Republic was in shambles and once again trapped under the oppressive yoke of Spanish rule – the very burden from which Oldenbarnevelt's lifelong political labors had delivered it.[33] George Buc's substitution in the passage just quoted of "to another forme" for "to a Monarchie" of course reflects his "proper" desire not to see the name of "Monarchie" sullied on the public stage. Yet we have to wonder how effective Buc is, for in the context of the play what form other than monarchy could Barnavelt possibly have in mind? What is more, it is quite interesting in itself that the king's censor would excise a reference to a country becoming a monarchy. After all, James's own writings admitted candidly that countries which now were monarchies had not always been so. This state of affairs, the King maintained, did not weaken his arguments in favor of absolute monarchy as the best and most natural form of government. So why would Buc change the play text on this score? Even though the word is uttered by the Arminian, republican conspirator, it seems undeniable that the playwrights have managed to give "Monarchie" a decidedly negative connotation by conveying that a transition from republic to monarchy is undesirable – why otherwise would the censor not applaud that aspect of Barnavelt's prediction?

Significantly, Buc's excision also signals a response to a shift in Massinger and Fletcher's use of historiographical method. There was a prohibition against the portrayal of living heads of state on the stage. Strictly speaking the ban should not apply to the Prince of Orange who, as general of the Republic's armed forces, is not a head of state. Nonetheless, Orange's princely title and ample reputation cause Buc to conceive of him at times as a head of state. Near the beginning of the drama, Buc diligently enforces the dictate against the portrayal of living princes on the stage with respect to the Prince of Orange. In the margin of the passage in which the prince is kept waiting outside the council chamber, Buc writes: "I like not this: neithe^{r} do I think y$^{t.}$ the pr. was thus disgracefully vsed. besides he is to much presented" (388–93). The last sentence is most relevant here because it displays a focus on "great men" and the portrayal of their actions, and hence follows the edicts of early humanist historiography. Yet, near the end of the drama, when Buc deletes "Monarchie" and replaces it with "another forme" he is clearly *not* protecting the Prince of Orange any more – the figure to whom this heinous act is attributed. Here Buc does not insist in the margin that Maurice would never do such a thing; indeed, it seems that Buc has no protective concern whatsoever for the "great man" Maurice. He clearly leaves open the possibility that Maurice might in fact bring about *a* constitutional change in the Republic (a grave accusation which the historical Maurits vehemently denied, and which Oldenbarnevelt claimed never to have made [Rowen, *Princes of Orange* 51; Motley, vol. III, 171]), as long as that change is not to a monarchy. In short, an interest in great personalities gives way to an interest in the public representation of the inception of the institution of a monarchy.[34] Uncannily, it was at the time of these events that Maurits became a "Prince" by right. Philip William, his older brother, died in Brussels on 20 February 1618, and Maurits officially became "Prince of Orange." The fact that hitherto Maurits had only been a count (*graaf*) is the type of detail that might easily have escaped the attention of two English playwrights; but not so. Grotius, one of Barnavelt's supporters, notes the change in a defiant and contemptuous speech. Vowing to defend the freedom he was born with, he says: "they dare not [arrest me]: / or if they should, I will not suffer it / I that haue without dread, ever maintaind / the freedom I was borne to, against all / that ever haue provoakd me, will not feare / what this old *Graue*, or this new *Prince* of *Orange* / dare vndertake" (3.5.1594–1600). And, finally, although Maurits was not in fact a monarch, "he *was* the head of a princely family which was widely thought to have monarchical ambitions, so that he offered a unique context within which the nature of contemporary monarchy might be atomised."[35]

The institutional shift is also strongly evident in a passage immediately following his arrest, in which Barnavelt, adopting the semblance of the humanist historian, draws a provocative analogy between the present and an episode in Roman history. "*Octauius*, when he did affect the Empire, / and strove to thread vpon the neck of *Rome*, / and all hir auncient freedoms, [took that course][36] / cutt of his opposites. / [that now is practisd on yo^u]: for the *Cato's* / and all free speritts slaine, or els proscribd / that durst have stird against him, he then sceasd / the absolute rule of all: [you can apply this]" (2434–40). The conspicuous shift in this example, of course, is again from republic to absolutist state (empire or monarchy). And again, the language used to convey this meaning suggests a strong distaste for absolutist forms of government. Absolutism tramples "free speritts" and "auncient [republican] freedoms" and "cutt[s] of his opposites." Notably, Barnavelt's example neither tries to establish Octavius and Cato as characters to which the audience is to have an emotional response, nor does it add anything to our knowledge of them. The names Cato and Octavius merely invoke well-known political values: the preservation of the republic and its freedoms versus the destruction of those freedoms. Barnavelt emphasizes that it is the Dutch Republic's very form of government that hangs in the balance – something which far transcends the life of any individual.[37]

Howard-Hill explains that for George Buc "the crucial line here was the appeal to the audience to 'apply' the analogy of Octavius and Cato to the present circumstances, which meant not only Barnavelt's situation in the play vis-à-vis Orange, but James, his assertion of absolute rule over the prerogatives of Parliament . . . and the severe restrictions on all forms of dissent during his reign" (Howard-Hill, "Buc" 59). Of course Howard-Hill is right, but we have to wonder if the deletion of "you can apply this" would make the intended analogy any less lucid to anyone who knew anything about humanist historiography or the universal credo that literature teaches by example. Indeed, the analogy between Octavius and Maurice obviously remains (despite the deletion of "that now is practisd on yo^{u}") for what else could Barnavelt possibly mean? And where there is one analogy. . . .[38]

James's theories of kingship usually differed notably from his practice,[39] but it was precisely those theories of absolutism and rule by divine right that both Parliament and the Church had to contend with on a regular basis. "Fears that [James] intended to rule England as [an] absolute monarch – subordinating the law of the land to [his] own wishes – were closely associated with the fact that absolutist theories were voiced with increasing frequency in the early seventeenth century, particularly by clergymen."[40] The danger was, many feared, that the King believed he had the ultimate right to exclude, whenever he deemed it necessary, Parliament, the Church, and the nation as a whole from discourses of power, and to mystify and privatize the decision making process in the person of the monarch. Jonathan Goldberg observes that when James spoke of "'the mystery of the Kings power'" before the Star Chamber in 1616, he meant by that "the center of the royal sphere of power, an inner sanctum from which all subjects were excluded – or almost all."[41] The language to warrant popular fears concerning Jamesian absolutism is already manifest in the King's *The Trew Law of Free Monarchies* (1598), but it is articulated particularly well in the 1610 Speech to Parliament. James maintained:

> it is sedition in subiects, to dispute what a King may do in the height of his power: But iust Kings will euer be willing to declare what they will do, if they will not incurre the curse of God. I wil not be content that my power be disputed vpon: but I shal euer be willing to make the reason appeare of all my doings, and rule my actions according to my Lawes.[42]

The possessive in "my Lawes" is not to be taken lightly here for the King firmly believed that all law originated with the monarch, and that he therefore was above the law (although he, paradoxically, also promised to obey it, even though the law could not compel him to do so).[43] For a Jacobean audience, the "auncient freedoms" in Barnavelt's speech must evoke, if not actually refer to, the freedoms contained in the ancient constitution or common law upon which James repeatedly tried to infringe with his royal prerogative. The fear was that the essence of James's ideology of kingship entailed the de-politicization of monarchial rule by barring the people from the decision making process. As "God's lieutenant" and "Father" of his country, the King declared himself willing to announce or even explain royal decisions to his subjects, but these decisions were to be final, absolute, and not a matter for political debate. The origin of political action would become shrouded in the monarch's mysterious and to others inaccessible relationship with God, to whom alone he was ultimately accountable in all matters.[44] Hence, despite often drawing on historical examples to buttress his claims, it should be stressed that James's arguments inevitably elide history and historical argumentation. It is this retreat into mystery and exclusivity, this evasion suggesting that "history was largely irrelevant to politics" (Sommerville, *Politics and Ideology* 49), that Massinger and Fletcher seek to impede in their play.

There was significant support for James's ideas, but, not surprisingly, they also met with much consternation and opposition among those who contended that the king's puissance originated with the people, who had freely transferred their power to the king, and who allowed him to rule with their *consent*. This view of kingship at least implied the possibility of the people's withdrawal of their consent.[45] As Richard Dutton contends, "the references [in *Barnavelt*] to 'auncient freedomes' and 'free speritts' and the accused dying 'a free man' might very well be construed as emotional appeals to (English) common law, against the 'absolute rule' of the 'Monarchie,' or James's insistence upon his divine right" (Dutton, *Mastering the Revels* 215). Massinger and Fletcher speak out strongly against deification and privatization and in favor of the recognition that power rises from below – from history – and does not descend from above, from a divine source. "[W]hat is this man, this *Prince*, this god ye make now," Barnavelt asks Bredero, "but what or hands haue molded, wrought to fashion, / and by or constant labors, given a life to?" (3.1.1129–31). Why "must we fall before him, now, adoare him / . . . worship the Image we set up orselves"? (1132, 1134). Such words, spoken publicly in a nation with a king who claimed his powers to be divine rather than historical, can only be construed as deeply subversive insofar as they make available a language that challenges James's ostensibly metahistorical theories head on. That the character that utters the heresies is finally found guilty of treason and beheaded does not in any way alter the fact that he enjoyed ample opportunity to parade across the Globe's stage.

IV

How is it that a play this subversive ever saw the light of day in a time when the royal family controlled the public playhouses? One way of answering the question is to point out that Massinger and Fletcher's drama *can* be read as a piece of pro-Jamesian political and religious propaganda.

There is good reason to believe that James exploited the developments in the Dutch Republic to shape not only his foreign policy with both the Netherlands and Spain but also to calm suspicions about his seemingly peculiar religious policies at home. Such exploitation was possible because in 1619 the complex debate on political and religious issues was shaped not only by internal considerations but also by England's relations with the Dutch Provinces and Spain.[46] *Barnavelt* reflects some of James's essential political and religious strategies. Despite the peace of 1604, traditional anti-Spanish and anti-Catholic feelings were still going strong in England. This popular sentiment, however, was nullified to some extent by James's desire to establish harmonious relations between the Churches of England and Rome, and also by his renewed efforts to marry the Prince of Wales to the Spanish Infanta Maria. As Nicholas Tyacke testifies, "By 1618 there was [again] talk of tolerating Catholicism, as a condition of the Spanish marriage. The concomitant of this would be a slump in demand for polemic against the popish Antichrist, and tighter government control over the diversity of Protestant practice" (Tyacke, "Puritanism" 127).[47] Furthermore, James already afforded the Arminians considerable toleration, even though the members of this sect, as noted earlier, were likened routinely to the Catholics because of their mutual rejection of Calvinist predestinarian views: Catholics and Arminians were equally charged with popery. James, however, approved of the Arminians' "lack of fanaticism," and their tradition of support for the royal prerogative.[48]

What is more, although first a Calvinist, James wanted to be thought of primarily as a peacemaker, not a religious ideologue. To that purpose he had married his daughter, Elizabeth, to the Protestant Elector Palatine, Frederick (a move generally applauded), and was now trying to balance the religious scales by marrying his son Charles into the Habsburg dynasty. The outbreak of the Thirty Year War in 1618 of course spoiled James's policy. When the Protestant citizens of the Bohemian Estates removed their Catholic ruler, Ferdinand II (a young Habsburg prince), and offered the position to Frederick, many Protestants in Europe hailed the move as a potentially crushing blow to Spanish dominance (Cogswell, "England" 113–14).[49] But James, despite his Protestant roots, was simultaneously outraged that a people would rise against their lawful monarch and deeply embarrassed by the affront to the Habsburg family by his own son-in-law. He therefore pleaded (in vain) with Frederick not to accept the crown. James's move baffled and angered many English Protestants.

The *Barnavelt* play found its narrow niche in this complex historical moment. One could argue that its proud Arminian protagonist was allowed on the stage because of the perceived lull in anti-Catholic rhetoric. But it is more likely that the censor perceived the Barnavelt character as wholly negative, and that the play therefore marks the historical moment in which James *publicly* reaffirmed his ties with Protestantism and asserts his opposition to the Arminian and Catholic religions. Such a reaffirmation had become necessary by 1619.

In the context of James's religious policy, Massinger and Fletcher's story of Barnavelt clearly counteracts the King's seemingly inexplicable decision (from a Protestant point of view) not to throw his support behind his son-in-law. It acts as a piece of pro-James religious propaganda. By allowing an overtly anti-Arminian play on the public stage, the censor seems to be saying to his audience that their King is very much anti-popery, even while the King is still pursuing a pro-Spanish marriage policy. As if there was any doubt, the play makes the link between Arminianism and Catholicism (and between Dutch and English politics of religion) explicit just before Barnavelt is beheaded. Scolding Barnavelt, one of the lords says:

> Examine all men
> branded wth such fowle syns as yo^{u} now dye for,
> and yo^{u} shall find their first stepp still, Religion:
> *Gowrie* in *Scotland*, 'twas his maine pretention:
> was not he honest too? his Cuntries Father?
> those fyery Sperrits next, that hatchd in England
> that bloody Powder-Plot; and thought like meteors
> to haue flashd their Cuntryes peace out in a Moment
> were not their Barrels loden wth Religion? (5.3.2938–46)

These analogies sound out of place coming from a Dutch lord, but they must have been music to an English government trying to certify publicly its anti-Catholicism to its suspicious citizens. To be sure, Massinger and Fletcher did not intend to be the monarch's mouthpiece; on the contrary, the government paid a significant price because the play's anti-Arminian stance allowed it to present an even more pronounced anti-absolutist point of view (even though, as we saw, the censor tried to tone down that point of view).

As Tyacke suggests, the apparent threat against Protestants in England did not materialize because of the "political crisis in the Low Countries, which was deemed to affect England's foreign policy interests" ("Puritanism" 127). James's decision, in part for theological reasons, to back Prince Maurits and the Calvinists against Oldenbarnevelt and the Arminians marks a resolute reversal of his religious policies (128). Yet when it came to the Dutch Republic James was clearly of two minds. He pursued the Spanish match, but he also followed Elizabeth's practice of supporting the Dutch war effort against Spain,[50] even though he shared his predecessor's view of the Dutch rebellion against the Spanish monarch as unlawful. But aside from these religious and ideological considerations, James understood quite well that until peace with Spain was somehow guaranteed England was better served by a small and strong but non-aggressive Dutch Republic (which, despite intense commercial rivalry, also happened to be an excellent trading partner) for its most immediate neighbor than by the presence of King Philip III's army and navy permanently deployed along the North Sea coast. England's support of the Dutch Republic, therefore, quite selfishly aimed to keep the Spanish forces at bay in the southern provinces, and to preserve a strong sense of unity within the Republic itself.[51] When in March of 1617 this unity became increasingly tested in the sharpening national religious and political debate between the Arminian and the Calvinist factions, James wrote to the States-General of the United Provinces in an effort to soothe the situation and warn against the "unhappy divisions, which we see ready to hatch forth in schism and faction formed among you, which are . . . pernicious to your state . . . [which] is only in its infancy[,] and that the basis of survival consists only in your union, first toward God and then toward faith among yourselves" (Akrigg, *Letters* 359). The Republic can hope to survive only if it holds firm "the universal consent of the Reformed Churches"; only then can "the close friendship which has reigned for so long a time between [the English] crown and [the] provinces" be maintained. James's words clearly blend good advice with a veiled threat.

By 1609 Oldenbarnevelt had achieved a truce with Spain, which he knew was conducive to foreign trade, the lowering of back-breaking wartime taxes, and much needed political stability.[52] Prince Maurits, on the other hand, was a military man who gained prominence through soldierly exploits. Peace with Spain would inevitably mean a decline of his power (Israel, *Dutch Republic* 60). For this reason, primarily, he opposed the peace and sided with England, which also benefited from the Dutch conflict with Spain. In the end, however, Maurits acquiesced to Oldenbarnevelt's drive for peace, and accepted the Twelve Year Truce with Spain. James's politics were revealed when in 1613 he invested Maurits with the Order of the Garter, both to honor the Prince and to bind him to a vigorous anti-

Spanish and anti-French policy (den Tex, *Oldenbarnevelt* 201). Bestowing such a great honor on Maurits but not on Oldenbarnevelt deliberately ignored the Advocate's invaluable contribution to the Dutch enterprise. As den Tex points out, James and Secretary Winwood longed for the fall of the Advocate, who intended clearly to pursue a Dutch foreign policy not controlled by the English king (*Oldenbarnevelt* 201).

Furthermore, James strongly objected to Oldenbarnevelt's "heretical" support for the Arminian faction of the Dutch Church. James, as the head of a Church of England that was inclined "towards the doctrines of Calvin of Geneva on such a disputed subject as predestination,"[53] had spoken out consistently and strongly against Arminian doctrine (which made a claim for a causal connection between the individual free will and salvation), and which was gradually gaining support in England itself.[54] James and Oldenbarnevelt had clashed as early as 1611 over the appointment of theologian Conradus Vorstius to the University of Leiden. Oldenbarnevelt had selected the German thinker[55] with the reasonable expectation that as a neutral outsider the theologian would be tolerant of the Arminian cause. James, however, believed that Vorstius was much too close to the Arminian position and responded by having the theologian's writings burned in London, Oxford, and Cambridge, and by demanding he be deposed and exiled. In case these demands were not met, he would file an open protest and sever the bond between the Provinces and reformed church communities of Germany, France, and England. In the end, King and Advocate both had to compromise, and Vorstius was dismissed but not banished, nor were his doctrines officially condemned in the Dutch Republic (den Tex, *Oldenbarnevelt* 184–8).

The Vorstius affair behind, James wrote to the Dutch States-General in 1617 and advocated elimination of certain religious topics from the sermon. For the sake of political and religious unity and "solid edification," he urged, Dutch ministers ought not to devote themselves "to preaching the manner of predestination . . . which is too high and too obscure for the ordinary people" (Akrigg, *Letters* 358). Not surprisingly, the King's convictions in this matter did not differ very much from those of his Ambassador, Dudley Carleton, outlined earlier. In 1617, James again revealed how profoundly disturbed he was by the growing religious schism in the Republic, which he felt threatened the very structure of the society. James was particularly alarmed by the chance that a torn and therefore militarily weakened Dutch Republic might facilitate the King's worst nightmare: an alliance between Spain and France (den Tex, *Oldenbarnevelt* 220).[56] In his letter of 20 March 1617, to the Dutch States-General, James urged that if, "by this time, the evil [Arminian doctrine] is so strong and so rooted among your people that it cannot be so promptly and readily eradicated, we beseech you at least to arrest the danger of it . . . until you can with a common mind convoke a national synod" (Akrigg, *Letters* 359).

Oldenbarnevelt and his supporters ignored the warning (den Tex, *Oldenbarnevelt* 220). Carleton, however, published the letter (an act which understandably outraged Oldenbarnevelt), and fueled the growing discontent in the Dutch provinces of Zeeland and Friesland (222). The domestic and foreign pressure on the religious question mounted on Oldenbarnevelt, and it was only Prince Maurits's circumspection (for fear of losing his office) that allowed Oldenbarnevelt to continue his opposition for another year (225). It is probably only a coincidence that, in August of 1618, about seventeen months after James had urged the arrest of the evil Arminian doctrine, Oldenbarnevelt was in fact arrested by Prince Maurits. Yet James and England clearly benefited insofar as they benefited from a renewal of hostilities between the Republic and Spain. "The drive against Oldenbarnavelt and the pro-Remonstrant regents ended by removing from power the group which had negotiated the Twelve Year Truce and forced it through. Maurits's *coup d'etat* was thus also an attack on the truce" (Israel, *Dutch Republic* 62).

If the arrest of Oldenbarnevelt was not performed at the explicit behest of James, the tremendous influence of the English delegation to the National Synod at Dort on 13 November of the same year can hardly be construed as a purely religious event that also happened to be a fortuitous political coincidence. Following James's instructions, the gathering at the Synod "proceeded to condemn the Arminian theology of grace, and affirm its Calvinist converse" (Tyacke, "Puritanism" 128). The double-edged character of James's religious policy is evident here: less than a year after the King relented to Spanish theologians who demanded greater tolerance for English Catholics if the marriage negotiations between Charles and Maria were to proceed, he helped destroy the Arminian religion at Dort. Without a doubt, intervention in the Synod constituted excellent public relations for a king who was losing the confidence of a portion of his Protestant constituency back home.

James's influence at Dort was quite apparent, but on other occasions he also operated behind the scenes. A letter written by Secretary Winwood to Carleton on behalf of James reveals that there was a private correspondence between the monarch and Prince Maurits in which they discussed and manipulated the direction the Dutch Republic was to take. In the letter, Winwood speaks of two identical letters, one addressed to the Dutch Parliament, which is to be delivered *only* after Maurits is given the opportunity to inspect the other copy. If the Prince is not satisfied with its content, Winwood tells Carleton, the letter to the Parliament must be "suppressed."[57] This subversion of proper protocol borders on state treason for we recall that Maurits, despite his stadtholdership, was merely a *servant* of the States General (a fact noted by Massinger and Fletcher [1.2.305–6]), and not their political equal or superior.[58] Certainly, Maurits had no authority to decide what should or should not be submitted to the States General. Indeed, Massinger and Fletcher's Barnavelt may not be far from the historical truth when he names "the King of *Britaine*" his "greatest Enemy" (4.5.1167–8).

Massinger and Fletcher's *Barnavelt* can easily be read as a piece of religious propaganda for the home front, a play denouncing Arminians and popery in order to calm jittery Protestants. Yet this religious message comes at a significant political price to James. For the much maligned Barnavelt is hardly an effective spokesman for Arminianism; his concern is with the political future of the Republic. Hence the Arminian-bashing engaged in by some of the Advocate's political opponents is largely ineffective; their charges of heresy barely cloud the substance of his political views.[59]

V

If it was the solemn task of the Master of the Revels to transform dramas into expressions of state ideology (or, at least, prevent subversive scripts from being staged), then he clearly failed in his duties in the instance of *Barnavelt*. At the very least, to reiterate Howard-Hill's observation, Buc should have magnified Orange. There should be at least a recognition, if not a celebration, of his victory. Yet the playwrights apparently see no cause for celebration. If at the close of Shakespeare's *Richard III* Henry Richmond is there to heal the wounds of civil strife and inaugurate a new peace, the final moments of *Barnavelt* are hollow, dark and grisly. The Prince of Orange, the figure who will lead the Dutch Republic after Barnavelt's death, is conspicuously absent (and has been so for the last two scenes, almost three hundred lines) as the inept executioner lops off not only the Advocate's head but also some of his fingers (an ahistorical detail added, no doubt, in part to underscore the nastiness of the whole affair). "You have strooke his fingers too," says one of the lords presiding over the execution, but, he adds with an apology that reeks of political expediency, "we forgive your haste" (2996–7).

The staging of the Advocate's untimely death is a subversive act, and the (fictional) detail of the butchered hand fiendishly satirizes the state's awesome power to disfigure or execute its citizens almost at will. As James Shapiro observes, the renaissance theater only rarely appropriated state-sanctioned methods of public execution for the public stage.[60] The theater habitually stages stabbings, shootings, poisonings, slitting of throats, but only rarely do we see characters decapitated, hanged, or burned at the stake

("Tragedies" 100). Playwrights had good reason not to simulate public executions. "[T]o imitate state spectacle," Shapiro explains, "could undermine the terrible power of officially sanctioned violence by showing it often enough to make it familiar or by resituating it within ethically and politically ambiguous contexts" (100). This explanation is indebted to the work of Foucault, who argued that instances of "public execution . . . coronation, entry of the king into a conquered city, the submission of rebellious subjects" belong to "a whole series of great rituals in which [state] power is eclipsed and restored."[61] The idea is not only that these types of events reestablish justice or order but that they *reactivate* state power. If Foucault is right about the importance of rituals for the maintenance of state power, and if Shapiro is correct in his assertion that renaissance dramatists shied away from reenacting state-sanctioned modes of execution in order not to compete with the state in this area, then Massinger and Fletcher's dramatic rendition of Barnavelt's death must be considered an infringement on that power. It cheapens and deflates the ritual through appropriation and repetition (in a fictional setting) and it lampoons the state by depicting it as inept in performing the very task designed to reactivate its power. "Haste" is perhaps the poorest excuse for such ineptitude.

The Prince of Orange's absence from the final scenes greatly emphasizes Massinger and Fletcher's unequivocally modern historiographical interest. As we saw in the previous chapter, Shakespeare and Fletcher's *Henry VIII* creates a space of ambiguity between agents and political actions, a distance which invalidates, or at least greatly complicates, Puttenham's conception of history as the actions of great men. But *Henry VIII*'s final scene does at least bring Henry and his infant daughter Elizabeth center stage, returning a visual sense of stability to political history. Massinger and Fletcher, on the other hand, withhold that visual spectacle, leaving the audience in part to ponder the truth of Barnavelt's chilling prediction: will the Prince of Orange take away the people's freedom and change the form of government from republic to another form? More importantly, however, the Prince's disappearance from the final scenes is highly suggestive of a passage in Foucault which I cited in the previous chapter. Foucault writes that "if it is true that Machiavelli is among the few . . . who conceived of the power of the Prince in terms of force relationships, perhaps we need to go one step further, do without the persona of the Prince, and decipher power mechanisms on the basis of a strategy that is immanent in force relationships."[62] Massinger and Fletcher took that step, leaving their audience in something of a dramatic as well as political void.

In terms of the history-play genre, all these factors indicate that Massinger and Fletcher's *Barnavelt* simply pressed further some of the changes already introduced by Shakespeare and Fletcher in *Henry VIII*.

The formal shift is even more obvious when we recall the typical Elizabethan history-play pattern as described by Alvin Kernan earlier. The order–chaos–order formula is still discernible in *Henry VIII* and *Barnavelt*, but its resolution is no longer due to the seizing of power by a single individual. The outcome of the competition between historiographies employed by Maurice and Barnavelt is indicative of this. The Machiavel Barnavelt, we can safely conclude, exposes the fraud of Maurice's providentialist historiography; and as a whole the drama withholds any evidence that God guides the hand of certain noble individuals, and crushes their heretical or rebellious opponents. The Machiavellian Barnavelt is destroyed but in the play he is *not* replaced (as he would have been in conventional providentialist historiography) with either another Machiavellian Prince (as in Shakespeare's Henry VI plays) or with a more noble figure as in *Richard III*. The Advocate's bloody beheading is followed by a perfunctory warning against vainglory, and then nothing: an empty stage, an abandoned site of a public execution.[63]

A return to the dialogue we engaged in with Leonard Tennenhouse in the previous chapter will put this in some perspective. Tennenhouse claimed that the drama and the state share rhetorical strategies idealizing state-authority. Several of Shakespeare's Elizabethan histories and comedies, he maintained, "transform patriarchal hierarchies into a state of disorder for the purpose of creating two bases for authority, and thus two competing hierarchies of power [e.g., the competition between Theseus and Egeus in *Midsummer Night's Dream*, a situation which also captures the style of Elizabeth I's rule, as well as the dual sources of her power], which only the monarch can hold together in harmonious discord. To this end, Shakespeare uses his drama to authorize political authority, and political authority as he represents it, in turn, authorizes art."[64] I agree that the cult of personality that virtually deified Elizabeth disseminated the view that only the queen could hold the factious state together; and I have already acknowledged that much Elizabethan historical drama is based on the order–chaos–order pattern. With the ascension of James I, however, Tennenhouse insists, monarchial politics changed because unlike his predecessor he did not need to acquire the signs and symbols of authorization. Elizabeth, we remember, derived her authority from *two* disparate sources: her blood connection to Henry VIII and the legal force of her father's will. When James became King of England these two forces were once again united: primogeniture and the queen's dying voice coincided. As a result, according to Tennenhouse, the genre of the history play was displaced by the masque and the romance, literary forms which more easily presented rulers as "the monolithic figure of state power" which the authors thought James – and which James thought himself – to be ("Strategies of State"

117). *Henry VIII* certainly includes a heavy dose of pageantry, aligning it closely with the masque form; but I agree with Peter Rudnytsky that most of the play's spectacle – for instance, the Field of the Cloth of Gold scene – creates an "atmosphere of uncertainty" rather than one of stability.[65]

It is easy to see that Massinger and Fletcher turn neither to romance nor to masque in *Barnavelt*. Indeed, far from searching for a literary form to express "the monolithic figure of state power," they, in apparently Elizabethan fashion – dramatic as well as historiographical – set against one another two "great men," each with his distinct source of power. However, unlike the Elizabethan model – again, dramatic as well as historiographical – they do not fully complete the pattern either by offering a figure who will temporarily triumph over adversity (and hold competing forces together in his person) or by trotting out Tennenhouse's "Jacobean" alternative: the Jamesian monolithic figure of state power. Indeed, in *Barnavelt* there is no genealogy to authorize art, as Tennenhouse would have it; there is no hereditary form of goverment. Instead Massinger and Fletcher greatly emphasize the clash between contrasting forms of government, one authoritarian, the other anti-authoritarian. Art here precisely challenges power's arbitrary link to genealogy. To claim, as one might, that the playwrights are merely adjusting their views to a foreign context is to avoid the explicit links the playwrights themselves as well as the pamphleteers draw between England and the Dutch Republic.

The concrete political impact of *Barnavelt* is of course extremely difficult to determine, but Tennenhouse is surely wrong to assert that "Only those performances could be authorised in London which in turn authorised the governing powers of that city" ("Strategies of State" 116). From the Master of the Revels' and Bishop of London's interventions we know that the play was viewed with considerable apprehension, a fact punctuated by this popular drama's absence from the printed renaissance corpus. There is little doubt that *Barnavelt* was still a seditious play after the authorities got through with it. If one views the supposedly providentialist Prince of Orange as a trusted ally or a lesser version of James, the former's clandestine and ruthless scheming tarnishes the reputation of divine right monarchy in general, and James in particular. If one prefers to consider the play's political stance, the message is even more aggressively critical of James's absolutist rhetoric and authoritarian style of rule. I do not think that George Buc or any representative of the government (if they saw it) would have judged the play a call to revolution; but it is reasonable to assume that if James had been able to presage the fateful events that were to take place outside the Banqueting House in Whitehall on 30 January 1649, he would never have allowed Barnavelt to march across the Globe stage.

6 *Perkin Warbeck* and the failure of historiography

. . . the historian in his bare "was" hath many times that which we can fortune to overrule wisdom. Many times he must tell events whereof he can yield no cause; or, if he do, it must be poetically.

Philip Sidney, *The Defence of Poesy*[1]

I

Some forty years after the publication of John Ford's *Chronicle History of Perkin Warbeck*, Charles II ordered the remains of the royal lodgings, annexed to the Tower, to be torn down and removed. When the workmen razed the external staircase that formed part of the link between the Royal Apartments and the Chapel of St. John, they uncovered "Under the bottom stair, at a depth of ten feet, . . . a wooden chest. In it were the skeletons of two children, the taller one lying on its back, the smaller one on top of it, face downwards."[2] The King's Principle Surgeon, John Knight, wrote in the same year that the bones "upon the presumptions that they were the bones of this king [the eldest son of Edward IV] and his brother Rich: D. of York, were by the command of K. Charles the 2nd put into a marble Vrn and deposited amongst the R; Family in H: 7th Chappel in Westminster at my importunity" (Williamson, *Mystery* 183).

The material connection between the discovery of the bones and Ford's play (printed in 1634) is frail at best,[3] except that the king's handling of the situation seeks to close the door on one of the great genealogical cruxes in English royal history, which also happens to be the dramatic centre of Ford's play: the fate of Richard Duke of York, King Edward's second son. It is perhaps no surprise that Charles, apparently undeterred by the many ambiguities surrounding the fate of Edward IV's sons, wasted no time in announcing the princely identity of the unearthed remains. The overhasty decision may have been motivated in part by the urge once and for all to confirm the legend that Richard III was responsible for the murder of *both* princes in the Tower, and thus to help substantiate the legitimacy of Henry Tudor's crown. Unlike Henry VII, Charles II faced no threats of Yorkist claimants to the throne. But as the newly restored king whose powers were severely restrained by a potent Parliament which included a number of vexatiously vocal republican members, Charles also had to confront grave challenges to his authority – indeed, one such challenge aimed to derail the succession of his brother James, heir to the crown.[4] Even for Charles, therefore, the supposed identification of both Edward and Richard must have tied up a historical loose end, and added welcome stability and continuity to the historical image of the Tudor–Stuart royal dynasty.

Although Charles II faced his own unique and complex set of historical circumstances, his greater interest in dynastic neatness than in historical accuracy sounds an echo of a time when there was acute apprehension about the legitimacy of Henry VII's crown, insofar as Henry's claim constituted the very basis of the providential view of English history as propounded by Tudor and Stuart governments. The Tudor government, we know, successfully solidified its hold over England, in part by propagating its self-serving view of English history through sponsoring and controlling the production of art, literature, pamphlets, entertainments, theatrical productions, and of course historical narratives. Historical narratives were encouraged to follow official ideology, which sometimes led to the historians' betrayal of their own historiographical principles, and which came at the expense of a balanced account.[5]

In its retelling of various remarkable incidents that took place in the precarious early years of the Tudor dynasty, Ford's play about Perkin Warbeck and Henry Tudor, by contrast, achieves an exceptional historiographical sophistication and independence, and startling honesty. First, the play presents a credible challenge to the official and widely accepted Tudor version of events which branded Perkin Warbeck, largely for ideological reasons, a villain and imposter. Secondly, the play stands as a corrective to the historiographical *practices* employed by renaissance historians writing about the Warbeck affair. This corrective is aimed at two pivotal facets of history-writing: the relation of "facts" to their context, as well as to the smothering impact of culturally preconceived narrative structures on those "facts." Thirdly, through an interrogation of genealogical claims and providential conceptions of history, Ford destabilizes declarations of royal ancestry and legitimacy. Fourthly, through the use of satire, Ford displaces Henry VII from the ideological center of the drama (and history), and thus debunks the popular "great men" version of history favored by the Tudor government. And, lastly, the play invites us to dwell on the theoretical and generic crux of whether *Perkin Warbeck* is a literary or an historical work. In this chapter I will argue that Ford's play can be understood simultaneously as a meditation on the powers and limitations of traditional historiographical practices, and as a work that foregrounds itself as an alternative mode of historiographical representation. The remainder of this chapter elaborates these four points. The first portion of the chapter will deal primarily with ideas of history; the second with the play.

II

In essence, the official Tudor version of the Warbeck story insists that the young man who landed on Scottish soil in 1495 proclaiming himself the Yorkist heir to the crown of England was in fact a misguided man from Flanders, a pawn abused and exploited by the enemies of England. This story, true or not, was the yarn most congenial to Henry Richmond, newly crowned Henry VII of England, whose right to rule depended squarely on the deaths of Edward V and his younger brother, the Duke of York. What is more, the whole of Tudor propaganda was geared toward the idea that it was the *sacred person* of Henry Tudor – "sent from heaven," as Ford puts it (3.1.36)[6] – who, newly married to Elizabeth of York, brought an end to God's punishment for the usurpation of Richard II, and who, through the happy union of the houses of York and Lancaster, inaugurated a new, peaceful chapter in English history (1.1.26). The frightful possibility that a Yorkist claimant with a superior birthright to Henry's might drag England back into the recent carnage of the Wars of the Roses was understood and feared by most. Hence, given how high the political stakes were, the Tudor regime concocted through patronage, censorship, and the dissemination of propaganda, a cultural and political climate in which it was to the advantage of historians to adopt a pro-Tudor version of the Warbeck episode; and we find it adopted in the labors of Raphael Holinshed, Edward Hall, Richard Grafton, Polydore Vergil, Francis Bacon, and Thomas Gainsford, among others.[7] Since the writings of these historians fed the appetite for historical knowledge of the vast majority of English men and women interested in the subject, it is no surprise that the public easily acquiesced to the Tudor spin on history, and Warbeck's devious role in it.[8] Ford suggests as much when he refers to the Warbeck affair in his prologue as a "known" story (15).

It is shocking therefore that Ford's *Chronicle History of Perkin Warbeck* is equivocal on the question of Warbeck's true origins: nothing in the play indicates conclusively that he is either Richard, Duke of York, or an imposter. Throughout the play, Warbeck eloquently maintains his birth claim, and none of his adversaries offers compelling evidence to prove him false. To make matters even more intriguing politically, the drama portrays Henry VII and Warbeck side by side and submits that it is virtually impossible for a commoner (and the theater audience?) to distinguish the founder of the Tudor line from the supposed pretender. The play's presentation of a lack of difference between Henry and Warbeck has direct bearing on divine right or providential and "great men" theories of history, for it denotes that the suits and trappings of kingship, the general ceremony, combined with a certain *acting* ability (those special "mysteries" into which King James sought to educate Charles in the *Basilikon Doron*),[9] make an ordinary person appear a king. It follows that if a common man can render himself indistinguishable from the king, the king himself has become unrecognizable and, in a sense, dispensable. Both providentialist and "great men" historiographical models are seriously weakened in the play because the recognizable centerpiece of each, the king (as hereditary ruler and God's anointed), loses some of the very aura that is supposed to differentiate him from his subjects. In the absence of such differentiation, the play indicates that the emphasis in the royal legitimation process falls less on the sacredness of personal or moral character or genealogy than on the *performance* of royal power and authority, especially as that performance is recorded for posterity by historians.

III

Ford's dramatic challenge to the official version of Warbeck's history is made possible in part by the proliferation of various methods of history-writing that took place in the sixteenth and early seventeenth centuries.[10] This fact has not yet been fully appreciated by modern criticism. Until Jonas Barish published his landmark article in 1970,[11] the prevalent view among critics was that Caroline audiences knew their history well enough not to be seduced by Warbeck's eloquence, royal bearing, and noble character, and to perceive him for the imposter he was. The implication here is, of course, that the audiences knew their *Tudor* version of history well enough, and that they would entertain no other. As it turns out, these critics themselves seem to accept the Tudor version, assuming that anything deviating from it has to be a historical ruse. These critics also suggest that Warbeck *had* to be a counterfeit, otherwise Ford "'would have been challenging the succession of the Stuarts, not to mention that of the Tudors.'"[12] The suggestion is ludicrous for it assumes that Ford was unwilling or incapable of mounting such a challenge. Barish deftly dispels these obviously prejudicial notions by privileging the play rather than the "official version of events sponsored by the ruling house," and by arguing that the drama can induce "us to unseat the received verdict on Perkin Warbeck" and "foster an ambiguity" without issuing an outright "challenge" to the established order (Barish, "*Perkin Warbeck*" 153, 152).[13]

Allowing the play to speak with its own, independent historiographical voice, Barish's balanced insight paves the way for a critical consideration of the historiographical theories and practices necessary for the production of alternative accounts of history capable of contesting the culture's governing version of the past. Ford's drama, we shall see, puts into practice a type of interpretative restraint exhorted in the very programmatic prefaces of a representative number of renaissance histories that recount the Warbeck affair, but which, ironically, are not put into *practice* in those same histories. The historians fail to practice the restraint they preach because such restraint tends to produce incomplete or imperfect and ideologically ambiguous narratives. I contend therefore that Ford's "literary" text, which *does* exercise interpretative restraint, is truer to renaissance historiographical principles than are the narratives of the historians who exhort those principles. The reason for the difference is that Ford, unlike his prose-writing colleagues, seems perfectly at ease with the realization that to "do" history means to problematize history-writing, to confront and acknowledge its limitations – not merely to elucidate the past. One strange result of all this is that Ford's play must be taken seriously as a complex historical document which serves not only as a historical representation but also as a text *about* what it means to produce such representations; as such, Ford's text is a meta-historical history play.

IV

Traditional wisdom contends that sound historical drama transcends or transforms historical reality into a primarily literary or aesthetic object. Peter Ure has argued that the question of Perkin's legitimacy becomes dissipated in Ford's *de*historicization of the subject. Ure maintains that the play offers essentially "a dramatic and literary experience" because the playwright's characterization of Perkin as convinced of his Yorkist heritage "appears independently of anything identifiable in the sources" ("Introduction" xlii, xliii). Ford, Ure propounds, "translates" narrative history into "a dramatic experience: one in which the spectators must measure the impact and appeal of Warbeck against the assured testimony of Henry and a whole range of witnesses, including the source-historians. It should be stressed that this is for the spectators primarily a dramatic and literary experience, not one in which they are asked to judge like a jury or a court of law" (xliii). Ure's position is provocative and requires a dual response. First we must consider the relationship between play and sources posited by Ure, and then determine what he means by "a dramatic and literary experience." Ure's claims, it seems, are based on the following assumptions: (1) that Ford's characterization of Warbeck is original (i.e., is not found in the sources, and that Ford's creation of Warbeck therefore is a "literary" or fictitious or ahistorical creation); (2) that Ford's audience would share this assumption; and (3) that there is a fundamental difference between a "literary" and a "historical" experience.

Some audience members, it is true, may have enjoyed the play purely as a dramatic or aesthetic fiction, but it is equally certain that a majority of playgoers had acquired through the popular narrative histories at least a basic knowledge of English history and the Tudor myth. F. J. Levy observes that already by the middle of

> the 1580's a typical Englishman must have found it more and more difficult to avoid having any knowledge of the past. Regardless of his purse or background, or his tastes, sooner or later he was bound to be exposed to history. A scholar would have his Camden, a courtier his Daniel or Drayton; a merchant his choice among historians, including Stow and Holinshed, while his apprentice could enjoy the ditties of Deloney. Any or all of them might have gone to the theater; or, if they lived in the country, not uncommonly the theater came to them.[14]

On the basis of such widespread knowledge of historical matters it seems mistaken to conclude that *Perkin Warbeck* provided primarily a "literary experience"; for the individuals described by Levy a viewing of Ford's play would have *had* to include a consideration of the historicity of the play's main character, and, inevitably, a judgment regarding his *legal* status vis-à-vis the Tudor dynasty. Ford himself expresses his estimation of his public's erudition when he refers to the Warbeck saga as "known" and "famous" in the prologue to the play (Prologue 15, 16). No doubt the reference to the story as "known," followed by a radically alternative version of it, is meant to provoke a historical judgment.

Secondly, Ford's rendition of Perkin Warbeck is not an imaginative, or fictitious or literary creation in the conventional sense intended by Ure.[15] It is arguable, if not simply wrong, to assert that Warbeck's unshakable faith in his Yorkist heritage is wholly *independent* of "anything identifiable in the sources" (Ure, "Introduction" xlii.); it all depends on *how* one reads those sources. A discerning reader (i.e., one who is not a Tudor apologist) will have little difficulty extracting evidence from the prose histories suggesting that Warbeck's cause may have been genuine. While almost all the sources denounce Warbeck as an imposter, they do so only after emphasizing certain qualities in him that precisely suggest he is *not* an imposter. It is as if the texts that speak out against Perkin Warbeck simultaneously and ventriloquistically speak out for him by speaking *of* him.[16] In a different context, Pierre Macherey argues successfully that

> If one is going to speak out against the people, effectively, one must speak *of* the people: they must be seen, given form, *allowed to speak*. Like eulogy, condemnation is not in itself enough: the ideological claim inevitably requires a presentation and a disclosure; then the argumentation turns into style. In proportion to its double meaning, [the] text makes possible a double reading: the reductive reading attends

only to the explicit; a different reading will try to extricate the conditions which make its utterance possible. (*Theory* 265)

As Stephen Greenblatt observes, when a culture records alien voices, even if it is for the purpose of studying, disciplining, correcting, and transforming them, the acknowledgment of the existence of those voices creates a "momentary sense of instability."[17] The treatment of the mysterious upstart from Flanders apparently warrants such treatment, with similar results. If the "pretender" is to be condemned, if the government is to speak out effectively against him, to study him, discipline him, and ultimately transform (i.e., expose) him, then he must be seen, given form, and be allowed to speak. Francis Bacon's assessment, for instance, of Warbeck as a man who, "himself, with long and continued counterfeiting and with oft telling a lie, was turned by habit almost into the thing he seemed to be, and from a liar to a believer" (Bacon, *History* 136) clearly condemns the man, but when we purge Bacon's judgment of its "official" prejudice (i.e., the word "counterfeiting"), his estimation reads something like this: Warbeck appears to believe himself to be who he says he is.[18] This, of course, would not be unusual if Warbeck was in fact the Duke of York. But there are more illuminating examples of this type of ventriloquism which, even while toting the government's line, express tremendous awe and wonder at the apparent authenticity of his majesty. A sense of admiration and amazement shines through powerfully in all the narratives, even though this sense is of course always officially repressed or repudiated in the end. A couple of examples will illustrate the point.

The words of Raphael Holinshed and Polydore Vergil, in particular, may have prodded Ford to create his controversial Warbeck figure. If we drop the word "counterfeit" from Holinshed's description, it underscores my paraphrase of Bacon: "[Perkin] kept such a princelie countenance, and so counterfeit the maiestie roiall, that all men in manner did firmelie beleeue, that he was extracted of the noble house and familie of the dukes of Yorke."[19] Polydore, the influential Italian humanist historian commissioned by Henry VII to write a history of Britain, also incessantly notes the falsity of Warbeck's claim, but admits that

The more the deceit was given an appearance of truth, the more people professed that they believed the youth to have escaped the hand of King Richard by divine intervention and had been led safely to his aunt [Margaret of Burgundy]. The rumour of so miraculous an occurrence rapidly spread to neighbouring countries and even more quickly crossed into England, where the story was not merely believed by the common people, but where there were many important men who considered the matter as genuine.[20]

A little later in his account Polydore notes: "the rumour of Richard, the resuscitated duke of York, had divided nearly all England into factions, filling the minds of men with hope or fear" (*Anglica Historia* 67), and that upon meeting Perkin in Flanders Sir "Robert [Clifford] forwith believed him to be of royal descent" (69).[21] The historian Edward Hall "adds an account of [Henry VII] sending spies to gather evidence, promising a reward to the person who would solve the *mystery* of Perkin's origin."[22] Such a move suggests that Henry himself may have been uncertain, or, at the very least, that he needed information to convince others. Readers of these accounts who possessed no independent evidence to the contrary may well have come to believe that Perkin Warbeck was indeed who he said he was. Holinshed goes so far as to report that Clifford "knew him to be Edwards sonne by his face, and other lineaments of his bodie" (*Chronicles* 506), even though Holinshed too insists repeatedly that Perkin is a fraud. Finally, and most spectacularly, Sir George Buc, who was writing his history of Richard III just a few years before Ford started on his play, used Clifford's assessment of Warbeck's appearance to come to a conclusion that flatly contradicts Holinshed's: "he had all the marks and tokens of the young Duke of York, and was *certainly* the second son of King Edward."[23] Buc's history did not find its way into print until after the publication of *Perkin Warbeck* in 1634, and we do not know if Ford ever saw the manuscript, but it seems reasonable to assume that if the cultural climate was such that Buc could so boldly affirm Warbeck's legitimacy, then Ford could surely contemplate the *possibility* of the same (without some extraordinary flight of imagination).

Nothing suggests that Ford had at his disposal special sources inaccessible to the historians. There is little doubt, however, that he interprets and presents the materials (often taken directly from Bacon and Gainsford) in a radically independent manner. Or, to put it in Hayden White's terms, Ford *refuses* the "pregeneric plot structures"[24] conventionally used in Tudor and early Stuart culture (and which are evident in the historical drama and narratives) to endow the events surrounding the founding of the Tudor regime with ideologically correct meaning. Like a revisionary historian heeding the ventriloquistic voices in his sources, Ford takes his "facts" directly from Bacon and Gainsford (and indirectly from Hall, Holinshed, Vergil, and More), and refashions them daringly into a dramatic/historiographical text that runs *against* the politico-historiographical grain.

None of this of course proves that Warbeck was the Duke of York; but those are not the stakes for which Ford is playing. All the above discussion recommends is that there is a *basis* in the sources for Ford's controversial presentation of the Warbeck character.[25] Which brings us to Ure's third assumption, which was that Ford's play underscores the fundamental difference between a "literary" and a "historical" experience. I would, however, stringently argue to the contrary, that Ford's "literary" play is an effort to instill precisely greater epistemological responsibility in the historian. The point is easily illustrated if we turn briefly to Sidney's *A Defence of Poetry*, where the author observes that the historian (in contrast to the poet) is "tied, not to what should be but to *what is*, to the particular truth of things" (221). On this particular point, virtually all renaissance historians shared Sidney's view. Addressing Prince Charles in his dedication of *The History of the Reign of King Henry VII,* Bacon, for instance, asserts that he has in no way idealized his subject: "I have not flattered him [Henry VII], but taken him to life as well as I could."[26] Buc's dedication to his *History of King Richard III* treats the issue in considerable detail:

> the historiographer must be veritable and free from all prosopolepsies and partial respects. He must not add nor omit anything, either of partiality or of hatred. All of which I have endeavoured to observe in the writing of this story, so that if my authors be sincere and faithful, my Muse is pure and innocent. For I have imitated the sceptic philosophers who of themselves affirmed nothing . . ." (Buc *History* 4)

And, finally, popular historian Holinshed in his *Chronicles* openly calls for interpretative restraint: "I haue in things doubtfull rather chosen to shew the diuersitie of their [other historians'] writings, than by ouer-ruling them, and vsing a peremptorie, to frame them to agree to my liking: leauing it neuerthelesse to each mans judgement, to controll them as he seeth cause."[27] These indeed are the stated and lofty intentions of most renaissance historians: to provide to the best of their ability an accurate written account of "what [was]" without adding or framing or distorting that account in any way.

In *The Defence*, however, Sidney also advances a derisive and highly skeptical image of the historian as one who is "laden with mouse-eaten records, authorizing himself (for the most part) upon other histories, whose greatest authorities are built upon the notable foundation of hearsay" (220). And of course it is *this* image, rather than the Sidneyan paragon of historical virtue, that so often captures the *practice* of historians Bacon, Buc, Grafton, Gainsford, Holinshed, and others. The contradiction is that most historians who confidently authorize their narratives upon mouse-eaten records and hearsay *also* uncomfortably acknowledge the difficulty, even the impossibility, of finding solid epistemological ground upon which to construct historical narratives. A couple of examples will illustrate the point.

In his previously mentioned dedication to Prince Charles, Bacon inserts an important qualification when he writes that he has protrayed Henry VII "*as well as I could, sitting so far and having no better light*" (italics added). This stipulation surely suggests that the history before the prince includes some things and events which the historian could not clearly perceive, and which may therefore fail to satisfy Sidney's standard for historical excellence. Whether Bacon's stipulation is a sign of professional integrity or an instance of political acumen, is difficult to say, but what is clear is that despite acknowledging his limitations as a historian, Bacon falls far short of indicating that his defects invalidate, or at least problematize, the labor he has performed. Bacon's work has a much fiercer critic in modern historian Roger Lockyer, who encounters in Bacon's history of Henry VII "a considerable gap between Bacon's theory of history-writing and his actual practice of it."[28] Lockyer points out that Bacon in theory believed in consulting original documents, but that he relied in practice "mainly on Hall's version of Polydore Vergil, supplemented by Richard Grafton's *Chronicle* and John Stow's *Annals*, all of which stood in a very incestuous relationship one to another." Despite his access to Sir Robert Cotton's famous manuscript collection, Bacon, incredibly, often put his trust in More's *History of Richard III*; and he relied on his own memory and the derivative work of John Speed, even when the documents could have been easily accessed in the Cotton collection (Lockyer, "Introduction" 16).

Like Bacon, Holinshed offers something of a disclaimer in a "Preface to the Reader." He too stresses the difficulties encountered in historical research, as well as the insuperable deficiencies inherent in the work of other historians:

> . . . I haue beene so carefull, that I haue spared no paines or helpe of freends to search out either written or printed ancient authors, or to inquire of moderne eie-witnesses for the true setting downe of what which I haue deliuered: *but I find such want in writers for the necessarie knowledge of things doone in the times past, and lacke meanes to obteine sufficient instructions by reporters of the time present*; and herewith the worthie exploits of our countriemen so manie, that it greeueth me I could not leaue the same to posteritie (as I wished) to their well deserued praise.[29] (italics added)

Richard Grafton's emphasis favors his own accomplishments as a historian, but he, too, admits his chronicle is "true without misreporting, [only in] *so farre as* the following of the best Aucthors & reporters & mine awne experience . . . could conceaue"[30] (italics added). George Buc inspires some initial confidence when he asserts that he can understand "obscure passages" and recognize stories "of little credit" and "fabulous and trivial romancers" contained in "the ancient and large histories," but our faith proves misplaced when we learn that although Buc did use Cotton's library (Kincaid "Introduction" 8), he relied mostly on More, Vergil, Grafton, Hall, Holinshed, and Stow "for the general story of Richard III and Henry VII" (Buc, *History* cxi). If Buc has these histories in mind when he speaks of "the ancient and large histories" – and there is every indication that he does – then he, like his colleagues, is still with those "whose greatest authorities are built upon the notable foundation of hearsay."

Sidney's negative assessment of historiographical practice, presenting what is a specific weakness in historical inquiry as its essential modus operandi, magnifies the problem to the point of hyperbolic sarcasm. Nonetheless, if Sidney's jeer unjustly highlights this particular flaw of historiography, the historians, conversely, seem in their *practice* to forget almost entirely the ambiguities and incompleteness of their sources when they come to the question of Warbeck's ancestry. The earliest authority of this score, Edward Hall, reports, for example, that Warbeck, in "his awne confession written with hys awne hande," wanted it to "be knowen, that I was borne in the toune of Turney in Flaunders, & my fathers name is Ihon Osbeck, which sayd Osbeck was coptroller of the sayde toune of Turney, & my mothers name is Katheryn de Faro."[31] Holinshed follows Hall almost verbatim, and Gainsford, too, finds little to disagree with, even though all three note that Perkin was "set fettered in a payre of stockes" and made to endure "innumerable reproches mockes & skorninges" before making his public confession. Gainsford goes so far as to establish a direct causality between Warbeck's rude treatment and his confession: upon being released from the stocks, he was "put to the racke, which made him not only confesse his pedigree and originall, but write it with his owne hands."[32] Even more startling is Bacon's adaption of the material. Whereas Hall, Holinshed, and Gainsford at least mention that the information concerning Warbeck's ancestry is extracted under duress, Bacon matter-of-factly incorporates it into Warbeck's biography, moves it prominently to the beginning of his discussion, and fails to mention its source altogether (*History* 132).

In his presentation of the confession material, Ford, by contrast, demonstrates the sound judgment and restraint the narrative historians advocate in the prefaces already quoted. Ford marvelously preserves the equivocal status of Perkin's lineage by introducing the content of the "confession" or "pedigree" into the play through the mouth of the morally controversial Lambert Simnel, who himself was an inept pretender to the English throne. Having confessed to treason in exchange for the King's mercy, Simnel now is the King's falconer and "Eat[s] from the king's purse" (5.3.45). In the play, Simnel urges Warbeck to be led by his example because Warbeck's "pedigree is published; you are known / For Osbeck's son of Tournay, a loose runagate, / A landloper" (23–5). Implicitly denying he ever made such a confession and refuting Simnel's testimony, Warbeck responds: "Baited to my death? / Intolerable cruelty! I laugh at / The duke of Richmond's practice on my fortunes" (27–9). What is more, Simnel himself undermines any credibility the published pedigree may have had when he later beseeches Warbeck to follow his example and "confess, and hope for pardon!" (52). Why urge Warbeck to confess if he has already done so? Those who obtained the first "confession" and published it all over London are obviously not convinced of its merit; *they* still have a gnawing suspicion that Warbeck may in fact be Richard of York, or at the very least they suspect that enough others still think so.[33] So, Ford appears to ask, why should the historian, the dramatist, and his audience not share in this suspicion?

This and other instances confirm that Ford's rendition of the Warbeck saga reveals a type of interpretative restraint missing from the historical narratives. More importantly, Ford's play seeks to do something other than offer its audience a purely "literary experience" in Ure's sense. Far from transforming history into a play without historical relevance (i.e., in which the audience is not asked to judge), Ford introduces historical data into a literary genre precisely to think about history and historical representation. Nonetheless, the term "literary" is useful here if we take it not in its conventional sense of "fictitious" or "invented," but in Hayden White's sense as a type of "plot" used by historians to order historical information for the purpose of making it accessible and comprehensible to audiences in the present. Indeed, exercising interpretative restraint for Ford means a withholding of the literary or ideological narrative – the Tudor plot – that is not warranted by the available historical facts.

As we saw in the case of Shakespeare and Fletcher's *Henry VIII* and Massinger and Fletcher's *Barnavelt*, Ford's play, too, withholds the literary (which, here, is also the historiographical) form which materialized from the Warbeck "content." This "content" of course was never ideologically neutral or shapeless. Regardless of the truth of Warbeck's contention, its very introduction was both provoked and contoured by the Tudor cultural climate even before Henry VII's official response. We saw in the chronicles that Warbeck was initially received with a sense of awe and puzzlement, but also with considerable suspicion because of the apparent threat he presented to the newfound political stability. Henry's official response is a piece of rationalist ideology buttressed by the theories of divine right, providentialism, and genealogy, and seeks to redefine the Warbeck "content" for Tudor culture, not least by destroying the sense of wonder felt by virtually all. Ford's drama underscores this eradication: when Warbeck is finally brought before the king and described as "the Christian world's strange wonder," Henry curtly observes, "We observe no wonder" (5.2.36, 37). Given the political success of the Tudor dynasty it is no surprise that its propaganda campaign (which of course extended far beyond the Warbeck matter) took hold of English subjects in a way that transformed Tudor ideology from a distinct set of ideas fostered by the ruling class to a nearly ubiquitous and somewhat amorphous set of ideas, beliefs, and values developing a life of their own in the fabric of daily existence. In the course of the sixteenth century, the legitimacy of Henry Richmond became a less acute political issue; and if we believe the historical narratives, plays, poems, and entertainments of the period, we see that the waning of Tudor ideological urgency on the succession question goes hand in hand with its widespread though mostly offhanded acceptance. The shift can be described schematically as one from a rationalist ideology to a more (though not wholly) cognitive ideology. In this climate, the Warbeck "content" undergoes yet another reshaping; for most of the sixteenth century Warbeck ceases to be an important character. He becomes the figure that everyone agrees was an imposter even though few are very clear why.

The importance of the ideological shift and its impact on history's "content" relates directly to the history–content–form (genre) question. Earlier we posited a strong link between literary forms and the "content" they need to embody. But "content" itself, we have just seen, is not an ideologically neutral set of building blocks out of which literary texts or historical narratives are fashioned. On the contrary, "content" itself contains something we may call "form" which is produced "under pressure of an inner need, of a collective psychological demand which, like everything else . . . has its social roots."[34] So as the form of "content" changes as "content's" status in culture or society is repositioned by ideological shifts, so the literary or historical forms which "house" that "content" are "changed, transformed, broken down, and revolutionized" (Eagleton, *Marxism* 22). What occurred in the case of *Warbeck* is that the collective inner need (a cognitive ideology no longer fueled by Tudor propaganda or cultural necessity) to comprehend the "content" of the Warbeck affair in the traditional manner had lost its grip on Jacobean culture – or, at least, on some of its members. Although the external, censorial pressure to exalt Henry VII and label Warbeck a fake and liar may still have been there when *Warbeck* was written, it is clear that the Tudor "inner logic" of the "content" of the Warbeck story – that which compels a certain understanding, that which produces a certain *kind* of story – had ceased to be valid for John Ford.

The concrete consequences of Ford's novel grasp of the Warbeck material are manifest in the form of the play itself. If, as we saw earlier, the typical Elizabethan history play plot follows the rebellion–chaos–restoration trajectory, then Ford's *Warbeck* deliberately aborts this generic form not merely by withholding restoration, but also by allowing the rebellion plot (Warbeck's) to withstand the ideological siege waged upon it by the Tudor plot. Ford's historiographical approach to the Warbeck enigma permits both plots to coexist fundamentally *unresolved* by insisting on the uncertainty of Perkin's identity even in death, and by Henry's failure to unmask his challenger. Ford disputes the "facts" ("content") as they appear in the historical narratives; but he also questions the historian's seemingly inconspicuous practice of imposing a master narrative upon that "content." The former is a problem of insufficient information; the latter brings to the fore a radical historical undecidability which occurs when historians are perceived to push their narratives beyond the epistemological limits of their inquiry. One way of understanding the conditions that enable Ford's text is to surmise that the anti-Tudor elements of the Warbeck saga were already latently present in the Tudor narratives, but that it took until well into the Stuart dynasty before residual Tudor ideology lost its grip and before a playwright could activate those elements and abandon Tudor forms of historical representation.

Does this mean that a withholding of generic narratives leads to objective historical truth? Ford does not seem to think so. His call for restraint, his call for the elimination of the historian as an ideological mediator, it turns out, is not an absolute but rather a *metaphor* that seeks to shift the importance away from the historian to the audience. In the dedicatory epistle to the play, Ford makes an arresting statement about the principles of restraint underlying his historiographical/dramatic practice: "In other labours you may read actions of antiquity discoursed; in this abridgement, you find the actors themselves discoursing: in some kind, practised as well what to speak, as speaking why to do" (4–7). The essential difference drawn here between historical drama and the narrative histories is that the narratives reach their audiences in a *mediated* fashion whereas the drama does *not*. In the play you are presented with the "actors *themselves*"; that is, according to the gloss of the Revels editor, the audience is confronted with "the *participants* in the historical action, with a quibble on 'stage-actors'" (italics added). These "actors" do not only know how to speak "well," they also know "why" they speak: they are granted an inner motivation. Ford's claim is of course wondrously ambitious, but before we dismiss as naive or hyperbolic his supposition that we can recreate history before our eyes, we should consider what exact insight he is trying to convey. First, it is unmistakable that Ford thinks of his play as *historical*, as opposed to what Ure referred to as a predominantly "literary experience." In the epistle to Cavendish, he writes: "Your Lordship is a most competent judge in expressions of such credit, commissioned by your known ability in examining and enabled by your knowledge in determining the *monuments of time*" (8–11; emphasis added). The italicized phrase has two relevant meanings: it designates the play-text as something that can hopefully withstand the test of time, but also as a memorial intended to "commemorate a notable person, action, or event."[35] Ford is suggesting that Cavendish has the expertise to decide whether *Perkin Warbeck* will become another *Iliad* but also that he possesses the erudition to determine whether the play is a credible historical account, i.e., a true monument of time.

Secondly, Ford's dramatic model, in which actors themselves discourse before an audience, has an uncanny resemblance to the ideal conception of historiography as advanced by Thomas Hobbes in his introduction to Thucydides' *The History of the Grecian War* (1628). Not only does Hobbes delineate the same theory of history as Ford, he describes it in remarkably similar theatrical language. Of the Greek historian Thucydides, who was revered by renaissance historians almost without exception, Hobbes writes:

> Thucydides . . . is accounted the most politic historiographer that ever writ. . . . He filleth his narrations with that choice of matter, and ordereth them with that judgment, and with such perspicuity and efficacy expresseth himself, that, as Plutarch saith, he maketh his auditor a *spectator*. For he setteth his reader in the assemblies of the people and in the senate, at their debating; in the streets at their seditions; and in the field, at their battles. So that look how much a man of understanding might have added to his experience, if he had then lived a *beholder* of their proceedings, and familiar with the men and business of the time: so much almost may he profit now, by attentive reading of the same here written. He may from the narrations draw out lessons to himself, and of himself be able to trace the drifts and counsels of the *actors* to their seat.[36]

Although, remarkably, one is speaking as a historian and the other as a playwright, the similarities between Hobbes and Ford are clear. Both believe it best to place before the audience a dramatic representation of the past. Neither author, however, believes that historical representation can be *equated* with history:[37] Hobbes's attentive reader may gain "almost" as much as if he had actually been there, and Ford acknowledges his "errors" (Prologue, 15), and the necessary abridgment of his account. The key to understanding the dramatic metaphor is that neither Ford nor Hobbes intends to speak *for* history by filling in the gaps in order to forge a master narrative. Ford's stated reluctance to discourse for his actors stems not from a naive belief that he can write objective historical truth but from a refusal to fill in the gaps to suit a Tudor–Stuart agenda. If Ford is uncertain about Warbeck's identity, then he will allow that uncertainty to be part of the dramatic presentation, however inconvenient it may be for any "official" teleology of history.

V

So far we have focused on the play's central equivocality – Warbeck's identity – and its exploitation by Ford in order to challenge conventional wisdom. But Warbeck is not the only character in the play who has difficulties establishing his identity with authority. In contrast with Warbeck, who relies almost completely on his charismatic personality to advance his aspirations, other characters in the play feel that they have history on their side when it comes to authenticating themselves. Ford here is principally concerned with Perkin's counterpart, Henry Richmond, and the murky origins of his dynastic pretensions. We may remind ourselves here that for many renaissance Englishmen history "was a source of self-definition" (Rackin, *Stages of History* 4). Historical interests – especially in genealogical and heraldic research (and occasionally forgery) – were relied on by individuals to hold on to a stable public (and private) persona in time of profound social flux. Rapid economic and social change fostered opportunities for financial gain (and loss) and facilitated the movement of individuals and families from one class to another as never before.[38] Here heraldry was of considerable utility to the upwardly mobile, because it afforded the *nouveaux riches* a certain respectability,[39] while many of the old families who had fallen on hard times desperately tried to maintain their social status by cashing in, whenever possible, often through marriage, on their genealogical heritage.

In the subplot of *Perkin Warbeck*, Ford offers a suggestive dramatization of the consequences when genealogy/historiography fail the individual. Dalyell, a courtier of lesser rank, wishes to marry Katherine, daughter of the Earl of Huntly, kinsman of the King of Scotland, James IV. The Earl, although sympathetic toward the youth's plight, is reluctant to grant him his daughter's hand, especially since the King has not yet married and may select her as his bride. Dalyell acknowledges the problem but then goes on to claim he is more than just a "noble subject":

> I could add more; and in the rightest line
> Derive my pedigree from Adam Mure,
> A Scottish knight, whose daughter was the mother
> To him that first begot the race of Jameses
> That sway the sceptre to this very day.
> But kindreds are not ours when once the date
> Of many years have swallowed up the memory
> Of their originals: so pasture fields,
> Neighbouring too near the ocean, are sooped up
> And known no more . . . (1.2.29–38)

The passage makes clear that Dalyell's blood ties to the Scottish royal family – a genealogical fact which ought to be conspicuous and celebrated – are entirely inconsequential, "sooped up" in the ocean of time. The passage spotlights history's selective memory, and, what is more, argues that kindreds *literally* cease to be ours when common ancestors are overlooked. The importance of historiography and/or genealogy in determining identity therefore cannot be underestimated, even while its failures are grave and chronic. Now Dalyell is a relatively insignificant character in the play's principal contest between Henry VII and Warbeck. Yet the references to "the race of Jameses" and the swallowed-up segments of family history of course encourage the audience to draw an analogy between Dalyell's "forgotten" link to the Scottish royal family and Perkin's supposed link to the York family. One consequence of such an analogy is the immediate realization that it is premature to reject Warbeck's claim simply because his family heritage cannot be established by empirical means. It is hard to believe that Ford included Dalyell in the play for any other reason.[40]

But if the analogy may caution against dismissing Perkin, it also works in the other direction, i.e., to unsettle the efforts of Henry VII, who has comparable difficulties establishing his royal pedigree. The troubles of the historical Henry of course did not pertain to his ancestry – that much about him was known – but to his tenuous right to the English crown. Henry's father, Edmund Tudor, had joined the Lancaster clan through marriage with Margaret Beaufort. Margaret was a descendant of one of John of Gaunt's "bastard" children, and even though the offspring had been officially legitimated by Richard II, they had been barred from the throne of England by Henry IV. Historians prudently note that Henry IV's addition to Richard II's patent of legitimation would probably not have stood up in a court of law; but, as one historian argues, "Henry VII and his contemporaries . . . probably did not know that the exclusion of the Beauforts was solely the work of Henry IV and of dubious validity" (Levine, M., *Tudor Problems* 33). What is more, even if the Beauforts were not barred from the succession, superiority in their line belonged to Henry's mother, Margaret, who was to outlive him. And to top it off, if, as Henry VI's followers contended, the Lancastrian title was based on Henry IV's descent from Henry III through Blanche of Lancaster (John of Gaunt's first wife), Henry VII (the great-grandson of Gaunt and his third wife, Catherine Swynford) did not even qualify as a bona fide Lancaster (Levine, M., *Tudor Problems* 33). And, finally, there was widespread belief that the Duke of Buckingham's claim through Thomas of Woodstock (youngest son of Edward III) should be given serious consideration. In sum, for those looking for cavils, Henry VII's right to the English throne can not have seemed much brighter than the feeble "summer's sun" that shined on Henry V's right to the throne of France.[41]

Indeed, Mortimer Levine exaggerates the case only slightly when he suggests that Henry's title to the crown was based not in law but in military conquest (*Tudor Problems* 34). Henry clearly understood this. Publicly and before Parliament, he wisely played up his Lancastrian roots (without addressing the debarment of the Beauforts) and, as he had agreed to before invading England, he married Edward IV's daughter, Elizabeth of York, in order to stress the end of the Wars of the Roses and to celebrate the Lancaster–York union. He also publicly called on the theory of divine right to prop up his claim to the crown. But it is clear that Henry's efforts to produce for himself a convincing royal genealogy were not enough to prevent a series of challenges to his royal authority. Ford's play alone documents the cases of Warbeck, Lord Stanley, and Lambert Simnel (c. 1487). The play also recounts the first Cornish Rising (1495), even though it does not fit the chronology. The episode in which "Ten thousand Cornish, / Grudging to pay your subsidies, have gathered / To a head" (1.3.129–31) has nothing to do with the Warbeck saga, and, although Henry deals with the rebels swiftly, it is a further sign of his uncertain authority over his subjects. Indeed, Ford addresses the question of Henry's lack of support head on in the third act. Christopher Urswick, the King's chaplain says to Henry: "How if king Henry were but sure of subject, / Such a wild runagate [Warbeck] might soon be caged, / No great ado withstanding" (3.3.49–51). Clearly, when Warbeck is at the height of his popularity the King is so little assured of the allegiance of his subjects that he is afraid to deal with the pretender openly.

There is a sense, then, in which Ford's Henry VII, because he lacks a ready-made royal genealogy, must continually produce his power and majesty for all to see. The play's opening speech at once lays the basis for this necessity: upon lamenting the presence of "the ghosts of York" which haunt his administration and private thoughts, Henry asserts that although he "sit[s] fast in his own royal birthright" and has healed the "bleeding wounds of England's slaughtered people," he yet feels like "a mockery-king in state" (1.1.1–14). Despite a public expression of his faith in his birthright, the challenge facing the King, as he conceives it, is to transform himself from a "mockery-king" into the genuine article. Like Henry V, who was the son of a usurper, who opted for a foreign quarrel, Henry VII must compensate for certain legal and genealogical deficiencies by publicly producing his royal power and authority. In Henry VII's case this means at least in part the unmasking of Warbeck the pretender.

These productions of Henry's royal persona are important not only because they are the means by which he must convince his contemporaries that indeed he is England's rightful monarch; they also come to constitute a historical record: they are Henry's opportunity to make his case before a Stuart audience. Ford's play is a representation or *simulation* of history in flux. The key lies in recognizing Hobbes's designation of historiography as supremely *dramatic* in its presentation. Moreover, Hobbes assigns to the reader (or spectator) of history the typically literary task of interpreting the meaning of the narrative before him. He "may from the narrations *draw out* lessons to himself, and *of himself be able to trace* the drifts and counsels of the actors. . . ." The historian will not interpret the events for him. Thus, for Hobbes, history is material or actual, its mode of presentation dramatic, and its reception literary in character.[42] Ford's play meets all the same requirements. Contrary to modern critics who are fond of defining historical drama as a genre which transforms historical matter into literature, Ford, in defining his play-text, does not name it a play *about* history but "a history couched in a play" (Prologue 14): a "true" (16) historical matter presented dramatically. This is more than a quibble on words; it clearly reverses the priority commonly given to the "literary" over the "historical." Thus Ford's play offers the *experience* which Hobbes deems history, with the understanding that the experience has an important literary or dramatic component.

Consequently, if we accept Ford's claim that his play is indeed a *chronicle history*, we must now receive Henry VII's efforts to authenticate himself at the expense of Warbeck's counterclaim, as history-in-progress, as opposed to history-after-the-fact. Let us therefore turn to the presentation and/or self-presentation of Henry and Warbeck to see how each tries to authenticate or historicize himself. A stunning instance of carefully orchestrated self-production occurs at the moment in the play when the Bishop of Durham couples Henry's legitimacy to public sentiment. Henry indicates he might show the traitor Stanley mercy, when Durham responds:

> You may, you may;
> And so persuade your subjects that the title
> Of York is better, nay, more just and lawful
> Than yours of Lancaster; so Stanley holds:
> Which if it be not treason in the highest,
> Then we are traitors all, perjured and false,
> Who have took oath to Henry and the justice
> Of Henry's title – Oxford, Surrey, Daubeney,
> With all your other peers of state and church,
> Forsworn, and Stanley true alone to heaven
> And England's lawful heir. (2.2.14–24)

A modern sensibility may not construe this speech as that unusual, but we must not lose sight of the fact that Durham is speaking these lines from a public stage to an audience ruled by a divine right monarch. The syllogism runs as follows: if the King shows mercy, then he will be perceived to be illegitimate (which is what Stanley the traitor believes), and which, in turn, would make traitors out of all the peers of state and church and would leave Stanley as the only just subject. But that, of course, is not permissible, and therefore Stanley must die. For an audience firmly believing in Charles I's right to rule (in part because of his descendance from Henry Tudor), it may have been disquieting to hear matters of legitimacy, loyalty, and legal and divine oaths made contingent upon an act of purely political opportunism. The execution of Stanley certainly is a production of the King's power, but it cannot have helped his cause for authenticity with Ford's audience.[43]

More striking even is the direct confrontation between Henry and Warbeck. Upon being captured by the English, Warbeck is presented to Henry VII as "the Christian world's strange wonder" (5.2.36). As an engineer of signs and their meaning, the King, however, is eager to match Perkin's outward appearance to the idea of Perkin as imposter, and corrects: "Daubeney, / We observe no wonder; I behold, 'tis true, / An ornament of nature, fine and polished, / A handsome youth indeed, but not admire him" (35–8). Henry is trying to be diplomatic about his encounter with Perkin in order to use it as an opportunity to establish a *difference* between himself and the claimant. In absence of compelling evidence of the Duke of York's death, the visualization of this difference is extremely important. After all, Henry's "sacred person" contains the "new soul" (1.1.26) of the commonwealth, whereas Warbeck is an empty shell, mere "shadow of majesty," a forgery (5.2.31–2, 131). As George Puttenham put it in a poem about Elizabeth I, "Out of her breast as from an eye, / Issue the rayes incessantly / Of her justice, bounty and might, / And reflect not, till they attain / The fardest part of her domain. / And makes each subject clearly *fee*, / What he is bounden for to be . . ." (emphasis added).[44] Warbeck, in fact, has been perceived in similar terms. When first introduced to Warbeck, James IV of Scotland exclaims: "How like a king a'looks! Lords, but observe / The confidence of his aspect! Dross cannot / Cleave to so pure a metal; a royal youth!" (2.3.73–5). This kind of language was of course quite common in Tudor efforts at mystifying the person of the monarch. But, face to face with his enigmatic rival, Henry finds it easier to denigrate Warbeck than to live up to ideological hyperbole himself. He turns the focus on the "inner" Warbeck and encourages him to "Turn now thine eyes, / Young man, upon thyself, and thy past actions! / What revels in combustion through our kingdom / A frenzy of aspiring youth hath danced / Till, wanting breath, thy feet of pride have slipped / To break thy neck" (5.2.47–52). How convenient would it be for Henry Tudor if Perkin emerged as a proud and ambitious youth, an unsympathetic and misguided overreacher. But nothing is further from the truth. By the time Henry and Warbeck meet, we are well aware that many characters in the play *see* in Warbeck what Henry wishes everyone would see in *him*. During the joint James IV – Warbeck invasion of England, for instance, the Bishop of Durham's refusal to meet James's demands leads the Scottish king to urge his soldiers to "Forage through / The [English] country; spare no prey of life or goods" (3.4.54–5). Immediately, Perkin tries to dissuade the King:

". . . I had never thought / The truth of mine inheritance with rapes / Of women, or of infants murdered, virgins / Deflowered, old men butchered, dwellings fired, / My land depopulated, and my people / Afflicted with a kingdom's devastation. . . . / Spare, spare, my dear, dear England" (59–64, 67). James retorts by stating that Perkin is ridiculous to be "careful of an interest / another man possesseth." But Perkin will not budge, nor will he oblige Henry Tudor's demand for "truth." You can break my neck, he tells the King, "but not my heart," and then daringly proceeds not to an assertion of his legal birthright to the English crown, but to drawing a surprising historical analogy between his current plight and Henry's just prior to Bosworth Field:

> Sir, remember
> There was a shooting in of light when Richmond,
> Not aiming at a crown, retired, and gladly,
> For comfort to the duke of Bretagne's court.
> Richard, who swayed the sceptre, was reputed
> A tyrant then; yet then a dawning glimmered
> To some few wand'ring remnants, promising day
> When first they ventured on a frightful shore
> At Milford Haven –
> . . . .
> Bosworth field:
> Where, at an instant, to the world's amazement,
> A morn to Richmond and a night to Richard
> Appeared at once. The tale is soon applied:
> Fate, which crowned these attempts when least assured,
> Might have befriended others like resolved. (5.2.58–66, 69–74)

The comparison of Henry VII to the tyrant Richard III is perhaps to be anticipated, but the suggested resemblance between Warbeck and Henry Richmond at the moment of his landing at Milford Haven is more complex. If, in a strictly legal context, Warbeck means to use the analogy to legitimate himself and delegitimate Henry he goes about it in an unnecessarily roundabout way. At first glance, the comparison between Richmond and Warbeck can only work in the latter's favor if Richmond is the legitimate monarch of England who had the right to overthrow Richard III (of York). But this of course cannot be if Perkin is the younger son of Edward IV. The only way this scenario can possibly make sense is if Warbeck's speech implies that Henry VII was ignorant of the fact that only one of Edward's sons had been murdered. That is, Richmond enjoyed the appearance of legitimacy because the rightful Yorkist heir to the throne was believed dead. Or, to put the matter even more favorably, Henry *was* the legitimate heir until the reemergence of Edward's son. But both scenarios tarnish

Warbeck's claim to the crown, for the first option would associate him with one who only has the appearance of legitimacy, and the second with one whose legitimacy is temporary.

It is much more probable that Warbeck's history lesson deliberately ignores the historical issues of legality and identity in favor of a consideration of the true forces that create kings who lack compelling royal genealogies: fate and resolved men who labor to "crown" their attempts even when they are "least assured" (as Richmond's were then, and Warbeck's are now). And Warbeck of course has a point. Not only was Henry's ascendancy based largely on victory in battle, but on a fortuitous victory at that. By any account, Richard III should have defeated Richmond at Bosworth, and would have done so if Stanley had not joined Richmond at the last hour, or if Richard had not been betrayed by Henry Percy, Earl of Northumberland, whose army was pledged to fight for Richard but who watched the carnage from a distance (Levine, M., *Tudor Problems* 31).[45] In any case, Warbeck is using one kind of historical argument (analogy) to defeat Henry's historical pretensions of another sort (genealogy, divine right). The end result is that Warbeck, without denying his own family heritage, insinuates the feebleness of *both* their genealogical claims.

Lord Daubeney rightly takes exception to the treasonous parallel drawn between Henry Richmond's state prior to defeating Richard III and Warbeck's present condition, but Henry says: "O, let him range: / The player's on the stage still, 'tis his part; / A' does but act" (5.2.67–9).[46] The King's casual dismissal of Warbeck's impressive histrionic show is certainly designed to make him appear confident. But if we take seriously Warbeck's deflation of genealogical pretensions, what else, besides putting on a good performance, is there? Henry incessantly belittles Warbeck as "prompted," "moulded," and "rehearsed"; and he urges him to abandon his "antic pageantry" and "appear / In your own nature" (88, 89). But, without the possibility of proving his identity genealogically, what other "nature" does the claimant possess? The only way Warbeck can convey his identity is to *stage* it.[47] Does this mean that Warbeck's eloquence and grand gestures are nothing but "the windy suspiration of forced breath" and the "actions that a man might play"? On the contrary, Warbeck's performance does denote him truly – or, more to the point here, there is in this case no way to determine that it does not. "Truth," Warbeck utters grandiosely, "in her pure simplicity wants art / To put a feigned blush on" (80–1). Whether this assertion is a part of the performance or evidence of absolute sincerity is irrelevant because it is beyond anyone's determination.

The pivotal moment in the scene occurs when the performances of Henry and Warbeck are judged side by side by a citizen. John A-Water, Mayor of Cork, one of Warbeck's followers who has been captured and who has confessed his "treason," is brought in and told to "Beg life, and cry aloud, 'heaven save king Henry!'" (5.2.112). But instead of leaping at the chance for life, John, though admittedly not a very bright fellow, makes the following, confounding speech: "Every man knows what is best, as it happens. For my own part, I believe it is true, if I be not deceived, that kings must be kings and subjects subjects. But which is which – you shall pardon me for that; whether we speak or hold our peace, all are mortal, no man knows his end" (113–17). Significantly, John is no social critic; he does not reject the basic structural opposition in the monarch–subject model, he merely confesses that he cannot tell the difference between king and commoner. So much for that special, tangible royal "authority" in a king's "countenance which [one] would fain call master."[48] So much for the claims of Henry VII's divine right or blood rule with which the play is littered.[49]

Shakespeare's Henry V also tries to underscore the king's humanity – a humanity shared with the common soldiers – on the eve of Agincourt. Henry V, however, stresses the king's likeness to his subjects precisely to affirm their fundamental difference, to elicit sympathy for and trust in the king's mysterious cause. John A-Water's words produce quite the opposite effect. They wipe out, from the subject's vantage point, the difference between king and subject to the point that monarch and pretender appear the same; through the Mayor of Cork, Ford satirizes the king's effort to be king. In a distinct echo of Shakespeare's Henry, who can ultimately only counter Williams's legitimate arguments by getting angry with him, Ford's Henry bruskly dismisses John by denigrating him: "We trifle time with follies." But "follies" such as these take on grave significance when recalled in the context of the Bishop of Durham's already noted assessment of the populace's impressionable nature. Clearly, Henry has utterly failed to convince a "typical" subject that his right to rule is self-evident and anchored in divine decree or law, or both. John simply cannot tell which end is up. Is Henry Richmond still but a "mockery-king in state"?[50]

Henry concludes the bizarre spectacle by agreeing with Daubeney that Warbeck must either learn "another language" or "The hangman's physic / Will purge this saucy humour" (135–6). The decision to execute Warbeck is of course supremely significant. A politic Henry had adopted a tolerant and merciful stance toward Warbeck and Lambert Simnel throughout the play. The most convincing way for Henry to *demonstrate* his superior royal birthright would have been to expose Warbeck as an irrelevant, misguided pretender; merely to execute him for unproven treason would not have eliminated all doubts, only served as a display of monarchial power. It has become clear, however, that Warbeck is incorrigible; he will not learn another language, not even to save his life. As long as Perkin lives his royal histrionics will haunt Henry. Ironically, only Warbeck's death can make

Henry's ghosts go away, and even then not completely, for what the historians say about him and what the people think will continue to matter.

So this is not Henry's ideal scenario. On his way to watch the execution, he offers his preferred moral of the story: "We gather this fit use: that public states, / As our particular bodies, taste most good / In health, when purged of corrupted blood" (5.3.217–19). The threat to the monarchy may have been subdued by the executioner's axe, but it is not at all clear whether false or true blood was spilled in the process. Nor has it been demonstrated that with Henry in charge the monarchy is in good health. Ford indicates as much in the play's epilogue: "Here has appeared, though in a several fashion, / The threats of majesty, the strength of passion, / Hopes of an empire, change of fortune; all / What can to theatres of greatness fall, / Proving their weak foundations" (1–5). Even with the elimination of Perkin, his (hi)story, as presented by Ford, demonstrates that "theatres of greatness" – a metaphor for "states" or "kingdoms" (Ure, "Introduction" 141n) – have "weak foundations." That is, Ford uses historical presentation to show not only that the official Tudor version of the Warbeck saga is ideologically biased, but also that historiography is incapable of satisfying those who insist that it supply the foundations (genealogical or otherwise) to prop up the earliest foundations of the Tudor state.

"No chronicle records his fellow," Lord Daubeney proclaims with derision as Warbeck is led to the scaffold. He means of course that Warbeck is an "impostor beyond precedent," but he also implies unwittingly that Warbeck is something of an inexplicable oddity, a figure whose stage presentation deviates crucially from the standard account found in the chronicles. What is more, from his special position as a character in a historical drama performed in the Stuart present, Daubeney functions both as an admonishing government agent and as a surveyor of the historical record. As censor he intimates that no historian (who values his life and liberty) will want to chronicle Warbeck as he has appeared in Ford's drama; and in the role of historian he confirms that no one has dared to ignore his thinly veiled warning. It is a palpable irony that Daubeney's voice rises from a text that contradicts him, and that has become part of the permanent public historical record of the Warbeck affair.

Daubeney's censorship is further significant in light of the widespread belief among renaissance historians and politicians that it was history's principal purpose to guide conduct in the present. We can understand this renaissance truism in two ways, either as a desire for transhistorical truth, or, cynically, as a lesson in the politicization of historiography. Perkin is vigorously inclined toward the latter when he expresses deep skepticism about the powers of historiography to preserve his cause. Already in the second act he implies the bias of contemporary historians: "I shall stand no blemish to this house / In chronicles writ in *another* age" (2.2.101–2; italics added). And shortly before death, he expresses the fear that historiography ("chronicle") will obscure the "truth": "But let the world, as all to whom I am / This day a spectacle, to time deliver, / And by tradition fix posterity, / Without another chronicle than truth, / How constantly my resolution suffered / A martyrdom of majesty' (5.3.70–5). But despite Warbeck's reservations, history was praised in the renaissance for its ability to illuminate the present, that is, to teach lessons. What is more, literature was perceived to have an even more universally accepted pedagogical authority. In fact, one of the historians who branded Warbeck a fraud, Thomas Gainsford relates how *Perkin Warbeck*, a play staged in London, "instructed those who cannot read."[51] Ironically, Gainsford refers in Heywood-like fashion not to Ford's drama but to another, now lost, play about the saga. Ford's play may well have instructed "those who cannot read," but it did (and does) so in ways intolerable to Gainsford and the state. The play gives the audience an opportunity to revisit the early hours of the Tudor state in order to witness "A Strange Truth," a "history couched in a play," and, without necessarily accepting Warbeck's version (for Warbeck's detractors like Henry and Durham have potent historical voices), to reclaim a portion of the past from the historians.

VI

I do not think that Ford believed that plays were necessarily or ordinarily more historical than narrative histories. But Ford's decision to set his dramatic account of the Warbeck story in direct competition with its narrative counterparts does promote a considered skepticism about the practical enterprise of many English renaissance historians and historiography in general. He focuses our attention on a gap between the historians' theories and their practice. He attributes the existence of this gap indirectly to the historian's sloppiness (reliance on erroneous sources), and directly to the political character of a generic plot implemented to promote the continuance of the Tudor–Stuart dynasty. Thirdly, Ford chastises the historians for not recognizing the fundamentally literary dimension of historical narrative. The culturally based plot codes make it impossible for the narrative historian to serve up Holinshed's "simple truth" or Sidney's "what is."

The anti-authoritarian thrust of Ford's play is in three parts. First, there is the play's opposition to government ideology. Although many of the narrative histories were not primarily products of aristocratic patronage, they were heavily indebted to Polydore Vergil's history of England, a work that *was* commissioned by the monarch, and they were shaped by government censorship as well as by the prevailing cultural climate which made them, as D. R. Woolf argues, quite orthodox.[52] The ideologies disseminated in these histories were internalized by a broad segment of the population, but they primarily served and preserved the interests of the ruling class. Ford's *Perkin Warbeck* contests those values insofar as it refashions the "content" of the Warbeck story into a new narrative, or, more accurately, narrative*s*. This refashioning is significant not merely because it is a form of dissension but also because it takes away symbolically the prerogative of history-writing from the ruling class and claims it for the public stage. Finally, *Perkin Warbeck* also deconstructs the historiographical and/or genealogical *models* relied on by English monarchs to assert their power over their subjects. In the late Jacobean and early Caroline period, Ford's revisionary narratives and deconstruction of historiographical modes of apprehension would have packed a considerable anti-authoritarian punch. The actual power of James I or Charles I did of course not depend on a rehashing of the Warbeck episode; but the ease with which power is exercised depends in some measure on monarchial control over processes of royal self-definition and self-legitimation, both of which come under attack in the play.

The only thing one can do at the end of the play is place one's trust in Henry – or not. Opting for Henry is no doubt the pragmatic thing to do – especially in retrospect, since he won and turned out to be an efficient ruler who brought much needed stability to the nation – but unlike many of his Elizabethan predecessors Ford does not appear to encourage alert members of his (reading) audience to do so. Ford's belated excursion into the history play genre abandons the well-known story line of the hero who *overcomes* a number of obstacles, growing in stature and legitimacy all the time, to emerge as victor and undisputed ruler in the fifth act. Henry VII executes Warbeck but he does not *overcome* him. The traditional literary model is never imposed on the basic story matter. Earlier we noted via Hayden White that many historians believe they "find" the *form* of their narratives in the historical events themselves, even though the most straightforward "descriptions of events *already* constitute interpretations of their nature" (*Tropics of Discourse* 95). To be sure, like any other historian's version of the past, Ford's narrative constitutes a historical interpretation; but in Ford's hands the narrative of the clash between Warbeck and Henry VII becomes a dramatization of fundamental undecidability of historical truth.

His play, Ford writes in the Prologue, is "A history of noble mention, *known*, / Famous, and true" (15–16; emphasis added). But clearly, history, as recounted in this drama, is not *known* in the way the readers of the Tudor chronicles knew it. Indeed, to call the history "known" and then to offer an account that departs from the known tale only stresses its difference from what the culture knows. As I hinted earlier, Ford is able to do this because

Tudor legitimacy had become a less pressing matter in the early decades of the seventeenth century than it had been in the years immediately following Bosworth Field, and because, as a consequence of that shift in emphasis, the generic plot codes designed to dramatize the importance of Tudor legitimacy had lost their hold over what people like Ford are able to think. Ford's historiographical difference manifests itself sharply because the competitive efforts by Henry VII and Warbeck to produce their legitimacy *foreground* the ways in which historiography itself functions as ideological production. In as much as *The Chronicle History of Perkin Warbeck* is a meta-historical history play, it is a double production of historiography; it reveals how historiography produces history, and also the process whereby ideology produces the historiographical forms which produce ideology. Such a foregrounding, if recognized by a Jacobean or Caroline audience, could have had actual implications for the ways in which political debates involving historical argumentation are settled. There is nothing "out of fashion" about that.

From the outset, I suggested that *Perkin Warbeck* should not be read as a direct political challenge to the *legitimacy* of Charles I's crown.[53] Surely, a number of Charles's powers were contested by the Commons throughout his reign, but his legal birthright to rule England was never in question. Moreover, if Ford intended to challenge Charles, it is hard to explain his dedication of the play to William of Cavendish, the Earl of Newcastle and "leader of the royalist armies in the North."[54] Still, Charles I, during whose reign *Warbeck* was published, should probably have been opposed to a play challenging the institution of monarchy.[55] James I of course had written solemnly and eloquently about divine right theory and the monarch's special relation to the law, but recent historians have argued convincingly that it was Charles for whom these theories proved most important in *practice*. James had almost always shown a willingness to forego his absolutist claims in order to reach political settlements with his Parliaments. Charles, on the other hand, embraced ideas of divine right and absolutism with such uncompromising vigor that he became rigid and incapable of successful political negotiation.[56] Legal and political hallmarks such as the Forced Loan of 1626, the parliamentary impeachment procedures against the unpopular royal favorite Duke of Buckingham, the Five Knights' Case, and the Personal Rule[57] corroded the authority of the crown and increased public perception of the monarch as one who believed himself to transcend the laws of the land. As Parliament sought assurances against royal infringements on the rights and liberties of the subject, Charles was typically more interested in reminding the Commons that his powers were divine, traditional (historical), and hereditary. He asserted contentiously: "I owe no account of mine actions but to God alone," and he "reminded parliament of the constitutional reality that they could not 'make or declare a law without my consent.'"[58] In particular during the period of the "personal rule," during which *Warbeck* was published, Charles's drive to achieve absolutism polarized English society. Perry Anderson notes that Charles restricted the conferral of privileges to the peerage and "the topmost stratum of urban merchants . . . The bulk of the gentry and the newer mercantile interests were excluded from the royal concert."[59] What is more, Charles utilized "every possible feudal and neo-feudal device in the quest for tax revenues capable of sustaining an enlarged State machine beyond Parliamentary control: revival of warships, fines for knighthood, use of purveyance, multiplication of monopolies, inflation of honours" (Anderson, "Kingship" 141). *Perkin Warbeck* may not discourse on these specific matters, but its treatment of historiography assumes an unquestionably anti-absolutist stand and frustrates polarization.

In any case, even if Charles's censor saw no need to excise potentially seditious parts of the play, the authors of the dedicatory verses printed in the 1634 quarto edition obviously felt uncomfortable endorsing a play about a sympathetic and majestic figure challenging the birthright of the founder of the Tudor dynasty. Two of the authors, as Anne Barton has pointed out, make it politicly clear that they do not support Warbeck's claim to be the Duke of York. A third "reduces him to a trickster who 'ran his wily ways,'" while the remaining two steer clear of the issue altogether.[60] No doubt it is possible that these authors were indeed convinced that Warbeck was an imposter. But we should not forget that in 1634, when *Warbeck* is published, we are closing in on the Civil War, and it is not unthinkable that during the contentious period that preceded it the verse writers were reluctant to commit themselves in print to a play giving a "pretender" more than his due.[61] Indeed, who other than the most daring would express support for Shakespeare's Henry Bolingbroke in writing when performances of *Richard II* coincided with the Earl of Essex's march on London?

Conclusion

Why precisely the number of history plays declines in the Stuart era is difficult to explain in historical terms, not least because even the most carefully construed exposé of historical conditions may fail to account for an individual author's choices or subtle changes in audience taste. Nonetheless, critics like Felix E. Schelling, William D. Briggs, Irving Ribner, Anne Barton, Leonard Tennenhouse, and others, have offered substantive reasons why the historical drama ceased to flourish just when it did. They have pointed to a loss of "national spirit" (occasioned by the accession of a foreign monarch and Spanish peace), the rise of foreign and satiric drama, "a general satiety with the [history play] type," Puritan attacks on history plays, censorship of historical subjects, and to changes in the way state authority presented and idealized itself. My response to what many have called the genre's "decline" has of course been to shift the discussion away from questions of aesthetics and to questions of historiographical theory and practice. Although our conclusions differ significantly, I am, on this score, indebted to the work of Irving Ribner, who also took seriously the import of historiography on the drama. The genre's "decline," Ribner maintains, results from too great an emphasis on romance elements, whereas I have come to the conclusion that it is a matter of too much historiography.

Ribner argues that the success of the history play genre depended on striking a careful balance between the authentic purposes of history and the dramatic need for romance themes.[1] When the history play "ceased to serve the didactic functions of history," it "lost the unity of purpose and design which made it significant as drama. When it was not held together by the power of romance themes, it became mere disjointed pageantry, such as Shakespeare's *Henry VIII*, which adds to the incoherence of Holinshed only the greatness of poetry" (Ribner, *English History Play* 271). For Ribner, historical drama requires romance themes, but should not allow its "historical" matter to become suppressed or inconsequential in the process. Ribner's inclusion of "romance themes" among the genuine purposes of history is remarkable because it moves him very close to endorsing Hayden

White's contention regarding the historian's crucial reliance on literary narrative to render "history" accessible. In any case, either the excessive presence *or* total absence of "romance themes" accounts in Ribner's argument for the Stuart history play's aesthetic decline.

Ribner's claims approximate to my own to a degree because, unlike some critics, he does not take it for granted that good drama must "transcend" the generic characteristics of its sources. Rarely is it suggested that literature takes on the formal features of other modes of text production: good literature always overpowers what it comes into contact with. Peter Ure's claim (discussed in chapter 6) that reading or viewing *Perkin Warbeck* is primarily a "literary experience," not a legal or historical experience is an outstanding expression of the latter position. Ribner, in arguing that the successful history play must stay true to the authentic purposes of renaissance historiography, asserts precisely the opposite. His explanation is based, nonetheless, on several assumptions that my study challenges. Ribner implies that it was a mistake for the playwrights to abandon their strong focus on the "careers of kings and nobles" as molders of history. Secondly, he maintains that historiography and historical drama without "romance themes" are disjointed and incoherent. In effect, he takes for granted that abandoning the governing rules of Tudor historiography and drama killed the genre in the Stuart era. We can all agree that the history play fared much better in the Tudor period than it did in the Stuart period, but Ribner's argument skews the real issue because it judges the Stuart history play by a set of standards extracted from the *Tudor* plays. Without apparent awareness of its anachronisity, Ribner simply charges that the conventions of Tudor historiography were so well suited to successful theatrical representation that they should never have been abandoned. That new, post-Elizabethan ways of thinking about historiographical representation are changing the form of the plays to suit new cultural, political, and philosophical priorities – that it is not a question of too much or too little romance – is never considered as a viable alternative.

Another failing of the critics is that they take as gospel John Ford's well-known pronouncement (c. 1630) concerning the history play's state of disfavor. Ford's pronouncement may in fact be the type of highbrow comment regarding audience taste we associate with Ben Jonson. In the prologue to *Warbeck*, Ford claims that "Studies have of this nature been of late / So out of fashion, so unfollowed, that / It is become more justice to revive the antic follies of the times than strive / To countenance wise industry" (Prologue 2–5). "Studies of this nature" need not strictly refer to history plays, and can also refer to "serious" drama in general, especially, since Ford contrasts his play with the "antic follies of the times," i.e., low comedy. But even if Ford is referring to the historical drama, then he is wrong, or at the very least misleading. Stuart audiences continued to cherish the Tudor history play genre, as is borne by the sparse record of public and court performances. The King's Men revived Shakespeare's *Henry V* (at court in 1605),[2] possibly *1 Henry IV* (1635) and *2 Henry IV* (1619 or 1620), *Richard II* (1631), and *Richard III* (1633).[3] Marlowe's *Edward II* was performed by Queen Anne's company sometime between 1615 and 1622 at the Red Bull. Title pages of other plays like the anonymous *King John* and *Thomas Lord Cromwell* refer to theatrical performances – "as they were (sundry times) *lately* acted by the Queenes Maiesties Players"[4] – and although this type of language of course offers no firm dates it does indicate Stuart stagings. What is more, Falstaff, Bardolph, Pistol, and Will Summers may fall into Ford's category of "antic follies," but there is nothing in *Richard II*, *Richard III*, *Edward II*, *Barnavelt*, or *Henry VIII* that would allow them to be classified in this way.

Even the apparent popularity of some Stuart plays belies our common understanding of Ford's pronouncement. Heywood's *If You Know Not Me* (part 1) was revived by Queen Henrietta's Company sometime between 1626 and 1637 (it also went through printings in 1605, 1606, 1608, and 1610), and *Henry VIII* was revived at least once, in the year 1628 (apparently with George Villiers, Duke of Buckingham, in attendance). There is no record of pre-revolution revivals of either *Warbeck* or *Barnavelt* but contemporary sources indicate that their initial performances met with considerable success. It seem reasonable to assume, therefore, that while nostalgic Stuart audiences had a significant appetite for Elizabethan revivals, there was also room for the intellectually charged historical dramas. If the genre had run its course by the time the theaters were closed, it was not because of an aesthetic decline but because the playwrights had taken the genre as far as it could go; they had first written historical plays and then written plays about the writing of history. Almost inevitably, once the productive process has been scrutinized and its way of evoking responses in the audience has been laid bare, its mystery and efficacy vanish, making spontaneous emotional responses a near impossibility. In this respect, it is virtually certain that by becoming increasingly sophisticated in its representation of the nature of historical representation, the history play wrote itself out of existence. Once the secrets of history-writing are exposed to the daylight of the theater for all to see, it is virtually impossible to go back and write some more old-fashioned history plays – except of course for purposes of nostalgia.

It is important therefore to move beyond the common thesis that the Stuart historical drama and renaissance historiography developed in opposite directions; that, as England entered the seventeenth century, historiography steadily gained in sophistication while the historical drama underwent a devastating aesthetic decline. It is certainly accurate that as historiography began to incorporate some useful antiquarian principles and increasingly focused its attention on secondary causes, it took on some of the features of what we now think of as modern historiography. But the danger here is to portray historiography's development as a unitary drive into the modern period and to erase in the process any medieval and renaissance properties that continued to flourish well into the seventeenth century. Even Holinshed's massive *Chronicles of England, Scotland, and Ireland*, generally perceived by literary critics as a bastion of Tudor orthodoxy, has recently yielded much greater political and methodological diversity than hitherto thought possible. Annabel Patterson's revelatory new book offers impressive grounds upon which to reconsider the familiar view of Holinshed as a "baggy and undisciplined" tome that, on the whole, promotes the *grand récit* of Tudor orthodoxy Tillyard and others professed to detect in it. Patterson argues that Holinshed's "bagginess" and failure to promote an aggressive pro-Tudor stance suggest that its editor conceived of history as "documentary history," and believed in the representation of "diversity of opinion" at a time when the English nation was no longer unified on questions of religion and politics.[5] If Holinshed's history was more advanced than we thought, some of the early seventeenth-century political histories at times turn to the kind of providentialism and didacticism we associate with medievalism and humanism.

In the sixteenth century, then, there was very little indication of a concerted effort to resolve the contradictions between antiquarian, providential, and humanist representations of history. These approaches to the past contradicted one another significantly, yet coexisted, "progressing" and often intermingling in unpredictable ways. The erasure of this diversity eliminates the latent opportunities for debate and opposition it created for dramatists and others. I have resisted a streamlined teleology of renaissance historiography and stressed how the coexistence of contradictory historiographies facilitates instances in the drama where their convergence creates sites of epistemological friction and ambiguity.

Just as I have been wary of strong teleologies of renaissance historiography, I have tried to show that the Stuart history play is not the aesthetic failure so many critics claim it is. But even as I have endeavored to portray the Stuart history as a fundamentally different kind of play than the Elizabethan history play – and not as its ugly stepchild – by pointing at the enriching effects innovations in renaissance historiography had on it, I do not want to leave the impression that I am merely inverting the trajectory of artistic decline and turning it into one of triumph. The Tudor period offers us instances of highly complex and self-conscious treatments of the character of historiographical representation. My discussion of *Henry V* sought to demonstrate just this point. But we saw that even much earlier texts like Bale's *King Johan* already contain profound moments of intersection between literature and history/historiography. In this play, the author is led by political and religious views to the appropriation of historical discourses for the explicit purpose of revising history in a literary medium. Structurally, what Bale does is not that different from Shakespeare, Ford, Fletcher, and Massinger. Indeed, my primary reason for including a discussion of *King Johan* is to preempt any easy generalizations about the *smooth* development and ever-growing sophistication of historical thought in the drama.

There are two further compelling reasons against reading the story of the Stuart historical drama as one of steady progress. The number of extant plays is too limited, and, secondly, some of the surviving texts do not betray a particularly intense desire to ponder the nature of historiographical representation. R. A. Gent's *The Valiant Welshman* (1615), Thomas Drue's *The Dutches of Suffolke* (1623), and Samuel Rowley's *When You See Me You Know Me* (1605), and even Thomas Dekker's *The Famous History of Sir Thomas Wyatt* (1603–5) instantly reveal that not all Stuart plays convey equal concern with the subtle questions of historical thought.[6] Thomas Drue's *The Life of the Dutches of Suffolke*,[7] for instance, written around the year 1623, does not exhibit any preoccupation with the historiographical sophistication and diversity we detected in *Henry VIII*, *Barnavelt*, *Warbeck* or even *If You Know Not Me* (which Drue's biographical history play resembles in some respects). Both *The Dutches of Suffolke* and *If You Know Not Me* depict, often in melodramatic fashion, the polemical Foxean reading of history that pits good Protestants against wicked agents of Rome; and both plays conclude with the death of Bloody Mary and the triumphant delivery of its respective persecuted but steadfast heroines, Princess Elizabeth and Katherine, Duchess of Suffolk. Drue never strays from this straight and narrow path, but Heywood's reliance on a one-sided rendering of history is complicated (as we saw in chapter 3) in thoughtful ways that qualify his representation of Elizabeth's ascendancy. Drue's play, on the other hand, avoids historiographical subtlety by tenaciously following the propagandistic, Foxean hard line. In Drue's play the constructed nature of historical presentation is meant to disappear; in Heywood's play that nature is brought to our attention.

Likewise, Samuel Rowley's *When You See Me You Know Me* looks back to Tudor history play conventions, rather than forward into the Jacobean era. From a historiographical vantage point *When You See Me*, which depicts the events from the birth of Prince Edward (the later Edward VI) and the death of Jane Seymour to the arrival of Charles V in London, contrasts keenly with Shakespeare and Fletcher's drama about the reign of

Henry VIII. If Shakespeare and Fletcher's sympathetic portrayal of the righteous Catherine of Aragon generates a genuine religious and historiographical ambiguity (her character is neither vilified nor effaced), Rowley's drama follows the same Foxean standard in evidence in *The Dutches of Suffolke* when it avoids any possible understanding for or tolerance of the Catholic cause. *When You See Me* gains its thematic unity from the clash between the authority of Rome and the royal supremacy of Henry VIII, a clash that governs only the opening action of Shakespeare and Fletcher's play. Significantly, the struggle for supremacy between crown and papacy – between the institutions of church and state – is embodied primarily in the figures of two powerful men, Henry VIII and Cardinal Wolsey. Unlike Shakespeare and Fletcher's hero, who is most conspicuous for his absence, Rowley's Henry VIII dominates most of the play's action with his legendary bluff and outbursts of anger. Indeed, while roaming the city of London in disguise to observe abuses and corruption amongst his subjects, Henry's involvement with and concern for his subjects is apparent in his lament (somewhat reminiscent of Shakespeare's Henry V's on the eve of Agincourt): "Fond heedelesse men, what bootes it for a King / To toyle himselfe and his high states affaires, / To summon Parliaments, and call together / The wisest heads of all his Prouinces: / Making statutes for his Subjects' peace. / That thus neglecting them, their woes increase."[8] What is more, the historical Wolsey had died in 1530, long before the events described in the play, which begin shortly before the birth of Prince Edward in 1537. In other words, Rowley resurrects this notorious agent of Rome – who boasts to Bonner that "whilst Harries life doth stand, / Hee shall be king, but we will rule the land" (C^r) – to give a very specific and familiar shape to the forces opposing English political and religious independence. And since it is a hallmark of much Tudor historiography to view historical controversy and development primarily in terms of the conflicts between powerful men, it is plain that Rowley is following this model aggressively, whereas Fletcher and Shakespeare's play clearly tends to enfeeble it.

A comparison between the Tudor and Stuart historical drama on the question of historiographical appropriation does not yield easy generalizations, but we can observe certain plain tendencies. The most noticeable difference in the representation of things historical in the renaissance drama is that as we approach and enter the seventeenth century, the drama's awareness of historiographical *variety* clearly intensifies. Stuart drama is generally more *deliberate* in its styling of historiographical representation. Tudor drama occasionally makes representation *an* issue, but in the Stuart plays treated here it is *the* issue. The Stuart drama does something we encounter only rarely in the Tudor drama, namely, it yokes heterogeneous approaches *together* in a unified dramatic discourse, for all to behold on the stage. This intense focus on historiography (as opposed to just history) was no doubt made possible by the veritable explosion in historical reading in the last decades of the sixteenth century which noticeably raised and widened the audience's level of historical consciousness.[9] This awareness made it much easier for the Stuart dramatists to politicize – or to disclose the already politicized nature of – historiographical discourse than it had been for their Tudor predecessors. Exactly how much the drama contributed to a growing public awareness of historical representation is difficult to determine, but late Elizabethan and Jacobean prohibitions against the printing of histories, the arrest of the players that put on *Richard II* during the Essex rising, the Bishop of London's decision to halt the performance of *Barnavelt*, Ben Jonson's troubles with the Star Chamber over the Roman history *Sejanus*, are only a few of the indicators of government's increasing fears about uncontrolled historiographical discourses.[10]

Despite governmental measures against unbridled productions of history, the plays discussed here are neither openly nor categorically subversive. Despite occasional and brief excursions into micropolitics, the plays discussed in this study do not involve themselves deeply in the nuts and bolts of specific laws or policies. To have done so would have invited censorship. On the whole these Stuart plays cannot be said to promulgate a cohesive ideological agenda; nor do they fit, individually, into clear political categories. Their subversive character resides in their appropriation and juxtaposition of multiple historiographical perspectives borrowed from a culture in which these perspectives already existed. Their juxtaposition, however, subversively foregrounds epistemological ambiguities in the production of versions of the past. It undercuts the premises upon which monolithic discourse relies, and therefore exercises a nebulous yet subtle potentially pervasive effect on all political discourse that appeals to history.

The concrete impact of such latent subversion cannot be measured accurately. Kernan once voiced his amazement that the censor permitted so many plays staging regicide.[11] This amazement is justified because these plays obviously intersected with the ongoing public debate on violent resistance to the crown, a debate in which King James himself, who had a lifelong fear of assassination, was a participant.[12] One way to answer the question why they were allowed to be staged is to say that pro-monarchy sentiments were considered so overwhelming that the government did not think a play would incite a citizen to regicide. Yet Charles I's fate demonstrates that the English people proved quite capable of killing a king, and who is to say that the stage murders of Richard II, Julius Caesar, Edward II, Duncan of Scotland, and Hamlet of Denmark – to name just a few – did not help to alter the mind of the people and make Charles's execution possible? In much the same way, the destabilization of historical discourses perpetrated in the Stuart drama may well have contributed to the piecemeal undermining of the authority of the crown, helping to prepare the end of the Stuart brand of royal absolutism.

Notes

PREFACE

1 Phyllis Rackin, *Stages of History: Shakespeare's English Chronicles* (Ithaca, NY: Cornell University Press, 1990), pp. 4, 13.
2 Iving Ribner, *The English History Play in the Age of Shakespeare* (Princeton: Princeton University Press, 1957), p. 27. Lily B. Campbell, *Shakespeare's Histories: Mirrors of Elizabethan Policy* (San Marino, CA: Huntington Library, 1947), pp. 8–17.

INTRODUCTION

1 Irving Ribner, *The English History Play in the Age of Shakespeare* (Princeton: Princeton University Press, 1957). Almost all studies of renaissance historical drama limit themselves to a consideration of Shakespeare's works. Among the most important studies of this kind are: M. M. Reese, *The Cease of Majesty: A Study of Shakespeare's History Plays* (London: Edward Arnold, 1961); Sigurd Burckhardt, *Shakespearean Meanings* (Princeton: Princeton University Press, 1968), pp. 144–205; Graham Holderness, *Shakespeare's History* (New York: St. Martin's Press, 1982); John Turner, Graham Holderness, Nick Potter, *Shakespeare: The Play of History* (Iowa City: University of Iowa Press, 1988); David Scott Kastan, *Shakespeare and the Shapes of Time* (Hanover, NH: University Press of New England, 1982); Phyllis Rackin, *Stages of History: Shakespeare's English Chronicles* (Ithaca, NY: Cornell University Press, 1990). Larry Champion's *"The Noise of Threatening Drum": Dramatic Strategy and Political Ideology in Shakespeare and the English Chronicle Plays* (Newark, Delaware: University of Delaware Press, 1990) does reach beyond Shakespeare but not beyond the Elizabethan period.
2 See Alvin B. Kernan, "From Ritual to History: the English History Plays," in *The Revels History of Drama in English*, 4 vols. (London: Methuen, 1975), vol. III, pp. 262–99, especially p. 264. Kernan argues that the historical drama exhibits a fundamentally conservative ideology vis-à-vis social order. In *The Idea of History in Early Stuart England: Erudition, Ideology and "The Light of Truth" from the Accession of James I to the Civil War* (Toronto: University of Toronto Press, 1990), D. R. Woolf makes strikingly similar claims for historiography when he submits that "obedience, duty, and deference to social and political hierarchy" were among its defining qualities (p. xiii).
3 Arthur B. Ferguson, *Clio Unbound: Perception of the Social and Cultural Past in Renaissance England* (Durham, NC: Duke University Press, 1979), p. 4.

4 William Shakespeare, *Henry V*, (The Arden Shakespeare), J. H. Walter (ed.) (London and New York: Methuen, 1985), 4.8.105–7.

5 David Scott Kastan, *Shakespeare and the Shapes of Time* (Hanover, NH: University Press of New England, 1982), p. 58.

6 Leonard Tennenhouse, "Strategies of State and Political Plays: *A Midsummer Night's Dream, Henry IV, Henry V, Henry VIII*," *Political Shakespeare: New Essays in Cultural Materialism*, Jonathan Dollimore and Alan Sinfield (eds.) (Ithaca and London: Cornell University Press, 1985), p. 121 (emphasis added).

7 Sigurd Burckhardt, *Shakespearean Meanings* (Princeton: Princeton University Press, 1968), p. 173.

8 Jonathan Dollimore and Alan Sinfield, "History and Ideology: The Instance of *Henry V*," *Alternative Shakespeares*, John Drakakis (ed.) (London and New York: Methuen, 1985), p. 225.

9 Terry Eagleton, *Marxism and Literary Criticism* (Berkeley and Los Angeles: University of California Press, 1976), p. 21. Also see Terry Eagleton, *Criticism and Ideology: A Study in Marxist Literary Theory* (London: Verso, 1976), pp. 80–5; Fredric Jameson, *Marxism and Form: Twentieth Century Dialectical Theories of Literature* (Princeton: Princeton University Press, 1976), pp. 401–7.

10 Eagleton quotes Trotsky, *Marxism and Literary Criticism*, p. 24.

11 Also see Eagleton, *Marxism and Literary Criticism*, pp. 22, 24, and *Criticism and Ideology*, pp. 84–5.

12 Hayden White, *Tropics of Discourse* (Baltimore: Johns Hopkins University Press, 1987), p. 82.

13 See Jonathan Dollimore, "Introduction: Shakespeare, Cultural Materialism and the New Historicism," *Political Shakespeare: New Essays in Cultural Materialism*, Jonathan Dollimore and Alan Sinfield (eds.) (Ithaca and London: Cornell University Press, 1985), p. 13.

14 Unless stated otherwise, references to Shakespeare are to *The Complete Works of Shakespeare*, David Bevington (ed.) (Glenview, IL and London: Scott, Foresman, 1980), and will be given in parentheses in the text.

15 Sir Philip Sidney, *The Defence of Poesy* in *Sir Philip Sidney*, Katherine Duncan-Jones (ed.) (Oxford and New York: Oxford University Press, 1989).

16 Sir Walter Ralegh, *The History of the World*, in *Selected Writings*, Gerald Hammond (ed.) (Harmondsworth, England: Penguin, 1986), p. 170.

17 Cf. John Turner et al., *Shakespeare: The Play of History*, pp. 1–2.

18 See, for instance, the "The Circulation of Social Energy" in Stephen Greenblatt, *Shakespearean Negotiations: The Circulation of Social Energy in Renaissance England* (Berkeley and Los Angeles: University of California Press, 1988), pp. 1–20. In cataloging different types of "acquisitions," Greenblatt is trying to articulate some generic principles that govern the dynamic exchanges between the theater and its cultural environment.

19 Walter Cohen, "Political Criticism of Shakespeare," *Shakespeare Reproduced*, Jean E. Howard and Marion F. O'Connor (eds.) (New York and London: Methuen, 1987), pp. 33–4.

20 See my "Shakespeare Criticism: 'It is a kind of history,'" *College English* 56: 3 (1994), pp. 335–6.

21 Frank Kermode, "The High Cost of New History," *The New York Review of Books*, June 25, 1992, p. 43.
22 E. W. M. Tillyard, *Shakespeare's History Plays* (New York: Collier Books, 1962), p. 17.
23 Tillyard, *The Elizabethan World Picture : A Study of the Idea of Order in the Age of Shakespeare, Donne, and Milton* (1943) (New York: Vintage Books, n. d.). For a judicious discussion of Tillyard's *Picture* in a historical context, see Graham Holderness, "Prologue: 'The Histories' and History" in Turner et al., *Shakespeare*, pp. 14–16.
24 Aristotle, *On Poetics and Style*, G. M. A. Grube (trans.) (New York: Bobbs-Merrill, 1958), p. 18.
25 For Aristotle, Sidney, and others who also wrote on this subject, it does not follow that therefore history deals in truth and poetry in falsehood. Rather, history and poetry concern themselves with different types of truth: history with the particular truth of things ("what men have done" [Sidney, *Defence of Poesy* 216]) and poetry with the "general truths" of things (Aristotle, *Poetics* 18).
26 Arnaldo Momigliano is one of White's more cogent critics when he argues that the rules of evidence distinguish historical writing from other forms of writing. "History is no epic, history is no novel, history is not propaganda because in these literary genres control of the evidence is optional, not compulsory" ("The Rhetoric of History and the History of Rhetoric: On Hayden White's Tropes," *Comparative Criticism: A Yearbook*, E. S. Shaffer (ed.) (Cambridge: Cambridge University Press, 1981), pp. 259–68, 261.
27 Hayden White, *The Content of the Form: Narrative Discourse and Historical Representation* (Baltimore and London: The Johns Hopkins University Press, 1990), p. 36 (italics added).
28 Terry Eagleton, *Ideology: An Introduction* (London and New York: Verso, 1991), p. 221. See further, Louis Althusser, "Ideology and Ideological State Apparatuses (Notes Towards an Investigation)," *Lenin and Philosophy*, Ben Brewster (trans.) (New York and London: Verso, 1971), pp. 127–86.
29 See Antonia Gransden, *Historical Writing in England II: c. 1307 to the Early Sixteenth Century* (Ithaca: Cornell University Press, 1982), p. 429
30 As Irving Ribner notes, "the coming of Henry VII to the English throne in 1485 gave a new impetus to historical writing, for among other things the right of the Tudors to the throne had to be demonstrated" (*English History Play* 4). Also see Gransden, *Historical Writing* pp. 429, 431; on ideologically motivated history, see Rackin, *Stages of History* pp. 3–4.
31 F. J. Levy, *Tudor Historical Thought* (San Marino, CA: The Huntington Library 1967), pp. 59–60.
32 John Bale, *King Johan*, Barry B. Adams (ed.) (San Marino, CA: Huntington Library, 1969), p. 25.
33 John Foxe, *The Actes and Monuments of John Foxe: A New and Complete Edition*, ed. Stephen Reed Cattley (ed.) (London: Seeley and Burnside, 1841), p. 513.
34 There may be a slight ambivalence in White's work on this point. In *Tropics of Discourse* he maintains that the fictional element in all historical discourses does not imply "the degradation of historiography to the status of ideology or propaganda" (99), but in *Content of the Form* he makes it quite clear there is no such thing as "'pure' interpretation."

35 Jonathan Dollimore has made a very strong case for a renaissance understanding of the cognitive view of ideology (*Radical Tragedy: Religion, Ideology and Power in the Drama of Shakespeare and His Contemporaries* [Chicago: University of Chicago Press, 1984], pp. 17–19).

36 Raymond Williams, *Marxism and Literature* (Oxford: Oxford University Press, 1990), pp. 121–7.

37 Steven Mullaney, *The Place of the Stage: License, Play, and Power in Renaissance England* (Chicago and London: University of Chicago Press, 1988), p. 49.

38 Robert Weimann, "Representation and Performance: The Uses of Authority in Shakespeare's Theater," *PMLA* 107 (1992), pp. 498–9 (italics added).

39 Jean E. Howard, *The Stage and Social Struggle in Early Modern England* (London and New York: Routledge, 1994), p. 31. Also see David Scott Kastan, "Proud Majesty Made a Subject: Shakespeare and the Spectacle of Rule." *Shakespeare Quarterly* 37 (1986), pp. 459–75.

40 Louis B. Wright, *Middle-Class Culture in Elizabethan England* (Chapel Hill: University of North Carolina Press), pp. 297–338, esp. pp. 298, 315–17, 334, 337.

41 See, for instance, Bryan D. Palmer, *Descent into Discourse: The Reification of Language and the Writing of Social History* (Philadelphia: Temple University Press, 1990). Palmer's basic argument is that life cannot be reduced to language, and that literary theory is no substitute for historical materialism.

42 For a discussion of the way in which ideology interpellates individuals as subjects of the state/culture, see Althusser, "Ideology," pp. 127–88, 170.

1 RENAISSANCE HISTORIOGRAPHY

1 D. R. Woolf, *The Idea of History in Early Stuart England: Erudition, Ideology and "The Light of Truth" from the Accession of James I to the Civil War* (Toronto: University of Toronto Press, 1990), p. xiii.

2 Annabel Patterson, *Reading Holinshed's Chronicles* (Chicago and London: University of Chicago Press, 1994).

3 William Shakespeare, *Henry V* (The Arden Shakespeare), J. H. Walter (ed.) (London and New York: Methuen, 1985).

4 For a cogent recent discussion of the moral ambiguity surrounding Henry, see Graham Bradshaw, *Misrepresentations: Shakespeare and the Materialists* (Ithaca, NY: Cornell University Press, 1993), pp. 34–63.

5 Anne Barton offers a succinct summary of some of the explanations for this decline suggested over the years. See Anne Barton, "He that Plays the King: Ford's *Perkin Warbeck* and the Stuart History Play," *English Drama: Forms and Development*, Marie Axton and Raymond Williams (eds.) (Cambridge: Cambridge University Press, 1977), p. 69. For additional explanations, see Irving Ribner, *The English History Play in the Age of Shakespeare* (Princeton: Princeton University Press, 1957), p. 266; Felix E. Schelling, *The English Chronicle Play: A Study in the Popular Historical Literature Environing Shakespeare* (New York: Macmillan, 1902), p. 275; G. K. Hunter, "Truth and Art in History Plays," *Shakespeare Survey* 42 (1989), p. 21; and Margot Heinemann's discussion of censorship in Middleton's *Mayor of Queenborough or Hengist, King of Kent* in *Puritanism and Theatre: Thomas Middleton and the*

Opposition Drama under the Early Stuarts (Cambridge: Cambridge University Press, 1982), p. 144.

6 My account of renaissance historiography is indebted to a number of modern studies. The most salient are: Paul Avis, *Foundations of Modern Historical Thought: From Machiavelli to Vico* (London: Croom Helm, 1986); Ernst Breisach, *Historiography: Ancient, Medieval and Modern* (Chicago and London: University of Chicago Press, 1983); Peter Burke, *The Renaissance Sense of the Past* (New York: St. Martin's Press, 1969); Eric Cochrane, *Historians and Historiography in the Italian Renaissance* (Chicago: University of Chicago Press, 1985); Arthur B. Ferguson, *Clio Unbound: Perception of the Social and Cultural Past in Renaissance England* (Durham, NC: Duke University Press, 1979); F. Smith Fussner, *The Historical Revolution in English Historical Writing and Thought, 1580–1640* (London: Routledge and Kegan Paul, 1962); Felix Gilbert, *Machiavelli and Guicciardini: Politics and History in Sixteenth Century Florence* (New York and London: Norton, 1984); Antonia Gransden, *Historical Writing in England II: c. 1307 to the Early Sixteenth Century*, (Ithaca, NY: Cornell University Press, 1982); Thomas M. Greene, *The Light in Troy: Imitation and Discovery in Renaissance Poetry* (New Haven and London: Yale University Press, 1982); B. A. Haddock, *An Introduction to Historical Thought* (London: Edward Arnold, 1980); Joseph Levine, *Humanism and History: Origins of Modern English Historiography* (Ithaca and London: Cornell University Press, 1987); F. J. Levy, *Tudor Historical Thought* (San Marino, CA: Huntington Library, 1967); Lawrence Manley, "Contextualism and the Role of Convention in Historiography," in *Convention, 1500–1750* (Cambridge, MA: Harvard University Press, 1980), pp. 203–40; Barbara J. Shapiro, *Probability and Certainty in Seventeenth-Century England: A Study in the Relationships Between Natural Science, Religion, History, Law, and Literature* (Princeton: Princeton University Press, 1983), pp. 119–62; D. R. Woolf, *The Idea of History in Early Stuart England: Erudition, Ideology, and "The Light of Truth" from the Accession of James I to the Civil War* (Toronto, Buffalo and London: University of Toronto Press, 1990).

7 See Leonard F. Dean, *Tudor Theories of History Writing* (Ann Arbor, MI: University of Michigan Press, 1947); Leonard F. Dean, "Bodin's *Methodus* in England Before 1625," *Studies in Philology* 39 (1942), pp. 160–66; Elizabeth Story Donno, "Old Mouse-Eaten Records: History in Sidney's *Apology*," *Sir Philip Sidney: An Anthology of Modern Criticism*, Dennis Kay (ed.) (Oxford: Clarendon Press, 1987), pp. 145–67. For a good survey of the subject see Paul Avis, *Foundations of Modern Historical Thought*.

8 Levy notes that grammar schools used history primarily as a source for rhetorical and literary conventions to be imitated (*Tudor Historical Thought* 40–50). It was not until 1623 that the first chair in history was established at Oxford. And its first occupant, Degory Wheare, still very much conceived of history in a primarily literary sense, as a source for lessons in moral conduct. Also see Gransden, *Historical Writing*, p. 427.

9 Levy writes that "A record of past events, to be sure, was included under the rubric of history, but so were other narratives. In fact, any truthful-seeming narrative might be called a history; the word could be used to mean no more than story." See Levy for examples, *Tudor Historical Thought*, pp. 13–14.

10 See my "Introduction" and Levine comments regarding William Caxton later in this chapter. Also see the induction to Shakespeare's *The Taming of the Shrew*, *The Complete Works of Shakespeare*, David Bevington (ed.) (Glenview, IL: Scott Foresman), Ind. 2. 137.

11 Woolf's equation of journalistic writing about current events and history will become relevant in my chapter on *The Tragedy of Sir John Van Olden Barnavelt*, a historical tragedy that deals with current events.

12 For a detailed overview of "The Advent of Humanism" and its effects on English historiography, see Levy, *Tudor Historical Thought,* pp. 33–78.

13 Raphael Holinshed, "Preface to the Reader," *Chronicles of England, Scotland, and Ireland*, vol. III (London: 1807 reprint); Richard Grafton, "To the Right Honorable Sir Wylliam Cecill Knight. . .," *A Chronicle at Large*, vol. I (London: 1809 reprint).

14 Annabel Patterson, *Shakespeare and the Popular Voice* (Oxford: Basil Blackwell, 1989), pp. 77–8. Patterson also compiles a list of mostly well-known events (several of them dealing with censorship) that show that "the government regarded English historical material as subject to its own control."

15 See Phyllis Rackin, *Stages of History: Shakespeare's English Chronicles* (Ithaca, NY: Cornell University Press, 1990), pp. 3–5.

16 They could follow one of two models offered by St. Augustine: they could structure their accounts on the Genesis model of the seven days of the Creation or on that of the four Monarchies, culled from the apocalyptic Books of Daniel and Revelation (Gransden, *Historical Writing* 455).

17 R. G. Collingwood, *The Idea of History* (1946) (London and Oxford: Oxford University Press, 1956), p. 54.

18 Also see Ferguson, *Clio Unbound*, who points out that although historical cyclicism is in theory contrary to versions of history as linear process, it in actuality left "plenty of room for developmental interpretation" (351–2). Theories of deterioration following an Age of Gold or of humanity's slow but steady rise from a "Stone Age existence to civil society" enjoyed substantial cultural currency, especially in the closing years of the middle ages (356).

19 George Cavendish, *The Life and Death of Cardinal Wolsey* in *Two Early Tudor Lives*, Richard S. Sylvester and David P. Harding (eds.) (New Haven and London: Yale University Press, 1990), p. 45.

20 But see Gransden, *Historical Writing*, for examples that suggest that when medieval historians needed to they could recognize and deal with anachronisms (455, 463, 465).

21 Levy makes this point with regard to two of the most popular English histories, Ranulph Higden's *Polychronicon* and the *Brut* (*Tudor Historical Thought* 45).

22 Thomas Blundeville's *The True Order and Methode of Wryting and Reading Hystories*, Hugh G. Dick (ed.) *The Huntington Library Quarterly* 2 (1940), pp. 149–70.

23 Polydore Vergil, *The Anglica Historia of Polydore Vergil*, vol. LXXIV, Camden Series, Denys Hay (ed. and trans.) (London: Royal Historical Society, 1950), p. 5.

24 See, for example, Levy's "The Advent of Humanism," in *Tudor Historical Thought*, pp. 33–78; Geoffrey Elton, "Humanism in England," *The Impact of Humanism on Western Europe*, Anthony Goodman and Angus MacKay (eds.)

(New York and London: Longman, 1990), 259–78; Peter Burke, "The Spread of Italian Humanism," in *The Renaissance Sense of the Past*, (New York: St. Martin's Press, 1969), pp. 1–22; Douglas Bush, *The Renaissance and English Humanism* (Toronto: University of Toronto Press, 1965); Thomas M. Greene, *The Light in Troy: Imitation and Discovery in Renaissance Poetry* (New Haven and London : Yale University Press, 1982); Johan Huizinga, *The Waning of the Middle Ages* (London, 1948).

25 Joseph Levine paraphrases Paul Oskar Kristeller's definition of humanism (*Humanism and History* 10).

26 See, for example, Paul Oskar Kristeller, *Renaissance Thought II: Papers on Humanism and the Arts* (New York, Evanston and London: Harper Torchbooks, 1965); and Joseph Levine, *Humanism and History*.

27 J. G. A. Pocock, *The Ancient Constitution and the Feudal Law: A Study of English Historical Thought in the Seventeenth Century* (1957) (Cambridge: Cambridge University Press, 1987), p. 4.

28 For a lucid account of the profound link between humanist rhetoric and the *vita activa*, see Victoria Kahn, *Rhetoric, Prudence, and Skepticism in the Renaissance* (Ithaca, NY: Cornell University Press, 1985), especially pp. 29–54.

29 Gransden notes that a handful of chroniclers with especially strong political agendas did produce "unitary works" (*Historical Writing* 427).

30 For the standard work on this topic, see Felix Raab, *The English Face of Machiavelli: A Changing Interpretation, 1500–1700* (London: Routledge, 1964).

31 Niccoló Machiavelli, *Discourses on the First Decade of Titus Livius* in *Machiavelli, The Chief Works and Others*, 3 vols., Allan Gilbert (trans.) (Durham, NC: Duke University Press, 1965), vol. I, p. 198.

32 Felix Gilbert, *Machiavelli and Guicciardini: Politics and History in Sixteenth Century Florence* (New York and London: Norton, 1984), p. 196.

33 Thomas More, *The History of King Richard III*, Richard S. Sylvester (ed.) (New Haven and London: Yale University Press, 1976), pp. 82–3. Strictly speaking, not More's *History of Richard III* but Edward Hall's *The Union of the Two Noble and Illustrae Famelies of Lancastre & York* (1548) is Shakespeare's source. Hall, however, simply copied More's account verbatim.

34 See Paul Avis, *Foundations*, pp. 46–51.

35 Francesco Guicciardini, *Ricordi*, Ninian Hill Thomson (trans.) (New York: S. F. Vanni, 1949), pp. 205, 207, 211.

36 Leonard F. Dean, "Sir Francis Bacon's Theory of Civil History-Writing," *English Literary History* 8 (1941), pp. 161–83, 179.

37 Quoted in Dean, ibid., p. 179.

38 For an exemplary discussion of the rise of the antiquarian movement in England see Joseph Levine, "The Antiquarian Enterprise, 1500–1800" in *Humanism and History*, pp. 73–106.

39 For a sustained discussion of Valla's treatment of language and rhetoric, see Kahn, *Rhetoric, Prudence, and Skepticism*, pp. 75–88.

40 Arnaldo Momigliano, "Ancient History and the Antiquarian," in *Studies in Historiography* (London: Weidenfeld and Nicolson, 1966), p. 3.

41 Also see Eric Cochrane, *Historians and Historiography in the Italian Renaissance*, p. 439.

42 Also see Woolf, *The Idea of History*, p. 205.

43 Also see, J. Levine, *Humanism and History*, pp. 99–100; and D. R. Woolf, "Erudition and the Idea of History in Renaissance England," *Renaissance Quarterly* 40 (1987), pp. 11–48, 16–17. The same distinction existed in Italian circles. See Eric Cochrane, *Historians and Historiography*, pp. 435–44.
44 Sir Philip Sidney, *The Defence of Poesy* in *Sir Philip Sidney*, Katherine Duncan-Jones (ed.) (Oxford and New York: Oxford University Press, 1989), p. 220.
45 Also see Breisach, *Historiography*, pp. 174–7.
46 John Stow, *The Survey of London*, H. B. Wheatley (ed.) (London and Melbourne: Everyman, 1987), p. 3. Woolf notes that Stow nowhere calls his work a "history." "The only 'history' in the books is a brief prefatory account of the ancient Britons and Romans" (*Idea of History* 22).

2 HISTORIOGRAPHY AND TUDOR HISTORICAL DRAMA

1 D. R. Woolf, *The Idea of History in Early Stuart England: Erudition, Ideology and "The Light of Truth" from the Accession of James I to the Civil War* (Toronto: University of Toronto Press, 1990), p. 32.
2 As Arthur B. Ferguson notes, "The humanists who did most of the thinking for Tudor England were not much given to theorizing about history – less, indeed, that their continental contemporaries" (*Clio Unbound: Perception of the Social and Cultural Past in Renaissance England* [Durham, NC: Duke University Press, 1979], p. 4).
3 Alvin B. Kernan, "From Ritual to History: the English History Plays," *The Revels History of Drama in English* 4 vols. (London: Methuen, 1975), vol. III, pp. 262–99, p. 264. Despite the neatness of Kernan's description, I do not cite it here to suggest these plays are simplistic but to identify their historiographical tendencies.
4 See Jonathan Goldberg, "Speculations: *Macbeth* and Source," *Shakespeare Reproduced*, Jean Howard and Marion O'Connor (eds.) (New York and London: Methuen, 1987), pp. 242–64; John Turner (and Graham Holderness, Nick Potter), *Shakespeare: The Play of History* (Iowa City: University of Iowa Press, 1988), pp. 85–149.
5 See Woolf, *Idea of History*, p. xiii.
6 I give the date (1634) of publication of *The Chronicle History of Perkin Warbeck*, but the play was written earlier, perhaps even as early as in the final days of the reign of James I, although a date in the late 1620s or early 1630s is more plausible (see Peter Ure, "Introduction," Revels edition of *The Chronicle History of Perkin Warbeck*, Peter Ure (ed.) (London: Methuen, 1968), pp. xxviii–xxx.
7 There is evidence that Bale revised and made additions to the play perhaps until just before his death in 1563. For a cogent treatment of the history of Bale's text, see Barry Adams, "Introduction," John Bale's *King Johan* (San Marino, CA: Huntington Library, 1969), pp. 1–19.
8 Geoffrey's account of the battle between King Arthur's army and Lucius Hiberius, for instance, includes detailed information about troop strength, names of commanders, and speeches made by Lucius and Arthur (Geoffrey of Monmouth, *The History of the Kings of Britain*, Lewis Thorpe [ed.] [New York: Penguin, 1966], pp. 247–52). As Lewis Thorpe points out, "One is tempted to say that this is romanticized history with a vengeance, until one remembers that

the battle never took place and that it is merely romantic fiction" (18). Geoffrey, however, also drew heavily on the chronicles of Gildas and Nennius (cited in the dedication), as well as on the works of Cicero, Juvenal, Lucan, Apuleius, Bede, and King Alfred (18, 19). Unfortunately, few fifteenth-and sixteenth-century readers had the expertise to distinguish between what Geoffrey found in chronicles and what he made up. The author certainly does not provide the reader with helpful clues.

9 David Bevington, *Tudor Drama and Politics: A Critical Approach to Topical Meaning* (Cambridge, MA: Harvard University Press, 1968), p. 99.

10 Not too much should be made of the "birth" image here. As Gransden has demonstrated, the genre of the historical romance – a fictional account of the exploits of a historic figure – flourished in England as early as the twelfth (in Geoffrey of Monmouth's *Historia Regum Britanniae*) and again in the sixteenth century (see Gransden, *Historical Writing*, pp. 459, 471–2. The difference between *King Johan* and medieval historical romances lies in the former's equal treatment of the categories "history" and "morality play," whereas the romance's connection to history is but nominal.

11 John N. King, *English Reformation Literature: The Tudor Origins of the Protestant Tradition* (Princeton: Princeton University Press, 1982), pp. 131–2.

12 John Bale, *Illustrium maioris Britanniae scriptorum Summarium* (Wesel: Derek van der Straten, 1548), and *Scriptorum Illustrium maiores Britanniae . . . Catalogus*, 2 vols. (Basel: Oporinus, 1557–9).

13 In *Theatre and Reformation: Protestantism, Patronage, and Playing in Tudor England* (Cambridge: Cambridge University Press, 1993), Paul Whitfield White shows that "playwrights of the English Reformation *did* operate under conditions and for the purposes comparable to those of the Protestant publicists . . . [and] were similarly involved in the dissemination of Protestantism" (7, 12–41).

14 David Scott Kastan, "'Holy Wurdes' and 'Slypper Wit': John Bale's *King Johan* and the Poetics of Propaganda," *Rethinking the Henrician Era: Essays on Early Tudor Texts and Contexts*, Peter C. Herman (ed.) (Urbana, IL and Chicago: University of Illinois Press, 1994), pp. 265–82.

15 John Bale, *The Image of both Churches* (Antwerp: Mierdman, 1545).

16 My account of Bale's religious views is indebted to Peter Happé and John N. King, "Introduction," *The Vocacyon of Johan Bale* (Binghamton, NY: Renaissance English Text Society, 1990), pp. 4–5, 13–16.

17 John Bale, *The Vocacyon of Johan Bale*, ll. 458–66 (italics added).

18 "Except for the thousand year period from the Nativity to Pope Sylvester II, during which time Satan remained bound and sealed in the bottomless pit (Apoc. 20.1–3), the faithful few in each age have been persecuted by the various manifestations of the general Antichrist – particularly the Papacy. This state of affairs is to continue until the glorious Second Coming and the descent of the New Jerusalem, understood in a spiritual sense as a return to the uncorrupted doctrine and practice of the primitive Church" (Adams, "Introduction" 59).

19 Edmund Spenser, *The Faerie Queene* (letter to Raleigh), Thomas Roche, Jr. (ed.) (New Haven and London: Yale University Press, 1981), p. 15.

20 Andrew Hadfield, *Literature, Politics and National Identity: Reformation to Renaissance* (Cambridge: Cambridge University Press, 1994), p. 78.

21 John Bale, *King Johan*, Barry B. Adams (ed.) (San Marino, CA: Huntington Library, 1969), ll. 1107–20. All references to the play are to this edition and will be given in parentheses in the text hereafter.
22 William Baldwin, *The Mirror for Magistrates*, Lily B. Campbell (ed.) (New York: Barnes and Noble, 1960), p. 64.
23 For a detailed discussion of the authors cited by Bale see Adams, "Introduction," pp. 27–31.
24 Thomas Greene, *The Light in Troy: Imitation and Discovery in Renaissance Poetry* (New Haven and London: Yale University Press), 12. Significantly, Greene also suggests that during the course of both the Italian and the English Renaissance both became increasingly skeptical of the concept of "authority," especially in historical context (265).
25 Antonia Gransden, *Historical Writing in England II: c. 1307 to the Early Sixteenth Century* (Ithaca: Cornell University Press, 1982), p. 428.
26 Indeed, the fact that Bale did not follow a legendary approach in *King Johan* is all the more striking since he did accept and expand upon the Brutus story elsewhere (Levy, *Tudor Historical Thought* 65–6).
27 Thomas Dekker, *Sir Thomas Wyatt* in *The Dramatic Works of Thomas Dekker*, 4 vols., Fredson Bowers (ed.) (Cambridge: Cambridge University Press, 1953), vol. I.
28 It is probable that Heywood was a co-author of *Sir Thomas Wyatt*, which may help explain the historical continuity from *Wyatt* to *If You Know Not Me*.
29 See Hadfield, who argues that the play "manipulate[s] Henry VIII" and that "representing two figures on stage, the historical King John and the abstracted Imperial Majesty, not only solves the problem of writing a historical-morality play, but it also shows the author to exploit the hyphen connecting them and attempt to influence the future actions of the Tudor dynasty" (*Literature* 79).

3 THOMAS HEYWOOD AND THE PRINCESS ELIZABETH

1 Thomas Heywood, *If You Know Not Me, You Know No Bodie; or, The Troubles of Queene Elizabeth*, *The Dramatic Works of Thomas Heywood*, 6 vols. (New York: Russell and Russell, 1964 [1874]), pp. 189–247. Page numbers will be given in parentheses in the text hereafter.
2 Alexander Leggatt, *Jacobean Public Theatre* (London and New York: Routledge, 1992). The play also went through eight editions between 1605 and 1639 (164).
3 Thomas Heywood, *Englands Elizabeth: Her Life and Troubles, During Her Minoritie, from the Cradle to the Crowne*, Philip R. Rider (ed.) (New York and London: Garland Publishing Inc., 1982).
4 The extent of Elizabeth's involvement in the rebellion is uncertain. According to Joseph Ridley, "Wyatt wrote to Elizabeth and Courtenay, telling them of his plan to put them on the throne. The letters were intercepted by the government's spies, who also intercepted the correspondence between the plotters and Noailles; but they could not discover any letter from Elizabeth or Courtenay to either Wyatt or the French ambassador" (*Elizabeth I: The Shrewdness of Virtue* [New York: Fromm, 1989], p. 56).
5 Peter Lake, "Anti-popery: the Structure of a Prejudice," *Conflict in Early Stuart*

England: Studies in Religion and Politics 1603–1642, Richard Crust and Ann Hughes (eds.) (London and New York: Longman, 1989), p. 80.

6 Heywood's third source, Faybian's *Chronicles*, does not mention Sir Henry. Even if some members of the audience understood that Beningfield was the same as Benefield or Bedingfield, it would help them very little since Sir Henry served both Mary and Elizabeth.

7 Madeleine Doran, "Introduction," *If You Know Not Me You Know Nobody* (Oxford: Malone Society Reprint, 1935), p. xviii. Also see pp. xi–xiii for her discussion of the prologue and its relationship to the play.

8 The prologue was first printed in Heywood's *Pleasant Dialogues and Dramas* (1637). It was added to the eighth and final edition of the play in 1639, but the first five lines that provide it with a context in *Dialogues and Dramas* are excluded.

9 *OED*, definition 1.

10 Roger Lockyer, *The Early Stuarts: A Political History of England 1603–1642* (London and New York: Longman, 1989), p. 14.

11 James in fact continued negotiations with Spain, culminating in the fateful journey to Madrid undertaken by Prince Charles and the Duke of Buckingham for the hand of the Infanta Maria in 1623. Again, people and Parliament fiercely resisted James's schemes.

12 The naming of the Wyatt rebellion and the overthrow of Queen Jane in such close proximity suggests that they occurred at the same time. The play, however, conflates the two events. Wyatt and his Protestant forces rebelled in January of 1554. Jane was executed around that time, but her reign ended earlier, on 19 July 1553.

13 Raphael Holinshed, *Chronicles of England, Scotland and Ireland*, 4 vols. (London: 1808 reprint), vol. IV, p. 140.

14 The Wyatt insurrection transpired shortly after the marriage negotiations between Mary and Philip II had been brought to successful conclusion in 1554. If spectators associated that marriage with the 1604 negotiations for the Infanta, the prominence of the Wyatt insurrection in the opening scene of the play could be construed as a veiled criticism of James's Spanish marriage politics.

15 Roger Lockyer, *The Early Stuarts*, p. 281. Lockyer quotes from *Letters of King James VI & I*, G. P. V. Akrigg (ed.) (London and Berkeley: University of California Press, 1984), p. 207. Akrigg attributes this letter to Henry Percy, Earl of Northumberland.

16 Also see J. Bruce (ed.), *The Correspondence of King James VI with Robert Cecil and others in England during the Reign of Queen Elizabeth* (Camden Society, 1860), *passim.*

17 G. P. V. Akrigg, *Jacobean Pageant or the Court of James I* (Cambridge, MA: Harvard University Press, 1962), p. 39.

18 Anne Somerset, *Elizabeth I* (New York: Knopf, 1991), p. 562.

19 James I. "A Speech, as it was Delivered in the vpper Hovse of the Parliament . . ." In *The Political Works of James I*, Charles H. McIlwain (ed.) (Cambridge, MA: Harvard University Press, 1918), pp. 274, 282.

20 Samuel R. Gardiner, *History of England from the Accession of James I to the Outbreak of the Civil War, 1603–1642*, 10 vols. (New York: AMS Press, 1965), vol. I, p.141.

21 Yet in the final stages of his reign, James exhibited a serious interest in Arminianism, a religion the tenets of which, particularly on issues of predestination and free will, were often equated with popery. See J. P. Sommerville, *Politics and Ideology in England 1603–1640* (London and New York: Longman, 1986), pp. 217–24.

22 For a discussion of the social and financial distress brought on by the war, see D. M. Palliser, *The Age of Elizabeth: England under the Later Tudors 1547–1603 Social and Economic History of England* (London and New York: Longman, 1985), pp. 26–8, and Alan G. R. Smith, *The Emergence of a Nation State: The Commonwealth of England 1529–1660* (New York and London: Longman, 1984), pp. 233–9.

23 John Foxe, *The Imprisonment of the Princess Elizabeth* (from *Acts and Monuments*) in *Tudor Tracts 1532–1588*, A. F. Pollard (ed.) (Westminster: Constable, 1903), p. 363. See also Holinshed, *Chronicles* (vol. IV, p. 135) for an almost identical version.

24 Georgianna Ziegler, "England's Savior: Elizabeth I in the Writings of Thomas Heywood," *Renaissance Papers 1980* (1981), pp. 29–37.

25 "Heywood and the Popularization of History," *Modern Language Notes* 43 (1928), pp. 287–93.

26 A cruder historical paradigm might sacrifice even more historical specificity and substitute "human being" for "ruler." The history would still include counsel for "princes," but only insofar as that counsel pertains to all Christians.

27 Hayden White, "New Historicism: A Comment," *The New Historicism*, H. Aram Veeser (ed.) (New York and London: Routledge, 1989), pp. 293–302.

28 *The Structuralists: From Marx to Lévi-Strauss*, Richard DeGeorge and Fernande DeGeorge (ed.) (Garden City, NY: Anchor Books, 1972), pp. 85–122.

29 See Jakobson, "Linguistics and Poetics," pp. 93–5 for examples.

30 White, H., "New Historicism," p. 300. My adaption of White consists of a refocusing of his analysis from the field of literary history to the field of history and historiography. It is difficult to assess whether Jakobson would accept White's redirecting the poetic function of language to the realm of associative meaning. However, there may be a precedent for White's maneuver in the linguist's assertion that in poetry "the internal nexus between sound and meaning changes from latent into patent and manifests itself most palpably and intensely" (Jakobson, "Linguistics and Poetics" 114).

31 Stephen Greenblatt, *Shakespearean Negotiations: The Circulation of Social Energy in Renaissance England* (Berkeley, Los Angeles: University of California Press, 1988), p. 66.

32 T. S. Eliot, "The Metaphysical Poets," *Seventeenth-Century Prose and Poetry*, 2nd edn., Alexander M. Witherspoon and Frank J. Warnke (eds.) (San Diego and New York: Hartcourt Brace Jovanovich, 1982), p. 1063.

33 Quoted in B. A. Haddock, *An Introduction to Historical Thought* (London: Edward Arnold, 1980), p. 80.

34 Sir Philip Sidney, *Sir Philip Sidney*, Katherine Duncan-Jones (ed.) (Oxford and New York: Oxford University Press, 1989), p. 221.

35 Sir Thomas North (trans.), *Plutarch's Lives of the Noble Grecians and Romans* (1579), 6 vols. (London, 1895), vol. I, p. 4.

36 For a provocative piece on the profound similarities between Amyot and Sidney,

see Elizabeth Story Donno, "Old Mouse-Eaten Records: History in Sidney's *Apology*," *Sir Philip Sidney: An Anthology of Modern Criticism*, Dennis Kay (ed.) (Oxford: Clarendon Press, 1987), pp. 147–67.

37 Jean Bodin, "Of the Choice of History, by Way of Preface," *The Conspiracy of Catiline* and *The War of Jugurtha*, Thomas Heywood (trans.) (1608) (London and New York: Constable, Knopf, 1924), p. 16.

38 Thomas Heywood, *An Apology for Actors* (New York: Johnson Reprint Corporation, 1972), sig. B4^r.

39 Jonathan Dollimore, *Radical Tragedy: Religion, Ideology and Power in the Drama of Shakespeare and his Contemporaries* (Chicago: University of Chicago Press, 1984), p. 22.

40 Terry Eagleton, *Criticism and Ideology: A Study in Marxist Literary Theory* (London: Verso, 1976), p. 85.

41 Irving Ribner, *The English History Play in the Age of Shakespeare* (Princeton: Princeton University Press, 1957), p. 27.

42 Hayden White, "The Historical Text as Literary Artifact" (1974), *Tropics of Discourse: Essays in Cultural Criticism* (Baltimore: The Johns Hopkins University Press, 1987), p. 99.

43 John Stubbs, *John Stubb's Gaping Gulf with Letters and Other Relevant Documents*, Lloyd E. Berry (ed.) (Charlottesville: University of Virginia Press, 1968), p. 91.

44 For a controversial yet important discussion of the queen's gender in the context of renaissance culture, see Louis Montrose, "'Shaping Fantasies': Figurations of Gender and Power in Elizabethan Culture," *Representing the Renaissance*, Stephen Greenblatt (ed.) (Berkeley, Los Angeles and London: University of California Press, 1988), pp. 31–64.

4 SHAKESPEARE, FLETCHER AND THE QUESTION OF HISTORY

1 Sir Henry Wotton, *Reliquiae Wottonianae*, quoted in appendix of *Henry VIII* (Arden Shakespeare), R. A. Foakes, (ed.) (London: Methuen, 1968), p. 180.

2 Irving Ribner, *The English History Play in the Age of Shakespeare* (Princeton: Princeton University Press, 1957), p. 290.

3 Shakespeare used the juxtaposition of historical accounts on several occasions. We encounter it, for instance, in the tension between Chorus and play action in Henry V (see Chris Fitter, "A Tale of Two Branagh's: *Henry V*, Ideology and the Mekong Agincourt," *Shakespeare Left and Right*, Ivo Kamps [ed.] [New York and London: Routledge, 1991], pp. 259–75), and also in *The Tempest* in the contradictory historical accounts of Prospero and Caliban relating how the island was settled (see Francis Barker and Peter Hulme, "Nymphs and Reapers Heavily Vanish: the Discursive Con-texts of The Tempest," *Alternative Shakespeares*, John Drakakis [ed.] [London and New York: Methuen, 1985], pp. 191–205).

4 George Puttenham, *The Arte of English Poesie*, Edward Arber (ed.) (Kent, OH: Kent State University Press, 1970), p. 54.

5 Arthur B. Ferguson, *Clio Unbound: Perception of the Social and Cultural Past in Renaissance England* (Durham, NC: Duke University Press, 1979), pp. 4, 5.

6 Alvin B. Kernan, "From Ritual to History: the English History Plays," *The*

Revels History of Drama in English, 4 vols. (London: Methuen, 1975), vol. III, p. 264.

7 Phyllis Rackin, *Stages of History: Shakespeare's English Chronicles* (Ithaca, NY: Cornell University Press), p. 54.

8 Georg Lukács, *The Historical Novel*, Hannah Mitchell and Stanley Mitchell (trans.) (Lincoln and London: University of Nebraska press, 1983), p. 151.

9 E. W. M. Tillyard, *Shakespeare's History Plays* (New York: Collier Books, 1962 [1944]), pp. 16–17.

10 William Shakespeare, *Henry V* (Arden edition), J. H. Walter (ed.) (London and New York: Methuen, 1985). All quotations are taken from this edition and will from now on be identified in parentheses in the text.

11 I am thinking here of studies like Tillyard's *Shakespeare's History Plays*, Lily B. Campbell's Shakespeare's *"Histories": Mirrors of Elizabethan Policy* (San Marino, CA: Huntington Library, 1958), and M. M. Reese's *The Cease of Majesty: A Study of Shakespeare's History Plays* (London: Edward Arnold, 1961).

12 See John Turner (and Graham Holderness and Nick Potter), *Shakespeare: The Play of History* (Iowa City: University of Iowa Press, 1988), p. 2. For other studies confirming a similar interest in Shakespeare as a historian (as opposed to a mouthpiece of state authority), see A. R. Braunmuller, "*King John* and Historiography," *English Literary History* 55 (1988), pp. 309–32; David Norbrook, "*Macbeth* and the Politics of Historiography," *Politics of Discourse: The Literature and History of Seventeenth Century England*, Kevin Sharpe and Steven N. Zwicker (eds.) (Berkeley, Los Angeles and London: University of California Press, 1987), pp. 78–116; Jonathan Goldberg, "Speculations: *Macbeth* and Source," *Shakespeare Reproduced: The Text in History and Ideology*, Jean E. Howard and Marion F. O'Connor (eds.) (New York and London: Methuen, 1987), pp. 242–64; David Quint, "'Alexander the Pig': Shakespeare on History and Poetry," *Boundary 2* 10 (1982), pp. 49–67; Herbert Lindenberger, *Historical Drama: The Relation of Literature and Reality* (Chicago and London: University of Chicago Press, 1975).

13 Larry S. Champion, "'Answere to this Perillous Time': Ideological Ambivalence in The Raigne of King Edward III and the English Chronicle Plays," *English Studies* 69 (1988), p. 127.

14 Stephen Greenblatt, "Invisible Bullets: Renaissance Authority and its Subversion, *Henry IV* and *Henry V*," *Political Shakespeare: New Essays in Cultural Materialism*, Jonathan Dollimore and Alan Sinfield (eds.) (Ithaca and London: Cornell University Press, 1985), pp. 18–47. Dollimore and Sinfield, "History and Ideology."

15 William Shakespeare, *1 Henry IV*, A. R. Humphreys (ed.) (London and New York: Methuen, 1985), 1.2.205. All subsequent citations to this text will be given in parentheses in the text.

16 A. R. Humphreys gives Ephesians v. 16 – "Redeeming the tyme, because ye dayes are euyll" as a source (p. 21 n.).

17 Karl Marx, *The Eighteenth Brumaire of Louis Bonaparte*, Lewis S. Feuer (ed.) (New York: Anchor Books, 1959), p. 320.

18 Louis Althusser, "Ideology and Ideological State Apparatuses (Notes Towards

an Investigation)," *Lenin and Philosophy*, Ben Brewster (trans.) (New York and London: Verso, 1971), pp. 127–86, 174.

19 Michael Sprinker, "Politics and Theory: Althusser and Sartre," *Modern Language Notes* 100 (1985), pp. 989–1011, 1003, 1007.

20 William Shakespeare, *2 Henry IV*, A. R. Humphreys (ed.) (London and New York: Methuen, 1980), 5.5.46. Subsequent references to the play will be to this edition and given in parentheses in the text.

21 Dollimore and Sinfield have noted the logical inconsistencies in Henry's argument ("History and Ideology" 221–3). They conclude: "Henry engrosses in himself the ideological coherence of the state and then, asked to take responsibility for the likely defeat of Agincourt, claims to be an effect of the structure which he seemed to guarantee" (223).

22 Alexander Leggatt, *Shakespeare Political Drama: The History Plays and the Roman Plays* (London and New York: Routledge, 1989), p. 136. Although the sentiment dates back to the middle ages and appears in political discourses, it is rarely found in popular drama or even in historical texts. Increasingly, however, we encounter it, defined ever more sharply, during the reigns of James and Charles (though not always explicitly in connection with the Stuart kings). See, for instance, Elizabeth Cary's *The History of the Life, Reign, and Death of Edward II. King of England, and Lord of Ireland. With the Rise and Fall of his great Favorites, Gaveston and the Spencers* (1627) (London, 1680). Cary writes: "The power Majestick is or should be bounded; and there is a reciprocal correspondence, which gives the King the obedience, the subject equal right and perfect justice, by which they claim a property in his actions; if either of these fall short, or prove defective by wilful errour, or by secret practice, the State's in danger of a following mischief" (68).

23 J. P. Sommerville, *Politics and Ideology 1603–1640* (London and New York: Longman, 1986), p. 49.

24 Alvin Kernan, "*The Henriad*: Shakespeare's Major History Plays," *Modern Shakespearean Criticism*, Alvin Kernan (ed.) (New York: Hartcourt Brace Jovanovich, 1970), p. 261.

25 Sigurd Burckhardt, *Shakespearean Meanings* (Princeton: Princeton University Press, 1968), pp. 194–5.

26 See, for example, R. C. Munden, "James I and 'the growth of mutual distrust': King, Commons, and Reform," *Faction and Parliament: Essays on Early Stuart History*, Kevin Sharpe (ed.) (London and New York: Methuen, 1978), pp. 43–72.

27 Joseph Candido, "Fashioning Henry VIII: What Shakespeare Saw in *When You See Me, You Know Me*," *Cahiers Élisabéthains* 23 (1983), pp. 47–59, 56, 57.

28 All references to Shakespeare and Fletcher's *King Henry VIII* are to the Arden Shakespeare, R. A. Foakes (ed.) (London: Methuen, 1968), and will be given in parentheses in the text.

29 Paul Dean, "Dramatic Mode and Historical Vision in *Henry VIII*," *Shakespeare Quarterly* 37 (1986), p. 177.

30 Frank V. Cespedes, "'We are one in fortunes': The Sense of History in *Henry VIII*," *English Literary Renaissance* 10 (1980), p. 415.

31 Matthew H. Wikander, *The Play of Truth and State: Historical Drama from*

Shakespeare to Brecht (Baltimore and London: Johns Hopkins University Press, 1986), pp. 46, 47.

32 I follow Stanley Wells and Gary Taylor in assuming that Shakespeare and Fletcher share the play's authorship. And I follow Frances Yates in maintaining that Fletcher and Shakespeare would have seen "eye to eye" on "the general approach to historical and contemporary problems in *Henry VIII*" (*Shakespeare's Last Plays: A New Approach* [London: Routledge and Kegan Paul, 1975], p. 67). What is more, I share Yates's conviction "that it is not a matter of great importance whether the whole play is actually written by Shakespeare or whether part of it is written by Fletcher." Whether the play – a play about disunified history – is the result of harmonious collaboration or of cross purposes, a Jacobean audience would be presented with the play, not with authorial intention(s). Even if the historiographical eclecticism (discussed in this chapter) stems from disagreements between Fletcher and Shakespeare, it is highly unlikely that a Jacobean audience would have attributed it to dual authorship.

33 Jean Bodin (trans. Thomas Heywood), "Of Choice of History, by Way of Preface." In Thomas Heywood's translation of *Sallust, The Conspiracy of Cataline and The War of Jugurtha* (1608) (London and New York: Constable, Knopf, 1924), p. 12.

34 Edmund Bolton, "Hypercritica, or a Rule of Judgment for Writing or reading our Histories" (1618?), *Critical Essays of the Seventeenth Century*, J. E. Spingarn (ed.) (Bloomington, IN: Indiana University Press, 1968), vol. I, p. 84.

35 Phyllis Rackin, *Stages of History: Shakespeare's English Chronicles* (Ithaca, NY: Cornell University Press, 1990), p. 13.

36 See J. G. A. Pocock's argument that apropos the king's relationship to the law, "historical criticism became one of the sharpest weapons of monarchy" (*The Ancient Constitution and the Feudal Law: A Study of English Historical Thought in the Seventeenth Century*, Cambridge: Cambridge University Press, 1987 [reissue], p. 17).

37 Leonard Tennenhouse, "Strategies of State and Political Plays: *A Midsummer Night's Dream, Henry IV, Henry V, Henry VIII*," *Political Shakespeare: New Essays in Cultural Materialism*, Jonathan Dollimore and Alan Sinfield (eds.) (Ithaca and London: Cornell University Press, 1985), p. 121.

38 Michel Foucault, *The History of Sexuality: An Introduction*, Robert Hurley (trans.) (New York: Vintage, 1980), p. 94. For my argument I am drawing on the chapter on "Method" (pp. 92–102).

39 Fredric Jameson, *The Political Unconscious: Narrative as a Socially Symbolic Act* (Ithaca, NY: Cornell University Press, 1982), p. 102.

40 This study is not the first to detect multiple voices in the play (see Peter L. Rudnytsky, "*Henry VIII* and the Deconstruction of History," *Shakespeare Survey* 43 [1991], pp. 46, 47), but it is the first to do so from the vantage point of various renaissance forms of historical representation.

41 Terry Eagleton, *Criticism and Ideology: A Study in Marxist Literary Theory* (London: Verso, 1982), pp. 84–5. Eagleton's point is that the "content" or "materials" out of which a play is fashioned possess a "form" even prior to their incorporation in the play. "Form" should not be understood as some type

of unchanging essence; on the contrary, "ideology produces the forms which produce it" (85).

42 Catherine Gallagher, "Marxism and The New Historicism," *The New Historicism*, H. Aram Veeser (ed.) (New York and London: Routledge, 1989), p. 37.

43 Stephen Greenblatt, *Shakespearean Negotiations: The Circulation of Social Energy in Renaissance England* (Berkeley and Los Angeles: University of California Press, 1988), p. 10.

44 In its original context, the quotation from Greenblatt does not pertain to *Henry VIII*, but I believe its force is relevant here. Also, I am partially conflating Greenblatt's categories of "acquisition through simulation" and "metaphorical acquisition" here (10). Such a conflation is warranted because the incorporation of historiography into the medium of the theater changes the status of historiography (i.e., from narrative history to something else) and is therefore not actual but metaphorical. Shakespeare's play does not become a history in the sense that the writings of Holinshed, Bacon, Foxe, Hall, Camden, et al. are histories; it remains a play that simulates certain historiographical practices.

45 In light of the play's epistemological uncertainty and lack of historiographical consensus, its subtitle, *All is True*, takes on a distinct irony. Howard Felperin, Peter L. Rudnytsky and others have pointed out that the subtitle "makes one wonder whether Shakespeare is not ironically hinting that we revise our conventional notions of historical truth, even of mimetic truth itself" (Felperin, "Shakespeare's *Henry VIII*: History as Myth," *Studies in English Literature 1500–1900* 6 [1966], p. 227) "or that 'all is true' means precisely that any interpretation of the past may be true if one thinks it so, and no point of view is allowed to contain or control all others" (Rudnytsky, "*Henry VIII*" 46). The play's "chosen truth" referred to in the prologue, therefore, must be conceived of not as a particular ideological reading of history, but as a pastiche of historiographical representations – a conception which, incidentally but not necessarily, may capture the dramatic practice of two authors, or of Shakespeare himself, who "was reading two or three histories at the same time, and taking ideas from more than one" (Foakes (ed.), *Henry VIII* xxxvi). Foakes points out that Shakespeare and Fletcher rely heavily on Holinshed's *Chronicles* (1587) and Foxe's *Actes and Monuments* (1597) for Act 5, but Halle's account of Henry VIII as well as John Speed's *The History of Great Britain* also contributed. George Cavendish's *Life of Wolsey*, on which John Stow's *Chronicles* (1565) draw, found its way into Shakespeare and Fletcher's play via Holinshed (Foakes, *Henry VIII* xxxv).

46 F. J. Levy, *Tudor Historical Thought* (San Marino, CA: The Huntington Library, 1967), p. 55.

47 Carl Stephenson and Frederick George Marcham (eds. and trans.), *Sources of English Constitutional History: A Selection of Documents from A.D. 600 to the Interregnum*, 2 vols. (New York and London: Harper and Row, 1972), vol. I, p. 304.

48 Pocock makes this point in the context of the growing importance of the interpretation of history in the struggles between monarch and parliament.

49 Richard Halpern, *The Poetics of Primitive Accumulation: English Renaissance Culture and the Genealogy of Capital* (Ithaca and London: Cornell University Press, 1991), p. 223.
50 James I, *The Trew Law of Free Monarchies* in *The Political Works of James I*, Charles McIlwain (ed.) (Cambridge, MA: Harvard University Press, 1918), pp. 61–2.
51 See Sommerville, *Politics and Ideology* (67–9) for the various legal solutions offered to the crux.
52 See John Guy, *Tudor England* (Oxford and New York: Oxford University Press, 1990), pp. 268–71, 331–6, 448–51.
53 Leonard Tennenhouse, "Strategies of State and Political Plays: *A Midsummer Night's Dream, Henry IV, Henry V, Henry VIII*," *Political Shakespeare: New Essays in Cultural Materialism*, Jonathan Dollimore and Alan Sinfield (eds.) (Ithaca and London: Cornell University Press, 1985), pp. 109–28.
54 D. R. Woolf, *The Idea of History in Early Stuart England: Erudition, Ideology, and "The Light of Truth" from the Accession of James I to the Civil War* (Toronto, Buffalo and London: University of Toronto Press, 1990), p. 16.
55 See Annabel Patterson, *Censorship and Interpretation: The Conditions of Writing and Reading in Early Modern England* (Madison: University of Wisconsin Press, 1984), pp. 52–115.
56 Raphael Holinshed, "Preface to the Reader," *Chronicles of England, Scotland and Ireland*, vol. III (London, 1808).
57 Holinshed places much greater stress on the "evidence" supplied by other witnesses, and he points out that "inquisitions were taken in diuerse shires of England of him" (*Chronicles* 658–60).
58 It has been suggested that Henry shrewdly ignores Wolsey's flaws because the Cardinal is carrying out policies of which Henry approves. However, we learn long before the pre-trial that Wolsey is privately negotiating foreign policy matters with Charles V (see 1.1.174–93).
59 See, for example, Jasper Ridley, *Henry VIII: The Politics of Tyranny* (New York: Fromm, 1986), pp. 122–3.
60 The passage is lifted from Foxe but with an interesting addition. The line "such things have been done" does not appear in John Foxe. The addition possibly suggests that Shakespeare and Fletcher want us to recall the Surveyor's testimony against Buckingham. The relevant passage in Foxe reads: "Do you not consider what an easy thing it is to procure three or four false knaves to witness against you? Think you to have better luck that way than your master Christ had?" (*The Actes and Monuments*, M. Hobart Seymour [ed.] [New York: Robert Carter and Brothers, 1856], p. 896).
61 Michel Foucault, *The History of Sexuality*, p. 95.
62 Stuart M. Kirkland observes a parallel here between *Henry VIII* and James I. James apparently praised Rochester, the royal favorite, "for employing Sir Robert Cotton, the antiquary, to search for precedents 'when as things were to be done in the State which he doubted whether they were lawful and expedient, and therefore did desire to have the example of former times for warrant'" ("*Henry VIII* and James I: Shakespeare and Jacobean Politics," *Shakespeare Studies* 19 [1987], p. 213).
63 The actual facts of the divorce are quite complex, and Shakespeare skips over

Henry's initial attempts (not included in Holinshed) first to challenge the dispensation bull granted by Pope Julius II on grounds that it contained faults, and then to challenge the Pope's power to grant such dispensations at all. For an elaboration of these and other points, see the "Introduction" to *The Divorce Tracts of Henry VIII*, Edward Surtz and Virginia Murphy (eds.) (Angers, France: Moreana, 1988), pp. i–xxxvi.

64 William Camden, *The History of the Most Renowned and Victorious Princess Elizabeth, Late Queen of England* (1615), Wallace T. MacCaffrey (ed.) (Chicago and London: University of Chicago Press, 1970), p. 3.

65 MacCaffrey, "Introduction" to Camden's *The History of the Most Renowned and Victorious Princess Elizabeth*, p. xxxi.

66 Following Holinshed, Shakespeare indicates that Wolsey was trying to slow the divorce process because he was against Henry marrying Anne Bullen, which he correctly feared would happen. Instead, he wanted Henry to marry "the Duchess of Alencon, / The French king's sister" (3.2.85–6), and believed that given time he would be able to persuade the King to do so.

67 Katherine does not explicitly call on providence to interpret her fate, but her capitulation, like Buckingham's, is marked by a declaration of her loyalty to king and God (3.1.180–1). She also expresses surprise and implicit doubt about the justice of her fate when she says she "little thought . . . / She should have bought her dignities so dear" (183–4). Her surrender, however, occurs after considerably more hardship and much more suddenly than Buckingham's. Whereas the Duke immediately realizes he cannot fight the forces against him, the Queen continues to put up a rational defense in her post-trial "counseling" session with Wolsey and Campeius. It is difficult, if not impossible, to see, however, how the Queen's consent to the divorce can be a plausible consequence of the arguments offered by the cardinals.

68 James's second son, Prince Charles, only eleven years old when his brother died, had lived in his brother's shadow, and was considered a disappointment. He was sickly, had a speech impediment, and was not hailed as a worthy heir to the throne of England.

69 John Donne, "Elegy upon the untimely death of the incomparable Prince Henry," John Donne: *The Complete English Poems*, A. J. Smith (ed.) (London and New York: Penguin, 1986).

70 Jasper Ridley, *Elizabeth I: The Shrewdness of Virtue* (New York: Fromm, 1989), p. 333.

71 James I, *Letters of King James VI & I*, G. P. V. Akrigg (ed.) (Berkeley and Los Angeles: University of California Press, 1984), pp. 207–8 (italics added).

72 Anne Somerset, *Elizabeth I* (New York: Knopf, 1991), p. 568.

73 Alan G. R. Smith, *The Emergence of a Nation State: The Commonwealth of England, 1529–1660* (London and New York: Longman, 1984), p. 379.

74 S. R. Gardiner, *History of England from the Accession of James I to the Outbreak of the Civil War 1603–1642*, 10 vols. (New York: AMS Press, 1965), vol. I, p. 79.

75 S. R. Gardiner, *History of England*, vol. II, pp. 114–15.

76 For outstanding recent accounts of Arbella Stuart's troubles, see Sara Jayne Steen, "Introduction," *The Letters of Arbella Stuart*, Sarah Jayne Steen (ed.) (Oxford: Oxford University Press, 1994), and Barbara Kiefer Lewalski,

Writing Women in Jacobean England (Cambridge, MA and London: Harvard University Press, 1993), pp. 67–92.

77 Also, both men allegedly engaged in subversive activities. Buckingham supposedly schemed to assassinate Henry VIII, and James (Shakespeare may or may not have known about this when he wrote the play) was "probably deeply implicated" (Akrigg, "Introduction," *Letters of King James* 9) in the Essex rebellion and after 1601 in secret correspondence with Robert Cecil to obtain the English crown.

78 James would certainly have identified with Henry VIII upon the Surveyor's claim that Buckingham planned to murder Henry with a dagger. Perhaps as a result of having witnessed multiple acts of violence as a child, James had "a morbid horror of death" and he "habitually wore a heavily quilted doublet for protection from the stilettoes of assassins" (G. P. V. Akrigg, *Jacobean Pageant or The Court of James I* [Cambridge, MA: Harvard University Press, 1962], pp. 6, 5). However, it is important to keep in mind that Henry VIII inquires after the legal grounds of Buckingham's claim before the surveyor brings up the possible assassination.

79 In a related irony, the "vain prophecy" falls properly into the domain of demonology, a subject about which James had become increasingly skeptical after becoming King of England. In his later years, Akrigg notes in *Jacobean Pageant*, James was apparently more apt to send witches "to the medical facility at Cambridge University for psychiatric study than burning them" (14) – or sending them to the scaffold as Henry does Buckingham. It is purely speculative to suggest that in implicitly comparing a judgmental Henry with a compassionate and understanding James, Shakespeare and Fletcher might be deflating the evidence against Buckingham even further.

80 Tennenhouse is surely mistaken to suggest that the playwrights have "no cause to engender sympathy for Katherine" ("Strategies of State," p. 123).

81 Nor will it do to view – as some critics have – the play's conclusion as a retreat from history into romance; Cranmer's vision may seem romance to us, not because it is, but because it belongs to a specific type of renaissance historical discourse, which, today, is no longer judged to be historical.

82 Also see Rudnytsky, "*Henry VIII*," p. 50. It is important to note here, with historian J. J. Scarisbrick, that "In the normal course of events, Anne would have mattered only to Henry's conscience, not to the history of England. She would have been used and discarded. . . . But, either because of virtue or ambition, Anne refused to become his mistress . . . and the more she resisted, the more, apparently, did Henry prize her" (*Henry VIII* [Berkeley and Los Angeles: University of California Press, 1970], p. 149). It is not unreasonable to assume that Anne finally agreed to become his mistress after assurances that she would become his wife. In the summer of 1531, Anne "began to behave in public as if she were his wife," and by 1532 (still a year before the actual divorce from Katherine) Henry was "living openly with Anne as husband and wife" (Ridley, *Elizabeth I*, pp. 203, 207).

83 Cespedes makes the same point in "'We are one in fortunes': The Sense of History in *Henry VIII*," pp. 432–3.

84 On this score, see Kim H. Noling, "Grubbing Up the Stock: Dramatizing Queens in *Henry VIII*," *Shakespeare Quarterly* 39 (1988), pp. 291–306. For an

antithetical view, see Tennenhouse, *Power on Display: The Politics of Shakespeare's Genres* (New York and London: Routledge, Chapman, Hall, 1986), p. 103.

85 Louis A. Montrose, "`Shaping Fantasies': Figurations of Gender and Power in Elizabethan Culture." In *Representing the English Renaissance*, Stephen Greenblatt (ed.) (Berkeley, Los Angeles and London: University of California Press), pp. 31–64, 47. See this essay for a detailed discussion of the peculiar political difficulties ensuing from the monarch's gender.

86 Judith H. Anderson, *Biographical Truth: The Representation of Historical Persons in Tudor-Stuart Writing* (New Haven and London: Yale University Press, 1984), p. 153.

87 For a reading emphasizing this aspect of the scene, see David Scott Kastan, *Shakespeare and the Shapes of Time* (Hanover, NH: University Press of New England, 1982), p. 137.

88 Alexander Leggatt, "*Henry VIII* and the Ideal England," *Shakespeare Survey* 38 (1985), p. 136.

89 Ernst H. Kantorowicz, *The King's Two Bodies: A Study in Medieval Political Theology* (Princeton: Princeton University Press, 1957 [1981]), p. 384. Kantorowicz goes on to explain that occasionally there was a subtle difference between "Officium" (the Office of the king) and "Dignitas" (the Dignity of the king) (384–5), but the distinction has no noticeable bearing on our discussion.

90 See, for example, Goldberg, "Speculations," p. 252.

91 Maurice Lee, Jr., *Great Britain's Solomon: James VI and I in His Three Kingdoms* (Urbana and Chicago: University of Illinois Press, 1990), p. 65.

92 Kim H. Noling, "Grubbing Up the Stock," p. 305.

93 Roy Strong, *The Cult of Elizabeth* (Berkeley and Los Angeles: University of California Press, 1977), p. 187.

94 See James I, *Trew Law of Free Monarchies*, pp. 53–70.

95 Strong also reports that the publication of Henry Peacham's *Minerva Britanna* (1612) "was prompted by one last fling with Elizabethan romance" (187). However, the book's dedication to Henry, the Prince of Wales and self-appointed revitalizer of Elizabethan mythology, only underscores how, by 1613, its system of representation had lost the one figure – Henry died in November of 1612 – that could have anchored it in political and historical reality. As another sign of the phoenix's diminished currency in 1612, Peacham assigns the emblem of the phoenix not to Elizabeth but to the Earl of Salisbury. And when, in "The Authors Conclusion," he does identify Elizabeth with the phoenix, he hardly emphasizes issues of continuity and immortality. His sentiment is one of loss and despair (*Minerva Britanna*, English Emblem Books no. 5, John Horden [ed.] [Menston, England: Scolar Press, 1969], pp. 19, 212).

96 Leonard F. Dean, *Tudor Theories of History Writing*, *Contributions in Modern Philology* no. 1 (Ann Arbor: University of Michigan Press, 1947), p. 4.

97 Indeed, Roy Strong draws directly on Cranmer's speech in the opening pages of his *The Cult of Elizabeth*, p. 15.

98 Thomas Blundeville, *The true order and Methode of wryting and reading Hystories*, Hugh G. Dick (ed.), Huntington Library Quarterly 2 (1940), p. 164.

99 But see Donna B. Hamilton's chapter on *Henry VIII* for an intriguing argu-

ment in favor of a topical reading (*Shakespeare and the Politics of Protestant England* [Lexington, KY: University of Kentucky Press, 1992]), pp. 163–90.

100 J. P. Sommerville, "James I and the Divine Right of Kings: English Politics and Continental Theory," *The Mental World of the Jacobean Court*, Linda Levy Peck (ed.) (Cambridge: Cambridge University Press, 1991), p. 63.

101 Sommerville, "James I," p. 57. For a brief but illuminating discussion of the clash between the different ideological positions, also see Sommerville, *Politics and Ideology*, pp. 86–111.

5 "NO MEETE MATTERS TO BE WRYTTEN OR TREATED VPON"

1 Philip Massinger and John Fletcher, *The Tragedy of Sir John Van Olden Barnavelt*, T. H. Howard-Hill (ed.) (Malone Society Reprints, 1979 [1980]). All quotations from the play are taken from this edition and hereafter given in parentheses in the text.

2 John L. Motley, *The Life and Death of John of Barneveldt, Advocate of Holland, With a View of the Primary Causes and Movements of the Thirty Years' War* in *The Complete Works of John L. Motley* (New York: Kelmscott Society Publishers, 1900) vol. XIV, p. 231.

3 The names of the two principals in this chapter – Oldenbarnevelt and Maurice – are variously spelled by different authors. In order to distinguish between the dramatic characters and their historical counterparts, I will refer throughout this chapter to the historical figure as Oldenbarnevelt (following Dutch spelling) and to the dramatic character as Barnavelt; and I will refer to the historical prince as Maurits (again, Dutch spelling) and to the character as Maurice.

4 When more than a year later, during casual after-dinner conversation, Dr. Junius, one of Oldenbarnevelt's judges, was asked by the Attorney-General of Utrecht how it was that the Advocate "had been hanging his head toward Spain, as not one word of that stood in the sentence," the judge merely suggested that the crime was "easily deduced from the sentence, because a man who breaks up the foundation of the state makes the country indefensible, and therefore invites the enemy to invade it. And this Barneveldt had done, who had turned the Union, religion, alliances, and finances upside down by his proceedings" (Motley, vol. XIV 230). Junius's answer reeks of party politics, and one may observe wryly that if all constitutional ministers imputed by the opposition party of bringing about fundamental changes by their proceedings were presumed to be treasonous, then there would have been few to escape the block.

5 For a discussion of anti-Spanish sentiments, see Thomas Cogswell, "England and the Spanish Match," in *Conflict in Early Stuart England: Studies in Religion and Politics*, Richard Cust and Ann Hughes (eds.) (London and New York: Longman, 1989), pp. 107–33, esp. pp. 111–12.

6 Elizabeth I, "A Declaration of the Causes Mooving the Queene of England to Give aide to the Defence of the People afflicted and oppressed in the lowe Countries," *Elizabethan Backgrounds*, Arthur F. Kinney (ed.) (Hamden, CT: Archon Books, 1975), pp. 187–211, 198.

7 In *Some Forerunners of the Newspaper in England, 1476–1622* (Philadelphia: University of Pennsylvania Press, 1929), Matthias Shaaber reports that at least three-quarters of all foreign news came from the Netherlands and France, p. 169.

Warren Chappell notes that "the first English-language news sheets appeared in Holland," *A Short of the Printed Word* (New York: Knopf, 1970), p. 129. Also see pp. 127–31.

8 Hyder E. Rollins, *A Pepysian Garland: Black-letter Broadside Ballads of the Years 1595–1639* (Cambridge: Cambridge University Press, 1922), pp. 105–9. Significantly, the balladist's suggestion that Oldenbarnevelt had hatched a murder plot against Maurits is purely fictitious, although rumors to that effect were floated during the trial. The reason for the rumors, John Motley suggests, was to persuade three of the twenty-four judges, who, although they were ready to convict the Advocate, were unwilling to go along with a death sentence. The tactic worked (Motley, vol. XIV 229).

9 Jan den Tex, *Johan van Oldenbarnevelt*, abridged edn ('s Gravenhage: Martinus Nijhoff, 1980), p. 265. Also see Carleton's letter to King James in G. P. V. Akrigg, *Letter of King James VI & I* (Berkeley: University of California Press, 1984), p. 366.

10 From two letters by Thomas Locke to Sir Dudley Carleton (the English ambassador to the Dutch Provinces) we know that the tragedy was first performed in London sometime between 14 August and 27 August of 1619, in all likelihood at the Globe (Gerald Eades Bentley, *The Profession of Dramatist and Player in Shakespeare's Time, 1590–1642* [Princeton: Princeton University Press, 1986], p. 416).

11 F. J. Levy, *Tudor Historical Thought* (San Marino, CA: Huntington Library, 1967), p. 165.

12 James I, *The Trew Law of Free Monarchies* in *The Political Works of James I*, Charles Howard McIlwain (ed.) (Cambridge, MA: Harvard University Press, 1918), pp. 58–61, 67. *Trew Law* was originally published in 1598 but reprinted shortly after James became King of England.

13 Ben Jonson, *Sejanus his Fall*, W. F. Bolton (ed.) (New York: Hill and Wang, 1966), p. 8. Jonathan Dollimore argues convincingly that the sentiment of the disclaimer is at odds with the play's action (*Radical Tragedy* [Chicago: University of Chicago Press, 1986], pp. 134–8).

14 Leonard F. Dean, *Tudor Theories of History Writing*, in *Contributions in Modern Philology* no. 1 (Ann Arbor, MI: University of Michigan Press, 1947), p. 8. See also, Annabel Patterson, *Shakespeare and the Popular Voice* (Oxford, and Cambridge, MA: Blackwell, 1989), pp. 80–1.

15 Pocock, *The Ancient Constitution and the Feudal Law: A Study of English Historical Thought in the Seventeenth Century* (Cambridge: Cambridge University Press, 1987), p. 259. See Kenneth C. Schellhase, *Tacitus in Renaissance Political Thought* (Chicago and London: University of Chicago Press), pp. 157–9.

16 Annabel Patterson, *Censorship and Interpretation* (Wisconsin: University of Wisconsin Press, 1984), p. 57.

17 D. R. Woolf, "Erudition and the Idea of History in Renaissance England," *Renaissance Quarterly* 40 (1987), pp. 11–48, 19. Woolf makes the same point in his *The Idea of History in Early Stuart England: Erudition, Ideology, and "The Light of Truth" from the Accession of James I to the Civil War* (Toronto and London: University of Toronto Press, 1990), p. 16.

18 Bodin strongly advised historians not to write about the present or recent past. Inevitably, he urged, "those that will write of the present, can hardlie write truly, but they must touch the credit and reputation of some men." Hence the historian either had to modify the "truth" to avoid touching the credit and reputation of certain men, because if he did not he would find himself and his work persecuted by those who considered themselves offended. And to the readers of histories Bodin says to avoid those who do write works that remember the living for, he asks, why would we turn to those historians for whom "to write what a man would not, was accounted dishonest: to write what he would, dangerous"? Chapter 4 of the *Method for the Easy Comprehension of History* (1566), trans. Thomas Heywood (1608), in Sallust's *The Conspiracy of Cataline* and *The War of Jugurtha* (London: Constable; New York: Knopf, 1924), p. 11. The sentiment is far from unique. Sir Walter Ralegh, who drew James I's ire over his apparent criticism of kings in *The History of the World*, for instance, stated "That whosoever in writing a modern History, shall follow Truth too near the heels, it may haply strike out his Teeth." From Ralegh's "Preface" to *The History of the World* (1617). Quoted in Levy, *Tudor Historical Thought*, p. 292.

19 E. K. Chambers, *The Elizabethan Stage* (Oxford: Clarendon Press, 1923), vol. IV, p. 263.

20 Wilhelmina P. Frijlinck, in the introduction to her edition of the play, *The Tragedy of Sir John Van Olden Barnavelt* (Amsterdam: Dorssen, 1922), p. xix, believes that it was the Lord Mayor of London who halted the performance. But Bentley rightly asserts that only the Bishop had such powers (*The Jacobean and Caroline Stage*, vol. III [Oxford: Clarendon Press, 1956], p. 417).

21 Frijlinck gives a convenient two-page summary of the deletions made by George Buc (Frijlinck, "Introduction" 84–5).

22 T. H. Howard-Hill, "Buc and the Censorship of *Sir John Van Olden Barnavelt* in 1619," *The Review of English Studies* 39 (1988), pp. 39–63.

23 The play was not printed until rediscovered by A. H. Bullen, who included it in his 1883 *Collection of Old English Plays* vol. II (London, 1883).

24 *Sir John Van Olden Barnavelt* (1.1.7–10).

25 Soldiers in "waiting pay" (*wartgeld*).

26 William W. Appleton, *Beaumont and Fletcher: A Critical Study* (London: George Allen and Unwin, 1956), pp. 89–90. Margot Heinemann believes "this may be due to the collaboration (Fletcher being much less critical politically than Massinger) or to some confusion of aim . . ." (*Puritanism and Theatre: Thomas Middleton and the Opposition Drama under the Early Stuarts* [Cambridge: Cambridge University Press, 1980], p. 204). Kathleen McLuskie sees the ambiguity as inherent "in the form of the play, which deals in the theatrical counters of pathos and heroism rather than the more complex concepts of Realpolitik" (*The Revels History of English Drama*, vol. IV [London: Methuen, 1981], p. 130).

27 Nicholas Tyacke, "Puritanism, Arminianism and the Counter-Revolution," in *The Origins of the English Civil War*, Conrad Russell (ed.) (London: Macmillan, 1973), p. 128. In the popular mind, Catholicism and Arminianism were often (incorrectly) equated.

28 Modern historians generally agree that Oldenbarnevelt deserves most praise in

the matter. Herbert H. Rowen writes that at "Forty years of age in 1587, [Oldenbarnevelt] was at the height of his powers of mind and will, ready as land's advocate to prove himself the equal of any statesman anywhere in his time. Although there were no such offices or titles, he became in practice both the prime minister and the foreign minister of the Dutch Republic for more than three decades. He provided the leadership of a single person which made government possible in a country with such dispersed authority . . . . He was the true creator of the Dutch Republic, adapting institutions inherited from the past for the work of republican government (*The Princes of Orange: The Stadtholders of the Dutch Republic* [Cambridge: Cambridge University Press, 1988], p. 37).

29 Significantly, one of the crucial differences between James I and Maurits is the former's ability to claim his crown on hereditary grounds. This difference between the two figures is practically eliminated when Maurice is named the "Father" of his country, making James I, as we will see in the second part of this chapter, an even more suitable target for the charges brought against Maurice.

30 Maurits was not a member of the tribunal.

31 John L. Motley, *The Life and Death of John of Barneveldt, Advocate of Holland*, in *The Complete Works of John L. Motley*, 17 vols. (New York: Kelmscott Society, 1902), vol. III, p. 234.

32 The passage in square brackets was deleted by the censor.

33 Historians generally agree that Maurits did a deplorable job in running the country. See, for example, two chapters, "The Debacle" and "No Monument for Maurits" in J. G. Kikkert, *Maurits van Nassau* (Weesp, Netherlands: Fibula-Van Dishoeck, 1985), pp. 130–50.

34 Gordon McMullan further suggests that the scene foregrounds "the possibility of subjects' autonomy and agency in face of absolutist claims. . ." (*The Politics of Unease in the Plays of John Fletcher* [Amherst, MA: University of Massachusetts Press, 1994], p. 88).

35 Richard Dutton, *Mastering the Revels: The Regulation and Censorship of English Renaissance Drama* (Iowa City: University of Iowa Press, 1991), p. 208.

36 The passages in square brackets were excised by the censor.

37 Note the sharp contrast between Massinger and Fletcher's overriding concern and that of George Chapman in *Caesar and Pompey* (1612–13?). In defeat, Pompey, who has doggedly defended republican values against the tyrannical Caesar, does not speak of the preservation of the body politic. On the contrary, the stoical Pompey candidly rejects all earthly institutions and announces: "I will stand no more / On others' legs, nor build one joy without me. / If ever I be worth a house again / *I'll build all inward*; not a light shall ope / The common outway. . ." (*The Plays and Poems of George Chapman*, T. M. Parrott [ed.] [London, 1910], vol. I, 5.1.203–7; italics added).

38 In the "Introduction" to his edition of *King John*, A. R. Braunmuller writes: "More readily than most other, plays on historical topics enter a covert, political dialogue with their own present; offering a shape for the past and a method for understanding historical process, a history play implicitly asks a contemporary audience to consider the shape of its present and how that present may be understood" (Oxford: Oxford University Press, 1988), p. 39.

39 Out of political necessity, James often showed himself more willing to compro-

mise with Parliament than his absolutist views might indicate. See Kevin Sharpe, "Introduction: Parliamentary History 1603–1629: In or Out of Perspective?" in *Faction and Parliament*, Kevin Sharpe (ed.) (London and New York: Methuen, 1978), pp. 1–42; R. C. Munden, "James I and 'the growth of mutual distrust': King, Commons, and Reform, 1603–1604," in the same volume, pp. 43–72.

40 J. P. Sommerville, *Politics and Ideology in England 1603–1640* (London and New York: Longman, 1986), p. 47.

41 Jonathan Goldberg, *James I and the Politics of Literature: Jonson, Shakespeare, Donne, and Their Contemporaries* (1983) (Stanford: Stanford University Press, 1989), p. 56.

42 Charles McIlwain (ed.), *The Political Works of James I* (Cambridge, MA: Harvard University Press, 1918), p. 310.

43 See *The Trew Law* in McIlwain, *Political Works*, pp. 62, 63.

44 James, Richard Halpern has recently argued, "denied that he had any direct link to God's will other than that provided by his own conscience, which was as other men's. . . ." This is probably so; and while this formulation introduces the possibility of the king's fallibility, it does not diminish his supreme authority over his subjects for the *substance* or *content* of the monarch's communications with God remain privileged – off limits to subjects, not to be disputed upon. Hence, Halpern is right to note that "For James, the divine right of kings is thus an almost purely virtual phenomenon. It invests the king with an unimpeachable political authority but provides no material means for safeguarding it and no spiritual means for ensuring that it will be exercised wisely" (*The Poetics of Primitive Accumulation: English Renaissance Culture and the Genealogy of Capital* [Ithaca and London: Cornell University Press, 1991], p. 227).

45 There are several important variations on the idea of rule by consent. See Sommerville, *Politics and Ideology*, pp. 57–85.

46 For concise overviews of Anglo-Dutch relations see H. P. H. Jansen, *Kalendarium Geschiedenis van de Lage Landen in Jaartallen* (Utrecht and Antwerp: Het Spectrum, 1971 [1982]); I. Schoffer et al., *De Lage Landen van 1500 tot 1780* (Amsterdam and Brussels: Elsevier, 1983).

47 In 1620 a secret agreement to marry Charles to the Infanta Maria was actually signed.

48 Roger Lockyer, *The Early Stuarts: A Political History of England 1603–1642* (London and New York: Longman, 1989), p. 117.

49 As Cogswell notes, the Habsburg family "might lose control of the Imperial crown, for a Protestant in Prague would for the first time create a Protestant majority in the Electoral College" ("England and the Spanish Match" 113).

50 Caroline Bingham, *James I of England* (London: Weidenfeld and Nicolson, 1981), p. 153.

51 In general, it was James's policy to maintain the war between the Dutch and the Spanish at a level most beneficial to England. While engaged in war neither Spain nor the Republic, both prominent mercantile powers, could fully compete with English merchants. At the same time, since James supported the Dutch cause financially, he did not want the fighting to escalate to the point where the Provinces became too large a burden on the English treasury. See Maurice Lee, *James I and Henry IV* (Urbana, Chicago and London: University of Illinois Press, 1970), pp. 71–96.

52 Jonathan I. Israel, *The Dutch Republic and the Hispanic World 1606–1661* (Oxford: Clarendon Press, 1982), p. 19.
53 Charles George, *The Stuarts: A Century of Experiment 1603–1714* (England: Blond Educational, 1973), p. 9.
54 Walter H. Frere reports how "the greater part . . . of the king's directions [1622] was designed to restrain preachers from controversial topics either of politics or of divinity. The rebellion [named Arminianism] against Calvinism, which began at Cambridge, had spread throughout the country." *The English Church in the Reigns of Elizabeth and James I. (1558–1625)* (London: Macmillan, 1911), vol. V, p. 382. Also see Nicholas Tyacke, *Anti-Calvinists: The Rise of English Arminianism* (Oxford: Clarendon Press, 1987), pp. 29–57.
55 Vorstius was more a Gomarust than an Arminian in that he emphasized the irresistibility of God's awesome and inscrutable powers, rather than God's love and justice which, as Arminius held, could be refused (den Tex, *Oldenbarnevelt* 169, 185).
56 Since the reign of Queen Elizabeth, the Dutch provinces had been central to the political stability (or lack thereof) between England, Spain, and France. English feelings toward the rebellious Dutch had always been ambivalent. Since Elizabeth and James both considered the provinces as a legal part of the Spanish empire, the Dutch were engaged in unlawful rebellion against their lawful ruler. On the other hand, the Dutch were Protestants, and England gained security from Spain's military sacrifice required to oppress the Dutch. As Maurice Lee notes, "France could not afford to see Spain conquer [the Dutch] – no more could England, for that matter. As long as the war between Spain and the Dutch went on, France would support the Dutch, and Franco-Spanish friendship would be impossible" (*James I and Henry IV*, 14).
57 *Letters from and to Sir Dudley Carleton During his Embassy in Holland, from January 1615, to December 1620* (London, 1757), p. 106. For an extended discussion of a secret conversation between Winwood and Maurits aimed at undermining Oldenbarnavelt see Motley, vol. xii, pp. 314–20.
58 Rowen points out that Maurits never attained the same status as his father, William the Silent. What changed was "his relationship to the States (the *provincial* assembly, for the stadtholdership never became a Generality office). Maurice was elected Stadtholder by the States and therefore became in law their servant, not their equal partner, like his father" (*Princes of Orange* 36).
59 Israel observes that historically, "The theological issues as such were of little concern to either the pro- or anti-Oldenbarnavelt factions . . . . [F]or many years . . . Maurits [did not show] any greater inclination towards strict Calvinist theology than did the Advocate. The forging of the Counter-Remonstrant party which eventually overthrew Oldenbarnavelt . . . was the result of sheer political opportunism and the harnessing of economic grievances to an ostensibly religious cause, true though that the theology played an indispensable part" (*Dutch Republic* 61).
60 "'Tragedies naturally performed': Kyd's Representation of Violence," *Staging the Renaissance: Reinterpretations of Elizabethan and Jacobean Drama*, David Scott Kastan and Peter Stallybrass (eds.) (New York and London: Routledge, 1991), pp. 99–113, 100. Shapiro finds two exceptions in Kyd's *The Spanish Tragedy*, in which Pedringano is hanged and Alexandro is almost burned at the stake.

61 Michel Foucault, *Discipline and Punish: The Birth of the Prison*, trans. Alan Sheridan (New York: Vintage, 1979), p. 48.

62 Michel Foucault, *The History of Sexuality* (New York: Vintage Books, 1980), p. 97.

63 I suppose that in part this ending may be tailored to an English audience more interested in the death of an Arminian than in the future of the Dutch Republic. But this misses the point: the play is not primarily about Arminianism or popery, and such a reading ignores all the political issues raised in it.

64 Leonard Tennenhouse, "Strategies of State and Political Plays: *A Midsummer Night's Dream*, *Henry IV*, *Henry V*, *Henry VIII*," *Political Shakespeare*, Jonathan Dollimore and Alan Sinfield (eds.) (Ithaca, NY: Cornell University Press, 1985), p. 111.

65 Peter L. Rudnytsky, "*Henry VIII* and the Deconstruction of History," *Shakespeare Survey* 43 (1991), pp. 43–57, 47.

6 PERKIN WARBECK AND THE FAILURE OF HISTORIOGRAPHY

1 Philip Sidney, *A Defence of Poesy* in *Sir Philip Sidney*, Katherine Duncan-Jones (ed.) (Oxford and New York: Clarendon Press, 1989), p. 224.

2 I follow the account given by Elizabeth Jenkins, *The Princes in the Tower* (New York: Coward, McCann and Geoghegan, Inc., 1978), pp. 196–7. The essential details of this account are corroborated by contemporary reports quoted in Audrey Williamson, *The Mystery of the Princes: An Investigation into a Supposed Murder* (Gloucester, England: Alan Sutton, 1981), pp. 183–4.

3 *Perkin Warbeck* was printed in 1634, some five years into Charles I's "personal rule," but may have been written and performed as early as 1622 (though a post-1625 date is more likely). For this reason, the performance of the play cannot be linked to any particular historical moment. I treat the play, therefore, as a document responding to certain royal tendencies prevalent throughout most of Charles's reign. See Peter Ure's "Introduction" to the Revels edition of *The Chronicle History of Perkin Warbeck*, Peter Ure (ed.) (London: Methuen, 1968), pp. xxviii–xxx.

4 The threat of succession of Charles II's Catholic brother, James, whose religious convictions (which were largely shared by Charles) were unacceptable to many in Anglican England, eventually led to the Whigs in the House of Commons passing a Bill of Exclusion in 1680, barring James from the succession. James himself went into exile in the Netherlands.

5 In her recent book, *Reading Holinshed's Chronicles* (Chicago and London: University of Chicago Press, 1994), Annabel Patterson makes a serious case that, although the *Chronicles* contain the *grand récits* of which critics like Tillyard were so fond, Holinshed resists that kind of orthodox historiographical totalization. Patterson may be correct, for much in Holinshed does not easily fit into a single overarching narrative, but all the evidence indicates that with rare exceptions Holinshed's readers did come away from the text with a sense of the Tudor view of history – the *grand récit*.

6 All quotations are from the Revels edition of *The Chronicle History of Perkin Warbeck*, ed. Peter Ure, and are parenthetically cited in the text.

7 This is not to suggest that these histories tell identical stories or always follow

party lines. Indeed, they reveal significant differences in the details (and their presentation) of the Warbeck story, as they disclose occasional doubts about the strength of Henry Tudor's claim to the English throne (in, for instance, Bacon and Holinshed), but none openly consider the possibility that Warbeck's claim should supercede Henry's.

8 That the Tudor account contributed to greater social stability in the lives of those readers was of course another crucial factor.

9 James I, *Basilikon Doron, or His Maiesties Instrvctions to his Dearest Sonne, Henry the Prince* in *The Political Works of James I*, Charles I. McIlwain (ed.) (Cambridge, MA: Harvard University Press, 1918), pp. 3–52.

10 Phyllis Rackin writes that "Historiographic writing no longer had a direct unequivocal relation with historical truth. Alternative accounts of historical events and opposed interpretations of their causes and significance now threatened each other's sensibility. . . ." (*Stages of History: Shakespeare's English Chronicles* [Ithaca, NY: Cornell University Press, 1990], p. 13).

11 Jonas A. Barish, "*Perkin Warbeck* as Anti-History," *Essays in Criticism* 20 (1970), pp. 151–71.

12 Donald K. Anderson quoted by Barish ("*Perkin Warbeck*" 152).

13 For a suggestive account of ways in which contemporary figures and events may be implicated by the play, see Dale B. J. Randall, *"Theatres of Greatness": A Revisionary View of Ford's "Perkin Warbeck"* (Canada: University of Victoria, 1986), pp. 19–26.

14 F. J. Levy, *Tudor Historical Thought* (San Marino, CA: Huntington Library, 1967), p. 234. See the whole chapter on "The Popularization of History," pp. 202–36.

15 A number of critics have taken up Ure's claim that Warbeck's unwavering belief in his royal identity was an ahistorical creation of Ford's genius. For these critics, the play's subtitle, *A Strange Truth*, obviously presents a bit of a problem: it cannot mean "historical truth" or "factual truth." Joseph Candido in "The 'Strange Truth' of *Perkin Warbeck*" (*Philological Quarterly* 59 [1980]) solves the difficulty by equating the "Strange Truth" with "the emotional 'truth' of [Perkin's] performance" and "aesthetic truth" (310, 311). Dorothy M. Farr (*John Ford and the Caroline Theatre* [New York: Barnes and Noble, 1979]) writes: "What Henry encounters here [in the character of Warbeck] is a new kind of truth – not truth as he and his world know it, measured by good sense and expediency, but truth to a man's own self and his conviction of what that self should be" (115). These readings, however, seem to be sophisticated though overly romantic updates on a traditional estimation of Warbeck as a "melancholic with the delusion of grandeur" (Lawrence Rabb, "Abnormal Psychology in John Ford's *Perkin Warbeck*," *Modern Language Notes* 51 [1936], p. 237), an estimation restated most recently by Ronald Huebert who asserts "Perkin Warbeck suffers from delusions of majesty" (*John Ford: Baroque English Dramatist* [Montreal and London: McGill-Queen's University Press, 1977], p. 67).

16 I borrow the concept of the "ventriloquistic text" from Annabel Patterson (*Shakespeare and the Popular Voice* [Cambridge, MA and Oxford: Blackwell, 1989], p. 41) who, in turn, borrows it from Pierre Macherey (*A Theory of Literary Production*, trans. Geoffrey Wall [London: Routledge and Kegan Paul, 1978], p. 265).

17 Stephen Greenblatt, "Invisible Bullets: Renaissance Authority and its Subversion, *Henry IV* and *Henry V*" in *Political Shakespeare: New Essays in Cultural Materialism*, Jonathan Dollimore and Alan Sinfield (eds.) (Ithaca, NY: Cornell University Press), pp. 18–47, 27. Greenblatt of course goes on to argue that "monological power" records such voices only to deny them ultimately. The unmasking of Warbeck as a false, illegitimate voice would certainly "deny" him and strengthen Tudor legitimacy and authority. The problem in the play is of course that Warbeck is executed, not unmasked.
18 Ure rejects this on the grounds that Bacon's explanation is only an explanation and "not a *description* of the behavior of the character in the play." The distinction has merit but should not lead one to conclude that "it is therefore hard to see why it should be presumed to have inspired Ford . . ." ("Introduction" xlii).
19 Raphael Holinshed, *Chronicles of England, Scotlande, and Irelande* (London, 1807 [1577]), vol. II, p. 504.
20 Polydore Vergil, *Anglica Historia*, Denys Hay trans. and ed. (London: Offices of the Royal Historical Society, 1950), Camden Series vol. LXXIV, p. 65.
21 See also Bacon, *History*, p. 138.
22 Arthur Noel Kincaid, Appendix C in Sir George Buc's *The History of King Richard III* (Gloucester, England: Alan Sutton, 1979), p. 327.
23 Sir George Buc[k], *The History of King Richard III*, Arthur N. Kincaid (ed.) (Gloucester, England: Alan Sutton, 1979), p. 144. Despite Buc's overt intention to rehabilitate the much maligned reputation of Richard III ("And my scope was to write this unhappy king's story faithfully and at large, and to plead his cause, and to answer and retell the many accusations and calumniations brought against him" [8]), it is hard to believe that he, as he was Master of the Revels for both James I and Charles I, would frivolously write anything that might be construed as criticism of the House of Stuart in favor of that of York.
24 Hayden White, *Tropics of Discourse: Essays in Cultural Criticism* (Baltimore and London: The Johns Hopkins University Press, 1978), p. 88. In general, these pregeneric plot structures are based on "the modes of relationships conceptualized in the myth, fable, and folklore, scientific knowledge, religion, and literary art, of the historian's own culture" (94). Here, specifically, the original force behind the story of the princes in the tower was no doubt largely political.
25 Lisa Hopkins goes a step further when she suggests that Ford and the circle of aristocrats to whom he routinely dedicated his works may well have believed that Warbeck was not an imposter at all (*John Ford's Political Theatre* [Manchester and New York: Manchester University Press, 1994], pp. 59–60).
26 Francis Bacon, *The History of the Reign of King Henry VII*, Roger Lockyer (ed.) (London: The Folio Society, 1971), p. 35.
27 Holinshed, "The Preface to the Reader," vol. III, no page number.
28 Lockyer's "Introduction" to his edition of Bacon's *Henry VII*, p. 16.
29 Holinshed, *Chronicles* vol. III, no page numbers.
30 Richard Grafton, *Chronicles* (London, 1807), p. viii.
31 Edward Hall, *Chronicle* (London, 1809 reprint), p. 488. See also Holinshed, p. *Chronicles,* 522. Most historians agree the confession is fraudulent, and Arthur Kincaid concludes: "That an almost certainly spurious confession had to be made for him seems to indicate that he never broke down sufficiently to give a

satisfactory confession which could have been simply verified, solving the matter. Yet he was sufficiently broke down to read a false confession" (*History of King Richard III*, 328).

32 Extracts from Thomas Gainsford's *True and Wonderfull History of Perkin Warbeck*. Appendix 1 of the Revels edition of the play, p. 175.

33 See Kincaid, p. 327 and Williamson, *Mystery*, pp. 161–72. It is of course not difficult today to find historians who argue persuasively that Warbeck was an imposter. Mortimer Levine, for instance, writes that "Though Warbeck's confession was made under *duress*, there is no reason to doubt its essential accuracy. Today it would take an incurable romantic to believe that Warbeck was indeed Edward IV's younger son." He goes on to say that "at the time, however, even Henry VII could not be sure he was an imposter. While it may have been common *assumed* that Edward V and little York had been murdered during Richard III's reign, the fact that their remains had not been found left room for *doubt*" (*Tudor Dynastic Problems, 1460–1571* [London: Allen and Unwin; New York: Barnes and Noble, 1973], p. 38. By the time Ford wrote his play the bodies still had not been found, nor had any other compelling evidence to substantiate the Tudor claim surfaced.

34 Terry Eagleton quotes Trotsky in *Marxism and Literary Criticism* (Berkeley and Los Angeles, University of California Press), p. 24.

35 *OED*, 4; also see "monumental," 5.

36 Thomas Hobbes, *The History of the Grecian War*, written by Thucydides (London: John Bohn, 1843), p. viii.

37 Francis Bacon's position is akin to Hobbes's and Ford's. While insisting that "under the name of Poesy I treat only of feigned history," and that "poesy is feigned history, as opposed to true history" (*A Selection of His Works*, pp. 406–7; also see *Advancement of Learning*, Bk. II, W. A. Wright [ed.] [Oxford: Clarendon Press, 1900], p. 102), Bacon nonetheless asserted that "Dramatic poesy is as History made visible, for it represents actions as if they were present, whereas History presents them as past" (*De Dignitate et Augmentis Scientarium* [1623]. In *A Selection of His Works*, Sidney Warhaft [ed.] [Indianapolis: The Odyssey Press, 1980], p. 407).

38 Lawrence Stone, *The Crises of the Aristocracy, 1558–1641*, abr. edn. (Oxford: Oxford University Press, 1967), pp. 21–61.

39 F. Fussner Smith, *The Historical Revolution. English Historical Writing and Thought 1580–1640* (London: Routledge and Kegan Paul, 1962), p. 42.

40 Philip Edwards shrewdly uses Dalyell's speech to undermine the conceptions of hereditary right (Warbeck's as well as Henry's), as it underlines "the unimportance of 'blood in veins'" ("The Royal Pretenders in Massinger and Ford," *Essays and Studies* 27 [1974], pp. 24–5).

41 *Henry V* (1.2.86). William Shakespeare, *The Complete Works of Shakespeare*, David Bevington (ed.) (Glenview, IL, and London: Scott, Forsman and Company, 1980).

42 It is crucial to understand that the "literary" reception of history does *not* transform history into literature in the sense of fiction. "Literary" simply refers to the way readers interpret history, not to what history is.

43 For a different reading of this passage, see Lisa Hopkins, who submits that "there is no hint of fault in the behavior of either Henry himself or of his coun-

sellors," and that the lords explicitly deny the superiority of the York title over that of Lancaster (*John Ford's Political Theatre* 49).

44 George Puttenham, *The Arte of English Poesy*, Edward Arber (ed.) (Kent, OH: Kent State University Press, 1988), p. 112.

45 Charles Ross, *The Wars of the Roses* (New York: Thames and Hudson, 1976), pp. 128–35.

46 Several renaissance monarchs, including Mary Queen of Scots, Elizabeth I, and James I, believed themselves to have been "set on stages in the sight and view of all the world" (quoted in Stephen Greenblatt, "Invisible Bullets", (44). See Jean Howard for a discussion of the "actor metaphor as a double-edged one" ("'Effeminately Dolent': Gender and Legitimacy in Ford's *Perkin Warbeck*," *John Ford: Critical Re-Visions*, Michael Neill [ed.] [Cambridge: Cambridge University Press, 1988], pp. 276–7, 270–1).

47 See Lisa Hopkins, "Acting the Self: John Ford's *Perkin Warbeck* and the Politics of Imposture," *Cahiers Élisabéthains* 48 (October 1995), pp. 31–5.

48 Kent in *King Lear*, ed. Bevington (1.4.27–8).

49 John Archer argues astutely that "Bacon's *Henry VII* monumentalizes another type of legitimacy, a sovereignty grounded in intelligence" (*Sovereignty and Intelligence: Spying and Court Culture in the English Renaissance* [Stanford: Stanford University Press, 1993], p. 135). The same proclivity for spying and secret diplomacy is certainly evident in Ford's play, but, much as in Bacon's history, although it allows Henry considerable success and the defeat of Warbeck, it does not affirm his own legitimacy claim (cf. Archer, p. 139). Part of the reason being that successes achieved in secret by definition do not lend themselves for public performance.

50 In her stimulating article, "'Effeminately Dolent': Gender and Legitimacy in Ford's *Perkin Warbeck*," Jean Howard works out the diminution of difference in a gender context. Howard argues that "Through the figure of Henry VII the play recapitulates the dominant practices of the history genre for representing the gender politics of patriarchal absolutism. But," she then goes on to point out, "Henry is not the protagonist; he is an anachronism, representing the only paradigm for monarchical legitimacy the culture credits, yet clearly being jostled from centre stage by a figure whose depiction represents an alternative mode of gender relations . . . ." (276). This other figure is, of course, Warbeck, in whose effeminate qualities (i.e. his passivity, his abhorrence of violence, his loving relationship with his wife) traditional differences between the masculine and the feminine become destabilized. Although Warbeck represents a subversive alternative to the hard-nosed patriarchalism of Henry VII, Howard rightly notes that Warbeck's inability to produce sufficient gender distinctions disqualify him as a satisfactory alternative, making him "not the solution to the problem, but its clearest articulation" through which "Ford shows how a patriarchal, absolutist culture unthinks itself" (264). In this fashion, Howard concludes, the play "hints at the increasing strain under which patriarchal absolutism laboured in the Caroline era and at the fear that the monarch could no longer maintain the differences underpinning the traditional social order."

51 Quoted from Ure's Appendix III, p. 181.

52 D. R. Woolf, *The Idea of History in Early Stuart England: Erudition, Ideology,*

and 'The Light of Truth' from the Accession of James I to the Civil War (Toronto, Buffalo, and London: University. of Toronto Press, 1990), pp. xii–xiii.

53 Although it seems not to have had any practical impact on Charles's reign at the time, the fact, as Lisa Hopkins reminds us, that Warbeck may have had children (Thomas Gainsford writes that Warbeck left Scotland with "Wife and family"), and that there was a group of Catholic aristocrats who, excluded from government, readily believed such rumors, is suggestive, and insinuates that Charles, like Ford's Henry VII, was still haunted by the ghosts of York (Hopkins, *John Ford's Political Theatre* 61).

54 Ure's note to the dedicatory epistle, p. 5. Donald K. Anderson makes the same point in "Kingship in Ford's *Perkin Warbeck*" in *English Literary History* 29 (1960), pp. 177–93, 191.

55 See Howard, pp. 264, 276–7.

56 See J. P. Sommerville, *Politics and Ideology in England 1603–1640* (London and New York: Longman, 1986), pp. 235–6. The King's aversion for negotiation with Parliament does not mean, as Kevin Sharpe points out, that early in his reign Charles already intended to govern England without (*The Personal Rule of Charles* [New Haven and London: Yale University Press, 1992]), p. 37.

57 After efforts to "raise money by Benevolence had been a complete failure," Charles decided to levy a forced loan to support the military efforts of his uncle, Christian IV of Denmark. "Forced loans, levied from individuals by privy seal letters" were nothing new, "but the 1626 levy was significantly different, since all subsidy payers were assessed for it, at the rate of five subsidies. It was, in other words, parliamentary taxation without parliamentary sanction, and as such it ran counter to many Englishmen's most deeply-held beliefs" (Roger Lockyer, *The Early Stuarts: A Political History of England 1603–1642* [New York and London: Longman, 1989], pp. 222–5). Also see Sommerville, *Politics and Ideology*, pp. 127–31. For other defining confrontations between crown and Parliament, see the Buckingham case (Roger Lockyer, *Buckingham* [London and New York: Longman, 1981], pp. 310–15), and the Five Knights' Case of 1627 (J. P. Kenyon, *The Stuart Constitution* 2nd edn. [Cambridge: Cambridge University Press, 1986], p. 89). The most recent study of Charles's personal rule is Kevin Sharpe's *The Personal Rule of Charles I*.

58 Charles Carlton, *Charles I: The Personal Monarch* (London, Boston, Melbourne, Henley: Routledge and Kegan Paul, 1983), p. 103.

59 Perry Anderson, *Lineages of the Absolute State* (1974) (London and New York: Verso, 1989), p. 140.

60 Anne Barton, "He that plays the king: Ford's *Perkin Warbeck* and the Stuart history play" in *English Drama: Forms and Development* (Cambridge: Cambridge University Press, 1977), p. 80.

61 See Kevin Sharpe, "Fear of the Censor?" in *Personal Rule*, pp. 682–3.

CONCLUSION

1 Irving Ribner, *The English History Play in the Age of Shakespeare* (Princeton: Princeton University Press, 1957), pp. 266–305.

2 J. H. Walter (ed.), *Henry V* (The Arden Shakespeare) (London: Methuen, 1968), p. lxiv.

3 Unless indicated otherwise, the facts regarding performance history are taken from Gerald E. Bentley, *The Jacobean and Caroline Stage*, 7 vols. (Oxford: Clarendon Press, 1941), vol. I.

4 E. K. Chambers, *The Elizabethan Stage*, 4 vols. (Oxford: Clarendon Press, 1923), vol. IV, p. 23 (emphasis added).

5 Annabel Patterson, *Reading Holinshed's Chronicles* (Chicago and London: University of Chicago Press, 1994), pp. 4–8.

6 These plays may not demand a great deal of interest from a study like this one, but that does not mean that they are unworthy of serious critical attention. Kim H. Noling's recent essay on Rowley's *When You See Me You Know Me*, for instance, underscores the importance of this play in our understanding of gender roles ("Woman's Wit and Woman's Will in When You Know Me, You Know," *Studies in English Literature, 1500–1900* 33 [1993], pp. 327–42).

7 Thomas Drue, *The Life of the Dutches of Suffolke* (London: J. Emery, 1631).

8 Samuel Rowley, *When You See Me You Know Me* in *The Tudor Facsimile Texts* (New York: AMS Press, 1970), D4^{r}.

9 F. J. Levy, *Tudor Historical Thought* (San Marino, CA: Huntington Library, 1967), p. 234.

10 See Annabel Patterson, *Shakespeare and the Popular Voice* (Oxford and Cambridge, MA: Blackwell, 1989), pp. 77–80. On *Sejanus*, see Jonathan Dollimore, *Radical Tragedy: Religion, Ideology and Power in the Drama of Shakespeare and his Contemporaries* (Chicago: University of Chicago Press, 1986), pp. 134–8.

11 Alvin B. Kernan, "The Plays and Playwrights," *The Revels History of Drama in English 1576–1613*, 4 vols. (London: Methuen, 1975), vol. III, pp. 264–5.

12 J. P. Sommerville, *Politics and Ideology in England, 1603–1640* (London and New York: Longman, 1986), pp. 10–12, 34–39, passim.

Bibliography

Adams, Barry, "Introduction," John Bale's *King Johan*, San Marino, CA: Huntington Library, 1969, 1–65.

Akrigg, G. P. V., *Jacobean Pageant or The Court of James I*, Cambridge, MA: Harvard University Press, 1962.

Akrigg, G. P. V. (ed.), *Letters of King James VI & I*, London, Berkeley: University of California Press, 1984.

Althusser, Louis, "Ideology and Ideological State Apparatuses (Notes Towards an Investigation)," *Lenin and Philosophy*, Ben Brewster (trans.), New York and London: Verso, 1971, 127–86.

"Contradiction and Overdetermination," *For Marx*, London: Verso, 1982.

Anderson, Donald K., "Kingship in Ford's *Perkin Warbeck*," *English Literary History* 29 (1960), 177–93.

Anderson, Judith H., *Biographical Truth: The Representation of Historical Persons in Tudor-Stuart Writing*, New Haven and London: Yale University Press, 1984.

Anderson, Perry, *Considerations on Western Marxism*, London: Verso, 1976.

Lineages of the Absolute State (1974), London and New York: Verso, 1989.

Appleton, William W., *Beaumont and Fletcher: A Critical Study*, London: George Allen and Unwin, 1956.

Archer, John, *Sovereignty and Intelligence: Spying and Court Culture in the English Renaissance*, Stanford: Stanford University Press, 1993.

Aristotle, *On Poetics and Style*, G. M. A. Grube (trans.), New York: Bobbs-Merrill, 1958.

Avis, Paul, *Foundations of Modern Historical Thought: From Machiavelli to Vico*, London: Croom Helm, 1986.

Bacon, Francis, *A Selection of His Works*, Sidney Warhaft (ed.), Indianapolis: The Odyssey Press, 1980.

Advancement of Learning, Bk. II, W. A. Wright (ed.), Oxford: Clarendon Press, 1900.

De Dignitate et Augmentis Scientarium (1623), *A Selection of His Works*.

The History of the Reign of King Henry VII, Roger Lockyer (ed.), London: The Folio Society, 1971.

The Advancement of Learning, *The Works of Francis Bacon*, vol. I, Basil Montagu (ed.), Philadelphia: Hart, 1853.

Baldwin, William, *The Mirror for Magistrates*, Lily B. Campbell (ed.), New York: Barnes and Noble, 1960.

Bale, John, *Illustrium maioris Britanniae scriptorum Summarium*, Wesel: Derek van der Straten, 1548.

King Johan, Barry B. Adams (ed.), San Marino, CA: Huntington Library, 1969.

Scriptorum Illustrium maiores Britanniae . . . Catalogus. 2 vols., Basel: Oporinus, 1557–9.

The Image of both Churches, Antwerp: Mierdman, 1545.

The Vocacyon of Johan Bale. Peter Happé and John N. King (eds.), Binghampton, NY: Renaissance English Text Society, 1990.

Barish, Jonas A., "*Perkin Warbeck* as Anti-History," *Essays in Criticism* 20 (1970), 151–71.

Barker, Francis and Peter Hulme, "Nymphs and Reapers Heavily Vanish: the Discursive Con-texts of *The Tempest*," *Alternative Shakespeares*, John Drakakis (ed.), London and New York: Methuen, 1985, 191–205.

Barton, Anne, "He that Plays the King: Ford's *Perkin Warbeck* and the Stuart History Play," *English Drama: Forms and Development*, Marie Axton and Raymond Williams (eds.), Cambridge: Cambridge University Press, 1977, 69–93.

Bentley, Gerald Eades, *The Jacobean and Caroline Stage*, 7 vols., Oxford: Clarendon Press, 1941.

The Profession of Dramatist and Player in Shakespeare's Time, 1590–1642, Princeton: Princeton University Press, 1986.

Bevington, David, *Tudor Drama and Politics: A Critical Approach to Topical Meaning*, Cambridge, MA: Harvard University Press, 1968.

Bingham, Caroline, *James I of England*, London: Weidenfeld and Nicolson, 1981.

Blundeville, Thomas, *The true order and Methode of wryting and reading Hystories*, Hugh G. Dick (ed.), *The Huntington Library Quarterly* 2 (1940), 149–70.

Bodin, Jean, "Of the Choice of History, by Way of Preface," Sallust, *The Conspiracy of Catiline* and *The War of Jugurtha*, Thomas Heywood (trans.) (1608), London and New York: Constable, Knopf, 1924.

Method for the Easy Comprehension of History (1566), Beatrice Reynolds (trans.), New York: Octagon Books, 1966.

Bolton, Edmund, "Hypercritica, or a Rule of Judgment for Writing or reading our Histories" (1618?), *Critical Essays of the Seventeenth Century*, vol. I, J. E. Spingarn (ed.), Bloomington, IN: Indiana University Press, 1968.

Bradshaw, Graham, *Misrepresentations: Shakespeare and the Materialists*, Ithaca, NY: Cornell University Press, 1993.

Braunmuller, A. R., "*King John* and Historiography," *English Literary History* 55 (1988), 309–32.

Braunmuller, A. R. (ed.), William Shakespeare, *King John*, Oxford: Oxford University Press, 1988.

Breisach, Ernst, *Historiography: Ancient, Medieval and Modern*, Chicago and London: University of Chicago Press, 1983.

Bruce, J. (ed.), *The Correspondence of King James VI with Robert Cecil and others in England during the Reign of Queen Elizabeth*, Camden Society, 1860.

Buc[k], Sir George, *The History of King Richard III*, Arthur N. Kincaid (ed.), Gloucester, England: Alan Sutton, 1979.

Bullen, A. H., *Collection of Old English Plays*, vol. II, London, 1883.

Burckhardt, Sigurd, *Shakespearean Meanings*, Princeton: Princeton University Press, 1968.

Burke, Peter, *The Renaissance Sense of the Past*, New York: St. Martin's Press, 1969.

Bush, Douglas, *The Renaissance and English Humanism*, Toronto: University of Toronto Press, 1965.

Camden, William, *The History of the Most Renowned and Victorious Princess Elizabeth, Late Queen of England* (1615), Wallace T. MacCaffrey (ed.), Chicago and London: University of Chicago Press, 1970.

Campbell, Lily B., *Shakespeare's Histories: Mirrors of Elizabethan Policy*, San Marino, CA: Huntington Library, 1947.

Candido, Joseph, "Fashioning Henry VIII: What Shakespeare Saw in *When You See Me, You Know Me*," *Cahiers Élisabéthains* 23 (1983), 47–59.

"The 'Strange Truth' of *Perkin Warbeck*," *Philological Quarterly* 59 (1980), 300–16.

Carlton, Charles, *Charles I: The Personal Monarch*, London, Boston, Melbourne, Henley: Routledge and Kegan Paul, 1983.

Carr, David, "Narrative and the Real World: An Argument for Continuity," *History and Theory* 25 (1986), 117–31.

Cary, Elizabeth, *The History of The Life, Reign, and Death of Edward II. King of England, and Lord of Ireland. with The Rise and Fall of his great Favorites, Gaveston and the Spencers* (1627), London, 1680.

Cavendish, George, *The Life and death of Cardinal Wolsey* in *Two Early Tudor Lives*, Richard S. Sylvester and David P. Harding (eds.), New Haven and London: Yale University Press, 1990.

Cespedes, Frank, V., "'We are one in fortunes': The Sense of History in *Henry VIII*," *English Literary Renaissance* 10 (1980), 413–38.

Chambers, E. K., *The Elizabethan Stage*, 4 vols., Oxford: Clarendon Press, 1923, vols. I and IV.

Champion, Larry S., "'Answere to this Perillous Time': Ideological Ambivalence in *The Raigne of King Edward III* and the English Chronicle Plays," *English Studies* 69 (1988), 117–29.

"The Noise of Threatening Drum": Dramatic Strategy and Political Ideology in Shakespeare and the English Chronicle Plays, Newark, DE: University of Delaware Press, 1990.

Chapman, George, *Caesar and Pompey* (1612–13?), *The Plays and Poems of George Chapman*, T. M. Parrott (ed.), London, 1910, vol. 1.

Chappell, Warren, *A Short History of the Printed Word*, New York: Knopf, 1970.

Cochrane, Eric, *Historians and Historiography in the Italian Renaissance*, Chicago: University of Chicago Press, 1985.

Cogswell, Thomas, "England and the Spanish Match," *Conflict in Early Stuart England: Studies in Religion and Politics*, Richard Cust and Ann Hughes (eds.), London and New York: Longman, 1989, 107–33.

Cohen, Walter, "Political Criticism of Shakespeare," *Shakespeare Reproduced*, Jean E. Howard and Marion F. O'Connor (eds.), New York and London: Methuen, 1987, 18–46.

Collingwood, R. G., *The Idea of History* (1946), London and Oxford: Oxford University Press, 1956.

Dean, Leonard F., "Sir Francis Bacon's Theory of Civil History-Writing," *English Literary History* 8 (1941), 161–83.

"Bodin's *Methodus* in England Before 1625," *Studies in Philology* 39 (1942), 160–66.

Tudor Theories of History Writing, Contributions in Modern Philology No. 1, Ann Arbor, MI: University of Michigan Press, 1947.

Dean, Paul, "Dramatic Mode and Historical Vision in *Henry VIII*," *Shakespeare Quarterly* 37 (1986), 1975–89.

Dekker, Thomas, *Sir Thomas Wyatt* in *The Dramatic Works of Thomas Dekker*, 4 vols., Fredson Bowers (ed.), Cambridge: Cambridge University Press, 1953, vol. I.

Dollimore, Jonathan, *Radical Tragedy: Religion, Ideology and Power in the Drama of Shakespeare and his Contemporaries*, Chicago: University of Chicago Press, 1984.

"Introduction: Shakespeare, Cultural Materialism and the New Historicism," *Political Shakespeare: New Essays in Cultural Materialism*, Jonathan Dollimore and Alan Sinfield (eds.), Ithaca and London: Cornell University Press, 1985.

Dollimore, Jonathan and Alan Sinfield, "History and Ideology: The Instance of *Henry V*," *Alternative Shakespeares*, John Drakakis (ed.), London and New York: Methuen, 1985, 206–27.

Donne, John, "Elegy upon the untimely death of the incomparable Prince Henry," *John Donne: The English Poems*, A. J. Smith (ed.), London and New York: Penguin, 1986.

Donno, Elizabeth Story, "Old Mouse-Eaten Records: History in Sidney's *Apology*," *Sir Philip Sidney: An Anthology of Modern Criticism*, Dennis Kay (ed.), Oxford: Clarendon Press, 1987, 145–67.

Doran, Madeleine, "Introduction," *If You Know Not Me You Know Nobody*, Oxford: Malone Society Reprint, 1935.

Drue, Thomas, *The life of the Dutches of Suffolke,* London: J. Emery, 1631.

Dutton, Richard, *Mastering the Revels: The Regulation and Censorship of English Renaissance Drama*, Iowa City: University of Iowa Press, 1991.

Eagleton, Terry, *Marxism and Literary Criticism*, Berkeley and Los Angeles: University of California Press, 1976.

Criticism and Ideology: A Study in Marxist Literary Theory, London: Verso, 1982.

Ideology: An Introduction, London and New York: Verso, 1991.

Edwards, Philip, "The Royal Pretenders in Massinger and Ford," *Essays and Studies* 27 (1974), 18–36.

Eliot, T. S., "The Metaphysical Poets," *Seventeenth-century Prose and Poetry*, 2nd edn., Alexander M. Witherspoon and Frank J. Warnke (eds.), San Diego and New York: Hartcourt Brace Jovanovich, 1982.

Elizabeth I, "A Declaration of the Causes Mooving the Queene of England to Give aide to the Defence of the People afflicted and oppressed in the lowe Countries," *Elizabethan Backgrounds*, Arthur F. Kinney (ed.), Hamden, CT: Archon Books, 1975, 187–211.

Elton, Geoffrey, "Humanism in England," *The Impact of Humanism on Western Europe*, Anthony Goodman and Angus MacKay (eds.), New York and London: Longman, 1990, 259–78.

Erickson, Peter, *Rewriting Shakespeare, Rewriting Ourselves*, Berkeley: University of California Press, 1991.

Farr, Dorothy M., *John Ford and the Caroline Theatre*, New York: Barnes and Noble, 1979.

Felperin, Howard, "Shakespeare's *Henry VIII*: History as Myth," *Studies in English Literature* 6 (1966), 225–46.

Ferguson, Arthur B., *Clio Unbound: Perception of the Social and Cultural Past in Renaissance England*, Durham, NC: Duke University Press, 1979.

Fitter, Chris, "A Tale of Two Branagh's: Henry V, Ideology and the Mekong Agincourt," *Shakespeare Left and Right*, Ivo Kamps (ed.), New York and London: Routledge, 1991, 259–75.

Ford, John, *The Chronicle History of Perkin Warbeck*, Peter Ure (ed.), London: Methuen, 1968.

Foucault, Michel, *Discipline and Punish: The Birth of the Prison*, Alan Sheridan (trans.), New York: Vintage, 1979.

The History of Sexuality: An Introduction, Robert Hurley (trans.), New York: Vintage, 1980.

Foxe, John, *The Imprisonment of the Princess Elizabeth* (from *Acts and Monuments*), *Tudor Tracts 1532–1588*, A. F. Pollard (ed.), Westminster: Constable, 1903.

The Actes and Monuments of John Foxe: A New and Complete Edition, Stephen Reed Cattley (ed.), London: Seeley and Burnside, 1841.

The Actes and Monuments, M. Hobart Seymour (ed.), New York: Robert Carter and Brothers, 1856.

The First Volume of the Ecclesiasticall History, London, 1576.

Fraser, Russell A. and Norman Rabkin (eds.), *Drama of the English Renaissance II: The Stuart Period*, New York: Macmillan; London: Collier Macmillan, 1976.

Frere, Walter H., *The English Church in the Reigns of Elizabeth and James I. (1558–1625)*, London: Macmillan, 1911, vol. V.

Frijlinck, Wilhelmina P., "Introduction," *The Tragedy of Sir John Van Olden Barnavelt*, Amsterdam: Dorssen, 1922.

Fussner, F. Smith, *The Historical Revolution in English Historical Writing and Thought, 1580–1640*, London: Routledge and Kegan Paul, 1962.

Gallagher, Catherine, "Marxism and the New Historicism," *The New Historicism*, H. Aram Veeser (ed.), New York and London: Routledge, 1989, 37–48.

Gardiner, Samuel R., *History of England from the Accession of James I to the Outbreak of the Civil War, 1603–1642*, 10 vols., New York: AMS Press, 1965, vols. I and II.

George, Charles, *The Stuarts: A Century of Experiment 1603–1714*, England: Blond Educational, 1973.

Gilbert, Felix, *Machiavelli and Guicciardini: Politics and History in Sixteenth Century Florence*, New York and London: Norton, 1984.

Goldberg, Jonathan, "Speculations: *Macbeth* and Source," *Shakespeare Reproduced: The Text in History and Ideology*, Jean E. Howard and Marion F. O'Connor (eds.), New York and London: Methuen, 1987, 242–64.

James I and the Politics of Literature: Jonson, Shakespeare, Donne, and Their Contemporaries (1983), Stanford: Stanford University Press, 1989.

Grafton, Richard, "To the Right Honorable Sir Wylliam Cecill Knight. . .," *A Chronicle at Large*, London, 1809 reprint vol. I.

Gransden, Antonia, *Historical Writing in England II: c. 1307 to the Early Sixteenth Century*, Ithaca, NY: Cornell University Press, 1982.

Greenblatt, Stephen, "Invisible Bullets: Renaissance Authority and its Subversion, *Henry IV* and *Henry V*," *Political Shakespeare: New Essays in Cultural Materialism*, Jonathan Dollimore and Alan Sinfield (eds.), Ithaca and London: Cornell University Press, 1985, 18–47.

Shakespearean Negotiations: The Circulation of Social Energy in Renaissance England, Berkeley and Los Angeles: University of California Press, 1988.

Greene, Thomas M., *The Light in Troy: Imitation and Discovery in Renaissance Poetry*, New Haven and London: Yale University Press, 1982.

Guicciardini, Francesco, *Ricordi*, Ninian Hill Thomson (trans.), New York: S. F. Vanni, 1949.

Guy, John, *Tudor England*, Oxford and New York: Oxford University Press, 1990.

Haddock, B. A., *An Introduction to Historical Thought*, London: Edward Arnold, 1980.

Hadfield, Andrew, *Literature, Politics and National Identity: Reformation to Renaissance*, Cambridge: Cambridge University Press, 1994.

Hall, Edward, *Chronicle*, London, 1809 reprint.

Halpern, Richard, *The Poetics of Primitive Accumulation: English Renaissance Culture and the Genealogy of Capital*, Ithaca and London: Cornell University Press, 1991.

Hamilton, Donna, B., *Shakespeare and the Politics of Protestant England*, Lexington, KY: University of Kentucky Press, 1992.

Happé, Peter, "Introduction," *Four Morality Plays*, Harmondsworth, England: Penguin, 1987.

Happé, Peter and John N. King, "Introduction," *The Vocacyon of Johan Bale*, Binghamton, NY: Renaissance English Text Society, 1990.

Heinemann, Margot, *Puritanism and Theatre: Thomas Middleton and the Opposition Drama under the Early Stuarts*, Cambridge: Cambridge University Press, 1982.

Heywood, Thomas, *An Apology for Actors*, New York: Johnson Reprint Corporation, 1972.

Englands Elizabeth: Her Life and Troubles, During Her Minoritie, from the Cradle to the Crowne, Philip R. Rider (ed.), New York and London: Garland Publishing Inc., 1982.

If You Know Not Me, You Know No Bodie, parts I and II, *The Dramatic Works of Thomas Heywood*, 6 vols., New York: Russell and Russell, 1964, 189–247, 251–351.

Hobbes, Thomas, *The History of the Grecian War*, written by Thucydides, London: John Bohn, 1843.

Holderness, Graham, *Shakespeare's History*, New York: St. Martin's Press, 1982.

Holinshed, Raphael, "Preface to the Reader," *Chronicles of England, Scotland, and Ireland,* 4 vols., London: 1807 reprint, vol. III, no page numbers.

Chronicles of England, Scotland and Ireland, 4 vols., London: 1808 reprint, vol. IV.

Holmes, George, *The Later Middle Ages: 1272–1485*, New York and London: Norton, 1966.

Hopkins, Lisa, *John Ford's Political Theatre*, Manchester and New York: Manchester University Press, 1994.

"Acting the Self: John Ford's *Perkin Warbeck* and the Politics of Imposture," *Cahiers Élisabéthains* 48 (October 1995), 31–5.

Howard, Jean E., "'Effeminately Dolent': Gender and Legitimacy in Ford's *Perkin Warbeck*," *John Ford: Critical Re-Visions*, Michael Neill (ed.), Cambridge: Cambridge University Press, 1988, 261–79.

The Stage and Social Struggle in Early Modern England, London and New York: Routledge, 1994.

Howard-Hill, T. H., "Buc and the Censorship of *Sir John Van Olden Barnavelt* in 1619," *The Review of English Studies* 39 (1988), 39–63.

Huebert, Ronald, *John Ford: Baroque English Dramatist*, Montreal and London: McGill-Queen's University Press, 1977.

Hunter, G. K., "Truth and Art in History Plays," *Shakespeare Survey* 42 (1989), 15–24.

Israel, Jonathan I., *The Dutch Republic and the Hispanic World 1606–1661*, Oxford: Clarendon Press, 1982.

Jakobson, Roman, "Linguistics and Poetics," *The Structuralists: From Marx to Lévi-Strauss*, Richard DeGeorge and Fernande DeGeorge (eds.), Garden City, NY: Anchor Books, 1972.

James I, *Basilikon Doron, or His Maiesties Instrvctions to his Dearest Sonne, Henry the Prince*, *The Political Works of James I*, Charles I. McIlwain (ed.) Cambridge, MA: Harvard University Press, 1918, 3–52.

Letters of King James VI & I, G. P. V. Akrigg (ed.), Berkeley and Los Angeles: University Of California Press, 1984.

The Trew Law of Free Monarchies, *The Political Works of James I*, Charles McIlwain (ed.), Cambridge, MA: Harvard University Press, 1918, 53–70.

"A Speech, as it was Delivered in the vpper Hovse of the Parliament . . ." *The Political Works of James I*, Charles H. McIlwain (ed.), Cambridge, MA: Harvard University Press, 1918, 269–80.

Jameson, Fredric, *Marxism and Form: Twentieth Century Dialectical Theories of Literature*, Princeton: Princeton University Press, 1976.

The Political Unconscious: Narrative as a Socially Symbolic Act, Ithaca, NY: Cornell University Press, 1982.

Jansen, H. P. H., *Kalendarium Geschiedenis van de Lage Landen in Jaartallen*, Utrecht and Antwerpen: Het Spectrum, 1982.

Jenkins, Elizabeth, *The Princes in the Tower*, New York: Coward, McCann and Geoghegan, Inc., 1978.

Jonson, Ben, *Sejanus his Fall*, W. F. Bolton (ed.), New York: Hill and Wang, 1966.

Kahn, Victoria, *Rhetoric, Prudence, and Skepticism in the Renaissance*, Ithaca, NY: Cornell University Press, 1985.

Kamps, Ivo, "Shakespeare Criticism: It is a Kind of History," *College English* 56:3 (1994), 335–6.

"Materialist Shakespeare: An Introduction," *Materialist Shakespeare*, Ivo Kamps (ed.), London: Verso, 1995.

Kantorowicz, Ernst H., *The King's Two Bodies: A Study in Medieval Political Theology*, Princeton: Princeton University Press, 1957.

Kastan, David Scott, *Shakespeare and the Shapes of Time*, Hanover, NH: University Press of New England, 1982.

"Proud Majesty Made a Subject: Shakespeare and the Spectacle of Rule," *Shakespeare Quarterly* 37 (1986), 459–75.

"'Holy Wurdes' and 'Slypper Wit': John Bale's *King Johan* and the Poetics of Propaganda," *Rethinking the Henrician Era: Essays on Early Tudor Texts and Contexts*, Peter C. Herman (ed.), Urbana, IL and Chicago: University of Illinois Press, 1994, 265–82.

Kenyon, J. P., *The Stuart Constitution* 2nd edn., Cambridge: Cambridge University Press, 1986.

Kermode, Frank, "The High Cost of New History," *The New York Review of Books*, June 25, 1992, 43.

Kernan, Alvin B., "*The Henriad*: Shakespeare's Major History Plays," *Modern Shakespearean Criticism*, Alvin Kernan (ed.), New York: Hartcourt Brace Jovanovich, 1970, 245–75.

"From Ritual to History: the English History Plays," in *The Revels History of Drama in English*, 4 vols., London: Methuen, 1975, vol. III, 262–99.

Kikkert, J. G., "The Debacle" and "No Monument for Maurits," *Maurits van Nassau*, Weesp, Netherlands: Fibula-Van Dishoeck, 1985.

Kincaid, Arthur Noel (ed.), Sir George Buc's *The History of King Richard III*, Gloucester, England: Alan Sutton, 1979.

King, John N., *English Reformation Literature: The Tudor Origins of the Protestant Tradition*, Princeton: Princeton University Press, 1982.

Kirkland, Stuart M., "*Henry VIII* and James I: Shakespeare and Jacobean Politics," *Shakespeare Studies* 19 (1987), 203–17.

Kristeller, Paul Oskar, *Renaissance Thought II: Papers on Humanism and the Arts*, New York, Evanston, and London: Harper Torchbooks, 1965.

Lake, Peter, "Anti-popery: the Structure of a Prejudice," *Conflict in Early Stuart England: Studies in Religion and Politics 1603–1642*, Richard Crust and Ann Hughes (eds.), London and New York: Longman, 1989

Lee, Maurice Jr., *James I and Henry IV*, Urbana, IL, Chicago, and London: University of Illinois Press, 1970.

Great Britain's Solomon: James VI and I in His Three Kingdoms, Urbana, IL and Chicago: University of Illinois Press, 1990.

Leggatt, Alexander, "*Henry VIII* and the Ideal England," *Shakespeare Survey* 38 (1985), 131–43.

Shakespeare Political Drama: The History Plays and the Roman Plays, London and New York: Routledge, 1989.

Jacobean Public Theatre, London and New York: Routledge, 1992.

Levine, Joseph, *Humanism and History: Origins of Modern English Historiography*, Ithaca and London: Cornell University Press, 1987.

Levine, Mortimer, *Tudor Dynastic Problems, 1460–1571*, London: Allen and Unwin; New York: Barnes and Noble, 1973.

Levy, F. J., *Tudor Historical Thought*, San Marino, CA: The Huntington Library, 1967.

Lewalski, Barbara Kiefer, *Writing Women in Jacobean England*, Cambridge, MA and London: Harvard University Press, 1993.

Lindenberger, Herbert, *Historical Drama: The Relation of Literature and Reality*, Chicago and London: University of Chicago Press, 1975.
Lockyer, Roger, "Introduction" to his edition of Bacon's *Henry VII*.
Buckingham, London and New York: Longman, 1981.
The Early Stuarts: A Political History of England 1603–1642, London and New York: Longman, 1989.
Lukács, Georg, *The Historical Novel*, Hannah Mitchell and Stanley Mitchell (trans.), Lincoln, NE and London: University of Nebraska Press, 1983.
Macherey, Pierre, *A Theory of Literary Production*, Geoffrey Wall (trans.), London: Routledge and Kegan Paul, 1978.
Machiavelli, Niccoló, *Discourses on the First Decade of Titus Livius* in *Machiavelli, The Chief Works and Others*, 3 vols., Allan Gilbert (trans.), Durham, NC: Duke University Press, 1965, vol. I.
McLuskie, Kathleen, *The Revels History of English Drama*, 4 vols., London: Methuen, 1981, vol. IV.
McMullan, Gordon, *The Politics of Unease in the Plays of John Fletcher*, Amherst, MA: University of Massachusetts Press, 1994.
Manley, Lawrence, "Contextualism and the Role of Convention in Historiography," *Convention, 1500–1750*, Cambridge, MA: Harvard University Press, 1980, 203–40.
Marx, Karl, *The Eighteenth Brumaire of Louis Bonaparte*, Lewis S. Feuer (ed.), New York: Anchor Books, 1959.
Massinger, Philip, and John Fletcher, *The Tragedy of Sir John Van Olden Barnavelt*, T. H. Howard-Hill (ed.) Malone Society Reprints, 1979.
Momigliano, Arnaldo, "Ancient History and the Antiquarian," *Studies in Historiography*, London: Weidenfeld and Nicolson, 1966, 1–39.
"The Rhetoric of History and the History of Rhetoric: On Hayden White's Tropes," *Comparative Criticism: A Yearbook*, E. S. Shaffer (ed.), Cambridge: Cambridge University Press, 1981, 259–68.
Monmouth, Geoffrey, *The History of the Kings of Britain*, Lewis Thorpe (trans.), New York: Penguin, 1966.
Montrose, Louis A., "'Shaping Fantasies': Figurations of Gender and Power in Elizabethan Culture," *Representing the English Renaissance*, Stephen Greenblatt (ed.), Berkeley, Los Angeles, and London: University of California Press, 31–64.
More, Thomas, *History of King Richard III* in *Richard III: The Great Debate*, Paul Murray Kendall (ed.), New York and London: Norton, 1965.
Morris, Brian, "Introduction" *The Taming of the Shrew*, Arden Shakespeare, Brian Morris (ed.), London and New York: Methuen, 1981.
Motley, John L., *The Life and Death of John of Barneveldt, Advocate of Holland, With a View of the Primary Causes and Movements of the Thirty Years' War, The Complete Works of John L. Motley*, vols. XII-XIV of 17, New York: Kelmscott Society Publishers, 1902.
Mullaney, Steven, *The Place of the Stage: License, Play, and Power in Renaissance England*, Chicago and London: University of Chicago Press, 1988.
Munden, R. C., "James I and 'the growth of mutual distrust': King, Commons, and Reform," *Faction and Parliament: Essays on Early Stuart History*, Kevin Sharpe (ed.), London and New York: Methuen, 1978, 43–72.

Nenner, Howard, *The Right to be King*, Chapel Hill, NC: University of North Carolina Press, 1995.

Noling, Kim H., "Grubbing Up the Stock: Dramatizing Queens in *Henry VIII*," *Shakespeare Quarterly* 39 (1988), 291–306.

"Woman's Wit and Woman's Will in *When You Know Me, You Know*," *Studies in English Literature, 1500–1900* 33 (1993), 327–42.

Norbrook, David, "*Macbeth* and the Politics of Historiography," *Politics of Discourse: The Literature and History of Seventeenth Century England*, Kevin Sharpe and Steven N. Zwicker (eds.), Berkeley, Los Angeles, and London: University of California Press, 1987, 78–116.

North, Thomas (trans.), *Plutarch's Lives of the Noble Grecians and Romans* (1579), 6 vols. London, 1895, vol. I.

Palliser, D. M., *The Age of Elizabeth: England under the Later Tudors 1547–1603. Social and Economic History of England*, London and New York: Longman, 1985.

Palmer, Bryan D., *Descent into Discourse: The Reification of Language and the Writing of Social History*, Philadelphia: Temple University Press, 1990.

Patterson, Annabel, *Censorship and Interpretation: The Conditions of Writing and Reading in Early Modern England,* Madison: University of Wisconsin Press, 1984.

Shakespeare and the Popular Voice, Oxford: Basil Blackwell, 1989.

Reading Holinshed's Chronicles, Chicago and London: University of Chicago Press, 1994.

Peacham, Henry, *Minerva Britanna*, English Emblem Books no. 5, John Horden (ed.), Menston, England: Scolar Press, 1969.

Pocock, J. G. A., *The Ancient Constitution and the Feudal Law: A Study of English Historical Thought in the Seventeenth Century*. Cambridge: Cambridge University Press, 1987 (reissue).

Puttenham, George, *The Arte of English Poesie*, Edward Arber (ed.), Kent, OH: Kent State University Press, 1970.

Quint, David, "'Alexander the Pig': Shakespeare on History and Poetry," *Boundary 2* 10 (1982), 49–67.

Raab, Felix, *The English Face of Machiavelli: A Changing Interpretation, 1500–1700*, London: Routledge, 1964.

Rabb, Lawrence, "Abnormal Psychology in John Ford's *Perkin Warbeck*," *Modern Language Notes* 51 (1936).

Rackin, Phyllis, *Stages of History: Shakespeare's English Chronicles*, Ithaca, NY: Cornell University Press, 1990.

Ralegh, Sir Walter, *The History of the World, Selected Writings*, Gerald Hammond (ed.), Harmondsworth, England: Penguin, 1986.

Randall, Dale B. J., *"Theatres of Greatness": A Revisionary View of Ford's "Perkin Warbeck*," Canada: University of Victoria, 1986.

Reese, M. M., *The Cease of Majesty : A Study of Shakespeare's History Plays*, London: Edward Arnold, 1961.

Ribner, Irving, *The English History Play in the Age of Shakespeare,* Princeton: Princeton University Press, 1957.

Ridley, Jasper, *Henry VIII: The Politics of Tyranny*, New York: Fromm, 1986.

Elizabeth I: The Shrewdness of Virtue, New York: Fromm, 1989.

Rollins, Hyder E., *A Pepysian Garland: Black-letter Broadside Ballads of the Years 1595–1639*, Cambridge: Cambridge University Press, 1922.

Ross, Charles, *The Wars of the Roses*, New York: Thames and Hudson, 1976.

Rowen, Herbert H., *The Princes of Orange: The Stadtholders of the Dutch Republic*, Cambridge: Cambridge University Press, 1988.

Rowley, Samuel, *When You See Me You Know Me*, *The Tudor Facsimile Texts*, New York: AMS Press, 1970.

Rudnytsky, Peter L., "*Henry VIII* and the Deconstruction of History," *Shakespeare Survey* 43 (1991), 43–57.

Scarisbrick, J. J., *Henry VIII*, Berkeley and Los Angeles: University of California Press, 1970.

Schellhase, Kenneth C., *Tacitus in Renaissance Political Thought*, Chicago and London: University of Chicago Press, 1976.

Schelling, Felix E., *The English Chronicle Play: A Study in the Popular Historical Literature Environing Shakespeare* , New York: Macmillan, 1902.

Schoffer, I., et al., *De Lage Landen van 1500 tot 1780*, Amsterdam and Brussels: Elsevier: 1983.

Shaaber, Matthias, *Some Forerunners of the Newspaper in England, 1476–1622*, Philadelphia: University of Pennsylvania Press, 1929.

Shakespeare, William, *Henry V*, Arden Shakespeare, J. H. Walter (ed.), London and New York: Methuen, 1985.

1 Henry IV, Arden Shakespeare, A. R. Humphreys (ed.), London and New York: Methuen, 1985.

2 Henry IV, Arden Shakespeare, A. R. Humphreys (ed.), London and New York: Methuen, 1980.

Henry VIII, Arden Shakespeare, R. A. Foakes (ed.), London: Methuen, 1968.

The Complete Works of Shakespeare, David Bevington (ed.), Glenview, IL and London: Scott Foresman, 1980.

Shapiro, Barbara J., *Probability and Certainty in Seventeenth-Century England: A Study in the Relationships Between Natural Science, Religion, History, Law, and Literature*, Princeton: Princeton University Press, 1983.

Shapiro, James, "'Tragedies naturally performed': Kyd's Representation of Violence," *Staging the Renaissance: Reinterpretations of Elizabethan and Jacobean Drama*, David Scott Kastan and Peter Stallybrass (eds.), New York and London: Routledge, 1991, 99–113.

Sharpe, Kevin, "Introduction: Parliamentary History 1603–1629: In or out of Perspective?" *Faction and Parliament*, Kevin Sharpe (ed.), London and New York: Methuen, 1978, 1–42.

The Personal Rule of Charles I, New Haven and London: Yale University Press, 1992.

Sidney, Sir Philip, *Sir Philip Sidney*, Katherine Duncan-Jones (ed.), Oxford and New York: Oxford University Press, 1989.

The Defence of Poesy, *Sir Philip Sidney*, Katherine Duncan-Jones (ed.).

Smith, Alan G. R., *The Emergence of a Nation State: The Commonwealth of England 1529–1660*, New York and London: Longman, 1984.

Smith, F. Fussner, *The Historical Revolution. English Historical Writing and Thought 1580–1640*, London: Routledge and Kegan Paul, 1962.

Somerset, Anne, *Elizabeth I*, New York: Knopf, 1991.

Sommerville, J. P., *Politics and Ideology in England 1603–1640*, London and New York: Longman, 1986.

"James I and the Divine Right of Kings: English Politics and Continental Theory," *The Mental World of the Jacobean Court*, Linda Levy Peck (ed.), Cambridge: Cambridge University Press, 1991, 55–70.

Spenser, Edmund, *The Faerie Queene* (letter to Ralegh), Thomas Roche, Jr. (ed.), New Haven and London: Yale University Press, 1981.

Sprinker, Michael, "Politics and Theory: Althusser and Sartre," *Modern Language Notes* 100 (1985), 989–1011.

Steen, Sara Jayne, "Introduction," *The Letters of Arbella Stuart*, Sarah Jayne Steen (ed.), Oxford: Oxford University Press, 1994.

Stephenson, Carl, and Frederick George Marcham (eds. and trans.), *Sources of English Constitutional History: A Selection of Documents from A.D. 600 to the Interregnum*, 2 vols., New York and London: Harper and Row, 1972, vol. I.

Stone, Lawrence, *The Crises of the Aristocracy, 1558–1641*, abridged edn., Oxford: Oxford University Press, 1967.

Stow, John, *The Survey of London*, H. B. Wheatley (ed.), London and Melbourne: Everyman, 1987.

Strong, Roy, *The Cult of Elizabeth*, Berkeley and Los Angeles: University of California Press, 1977.

Stubbs, John, *John Stubbs' Gaping Gulf with Letters and Other Relevant Documents*, Lloyd E. Berry (ed.), Charlottesville: University of Virginia Press, 1968.

Surtz, Edward, and Virginia Murphy, "Introduction," *The Divorce Tracts of Henry VIII*, Edward Surtz and Virginia Murphy (eds.), Angers, France: Moreana, 1988, i-xxxvi.

Tennenhouse, Leonard, "Strategies of State and Political Plays: *A Midsummer Night's Dream, Henry IV, Henry V, Henry VIII*," *Political Shakespeare: New Essays in Cultural Materialism*, Jonathan Dollimore and Alan Sinfield (eds.), Ithaca and London: Cornell University Press, 1985, 109–28.

Power on Display: The Politics of Shakespeare's Genres, New York and London: Routledge, Chapman and Hall, 1986.

Tex, Jan den, *Johan van Oldenbarnevelt*, abridged edn., 's Gravenhage: Martinus Nijhoff, 1980.

Tillyard, E. W. M., *The Elizabethan World Picture : A Study of the Idea of Order in the Age of Shakespeare, Donne, and Milton* (1943), New York: Vintage Books, n. d.

Shakespeare's History Plays (1944), New York: Collier Books, 1962.

Turner, John, and Graham Holderness, Nick Potter, *Shakespeare: The Play of History*, Iowa City: University of Iowa Press, 1988, 85–149.

Tyacke, Nicholas, "Puritanism, Arminianism and the Counter-Revolution," *The Origins of the English Civil War*, Conrad Russell (ed.), London: Macmillan, 1973, 119–43.

Anti-Calvinists: The Rise of English Arminianism, Oxford: Clarendon Press, 1987.

Ure, Peter, "Introduction" to the Revels edition of *The Chronicle History of Perkin Warbeck*, Peter Ure (ed.), London: Methuen, 1968.

Vergil, Polydore, *The Anglica Historia of Polydore Vergil*, vol. LXXIV, Camden Series, Denys Hay (ed. and trans.), London: Royal Historical Society, 1950.

Weimann, Robert, "Representation and Performance: The Uses of Authority in Shakespeare's Theater," *PMLA* 107 (1992), 497–510.

Wells, Stanley, Gary Taylor, John Jowett and William Montgomery (eds.), *William Shakespeare: The Complete Works*, Oxford: Clarendon Press, 1986.

White, Hayden, "The Historical Text as Literary Artifact" (1974), *Tropics of Discourse: Essays in Cultural Criticism*, Baltimore: The Johns Hopkins University Press, 1987.

"New Historicism: A Comment," *The New Historicism*, H. Aram Veeser (ed.) New York and London: Routledge, 1989.

The Content of the Form: Narrative Discourse and Historical Representation, Baltimore and London: The Johns Hopkins University Press, 1990.

White, Paul Whitfield, *Theatre and Reformation: Protestantism, Patronage, and Playing in Tudor England*, Cambridge: Cambridge University Press, 1993.

Wikander, Matthew H., *The Play of Truth and State: Historical Drama from Shakespeare to Brecht*, Baltimore and London: The Johns Hopkins University Press, 1986.

Williams, Raymond, *Marxism and Literature*, Oxford: Oxford University Press, 1990.

Williamson, Audrey, *The Mystery of the Princes: An Investigation into a Supposed Murder*, Gloucester, England: Alan Sutton, 1981.

Winwood, Sir Ralph (secretary), *Letters from and to Sir Dudley Carleton During his Embassy in Holland, from January 1615, to December 1620*, London, 1757.

Woolf, D. R., "Erudition and the Idea of History in Renaissance England," *Renaissance Quarterly* 40 (1987), 11–48.

The Idea of History in Early Stuart England: Erudition, Ideology and "The Light of Truth" from the Accession of James I to the Civil War, Toronto: University of Toronto Press, 1990.

Wright, Louis B., "Heywood and the Popularization of History," *Modern Language Notes* 43 (1928), 287–93.

Middle-Class Culture in Elizabethan England, Chapel Hill: University of North Carolina Press, 1935.

Yates, Frances, *Shakespeare's Last Plays: A New Approach*, London: Routledge and Kegan Paul, 1975.

Ziegler, Georgianna, "England's Savior: Elizabeth I in the Writings of Thomas Heywood," *Renaissance Papers 1980* (1981), 29–37.

Index